BOTTEGHE OSCURE READER

Marguerite Caetani   *Photograph by Jane Sprague*

BOTTEGHE OSCURE
READER

Edited by GEORGE GARRETT
with the assistance of KATHERINE GARRISON BIDDLE
Introduction by GEORGE GARRETT

WESLEYAN UNIVERSITY PRESS
Middletown, Connecticut

The Publisher gratefully expresses appreciation to Lelia Caetani Howard, daughter of Maguerite Caetani, for the use of copyrighted materials and for her recommendations.

Library of Congress Cataloging in Publication Data

Garrett, George P   1929–   comp.
   Botteghe oscure reader.

   English, French, German, Italian, or Spanish.
   1. Poetry, Modern—20th century. I. Title.
PN6099.G37   808.8   73-15006
ISBN 0-8195-4071-4
ISBN 0-8195-6033-2 (pbk.)

Manufactured in the United States of America
First edition

CONTENTS

Texts are arranged by language and in chronological order of original publication. When more texts than one are derived from the same issue, the authors are given in alphabetical order.

v

ix

ACKNOWLEDGEMENTS

The publisher gratefully acknowledges the permission of the authors, their representatives, and their publishers to reprint their works in this volume.

Ischia by W. H. Auden copyright © 1948 by Botteghe Oscure; reprinted by permission of the author and Curtis Brown, Ltd.

A Day in the Dark by Elizabeth Bowen reprinted by permission of Curtis Brown, Ltd.

when faces called flowers . . . by E. E. Cummings, in *Complete Poems 1913–1962*, reprinted by permission of Harcourt Brace Jovanovich, Inc.

Pride and *An Angel* by Walter de la Mare reprinted by permission of The Literary Trustees of Walter de la Mare and The Society of Authors as their representative.

Valentino by Natalia Ginzburg reprinted by permission of the author and Giulio Einaudi Editore.

The Devil is a Protestant by Robert Graves reprinted by permission of the author and A. P. Watt & Son.

Ostia Antica by Anthony Hecht, in *The Hard Hours* (Copyright © 1967 by Anthony E. Hecht), reprinted by permission of the author and Atheneum Publishers.

A Girl in a Library and *Conversation with the Devil* by Randall Jarrell reprinted by permission of Farrar, Straus & Giroux.

Besonders die kleinen Propheten by Uwe Johnson, in *Karsch und Andere Prosa*, reprinted by permission of Suhrkamp Verlag; all rights reserved.

Outside and In by C. Day Lewis, in *Poems 1943–1947*, published by Jonathan Cape, Ltd., reprinted by permission of A. D. Peters & Company.

How the River Ninfa Runs Through the Ruined Town Beneath the Lime Quarry by Archibald MacLeish, from *The Wild Old Wicked Man* copyright © 1966, 1968 by Archibald MacLeish; reprinted by permission of the author and Houghton Mifflin Company.

"The Shimmer of Evil", *Love's Progress* and *Elegy* by Theodore Roethke copyright © 1955 by The New Republic, Inc.; reprinted by permission of Doubleday & Company, Inc.

INTRODUCTION

To tell the truth, nobody really misses a defunct literary magazine very much. Little magazines and quarterlies come and go, good and bad and wonderfully indifferent ones, flashy or drab, some briefly respected and all mostly ignored, each seemingly irreplaceable, yet all of them ordained to vanish, sooner or later, without so much as a single bright puff of smoke to testify to the magic of having been here at all. And then they become *documents*, sometimes in uniformly bound and lightly dusty sets, placed in at least some of the better libraries, fixed forever in chronological order, with a beginning and a middle and an end in time, perhaps to be a source of accidental pleasure for a new generation of lonesome browsers of library stacks and maybe even a challenge (to stake out a quick claim) to those tireless literary prospectors and promoters whose durable, exploitative industry depends so largely upon the rediscovery and refurbishing of forlorn ghost towns.

Which is to say, if the truth is to be told, that most literary periodicals (like most of us who write for them) are, by doom and by definition, more important dead than alive.

None of the above is true about *Botteghe Oscure*. It was urgently important while it was alive, and now that it has been gone for more than a decade, it is sorely missed.

Twice a year *Botteghe Oscure* appeared and flourished in a total of twenty-five volumes published between 1948 and 1960.

Except for its slightly different, natural parent, *Commerce* (1924–1932), there was no other publication even remotely like it. And when it was finished, when it was gone for good, there was suddenly —and remains until now—a raw vacant place where it had been, an absence deeply distressing to those who admired and respected the magazine. Even after all this time, a tumultuous time, it is hard to believe, to accept the brute fact that *Botteghe Oscure* has ceased to be. One cannot really imagine it. Whatever we cannot imagine is not true.

Which is to say that although the text and form and physical dimensions of *Botteghe Oscure* are fixed now within measurable limits of shelf space for the sequence of volumes and a final index (not to mention the twelve separate books and pamphlets issued by *Botteghe Oscure*), there is something else, an immeasurable and unspent energy, a lively and restless spirit, which persists, simply refusing to lie down, lie still, and play dead.

The purpose of this book is to invoke and to celebrate that spirit.

One proof of the present vitality of *Botteghe Oscure* can be found in the form which this volume had to assume. Often a form can be imposed, by design, and maintained by skill, authority, and sleight of hand. But sometimes there is a form which cannot be chosen and demands to be discovered and honored. It was not possible—and so nobody considered the notion very long or very seriously—to arrange a conventional anthology purporting to present "the best of *Botteghe Oscure*." The results of such a common and often effective strategy would have been a crude distortion of the truth and the spirit of the magazine. The only honest form for this book to take on was precisely what it is, a *reader*, itself organized and arranged in very much the same way and of roughly the same size as the individual published issues, a rather strictly representative selection taken from the magazine's whole history, at once a celebration of its unique character and a reintroduction to the whole scheme and system. Any gathering calling itself "the best of *Botteghe Oscure*" would inevitably have become an incomplete and inaccurate assembly of international literary celebrities, something *Botteghe Oscure* was not and never intended to be. And even in that limited and typical sense, it would be hopelessly inadequate. Mundane publishing requirements would have jostled many illustrious names out of its pages. More pertinent, such a method would do a very serious injustice to Marguerite Caetani's superb indifference to the idle whims of literary fashions and to the rising and falling of reputations in the literary marketplace. Though a great many distinguished writers, some already undeniably famous and others subsequently to be so, were published in *Botteghe Oscure*, there was always ample place and space for the young, the new, the unknown and undiscovered, and (yes) for the forgotten and ignored. It is easy to see now that a sense of discovery was at the heart of Marguerite Caetani's constant and informing editorial spirit, discovery together with the delight of recognition. The one uniform and rigorous criterion was quality. To attempt now to impose deliberately one's own critical tastes and notions, stripmining the contours of *Botteghe Oscure* for "the best," would be not only false and unjust, but foolishly presumptuous. All the poems and stories included here are genuinely distinguished, but they are also merely representative of the distinction evident in each of the published volumes. It follows, then, that there are not a few but a great many poems and stories by very fine writers which are not and could not be included here. That necessity is, it seems to me, a simple tribute to the Princess Caetani and the extraordinary magazine she created and edited. The reader is cheerfully referred to the *Botteghe Oscure Index* (1964) and from there directly to the twenty-five volumes.

If this gathering can offer that much impetus and direction, it will have justified itself and honored its primary purpose.

It might have been possible to include more contributors by other sorts of distortion. For example, this reader could have violated a basic principle of the magazine and confined itself to English-language writers or, indeed, only to American writers. Even such a limited gathering would have been impressive, but it could not be honestly representative. Another possibility might have been to limit the poets, for example, to one poem apiece. But, with a very few exceptions, Marguerite Caetani almost invariably chose to publish several poems, or several pages of poetry, by the individual poets she selected for the magazine. And so it seemed proper to follow her practice and to include the selections as they originally appeared in *Botteghe Oscure.*

The sequence of this book is chronological; that is, the order of appearance follows the order in which the poems and stories appeared; and, insofar as possible and without being rigidly mathematical about it, I have tried to offer a reasonable and various distribution of works taken from all the issues, first to last. Similarly, the sections of the book, arranged in language groups, correspond to the customary arrangement of the individual volumes of *Botteghe Oscure.* In each issue there were five basic language sections—American, English, French, Italian, and (alternately) German and Spanish. Within the boundaries of the separate languages there was a good deal of translation, from one language to another, and also from other languages and periods, including works translated from Latin and Greek, from Polish, Dutch, Korean, and Portuguese.

As a part of his graceful essay, "Requiem for a Literary Haven," first published in 1960 in *Saturday Review* and later reprinted, slightly revised, as the "Introduction" to the *Botteghe Oscure Index*, Archibald MacLeish listed some of the vital statistics of *Botteghe Oscure.* During its twelve years the magazine published work by some 650 writers "of thirty-odd nationalities, including 28 writing in Spanish (Spaniards, Mexicans, Cubans and South Americans), 39 writing in German (Germans, Austrians, Swiss), 98 writing in French (French, Belgians and Swiss) and 362 writing in English (more than half of them American and the rest British, Canadian, Australian, New Zealander) with five Filipinos, four Indians and a scattering from a dozen other countries." In terms of space allotted to language groupings (as distinct from number of authors), there was always a fairly even balance. Curiously, the impact of the multilingual volumes was more a sense of coherence than of any kind of confusion. What was, in fact, separated first by language and further by a variety of national boundaries and a consequent diversity of experiences and traditions, was here joined together into a real spirit of unity, a community which would have been rare enough at any time, but was and remains all the more remarkable for happening in the grim postwar years and the decade of the Cold War.

Botteghe Oscure had ended for us when the tumult and shouting of the Sixties developed. But something had already happened in the years before, something which has become more evident since then. For while there has been no true peace and while nations and peoples have been set against one another, nevertheless there has come to be a very real sense, in fact and in spirit, of the global community widely shared by artists and writers. This sense of community has not only endured enormous pressures, but has grown steadily stronger, stronger and firmer than, perhaps, at any time in our history since the late Middle Ages and the early Renaissance. Widespread and fairly prompt translation—of poems and stories, books, plays, and films—has certainly been a part of the restored awareness of each other, but beyond that literal means of communication, we more and more influence and inspire each other by example and through shared experience. We have come to know, slowly enough but with an invincible certainty, that we need each other and that we are in each other's hands. It would be outrageous to assert that the richly various literary community manifest in *Botteghe Oscure* was a major force in creating this renewed awareness of the larger human context of contemporary literature. But it is not too much to say that from the first issue onward *Botteghe Oscure* was early and tangible evidence, and, as such, against the apparent grain of the times, of the evolving communal artistic spirit of the future.

Behind that spirit of international community was the flesh and spirit of Marguerite Caetani, whose dedication and generosity were unflagging. Through its years *Botteghe Oscure* reflected her character and sensibility. Few publications, even the best of them, so fairly and accurately represent the imagination of their creators. Yet she was never rigid or dominating as an editor, and, indeed, she was never really alone at the task of gathering and publishing each issue. She had able assistance, assistant editors on record like Giorgio Bassani and Ben Johnson and Eugene Walter; and there were other young editorial assistants who had the privilege of working for her and the magazine at one time or another.

Above all she had the aid of many writers from all over the world, writers she knew and respected, ones whom she had published and encouraged and who, in turn, encouraged others to send their manuscripts to Rome or, if lucky enough to be there, to call upon her and to avail themselves of the hospitality at the Palazzo Caetani or at beautiful Ninfa. There is a whole story (*story* more than *study*) to be written some day by the scholars, a double history of the magazine and of the woman who created and sustained it. Much of this history rests in the separate memories of the many writers who knew her, personally and through correspondence, and who came also to know of each other and each other's work through her and the magazine. In his essay Archibald MacLeish, who knew her well, said it eloquently and accurately. "It is difficult to speak of Marguerite Caetani as a person now she is dead: her memory is too living in too many minds—her delighted spirit. But the achievement is something else: one can speak of that. In an ignorant, nationalistic, and fanatical time, paralysed by public hatreds, she kept a small flow of international literature alive and gave hundreds of young writers, in the loneliness of their defeated work, the hope that they too might become a generation—perhaps the first of all the literary generations to inherit the wholeness of the world."

The achievement has, if anything, grown in stature through the years of absence. The times are no better; MacLeish could be describing them from this morning's paper. But, already in a short span of time, what was clearly hope has become more clearly promise. And what was promise, in the work of so many of the writers for *Botteghe Oscure*, has become achievement. Thus her achievement is larger now, more permanent, than one might have believed possible only a few years ago.

Which is to say that one of the valid reasons why *Botteghe Oscure* has escaped the common fate of literary magazines is that its uncommon story is far from finished. It goes on not only in the memories of the writers who found themselves, and each other, in print in its pages, but also, widening but not diminishing, in the influence which they may have upon others, directly or indirectly. What we are thinking of is energy, not spent or dissipated, but growing in cumulative power. This book is, then, intended to be only one part of a continuing story, a brief celebration of a great magazine and the lively spirit of it. Most of the honor and gratitude due for the preservation of *Botteghe Oscure* into our present time belongs to Katherine Garrison Biddle, who, as literary executor for Marguerite Caetani and as a poet of distinction herself, has acted with a generosity at once firm and modest, serving always more as a guide to than the guardian of the living spirit. In particular, Mrs. Biddle's gentle criticism and gracious encouragement, offered to me and to all others concerned with the preparation of this volume, have been, purely and simply, invaluable. The extent to which this book may now achieve its larger aims derives chiefly from her care and wisdom. Its faults, its editorial flaws and weaknesses, are all my own; but happily, I am convinced, these are bound to be irrelevant when measured against her dedicated contribution and against the abundant energy still flowing from the original source.

GEORGE GARRETT

BOTTEGHE OSCURE READER

CONRAD AIKEN

THE CLOVER

The tiger gash of daybreak rips the night
under palmetto leaves drips the first light
the dream is broken the word of water spoken
and the dream fills with the golden scream
of the unknown bird in the fountained park
hark hark hark hark screaming beneath dark leaves
and the wild hour is strange and pain strange too
as also too that love to pain should change
the pure love-pattern into deep life-pattern change.
"O love O love O love that in the mountains took
this simple heart, coeur simple, *beside the mountain brook*
and broke the goldenrod for summer speech
brimming with water-gold the heart of each,
with what ascending steps carved in the light
climbing the hyaline we have come to this
animal world invented in a kiss!"
And then the tiger gash of pain
the malicious bird screams in the dark again
now at the window screams now at the breast
this breast that lives and gives.

"Pray Time what is our shame
or what this blessedness without a name
that the unknown of love should come to this
birth and afterbirth embodied in a kiss?

3

And this child born in pain of me
this small pale soul that wails in fear of light
what shall I be to him or he to me
now that the dual world is sundered into three?
All's lost in finding, we are washed away
like shoreless mariners this bed our ship
nor in this voyage shall we one harbour find
but separately and alone, love as we may,
seek our own soulshaped landfall under hostile day.
Farewell dear voyager — already you depart
who but a moment since lay in my heart."

And the red leaf turns, turns, in a circle of dust
in the shaft of light that has come and gone
and the light is turned, turns, in a ring of darkness
the mind of night that dreams of waking
and the time turns as sand by the hand is turned
circle in circle ring within ring
reason at work in season and season in reason
till again the finger writes in a circle of dust
and again the same leaf turns in a ring of dust
in the shaft of light that has come and gone,
and the world, my love, comes round
round as the dance of druid oaks in spring
or the ritual song the pinkwinks sing,
the world is round as a ring.

For see, he brings you now his fourleafed clover
who is already as you bear again your lover
and the clear pink-tipped blossoms too
those that he loves
clusters that smell like cloves.
As much as you he loves, as much as you
and as you turn upon the bed
on the pale pillow turn your head
you see (and smile) the something new
that lights and listens in your child as if

your own eyes there burned back at you
and if with love yet with a different view.
For in that look, that probing interchange,
hovers the idea perceptible to each
shines between the eyes but without speech
that you surrender now your soverignty
yet with a kind of acquiescent glee,
you whose wings still mount in wider gyre
over the world's darkness, yet know how soon
time's gift but also yours
the child's must further range and higher.
This too is a departure this accolade of clover
but also although no mention made
without a kiss it is conveyed
although perhaps each wished a kiss
that now henceforward far though the voyage take
each on his destined journey, he will keep
your heart, your mind, your thought, your love
enringed in his:
your flight no matter where
will be ensphered and move in his:
no matter no how high and faint it soar
or low and lost at last it fall,
his love pursues and understands it all.
Thus, in silence, in the May-morning light,
the mutual accolade.

And yes! you guessed, whose generous gesture made
his young dream feel the wing-beat's power
shuddering imagination in that hour
for flaming wheel and falcon tower
over the ruined infernos and gutted heavens
and obliterated purgatories of a world
overwhelmed and overwinged
in rung and ring and rise of mind
by feather and ecstacy and blood —
and yes! you knew and meant

if your own journey went
too early and too cheated underground
and O poor love for only treason's reason
too soon too dark in the alien spring
the alien much-loved chinaberry season
that he would join you there his whole soul's vision
flung down with the handflung dust and the windlost voice
chanting the last verse
passionately in your grave. For there it stayed
and there it stays, and there rejoined
to the lost heart, as the slow seasons made
their havoc, from ruin to ruin it too decayed
fell with you lightly into dust, you two
becoming dust together. But not forgetful
and not in sleep, if the dust sleeps is thought to sleep,
for now his sight was yours, dedicated to you —

who while he lives will be your secret lover
(listen, his footstep coming against the whisper
buena ventura *whispering of the spanish moss)*
and to the dark grave brings the clear-stemmed clover
O lost love in this token
sharing with you forever but no word spoken
beyond the chinaberry-shadowed wall
and the alien ghostly spring
(you still can hear the beating wing)
that moment's magic, the May-bright morning,
when you evoked so long ago
the rings and rituals of your light:
the leaf turning turning in a circle of fire
the finger writing writing a word of fire
and the mind of night dreaming divine delight:
for the world my love comes round
the silent dance of ancient oaks in spring
and the ritual song the enchanted pinkwinks sing
the world is round as a ring.

E. E. CUMMINGS

POEM

when faces called flowers float out of the ground
and breathing is wishing and wishing is having —
but keeping is downward and doubting and never
— it's april (yes, april; my darling) it's spring!
yes the pretty birds frolic as spry as can fly
yes the little fish gambol as glad as can be
(yes the mountains are dancing together)

when every leaf opens without any sound
and wishing is having and having is giving —
but keeping is doting and nothing and nonsense
— alive; we're alive, dear: it's (kiss me now) spring!
now the pretty birds hover so she and so he
now the little fish quiver so you and so i
(now the mountains are dancing, the mountains)

when more than was lost has been found has been found
and having is giving and giving is living —
but keeping is darkness and winter and cringing
— it's spring (all our night becomes day) o, it's spring!
all the pretty birds dive to the heart of the sky
all the little fish climb through the mind of the sea
(all the mountains are dancing; are dancing)

7

MARIANNE MOORE

AT REST IN THE BLAST

Like a bulwark against fate,
　　By the thrust of the blast
　Lead-saluted;
Saluted by lead?
As though flying
　　Old Glory full mast.

Pent by power that holds it fast —
　　A paradox... Hard-pressed,
　You take the blame
　And are inviolate —
　　Down-cast but not cast

Down. Some bind by promises,
　　But not the tempest-tossed —
　Borne by the might
　Of the storm to a height,
From destruction;
　　At rest in the blast.

WILLIAM CARLOS WILLIAM

THE BIRTH OF VENUS

*Today small waves are rippling, crystal clear, upon the pebbles
at Villefranche whence from the wall, at the Parade Grounds of
the Chasseurs Alpins, we stood and watched them; or passing
      along
the cliff on the ledge between the sea and the old fortress, heard
the long swell stir without cost among the rocks' teeth. But we*

*are not there! — as in the Crimea the Black Sea is blue with
      waves
under a smiling sky, or be it the Labrador North Shore, or
      wherever
else in the world you will, the world of indolence and April; as,
November next, spring will enliven the African coast southward
and we not there, not there, not there!*

*Why not believe that we shall be young again? Surely nothing
could be more to our desire, more pebble-plain under a hand's
      breath
wavelet, a jeweled thing a Sapphic bracelet, than this. Murder
staining the small waves crimson is not more moving — though
      we strain
in our minds to make it so, and stare.*

9

Cordite, heavy shells falling on the fortifications of Sebastopol,
fired by the Germans first, then by the Russians are indiffe-
rent to
our agony — as are small waves in the sunlight. But we need
not elect
what we do not desire. Torment, in the daisied fields before
Troy
or at Amiens or the Manchurian plain is not

of itself the dearest desired of our world. We do not have to die,
in bitterness and the most excruciating torture, to feel! We can
lean on the wall and experience an ecstacy of pain, if pain it
must
be, but a pain of love, of dismemberment if you will, but a pain
of almond blossoms, an agony of mimosa trees in bloom, a

scented cloud! Even, as old Ford would say, an exquisite
sense of
viands. Would there be no sculpture, no painting, no Pintu-
ricchio, no
Botticelli — or frescos on the jungle temples of Burma (that the
jungles
have reclaimed) or Picasso at Cannes but for war? Would
there be
no voyages starting from the dunes at Huelva —

over the windy harbor? No Seville cathedral? Possibly so. Even
the quietness of flowers is perhaps deceptive. But why must
we suffer
ourselves to be so torn to sense our world? Or believe we
must so
suffer to be born again? Let the homosexuals seduce whom
they will
under what bushes along the coast lines of the Middle Sea

rather than have us insist on murder. Governments are defeats,
    distor-
tions. I wish (and so I fail). Notwithstanding, I wish we might
learn of an April of small waves — deadly as all slaughter,
    that we
shall die soon enough, to dream of April, not knowing why we
    have been
struck down, needless of what greater violence.

WALLACE STEVENS

A HALF DOZEN SMALL PIECES

I

WHAT WE SEE IS WHAT
WE THINK

At twelve, the disintegration of afternoon
Began, the return to phantomerei, if not
To phantoms. Till then, it had been the other way;

One imagined the violet trees but the trees stood green
At twelve, as green as ever they would be.
The sky was blue beyond the vaultiest phrase.

Twelve meant as much as: the end of normal time,
Straight up, an elan without harrowing,
The imprescriptible zenith, free of harangue,

Twelve meant as much as: the end of normal time,
Of violet gray, a green violet, a thread
To weave a shadow's leg or sleeve, a scrawl

On the pedestal, an ambitious page dog-eared
At the upper right, a pyramid with one side
Like a spectral cut in its perception, a tilt,

And its tawny caricature and tawny life,
Another thought, the paramount ado...
Since what we think is never what we see.

II

A GOLDEN WOMAN IN A SILVER MIRROR

Suppose this was the root of everything.
Suppose it turned out to be or that it touched
An image that was mistress of the world.

For example: Au Château. Un Salon. A glass
The sun steps into, regards and finds itself;
Or: Gawks of hay... Augusta Moon, before

An attic glass, hums of the old Lutheran bells
At home; or: In the woods, belle Belle alone
Rattles with fear in unreflecting leaves.

Abba, dark death is the breaking of a glass.
The dazzled flakes and splinters disappear.
The seal is as relaxed as dirt, perdu.

But the images, disembodied, are not broken.
They have, or they may have, their glittering crown.
Sound-soothing pearl and omni-diamond,

Of the most beautiful, the most beautiful maid
And mother. How long have you lived and looked,
Ababba, expecting this king's queen to appear?

III

THE OLD LUTHERAN BELLS AT HOME

These are the voices of the pastors calling
In the names of St. Paul and of the halo-John
And of other holy and learned men, among them
Great choristers, propounders of hymns, trumpeters,
Jerome and the scrupulous Francis and Sunday women,
The nurses of the spirit's innocence.

These are the voices of the pastors calling
Much rough-end being to smooth Paradise,
Spreading out fortress walls like fortress wings.
Deep in their sound the stentor Martin sings.
Dark Juan looks outward through his mystic brow...
Each sexton has his sect. The bells have none.

These are the voices of the pastors calling
And calling like the long echoes in long sleep,
Generations of shepherds to generations of sheep.

Each truth is a sect though no bells ring for it.
And the bells belong to the sextons, after all,
As they jangle and dangle and kick their feet.

IV

QUESTIONS ARE REMARKS

In the weed of summer comes this green sprout why.
The sun aches and ails and then returns halloo
Upon the horizon amid adult enfantillages.

Its fire fails to pierce the vision that beholds it,
Fails to destroy the antique acceptances,
Except that the grandson sees it as it is,

16

Peter the voyant, who says « Mother, what is that » —
The object that rises with so much rhetoric,
But not for him. His question is complete.

It is the question of what he is capable.
It is the extreme, that expert aetat. 2.
He will never ride the red horse she describes.

His question is complete because it contains
His utmost statement. It is his own array,
His own pageant and procession and display,

As far as nothingness permits... Hear him.
He does not say, « Mother, my mother, who are you »,
The way the drowsy. infant, old men do.

V

STUDY OF IMAGES I

It does no good to speak of the big, blue bush
Of day. If the study of his images
Is the study of man, this image of Saturday,

This Italian symbol, this Southern landscape, is like
A waking, as in images we awake,
Within the very object that we seek,

Participants of its being. It is, we are.
He is, we are. Ah, bella! He is, we are,
Within the big, blue bush and its vast shade

At evening and at night. It does no good.
Stop at the terraces of mandolins,
False, faded and yet inextricably there,

17

The pulse of the object, the heat of the body grown cold
Or cooling in late leaves, not false except
When the image itself is false, a mere desire,

Not faded, if images are all we have.
They can be no more faded than ourselves.
The blood refreshes with its stale demands.

VI

STUDY OF IMAGES II

The frequency of images of the moon
Is more or less. The pearly women that drop
from heaven and float in air, like animals

Of ether, exceed the excelling witches, whence
They came. But. brown, the ice-bear sleeping in ice-month
In his cave, remains dismissed without a dream,

As if the centre of images had its
Congenial mannequins, alert to please,
Beings of other beings manifold —

The shadowless moon wholly composed of shade,
Women with other lives in their live hair,
Rose — women as half-fishes of salt shine,

As if, as if, as if the disparate halves
Of things were waiting in a betrothal known
To none, awaiting espousal to the sound

Of right joining, a music of ideas, the burning
And breeding and bearing birth of harmony,
The final relation, the marriage of the rest.

18

CLINCH CALKINS

HYMN TO THE WINTER SOLSTICE

The sun stands still in the vast
Then starts his return.

It is for me that the sky explodes into fire and rose of the
winter solstice.
For me hangs December's planet above the linear moon in
the mauve of the evening;
Galaxies troop through the night, the outer galactic systems
recede in numberless armies.

For me the year and the night divide into two, become equal,
half living, half dying.
The past is bent back. The future wheels in, is instant and
instantly over, imperceptibly present,
Made finite in season, month, day, hour, minute and second
of change from coming to gone
From taut into slack into lowered; calyx to mould.

From brown spill of new beech leaf, from foal in the stable,
lamb on the meadow or plain, to their passing;
The readying shift of the fledgling from nest to twig's ledge,
thence to hedge, then to flying and singing;

19

*From shimmer of plumage in mating, till the long flight is
   over;*
*From spear of the root into earth, through labor to harvest,
   from banquet to valedictorian:*

*This is all mine for my own private seeing and hearing,
(Man's being mine) for self-abnegation of worship —
From greater to small, from space into star into atom;
From intoxication to grape, from grape through the vine
   back to grape-seed;
From smaller to larger, from passion to love, from life into
   welcoming death.*

DAVID IGNATOW

KING DAVID

How else except that he had walked out
of his palace chamber in despair
with the day's work — it came to the same thing
always, success, success monotonously;
was there never a doubt to enter one's head
that all was not well, just this suspicion
of success? — and saw Bathsheba bathing.
He leapt at it, a new vision, a new chance
to prove himself in a new environment;
and beckoned her to him by his royal fools,
and proved what? That he was liable to do
anything, even to murder; and success was murder;
and that he had done as much as he could accomplish
in his whole life: a stillborn and a live child
of rape to take over at his death
and to prove what again? That it was murder
and always murder that succeeded.
Solomon has not had his peer since his brother's death.

BATHSHEBA

I gave myself to David with a hard, silent,
dry womb, as in a death chamber; and it was so.
He gave birth upon me to death, to know better
the evil of his doing; and after Uriah's death,
after my husband's murder, I wept because I
having to live had to bear this burden
in some degree; and David took me and I affirmed
life again in despite of him, as if in Uriah's
memory, and for his sake; and brought up a child
who would make lust and all other sensual pleasure
his greatness and his ruination, in the hateful image
of his father, the king.

Then what was the nation?
Then what had Uriah fought for, kept from me
for months? Because of his absence my love
had reached out to him absentmindedly
in the garden.

MYSTIQUE

No man has seen the third hand
that stems from the center, near the heart.
Let either the right of the left prepare
a dish for the mouth, or a thing
to give, and the third hand will deftly
and unseen enter to change the object
of our hunger or of our giving.

IN YOUR DREAMS

Oh God, if I was born to be dead
why was I not ended in advance?
If life is to be sand and salt
what is the power that moves me to complain?
The withheld sweetness that it can surmise
from pain?
      Pluck out the root of planted
bitter herb, sunk in my love for you,
sweet source, if sand and salt is my domain.
You are the soil of my distress,
to bid me live, but like a barren grain.
Be one with me in your desires,
and seek a simple child in your dreams.

RANDALL JARRELL

A GIRL IN A LIBRARY

An object among dreams, you sit here with your shoes off
And curl your legs up under you; your eyes
Close for a moment, your face moves toward sleep...
You are very human.

                    But my mind, gone out in tenderness,
Shrinks from its object with a thoughtful sigh.
This is a waist the spirit breaks its arm on.
The gods themselves, against you, struggle in vain.
This broad low strong-boned brow; these heavy eyes;
These calves, grown muscular with certainties;
This nose, three medium-sized pink strawberries
— But I exaggerate. In a little you will leave:
I'll hear, half squeal, half shriek, your laugh of greeting —
Then, decrescendo, bars of that strange speech
In which each sound sets out to seek each other,
Murders its own father, marries its own mother,
And ends as one grand transcendental vowel.

(Yet for all I know, the Egyptian Helen spoke so.)
As I look, the world contracts around you:
I see Brunnhilde had brown braids and glasses
She used for studying; Salome straight brown bangs,
A calf's brown eyes, and sturdy light-brown limbs
Dusted with cinnamon, an apple-dumpling's.

24

Many a beast has gnawn a leg off and got free,
Many a dolphin curved up from Necessity —
The trap has closed about you, and you sleep.
If someone questioned you, What doest thou here?
You'd knit your brows like an orangoutang
(But not so sadly; not so thoughtfully)
And answer with a pure heart, guilelessly:
I'm studying...
              If only you were not!
Assignments,
        recipes,
              the Official Rulebook
Of Basketball — *ah, let them go; you needn't mind.*
The soul has no assignments, neither cooks
Nor referees: it wastes its time.
                  It wastes its time.
Here in this enclave there are centuries
For you to waste: the short and narrow stream
Of Life meanders into a thousand valleys
Of all that was, or might have been, or is to be.
The books, just leafed through, whisper endlessly...
Yet it is hard. One sees in your blurred eyes
The «uneasy half-soul» Kipling saw in dogs'.
One sees it, in the glass, in one's own eyes.
In rooms alone, in galleries, in libraries,
In tears, in searchings of the heart, in staggering joys
We memorize once more our old creation,
Humanity: with what yawns the unwilling
Flesh puts on its spirit, O my sister!

So many dreams! And not one troubles
Your sleep of life? no self stares shadowily
From these worn hexahedrons, beckoning
With false smiles, tears?...
                Meanwhile Tatyana
Larina (gray eyes nickel with the moonlight
That falls through the willows onto Lensky's tomb;

25

Now young and shy, now old and cold and sure)
Asks, smiling: « But what is she dreaming of, fat thing? »
I answer: She's not fat. She isn't dreaming.
She purrs or laps or runs, all in her sleep;
Believes, awake, that she is beautiful;
She never dreams.

                    Those sunrise-colored clouds
Around man's head — that inconceivable enchantment
From which, at sunset, we come back to life
To find our graves dug, families dead, selves dying:
Of all this, Tanya, she is innocent.
For nineteen years she's faced reality;
They look alike already.

                         They say, man wouldn't be
The best thing in this world — and isn't he? —
If he were not too good for it. But she
— She's good enough for it.

                         And yet sometimes
Her sturdy form, in its pink strapless formal,
Is as if bathed in moonlight — modulated
Into a form of joy, a Lydian mode;
This Wooden Mean's a kind, furred animal
That speaks, in the Wild of things, delighting riddles
To the soul that listens, trusting...

                         Poor senseless Life:
When, in the last light sleep of dawn, the messenger
Comes with his message, you will not awake.
He'll give his feathery whistle, shake you hard,
You'll look with wide eyes at the dewy yard
And dream, with calm slow factuality:
« To day's Commencement. My bachelor's degree
In Home Ec., my doctorate of philosophy
In Phys. Ed.

               [Tanya, they won't even scan]
Are waiting for me... »

                    Oh, Tatyana,
The Angel comes: better to squawk like a chicken

26

Than to say with truth, « But I'm a good girl, »
And Meet his Challenge with a last firm strange
Uncomprehending smile; and — then, then! — see
The blind date that has stood you up: your life.
(For all this, if it isn't, perhaps, life,
Has yet, at least, a language of its own
Different from the books'; worse than the books'.)
And yet, the ways we miss our lives are life.
Yet... yet...
                    to have one's life add up to yet!

You sigh a shuddering sigh. Tatyana murmurs,
« Don't cry, little peasant »; leaves us with a swift
« Goodbye, goodbye... Ah, don't think ill of me... »
Your eyes open: you sit here thoughtlessly.

I love you — and yet — and yet — I love you.

Don't cry, little peasant. Sit and dream.
One comes, a finger's width beneath your skin,
To the braided maidens singing as they spin;
There sound the shepherd's pipe, the watchman's rattle
Across the short dark distance of the years.
I am a thought of yours; and yet, you do not think...
The firelight of a long, blind, dreaming story
Lingers upon your lips; and I have seen
Firm, fixed forever in your closing eyes
The Corn King beckoning to his Spring Queen.

A CONVERSATION WITH THE DEVIL

Indulgent, or candid, or uncommon reader
— I've some: a wife, a nun, a ghost or two —
If I write for anyone, I wrote for you;
So whisper, when I die, We was too few;
Write over me (if you can write; I hardly knew)

That I — that I — but anything will do,
I'm satisfied... And yet —

                     and yet, you were too few:
Should I perhaps have written for your brothers,
Those artful, common, unindulgent others?

Mortal men, man! mortal men! So says my heart
Or else my belly — some poor empty part.
It warms in me, a dog beside a stove,
And whines, or growls, with a black lolling smile:
I never met the man I didn't love.
Life's hard for them... these mortals... Lie, man, lie!
Come, give it up — this whining poetry;
To any man be anything. If nothing works,
Why then, Have Faith.
                  That blessed word, Democracy!

But this is strange of you: to tempt me now!
It brings back all the past: those earliest offers
— How can I forget? — EACH POEM GUARANTEED
A LIE OR PERMANENTLY IRRELEVANT.
WE FURNISH POEMS *AND* READERS. *What a slogan!*
(I had only to give credit to « my daemon »;
Say, confidentially, « dictated by the devil. »)
I can still see my picture in that schoolroom.
And next — who has it now? — The World's Enormity,
That novel of the Wandering Jewess, Lilith,
Who went to bed with six millennia.
(It came complete with sales, scenario,
And testimonials of grateful users:
Not like a book at all... Beats life...)
                     Beats life.
How ill we knew each other then! how mockingly
I nodded, « Almost thou persuadest me, »
And made my offer:
                  « If ever I don't say
To the hour of life that I can wish for: Stay,

Thou art so fair! *why, you may have my —*
Shadow. »
                    Our real terms were different
And signed and sealed for good, neither in blood
Nor ink but in my life: Neither to live
Nor ask for life — *that wasn't a bad bargain*
For a poor devil of a poet, was it?
One makes a solitude and calls it peace.
So you phrased it; yet — yet — one is paid:
To see things as they are, to make them what they might be —
Old Father of Truths, old Spirit that Accepts —
That's something... If, afterwards, we broke our bargain —

He interrupts: But what nobility!
I once saw a tenor at the *Opera Comique*
Who played the Fisher — of Pearls or else of Souls.
He wore a leopard-skin, lay down, and died;
And sang ten minutes lying on his side
And died again; and then, applauded,
Gave six bows, leaning on his elbow,
And at the seventh started on his encore.
He was, I think, a poet.
                    Renounce, renounce,
You sing in your pure clear grave ardent tones
And then give up — whatever you're afraid to take,
Which is everything; and after that take credit
For dreaming something else to take its place.
Isn't what is already enough for you?
Must you always be *making* something?
Must each fool cook a lie up all his own?
You beings, won't even being disgust you
With causing something else to be? *Make, make —*
You squeak like mice; and yet it's all hypocrisy —
How often each of you, in his own heart,
Has wiped the world out, and thought afterwards:
No need to question, *now*: « If others are, am I? »
Still, I confess that I and my good Neighbor

Have always rather envied you existence.
Your simple conceits! — but both of us enjoy them:
« Dear God, make me Innocent or Wise, »
Each card in the card-catalogue keeps praying;
And dies, and the divine Librarian
Rebinds him —

             rebinds? that's odd; but then, He's **odd**
And as a rule —

           I'm lying: there's no rule at all.
The world divides into — believe me — facts.

I see the devil can quote Wittgenstein.
He's blacker than he's painted.

             Old ink-blot,
What are you, after all? A parody.
You can be satisfied? then how can I?
If you accept, is not that to deny?
A Dog in a tub, who was the Morning Star!
To have come down in the universe so far
As here, and now, and this — and all to buy
One bored, stoop-shouldered, sagging-cheeked particular
Lest the eternal bonfire fail —

           ah Lucifer!

But at blacker an embarrassed smile
Wavers across his muzzle, he breaks in:
It's odd that you've never guessed: I'm through.
To tempt, sometimes, a bored anachronism
Like you into — but why should I say what?
To stretch out by the Fire and improvise:
This pleases me, now there's no need for me.
Even you must see I'm obsolescent.
A specialist in personal relations,
I valued each of you at his own worth.
You had your faults; but you were bad at heart.
I disliked each life, I assure you, for its own sake.
— But to deal indifferently in life and death;

To sell, wholesale, piecemeal, annihilation;
To — I will not go into particulars —
This beats me.
                    To *men, now,* I should give advice?
I'm vain, as you know; but not ridiculous.
Here in my inglenook, shy, idle, I conclude:
I never understood them: as the consequence
They end without me ...
                    « Scratch a doctor
And find a patient, » I always used to say.
Now that I've time, I've analyzed myself
And find that I am growing, or have grown —
Was always, perhaps, indifferent.
It takes a man to love or hate a man
Wholeheartedly. And how wholeheartedly
You act out *all that is deserves to perish!*
As if to take me at my word — an idle *mot*
That no one took less seriously than I.
It was *so,* of course; and yet — and yet —

I find that I've grown used to you. Hell gives us habits
To take the place of happiness, alas!
When I look forward, it is with a pang
That I think of saying, « My occupation's gone. »

But twelve's striking: time to be in bed.

I think: He's a changed — all this has shaken him.
He was always delicate: a spirit of society,
A way to come to terms —
                    now, no more terms!
Those pleasant evenings of denunciation!
How gratefully, after five acts' rejection,
A last firm shake and quaver and statistic,
He'd end, falsetto: « *But let's be realistic* » —
Had he, perhaps, exaggerated? He had exaggerated ...
How quietly, a little later, he'd conclude:

31

« *I accept it all.* »
                    And now to be unable
To accept, to have exaggerated —
                              to do anything:
It's hard for him. How often he has said,
« *I like you for always doing as you please* » —
He couldn't. Free will appealed so much to him;
He thought, I think: If they've the choice...
He was right. And now, to have no choice!

WILLIAM WEAVER

ON EARTH AS IT IS

The Professor spent all of the day in his room, in silence. The silence belonged to him, but the room did not, for he was alone in the world, and the place he occupied now was only the last in a series of furnished, rented rooms that had housed, but not welcomed him in his long career since he had left his remote province and come to the Capital to teach in the Industrial High School.

Now for years he had been retired, and with his retirement had begun that physical process which gradually and inexorably had made him what he was: large, disorderly, and lost. His body had gone beyond him and, while it had not acquired a will of its own, it had gained an almost complete independence of the Professor's; so that he could begin the simplest of actions — picking up a glass, for example — with no assurance that the movement would be completed as he had intended. Much of his meager income went to pay for broken crockery or to repair furniture that his unwieldy bulk had maimed.

But in all this bodily decay, his mind remained sound. It lived in his body as an abandoned prince might inhabit the ruins of his palace, and the Professor felt himself to be a kind of prisoner, jailed in his own flesh, where news of the outside world reached him rarely and in garbled form.

His mind was alive, but like a shrub left to itself, it had grown wild. His eyes ranged about the somber room, where a hundred different roomers had created not a personality, but a thick anonymity, and he saw nothing, or vague things, shapes, scraps of the past, a world where the Professor had been young and thin, and if he had not been happy, he had at least been ordinary, and that seemed happines to him now.

He did not dislike his landlady, still he communicated with her only slightly. She was responsible for feeding him and, her inherent barriers of modesty having long since been obliterated by necessity, she even helped him dress himself on occasion.

Her duties, however, were performed in silence. He spoke only with difficulty, and therefore with displeasure. And the landlady, used to his ponderous silence, controlled her natural inclination to talk. Moreover, since she knew that for years he had read nothing and had seen no one, she would have been at a loss for something to say; they had no meeting place.

Hence it was strange, and in a small way typical of the strange day that followed, when one mornig the landlady greeted him heartily, opened wide the window, and said:

« It's a lovely day, Professor. A lovely fall day ».

The seasons meant nothing to him; changes of weather never penetrated him, and for this reason the window was kept closed always. Now he looked at it with a slight curiosity — days had passed since he had looked out last — and he saw the dingy white curtains stir in a breeze, as the leaves outside stirred lazily, twirled with an indolent grace, like young girls strolling.

« There may not be any more of these lovely days for quite a while », the landlady continued, « why don't you just go out and take a little walk? »

He was moved by the thought, and moved also by the sight of the street, the line of tall and delicate trees. « Yes »,

he agreed, surprised by the sudden ease with which he had
pronounced the word.

« Wonderful », the landlady concluded, her mind alive
with plans for dusting and straightening up, turning the
mattress and washing the mirrors. « Now you'd better just take
a light coat or something. And don't go too far and get over-
heated. You could go to the park and sit on a nice bench,
and if you didn't feel just right, you could ask some young
person to help you. Don't be ashamed of that. There's no
disgrace in being old. You're not the oldest person in the
world, you know », she said cheerily.

Oh yes, I am, he wanted to say, but he knew better
than to attempt so much.

With her help and with his own unexpected energy, he
was soon dressed and ready to venture out. She forced his
arms into the sleeves of a coat, as she might have stuffed a
bulky pillow into its case, and put a cap on his head (he
didn't want it, but it was easier to give in), then she directed
him through the apartment to the front door and set him
on his way.

But he did not go to the park. Propelled by an obstinacy
to make this walk his own, he took a different direction. He
followed the street until the trees ended and he was in the
square.

The landlady had purposely not suggested the square
because she had been afraid of traffic, yet at this mid-morning
hour the city had settled down to its business and the streets
were virtually deserted, both by machines and by human
beings. In spite of the date (the end of October), there were
still a few tables set out hopefully in front of the caffè, and
at one of them the Professor, with practiced patience, settled
his weight into an iron chair.

The waiter approached him with deference, not knowing
who the Professor was, but feeling at the same time a respect
for the mere size and silence of the old man, as if he were
a national monument, or some object from the past which,

without being beautiful, is imposing and therefore to be respected.

« Coffee », the Professor managed to say well enough to be understood. In a minute the waiter was back with the cup, which he set carefully on the table.

But the Professor allowed the coffee to grow cold while he surveyed the square. He could not think when he had seen it last, and now its beauty struck him with new force: it was not a square at all, he realized, but an enormous, irregular circle, pointed in the center with a graceful obelisk commemorating nothing, and dominated by a pair of baroque churches, unidentical twins, whose curving domes, whose time-stained columns brought tears to the old man's eyes.

The past, he thought, how typically generous of them. To build two churches, not because they needed them, but because two would be more lovely than one.

This sudden moment of beauty seemed to him a part of the day, the weather. Now the few people that moved across the square, anonymous in the distance, walked with a grace and a decision that he found also beautiful. They are all so thin, he thought.

He was reluctant to move, even to turn his head, from this view. Beyond the obelisk, at the far end of the square, there was a patch of green, the hills of the Public Gardens, their pines towering over the orange-golden square.

The waiter reappeared, and the Professor, afraid that perhaps he had been sitting too long at the table, swallowed his coffee, miraculously spilling none of it. Then, to complete this performance of nonchalance, he took up a newspaper that some earlier customer had left on the table and pretended to read. The waiter withdrew again.

The old man would have replaced the paper at once but, as if by accident, a few words — part of a headline — caught his attention, the cryptic phrase *Student's Tragedy*, which reminded him of many things and assembled, like bits of a puzzle, some of those fragments of the past that lay always scattered in his thoughts. And in the spirit of this awakening, that had begun with the weather and the unremembered loveliness of the square, he began to read the article. His awkwardness, as he handled the paper, was even greater than usual because of the object's unfamiliarity; he had not seen print for years, and the words came alive before his eyes. He did not readily understand.

« *The twenty-year-old law student X...*, *son of the well-known lawyer of this city* », the Professor read, forcing himself to comprehend the strange phrasing, « *resident at number 121 R... Street, took his own life last night in a still unexplained gesture which has left his devoted family plunged in grief. The suicide would seem to have been without motive, since the young man was highly personable, popular, and successful in his studies. A statement by the father of the unfortunate youth did, however, disclose that the boy had for some weeks been suffering from a form of melancholia, the source of which remains obscure...*

When he had finished the article, his eyes already were stinging with tears. And he learned with surprise that, even after the arid years, his body wept easily. He was unable to let go of the paper; his shaking hand, with a private volition, kept holding the printed sheet, while his eye continued to wander over the enemy words.

He was weeping not only for the dead boy, but for himself: that such a tragedy should have taken place in this weather, that he should learn about it on this day and in this square. He felt a personal offence, a savage wound that made all his spirit rebel.

With a rough gesture he wiped his eyes on the sleeve of his coat, then looked to see if the waiter had returned. No, the Professor was still alone. Again he turned to the paper, wanting to read the article again, to draw himself closer to the unhappy boy, who had cut off his own life as if it had been no more than an ugly, awkward limb (the Professor thought of all this). But instead, he saw another headline, and again without knowing how or why, he was reading:

Ghastly Crime in Workers' Quarter — Man Strangles Erring Wife. Residents in N... street were awakened in the early hours of this morning by a series of screams, coming from a window of the apartment house at number 23. At first the neighbors thought it was merely a quarrel, but later when they began to distinguish clearly the words « help » and « murder », they thought it was best to intervene. Unfortunately their intervention was too late; the inhabitant of apartment A-44 had already killed his wife, whom he had apparently surprised earlier in an illicit relation. The third party in the affair remains unknown, though the police have every confidence that he will soon be found to testify. The name of the victim is Rosa L...

Now his pity had ceded to anger, a ravenous rage that consumed all thought of time or place, that drove him to read further. Now his one desire was to plumb fully the monstrosity of this day that had been thrust upon him.

Obscure Death at Memorial Bridge, he read, *Police are investigating the circumstances connected with the death of an elderly man, whose body was found on the bank of the river near the Memorial Bridge. The body, as yet unidentified, was discovered last night by a member of the vice squad assigned to the area; he estimates the age of the victim at about fifty or sixty years. The peculiar position of the cadaver and certain signs of violence lead to the supposition of foul play. Investigations, a Department spokesman said, will continue.*

« Reading about the murders? » a pleasant voice asked. It was the waiter, who had come back. « It certainly is a terrible business, now isn't it? »

The Professor could think of no words to say; all his revulsion was locked within him speechless, an animal caged by his ribs, raging for freedom, for expression. Glancing up, he saw the sky darkening over his head. He wanted the waiter to go away. He looked with hatred at the bus that lazily, half-empty, passed on its regular route through the square.

Beyond the churches lay the heart of the city, and behind him stretched its largest residential district, houses on quiet streets. This was where he lived. Suddenly he was frightened by the silence and by all the false surface of calm which covered the city like a deceptive glove. He knew: it was a city of terror, everything around him lay in ambush.

He took a coin from his pocket and put it on the table, then stood up, wavering for a moment as if deciding himself for flight.

At first he walked erratically, without knowing where his direction lay, past houses with gardens where nurses sat watching children, who played on the ground already hardening with winter. Until, all at once, he saw the name of the street, stamped in marble, and it shocked him. He knew where he was. It was the address of the student, the suicide. *His house* was the Professor's destination, though he could not yet say why. There was something he had to see or know.

The house, when he found it at last, was like all the others on the street: there was an iron fence about the garden and a high ornamental gate, where a trailing vine, unflowering at this season, ran through the iron bars as if to deprecate their severity. The villa itself had obviously been built about a half-century before in the most expensive style of the period, elaborate without elegance, large without grandeur.

The Professor could imagine the interior, a forest of over-furnished rooms, draped windows, closed doors, and the family which tried to live up to the pomposity of the building. He saw the son, who was dead now, and how he must have walked through that heavy air, feeling himself a stranger, wanting to escape to some country he could not have known.

One of the windows was open. And the old man imagined it had been the boy's; the family would be airing the room, as if to clear away the breath of the suicide. He pictured the room: a museum of meaningless relics, kept in place by an insistent mother who shared their meaninglessness, patient and preoccupied, unwilling to admit that she preferred her docile daughter to that son, so remote always from the rest of them, who had so proudly turned his back to life.

The Professor knew that the family would be hating this event and the dead son for what he had done to them, putting them in an embarassing position, making them public — his final revenge. For them what had happened was a scandal, not a tragedy.

And now as the old man looked at the window, fixing it with his silent stare, it seemed to become human, a mouth, stifling a cry, longing to shout some youthful, long-restrained word of contempt or defiance or desire.

Then a woman opened the front door of the villa and stood on the step, glaring at the Professor, as if to say: you've seen enough, go away. Offended, he looked down at himself, then moved off, with the heaviness of some prehistoric beast moving towards extinction.

He walked the length of the street, a gauntlet of similar villas, all of them human and ugly to him, crowded with death and smothered cries, with sons and with mothers.

The strength that forced him forward was not his, did not come from his great, weak body, but rather from his emotion; it was the boiling of his blood, the stir of his thoughts that kept him in motion. He had to find that other place, an apartment house in the workers' quarter, a street whose name he had never heard. It had not been in existence in those distant days when he had walked about freely. The thought pierced him how, in that time, he had walked everywere thoughtlessly, seeing nothing, and now that he had finally been gifted with sight, on this day, he could move only in difficulty and pain.

From time to time he leaned against a building to rest, shutting his eyes so as not to bear the glances of curious passers-by. At one point a group of children shouted something at him, words of insult in a meaningless sing-song that seemed vaguely familiar. Once or twice he had to ask directions, and the huge effort to say the strange street-name tired him almost as much as the walking had.

Finally, when he had passed the old railroad station and the cathedral, he reached a wholly new quarter of the city, a series of buildings constructed perhaps twenty years before, but constructed so badly that already they were no more than ruins, their once brightly-colored façades now dingy and grotesque, with an air of prostitutes, prematurely aged.

And the street itself, when he arrived there at last, was full of an unpleasant excitement he could not define. At first he thought it might still be an effect of the murder, a vicarious challenge, a thrill that these hurrying people (most of them women) felt urging them on through a life that had miraculously ceased to be quotidian. But as he rested and observed with greater care the traffic and the laughter and shouts, he realized that this was the normal behavior of the street. Every window and door stood open; in this complete absence of privacy, the inhabitants seemed then to hurry and shout in a futile effort to assert themselves and to hold themselves together as individuals.

Number twenty-three was at the corner. Otherwise it was exactly like number twenty-one and number twenty-two. The windows greeted him in rows, like a ragged army, the panes patched and cracked, or absent, strung with drying clothes which were already being dirtied by the dust of the street, and with faces that shouted or emptily watched the others who passed. A child caught his eye in inexplicable invitation.

Where had it been? He looked carefully at every window, seeking some particular sign of guilt. Nothing. Whatever he saw — windows, faces, façades — showed the signs of a life that had settled down into horror, resigned itself, given up. Nothing was innocent any more. He turned to the people that walked past him: some of them must have known everything: that woman pushing a rickety baby-carriage might have been the victim's confidante (he imagined them shopping

together or drinking their coffee at mid-morning, spreading
out their secrets like a greasy pack of cards); or one of these
hurrying men, all of them so alike, their faces as worn as
their suits, might have been the other one, the nameless
lover, worried now only by his own silence and the lust he
would have to appease elsewhere.

For now the whole street seemed stirred by this sexual
force that had driven one of them at last to kill and another
to die. What haven't these windows heard? he thought.

And suddenly the streets were empty; as if by a signal,
they had become mere littered caverns. It was the hour for
eating. His own body, which was beyond all hungers, felt
nothing, but he could imagine all of those others, crowded
into rooms, curved over tables in silence, or talking perhaps
of the crime, whetting their appetites with its novelty.

He had to leave this silence still charged with lust, a
desire that swept through the street like a devouring wind.
He forced himself into motion again, looking at nothing, his
head down, so that he could see only the intersecting lines
of pavements that he followed as if he were wandering in a
maze and had long renounced all hope of exit.

But finally he reached, not an exit, a stopping-place.
White, broad, the bridge spanned the river in a quiet part
of the city, deserted at this noon hour. At one side, around
the monument to the dead soldiers that the bridge itself
commemorated, there was a small park, some trees and a
few benches that lined the river, where a low railing did
not obscure the view.

It was this view he watched from where he sat, the river
unwinding itself past him with a slowness, a laziness that
was maddening and, he thought, malevolent. Was it filled with
blood and bodies? It seemed to him an enormous wound in
the city, open and unhealing.

And yet, as time passed and he continued to stare at the
water, its tranquil flow began inevitably to have a calming
effect on him. He felt a provisional ease which at first he

could not explain, then with a shock, he knew that it came from the absence of human beings. He was alone. The trees, still green in this false autumn warmth, stood around him, solid, unmoving, at peace. He heard a sound somewhere in the distance and imagined that it was a bird. He would have been glad to sleep.

But at that very moment from somewhere — nowhere? — a man appeared. To the Professor this newcomer came with all the force of an apparition. A man, nondescript, short, poorly dressed, with a face that expressed nothing if not absence, shuffled across the bridge, then followed the path along the river until at last he was almost directly in front of the Professor's bench. He stopped to lean against the rail.

There was an unhealthiness in this new face that woke the Professor again and shattered his tenuous calm. That face was alive, human, repulsive. The old man felt again all his horror and disgust erupt within him; this new face summed up the city, its illness, all the Professor had seen that day and wanted never to see again.

He rose from the bench, with a slow and decided movement. Almost with courtesy, he extended his hand towards the stranger, but in an instant, that heavy hand became a weapon, and in the time it took for him to draw a breath, the stranger had fallen in silence into the river, which slowly swept him away.

JAMES MERRILL

THISTLEDOWN

First clan of autumn, thistleball on a stem
Between forefinger and thumb,
Known for the seeds
That make a wish come true when the light last of them,
Into air blown, subsides,

Feathery sphere of seeds, frail brain
On prickly spine,
I feared their dissipation, seeds of that crown aspin,
Words from a high-flown talker, pale brown
Thistledown;

Yet when, bewildered what to want
Past the extravagant
Notion of wanting, I puffed
And the soft cluster broke and spinning went
More channels than I knew, aloft

In the wide air to lift its lineage,
Ha! how the Scotch flower's spendthrift
Stars drifted down
Many to tarn or turf, but ever a canny one
On the stem left

To remind me of what I had wished:
That none should have clung, lest summer, thistle-bewitched,
Dry up, be done
— And the whole of desire not yet into watched
Air at a breath blown!

OLIVE GROVE

The blue wave's slumber and the rocky brow
Almost submerged where while her father slept
Sleep of the blue wave from his forehead leapt
The goddess, dropped her gift, this silvery bough,

On him who among olives drowses now
Among these drowsing boughs their trunks express,
Pale paint from tubes so twisted, emptiness
Might sooner have put forth the slumbering green

Than these whose gnarled millenium bestows
(Upon his slumber tentatively marine
For whom endurance, lacking theirs, had been
Too bare an ikon of the mind's repose)

A dream, not of his dreaming that would wean
Roots from deep earth, rather of how each delves
To taste infusions by whose craft ourselves,
Once dreams in the mind of earth, like olive-trees,

Houses, the sleeper and his smile, the quais
And tall sail bent on the blue wave, have grown
Out of the scalding center that alone
Is wakeful for its melting images.

WILLIAM JAY SMITH

THE DESCENT OF ORPHEUS *

A cockatoo with nervous, quick cockade
Consumes the cones upon a tree of fire
Whose branches cast a giant, trembling shade
Upon the earth, and on the gilded lyre
Of Orpheus, who wanders underground,
And is consumed, and is consumed by fire.

Hear him, O wild singer, as he moves
Below the helmèd hills:
« We cannot live like this, we must empty
Ourselves of living: we must go down
Through Death's blue acres to the roots of things,
Life's darker surfaces, where huge hot springs
Break from stone.
                    We must seek Love
At the center of fire ».

                         And through a tangled wood,
Past triple-branching flame, he goes.

---

* Phi Beta Kappa Poem, *Columbia, 1951.*

48

Knowledge which is powerful will take
Man down those worn rock ways
Below the ground, into the dark god's
Kingdom, fire-dominion:
He must learn,
Like Orpheus, he cannot turn
But turning find
His sweet love vanished, and descend
Where days are nothing, and dreams end,
And broad and burning rivers flow;
And yet must turn,
And turning, ask,
« What shall I do without her?
Che farò? »

         And wanders on
Beyond all light,
From total darkness into night,
Bearing his flaming shield, his lyre.

Here at the cave's gray mouth,
The grave's green edge,
We watch the cockatoo, and cry: Return,
Return to us among the living.

         O so much
Is lost with every day: the black vanes
Turn in an angry wind, the roses burn
To ashes on a skeleton of wire;
Sun is mirror to the fire,
And earth, reflected, crumbles at our touch.

WILLIAM GOYEN

THE FIGURE OVER THE TOWN *

What I thought for so long was my doom but, I know now, is my hope, and all our's, takes the shape — or took it long ago when it was first branded upon my brain — of a huddled figure of a man aloft a flagpole. It took me a long time to see this meaning, and by the way of so much error and blind stumbling through half the experience of my life and through, it seems, half a race of lovers who fell into or were drawn upon my path.

Now each man, an army unto himself, carries with him both the artillery to kill or the flag to raise to truce — human relations have seemed to me like one eternal battle — we fight with the mind, with the heart, and with the loins, fierce weapons, or we simply come upon a man where he is working quietly at his task in the fields and slay him at his work. We draw back from him, perhaps astonished, are accused, flee branded by the murder and are 'protected' by the brand from murder or from revenge by other hands. Fugitive, we carry the brand upon our bodies and we wander over the face of the earth, with our burden which is to reconcile the passions of hate and love, and to understand the evil act.

In the town of my beginning, in my boyhood, I saw this

---

* From a Novel: *Half a Look of Cain.*

50

masked figure sitting aloft. It was never explained to me by
my elders, who were thrilled and disturbed by this figure,
too, who this figure was, except that he was called 'Shipwreck
Kelley' and that the days and nights he sat aloft were counted,
kept a record of, on calendars in the kitchens of small houses
and in the troubled mind. Shipwreck Kelley fed the fancy
of an isolated small town of practical folk whose day's work
was hard and real enough.

It was at the time of a war; and since the night this figure
was pointed out to me from the roof of our little shed where
my father sheltered grain and plowing and planting imple-
ments, his shape has never let me alone; and it has seemed
that in every critical or significant experience of my life this
shape has suddenly appeared before me, to deliver me or to
rob me, so that I have come to see that it is the dominating
emblem of my life, as often a lost lover is, or the figure
of a powerful parent, or the symbol of a Faith as the Scallop
Shell was for so many, at one time, or the Cross. The life
of a man, then, can be the search for the identification or
the definition of such an image which it seems his lot to carry
through the world in the time of his life, and to make, finally,
a choice in favor of it or against it. Beginning with a secret,
a personal image, he carries it out into the world and tries
to progress it, using it, testing its validity, its human, univers-
al use, relating it to the world, to human life, as well as
to his own life. All things become related to this central
image, seem to take their meaning from it and to give mean-
ing to it; it can be an instrument, then, of order and enlighten-
ment where our daily human acts seem to lie so in fragment,
so half in darkness and so often meaningless. This image can
be one of light and not a dark and malign one which sorcerers
must exorcise us of, or an engine of destruction and evil.
Men must have images, for themselves and to lend to many
men, and the thieves who rob us of them or explain them
away in their own terms are the killers of men's fancy, they
are the creators of a 'reality' in which a society cannot breathe
and in which the 'reason' they wish to substitute for 'un-

reason' is a machine which grinds like an ice-maker in the brain and freezes the human affections.

It was in a time of a War I could not understand, being so very young, that my father came to me at darkening, in the beginning wintertime, and said, 'Come with me to the Patch, Son, for I want to show you something'. The Patch, which I often dream about, was a mysterious fencedin plot of ground, about half an acre, where I never intruded. I often stood at the gate or at the fence and looked in through the octagonal lenses of the chicken-wire and saw how strange this little territory was and wondered what it was for. There was the shed in it where implements and grain were stored, and nothing was ever planted here nor any animal pastured here; nothing, not even grass or weed, grew here, it was just plain common ground. This late afternoon, just at the moment of darkening, my father took me into this little pasture and led me to the shed where he hoisted me up to the roof. He waited a moment while I looked around at all the world we lived in and had forgotten that it was so wide and housed so many in dwellings quite like ours. Later, when my grandfather, my father's father, took me across the road and railroad tracks into the large pasture that was so great I had thought it, from a window of the house, the whole world, where a little circus had been set up as if by magic or by a dream of mine in the night before, and raised me up to sit on the broad back of a sleepy elephant, I saw the same sight and not only recalled the night I stood on the roof of the shed but also what I had seen from there, that haunting image, and thought I saw it again, this time on the lightning-rod of our house ... but no, it was that crowing cock that always stood there, eternally strutting out his breast and at the break of crowing.

My father waited a while for me to arrange myself to air and height — he saw how wobbly I was — and then when he saw I had steadied myself and was fixed on the sight he had brought me to see, he said, 'Well, Son, what is that you see over there, by the Methodist Church?' I was speechless and could only gaze; and then I finally said to him, not moving, 'Something is sitting on the flagpole on top of a building'.

'It is just a man', my father said, 'and his name is Shipwreck Kelley. He is going to sit up there for as long as he can stand it'.

When we came in the house, I heard my father say to my mother, lightly, 'I showed Son Shipwreck Kelley and I think it scared him a little'. And I heard my mother say, 'It seems a foolish stunt, and I think maybe children shouldn't see it'.

All that night Shipwreck Kelley was on my mind. When it began raining in the very deepest night, I worried about him in the rain, and I went to my window and looked out to see if I could see him. When it lightened I could see that he was safe and dry under a little tent he had raised over himself and gathered around him. Later I had a terrible dream about him, that he was falling, falling, and when I called out in my nightmare of Shipwreck Kelley, they came to me and patted me back to sleep, not knowing that I dreamt of him again.

He stayed and stayed up there, the hooded flagpole sitter, and when we would go into town and walk under him I would not look up as they told me to; but once when we stood across the street from the building where he was perched, I looked up and saw how high he was in the air and he waved down at me with his cap in his hand. Why would he not show his face?

Everywhere there was the talk of The War, but where it was or what it was I did not know. It seemed only some huge appetite that craved all our sugar and begged from the town its goods so that people seemed paled and impoverished by it, as though it were some sickness that infected them and it made life gloomy, that was the word. One night we went into the town to watch them burn Old Man Gloom, a monstrous strawman with a sour turned-down look on his face and dressed even to the point of a hat on — it was the

Ku Klux Klan who lit him afire — and above, in the light of the flames, we saw Shipwreck Kelley waving down his cap to us. He had been up eighteen days.

He kept staying up there. More and more the talk was about him, with the feeling of The War beneath all the talk. It seemed a scarey and an evil time. People began to get restless about Shipwreck Kelley and to want him to come on down. 'It seems *morbid*', I remember my mother saying. What at first had been a thrill and an excitement for the town — the whole town was there every other day when the provisions basket was raised up to him, and the contributions to it were extravagant, fresh pies and cakes, fresh milk, little presents, and so forth — became an everyday sight, like spires on churches and weathervanes on houses; then he seemed ignored and forgotten by the town except for me who kept a vigil with him and a constant watch on him, secretly; then finally the town became so disturbed by him, for he seemed to be going on and on, he seemed, now, an intruder — who could feel unlooked at or unhovered over in his house with this figure over everything that happened below in it — it was discovered that Shipwreck was spying on the town through binoculars! — and towards the last there was an agitation in the town to bring him down and the City Council met to this end. There had been some events of irregularity in the town which the town had laid to the general lawlessness and demoralizing effect of The War: some robberies, the disappearance of a young girl, Sarah Nichols, the beauty of the town; but it was said she ran away to find someone in The War; and one Negro was shot in the woods, which could have been the corrective work of the Ku Klux Klan who had their reasons. The question, at the City Council meeting was, *who gave Shipwreck Kelley permission to go up there?* No one seemed to know; the merchants said it was not for advertising, or at least no one of them had arranged it, though after he was up various of them tried to use a good thing to advertise their products, *Egglay or Redgoose Shoes* or *Have a Coke at Robbins Pharmacy* — and why not? The Chamber of Commerce had not brought him, nor the Women's Club; maybe the Ku Klux had, to warn and tame the Negroes, for they were especially in awe of Shipwreck Kelley; but the Ku Klux were as innocent as all others. The Pastor of the church was reminded of the time a bird had built a nest on the church steeple, a huge foreign bird, and had delighted all the congregation as well as it had given him subject for several sermons; how all the congregation came out on the grounds to adore the bird who, in time, became suddenly savage and dived down to pluck the feathers from women's Sunday hats and, finally, appeared fiercely in Church during Sermon and shrieked; and they had to bring him down by calling the Fire Department who found his nest full of rats and mice, half-devoured, and no eggs at all ... the subject for another series of sermons by the Pastor, drawing as he did his topics from real life.

As the flagpole sitter had come to be regarded as a defacement of the town landscape, an undesireable, unsightly object, a tramp, like a transient bird, it was suggested that the Ku Klux build a fire in the square and ride round it on their horses and in their sheets, firing their guns into the air, the way they did in their public demonstrations against immorality, sensationalism and perversity: and to force Shipwreck Kelley down. Perhaps he was going to be a wartime suicide. If this failed, it was suggested that someone be sent up on a fireman's ladder to reason with Shipwreck. Now he was regarded as an enemy to the people of the town and more, as a *danger* to the town, and even more, as a kind of criminal, who had at first been so admired and respected for his courage, and so desired, even; for many had been intoxicated and infatuated with him, sending up love-notes and photographs of themselves in the provisions basket, which Shipwreck had read, obviously, and had later sailed down in the form of winged planes — some religious fanatics said they were in the form of the Cross — for anyone to pick up and read on the ground, to the embarassment of this one and that.

The town had been ready for any kind of miracle or

sensation, obviously, or just for something to be excited or outraged by. A fanatical religious group took Shipwreck Kelley as the Second Coming, the old man called Old Man Nay, who lived on the edge of the town in his boarded-up house and sat at one open window with his shotgun in his lap watching for the Devil, unnailed his door and appeared in the town to announce that he had seen a light playing around Shipwreck at night and that he was some phantom representative of the Devil and should be banished by a raising of the Cross; but it was explained by others that what he saw was St. Elmo's Fire, a natural phenomenon. Whatever was given a fantastical meaning by some was explained away by others as of natural origin and cause, and what was right and who was to believe what? An Evangelist of the town who called himself 'The Converted Jew' (He was now a Baptist) had, at the beginning, requested of Shipwreck Kelley by a letter in the basket, the dropping of leaflets, a sample of which was pinned to the letter. The leaflet, printed in red ink, said across the top in huge letters: WARNING: YOU ARE IN GREAT DANGER! Below was a long message to sinners. If Shipwreck would drop these messages upon the town he would be aiding in the salvation of the wicked. 'The Judgments of God are soon to be poured upon the Earth! Prepare to meet God before it is too late! Where will you spend Eternity? What can you do to be saved? How can we escape if we neglect so great salvation (Heb. 2:3)?' But there was no reply from Shipwreck, which was evidence enough for The Converted Jew to know that the was on the Devil's side; and so he held some meetings at night in the square, under the shadow of the flagpole, with his little group passing out the leaflets. 'Lower Cain!' he bellowed. 'You Sinners standing on the street corner running a long tongue about your neighbors; you show-going, card-playing, jazz-dancing brothers, God love your soul, you are a tribe of sinners and you know it and God knows it, but He loves you and wants you to come into his tabernacle and give up your hearts that are laden with wickedness. If you look in the Bible, if you will turn to

the chapter of Ezekiel, you will find there about the fallen
Angel, Lucifer was his name, and how his clothing was sewn
of emeralds and sapphires, for he was very beautiful; but
friends, my sin-loving friends, that didn't make any dif-
ference: 'How are thou fallen from Heaven, O Lucifer, son
of the morning', the Bible reads. And it says there that
the Devil will walk amongst us and that the Devil will sit
on the rooftops; and I tell you we must unite together to
drive Satan from the top of the world. Listen to me and
read my message, for I was the rottenest man in this world
until I heard the voice of God in my ear. I drank, I ran
with women, I ran after thrills of the flesh ... and I admonish
you that the past scenes of earth *shall be remembered in
Hell...*'

The old maid, Miss Hazel Bright, who had had one
lover long ago and he, a cowboy named Rolfe Sanderson,
had gone away and never returned, told that Shipwreck was
Rolfe come back, and she wrote notes of poetic longing up
to him which she put in the provisions basket. Everybody
used Shipwreck Kelley for his own purpose, and so he, sitting
away from it all, apparently serene and in his own dream
and idea of himself, became the lost lover to the lovelorn,
the Saint to the seekers of Salvation, the damned to the lost
and guilty, the scapegoat of the guilty-minded, the exposer
of the guilty, the reminder of love, of evil, of the lost, of
hope, of guilt.

But the town went on tormenting him; they could not
let him alone. They wished him to mean their own dream
or hope or lost illusion or they wished him to be what destroy-
ed hope or illusion: they wanted something *to get their hands
on*, around the loins if he would love them, around the neck
if he would not; they wanted something to avenge some
dark misgiving in themselves or to take to their deepest
bosom, into the farthest cave of themselves where they would
take no other if he would come and have them for them-
selves alone. They could not leave him alone. They plagued
him with loveletters and when he would not acknowledge

their professions of love, they wrote him messages of hate and insult. They told him their secrets and when he would not show himself to be overwhelmed by their secrets, they accused. him of keeping secrets of his own. They professed to love him, to be willing to follow him, leaving everything behind; but when he would not answer to come with him, they told him how they wished he would fall and knock his brains out. They could not make up their minds and they tried to destroy him who had made up his, whatever it was he had made up his mind to.

Merchants tormented him with proposals and offers — would he wear a Stetson Hat all one day, tipping it and waving it to the people below; would he hold, if just for fifteen minutes every hour, a streamer with words on it proclaiming the goodness of their lightbread, or allow balloons, spelling out the name of something that ought to be bought, to be floated from the flagpole? Would he throw down Life-savers? Many a man, and most, would have done it, to give a simplified and easily understandable reason for what his behavior was about, pacifying the general observer with some reason for what was done, and broad in the public eye, and in the general observer's own terms (or the general observer would not have it); and so send the public attendant away undisturbed and easy, with the feeling that all the world was really just as he, cheating a little here, disguising a little there, everybody was, after all, alike, so where the pain, and why?

But Shipwreck Kelley gave no answer. Apparently he had nothing to sell, wanted to make no fortune, to play no jokes or tricks, apparently he wanted just to be let alone to do his job; but because he was so different, they would not let him alone until they could, by whatever means they could muster, make him undifferent and quite like them-selves, or cause him, at least, to recognize them and pay them some attention. Apparently he was not camping up there for the fun of it, for if so why would he not let them all share in it, they would do that; or maybe he was there

58

for the pure devilment of it, like a cat calm on a chimney-top... or for some very crazy and not-to-be-tolerated reason of his own, which everyone tried to make out, hating secrets as people do who want everything in the clear — where they attack it and accuse it and take high moral dudgeon against it.

Was it Cray McCreery up there — had somebody made him another bet — one time he had walked barefooted to the next town, 18 miles, because of a lost bet; but no, Cray McCreery was found, as usual, in the Domino Parlor. Had any crazy people escaped from the Asylum? They were counted and found to be all in, home. The Mind Reader, Madame Fritzie, was importuned: she could not find out one thing. There seemed, she said, to be a dark woman in the picture, and that was all she contributed, « I see a dark woman... »; and as she had admonished so many in the town her recurrent vision of a dark woman, there was either an army of dark women tormenting the minds of men and women in the world, or only one, which was Madame Fritzie herself. She could have made a fortune out of the whole affair if she had had her wits about her to see the right things. More than one Ouija Board was put questions to, but the answers were either indistinguishable or not to the point... the way people go to supernatural sources for explanations which natural ones will not yield.

Dogs howled and bayed at night and sometimes in the afternoons; hens crowed; and the sudden death of children was laid to the evil power of Shipwreck Kelley over the town.

A masked buffoon came to a party dressed as Shipwreck Kelley, and for awhile he caused increasing uneasiness among the guests until three of the men at the party decided to take subtle action rather than forcibly unmask the stranger and reported the incident to the Police on the telephone. The Police told them to unmask him by force and they would be on their way. When the Police arrived they found it had turned out to be Marcus Peters, a practical joker with the biggest bellylaugh in town and past president of the Lion's

Club, and everybody could have known all along that the imposter was he if he had only laughed.

A new little language evolved in the town: 'You're crazy as Shipwreck'; 'cold as a Flagpole Sitter's...'; 'Go sit on a flagpole'; and a high school girl riding home from a dance said to the football player whose lap she was sitting on, 'What do you think I am, a flagpole sitter?'

There were so many little felonies and even big offenses of undetermined origin in the Police records of the town, and Shipwreck was a stimulus to fresh inspection of unsolved misdemeanors. He drew up to him, as though he attracted blame, the suspicions of the town, and he absorbed them like a filter, as though he might purify the town of its wickedness. If only he would send down some sign of response to what had gone up to him. But he would not budge; and now he no longer even waved down to the people below as he had during the first good days. Shipwreck Kelley had utterly withdrawn from everybody. What the town finally decided to do was to put a searchlight on him at night to keep watch on him.

What with the searchlight on the flagpole sitter, the whole thing took a turn, as ideas do which seem for a while insupportable but, in another light, obsessive as they are, become an excuse for ribald, hysterical, devil-may-care attitude towards it. The town began to be gay with Shipwreck. When a little wartime Carnival came to the town, it was invited to install itself in the square by the flagpole sitter, and a Bazaar was added to it by the town. The spirit of Shipwreck had to be, it was admitted, admired; for after a day and night of shunning the gaiety and the mockery of it all, he showed his good nature and his good sportsmanship — and even his daring — by participating! He began to do what looked like acrobatic stunts above the town, as though he were an attraction at the Carnival. But what would the people do, after awhile, again, but turn against him and say he was, as they had said at first, a sensationalist? Still, I loved it that he had become active, this idea, I loved it that *my* idea participated in the whole show, that it was not a static and stagnant, fastidious, precious and Olympian idea, that Shipwreck did not take on a self-righteous or pompous or persecuted air about it all; although my secret conception of him was a tragic one. I was proud that the idea fought back — otherwise it was like Old Man Gloom: a shape of straw and sawdust in man's clothing: let them burn him, gloom only stood there, among the executioners, watching its own effigy and blowing the flames. I see now that what I was watching was the conflict of an idea with a society; and I am sure that the idea was bred there by the society, raised up there, even, by the society that opposed it, and not removed from it; in short, that society was in the flagpole sitter and he was in the society of the town. But the difference was that the flagpole sitter was thinking in terms of the community, I believe, while the town was thinking only in terms of itself.

There was the little carnival around him. One concession called 'Ring Shipwreck's Bell' invited customers to try to strike a bell at the top of a tall pole resembling Shipwreck's and with a replica of him on top by hitting a little platform with a rubber-headed sledge hammer. There were other concessions where people could throw darts at a target resembling a figure on a pole. The Ferris Wheel was put up so close to Shipwreck that when its passengers reached the top for a magical instant they could almost reach over and touch his body. Going round and round, it was as if one were soaring and rising up to him only to fall away, down, from him; to have him and to lose him; and it was all felt in a marvellous and whirling sensation in the stomach which made this experience the most vaunted one of the show. This must have tantalized Shipwreck and it must have seemed to him that all the beautiful and desirable people in the world rose and fell around him, to give themselves to him only to withdraw from him untaken and ungiven, in a flashing wheel of faces, eyes and lips and tongues stuck out to him and sometimes a thigh shown him or a hand offering a breast or sex, and then burning away, like the temptation of Saint Anthony.

His sky at night was filled with voluptuous images of flesh and desire, and often he must have seen the faces, he thought, of those he had loved and possessed, turning round and round his head to torment him — or was it his brain, filled with this burning wheel? But there were men on the wheel who made profane signs to him and women who stuck out their rumps at him, fingering their nose. Soon he raised his tent again and obscured himself from his tormentors and the tormented. But what specifically caused this withdrawal, was the attempt of a drunken young man to shoot him. This young man named Maury rode a motorcycle around the town at all hours and loved the mean streets of the town and the good women who gave him ease on them, especially the fat ones, his mania. One night he stood at the window of the hotel and watched the figure on the pole that seemed to flash on and off, real and then unreal, with the light of the electric sign beneath the building. He took deep drags off his cigarette and blew the smoke out the window towards Shipwreck; then he blew smoke rings as if to lasso Shipwreck with them, or as if his figure were a pin he could hoop with rings of smoke. 'You silly bastard', he had muttered, 'where have I seen you before', between his half-clenched teeth, the way he spoke that made him so seductive to people, and fired. Shipwreck turned away, once and for all. But he had not turned away from me.

With all this in my mind, I, the silent observer, watching from my window or from any high place I could secretly climb to, witnessed the conflict of sides and the tumult of the town. One night in my dreaming of Shipwreck Kelley — it happened every night, this dream, and in the afternoons when I had to take my nap, and it had gone on so long, this dreaming of him that it seemed, finally, that he and I were friends and that we met in the rendezvous of my dream where he had come down secretly to me in the little pasture — years later I would know what all our conversations were about, but not for many years and after so much — he lived, alive and real in my room where the dreaming of him happened, he was the only one in the world who knew me — the people of the town came to me and said, 'Son, we have chosen you to go up the flagpole to Shipwreck Kelley and tell him to come down. In my dream they led me, with cheers and honors, to the top of the building and stood below while I skinnied up the pole. Shipwreck's tent was up, for it was raining in my dream; but a great black bird was circling over the tent. As I went up the pole I noticed crowded avenues of ants coming and going. And when I went into the tent, I found him gone. The tent was as if a tornado had struck inside it and wrecked the whole world of it; there were piles of rotten food — he had not eaten any of the provisions they had sent up — shreds of letters torn and retorn a score of times were as small as flakes of snow; photographs pinned to the walls of the tent were marked and scrawled over until they looked like photographs of fiends and monsters; corpses and drifts of feathers of dead birds that had flown, in their night flights, into the tent and gone so wild in fright that they had beaten themselves to death against the sides of the tent. There was a floor of feathers and decaying food and the litter of torn letters. And over it all was the vicious traffic of insects that had found the human remains in the way they sense what human beings have left and come from miles away to get it. What would I tell them below who were now *crying* up to me, 'What does he say, what does Shipwreck Kelley say, Son?' and there were whistles and Indian calls and an increasingly thunderous chant of *'Bring him down! Bring him down! Bring him down!'* What would I tell them? I was glad he had gone; but I would not tell them that, yet. In the tent I saw one thing that was not touched or changed by Shipwreck: a piece of paper with printed words in red ink, and across the top the huge words: WARNING: YOU ARE IN GREAT DANGER!

Then, in my dream, I went to the flap of the tent and stuck out my head. There was a searchlight upon me through which a delicate curtain of light rain fell; and through the lighted curtain of rain that made the people below seem to be far far under shimmering and jeweled veils, I shouted down upon all the faces of the multitude which was dead quiet now, 'He is not here. Shipwreck Kelley is not here'.

There was no sound below from the crowd who did not, at first, believe what I said. They waited, then one voice bellowed up, 'Tell him to come down!' to make me say again what they would not yet believe; and others joined this voice until, again, the crowd roared, 'Tell him we will not harm him; only tell him he has to come down!' Then I waved down at them to be quiet, in the gesture of Shipwreck Kelley's salute as he had waved down at people on the sidewalks and street. They hushed to hear me again. Again I said, this time in a voice that was not mine but in my dream it sounded large and round and resounding, 'Shipwreck Kelley is not here, his place is empty'.

And then, in my magnificent dream, I closed the flap of the tent and settled down to make Shipwreck Kelley's place my own, to drive out the insects, to erase the obliterating marks on the photographs, and to piece together, with infinite and patient care, the fragments of the letters to see what they told. It would take me a very long time, this putting together again what had been broken into pieces and by so many lovers and killers; but I would have a very long time to give to it, and I was at the source of the mystery, removed and secure from the chaos of the world below that could not seem to make up its mind and tried to keep me from making up my own.

My dream ended here, or was broken, by the hand of my mother shaking me to morning; and when I went to eat breakfast in the kitchen, I heard them saying that Shipwreck Kelley had signalled that he wanted to come down early that morning, around six o'clock — he had come down in his own time — and that he had come down very very tired, having set a world's record of forty days and nights, the length of the flood. I did not tell my dream, for I had no power of telling; but I knew that I had a story to one day shape around the marvel and mystery that ended in a dream and began in the world that was to be mine. I would either run through my life groping like a child for a child's lost image, or rise out of it into a strong manhood and, like a man, kill it. What I had to start with, to examine and to clarify, was an idea and a dream which, working upon each other and together or against each other, might grow and grow, if it was healthy and valid, drawing more and more life into it and giving up, fragment by fragment, a meaning to life; or sicken and wither, withering me into a victim of it instead of a champion of it, drive me on in vengeance what was once a heroic shape and might have made me a hero and a savior, until I carried vengeance out against myself — or destroyed, in that final courageous look, the image. My life, its pattern, was to be the manipulation of this idea in the world, in society; to carry it through the world, to progress it as idea. And the movement of this idea, the march and gait of it, the moving or the halting of it, measured my life.

Was it a murderous image or a benevolent one? Would it make me a fanatic? Would I be its victim, living by a kind of ventriloquism? Would it be a weapon, this idea, striking out through me? Would it be a straw and sawdust figure which I would forever thrust out before me, between me and my experience — a buffer idea — I hiding behind it, a corpse of straw and sawdust shadowing me and keeping me in its dark shadow — was I the carrier of a corpse, as though it were clasped upon my back, going hunched under it through my life, cursed by it which was dependent upon me for its life, this dead image I would not bring down to bury, draining me and wearying me and sapping my blood life out of me?

There is that long story to tell.

CONRAD AIKEN

THE WALK IN THE GARDEN

I

Noting in slow sequence by waterclock of rain
or dandelion clock of sun
the green hours of trees and white hours of flowers:
annotating again the « flower-glory of the season,
a book that is never done, » never done:
savoring phrases of green-white, mock-white,
while the ancient lyre-tree, the ancient plum,
adds for another May its solar sum
in silent galaxies of bloom:
it is here, interpreting these, translating these,
stopping in the morning to study these,
touching affectionately the cold bark
of the seven-branched tree, where bees
stir the stars and scatter them down:
it is here, in these whitenesses of thought,
poring over these pages of white thought,
that we ponder anew the lifelong miracle:
the miracle that in these we best remember,
and in wisdom treasure best,
the lost snows of another December,
and the lost heart, and the lost love.
What matter that we are older, that we age?

Blest that we live this morning, blest
that still we read the immortal book
and in time's sunlight turn another page.

II

Shall we call it, then, the walk in the garden?
the morning walk in the simple garden? But only if by this
    we mean
everything! The vast daybreak ascends the stairs of pale silver
above a murmur of acacias, the white crowns
shake dark and bright against that swift escalation of light,
and then, in intricate succession, the unfolding minutes and
    hours
are marked off by the slow and secret transactions
of ant and grassblade, mole and tree-root,
the shivering cascade of the cicada's downward cry, the
    visitation
(when the brazen noon invites) of that lightninged prism
the hummingbird, or the motionless hawkmoth.
Listen! The waterclock of sap in bough and bole,
in bud and twig, even in the dying
branch of the ancient plum-tree, this you hear, and clearly,
at eleven, or three, as the rusted rose-petal
drops softly, being bidden to do so, at the foot of the stem,
past the toad's unwinking eye! Call it
the voyage in the garden, too, for so it is:
the long voyage home, past cape and headland
of the forgotten or remembered: the mystic signal
is barely guessed in the spiderwort's golden eye, recognized
tardily, obscurely, in the quick bronze flash
from the little raindrop left to wither
in the hollow of a dead leaf, or a green fork
of celandine. For in this walk, this voyage,
it is yourself, the profound history of your « self, »
that now as always you encounter. At eleven or three

it was past these folded capes and headlands, these decisions
     or refusals,
these little loves, or great,
that you once came. Did you love? did you hate?
did you murder, or refrain from murder, on an afternoon
of innocent cirrus in April? It is all recorded
(and with it man's history also)
in the garden syllables of dust and dew:
the crucifixions and betrayals,
the lying affirmations and conniving denials,
the cowardly assumptions, when you dared not face yourself,
the little deaths, and the great. Today
among these voluntary resumptions you walk a little way
toward tomorrow. What, then, will you choose to love or
     hate?
These leaves, these ants, these dews, these steadfast trifles,
     dictate
whether that further walk be little or great.
These waiting histories will have their say.

III

But of those other trifles, the too intrusive,
the factual, the actual, that are too intrusive,
too near, too close, too gross, for deeper meaning:
what of these, what will memory make of these?
Will these too yield in time to the magic of translation?
The bobby pins, the daily news, the paper clips, even
the stuffed two-headed calf once seen in a pawnshop window;
as indeed also the crumpled letter, furtively
dropped in the ash can at the corner,
yes, and the torn half of the movie ticket, bright pink,
found inadvertently in the breast pocket, to remind you —
but meanly — of other days of afternoon rain:
how will you profitably rehearse these,

how will you (otherwise than here!) rehearse these, and to
    what end
of reconstruction? for what inspired reinterpretation
of the lost image, the lost touch?
Useless, here, the immediate, the factual, the actual:
the telephone remains silent when most you wish to hear
    it:
the May morning, or is it August or September,
remains empty, infertile, at precisely that instant
when your heart — if that is what you mean by heart —
would invoke a vision.

                    Blessing enough, indeed, it might have
    been,
but not under peach-tree or lyre-tree,
in the persistence of the radio's tremolo
and the listening silence of an empty room:
blessing enough if in these should quietly have spoken,
in answer to that invocation, the not-voice of voice,
the now almost unknown and unfamiliar voice,
the voice at first not recognized when heard:
blessing enough if in these
indifferent accidents and meaningless impromptus
the angelic not-you should open the door
and angelically enter, to take slow possession
of the room, the chairs, the walls, the windows,
the open piano with its waiting keys,
and the poor bed under the forgotten picture,
but possessing also
the divine touch that in the radiant fingertips
could at once create, with a magician's eloquence,
nothing from something, or something from nothing:
as, out of the untouched piano,
a shabby chord, a threadbare tune, the banal air
squealing from the midnight jukebox, where,
at the corner saloon, over the tepid beer,
you sit and stare,

69

remembering how the days have become years,
and the minutes hours,
and the false sunlight is distilled to tears
in the sentimental involutions of a shared sound:
yes, and the touch of the fingertip, once, on the back of the
      hand,
or, for a braver instant, tentatively, along the line of the
      cheek:
but no, these are all a broken imagination only,
the one and only heart remains lonely,
the morning remains silent, cannot speak,
muted by the ridiculous trifles, the preposterous trifles,
that stammer between the past and you.
Only, in the thinking hands, for a moment,
the persistent stupid bloodstream vaguely traces —
as if on air, as if on air —
the lost touch, the lost image, the chimerical future:
praying, now, for the illusion of an abstract love.

IV

The illusion of an abstract love? Say, rather,
it was the loves and hates that were illusion,
and all that accompanied them: items of fatigue
or of dubious regret, denials and acceptances,
these it is that are as clouds
gone deathward over the morning, lost, dislimned,
and now recoverable only, if at all,
in the remembered crevice in the remembered garden wall:
abstracted out of space, abstracted out of time,
but now reset, by the morning walk in the garden,
in crystal rhyme.
In these rich leaves, which are not only leaves
of lyre-tree or pomecitron, but also leaves
of a living book that is never done:
from winter to summer, from spring to fall:

in these we keep them all.
Here is that abstract love which we would find
wherein all things become imperishable mind:
the numberless becomes one, the brief becomes everlasting,
the everlasting opens to close
in the perishing of the raindrop on the rose:
violence is understood, and at last still,
evil is fixed and quiet as a tree or hill,
but all alike acceptable and one
and in one pattern made to move, or not to move,
by the illusion, if it is illusion,
of an abstract love.
Touch now again the serpent skin of the lyre-tree:
stoop now again, a hummingbird,
to the magic of the mock-orange:
count again by waterclock of rain
or dandelion clock of sun
the slow days of trees, the quick hours of flowers:
this time, this matin-song, this love, is yours, is ours,
a book that is never done, never done.

THEODORE ROETHKE

« THE SHIMMER OF EVIL »

Louise Bogan

The weather wept, and all the trees bent down;
Bent down their birds: the light waves took the waves;
Each single substance glittered to the stare;
Each vision purely, purely was its own:
— There was no light; there was no light at all:
(Stones heavy; stones, stone.)

Far from the mirrors all the bushes rang
With their hard snow; leaned on the lonely eye;
Cold evil twinkled tighter than a string; a fire
Hung down: And I was only I.
— There was no light; there was no light at all:

Each cushion found itself a field of pins,
Prickling the wishes with confusion's ire;
Hope's holy wrists: the little burning boys
Cried out their lives an instant and were free.
— There was no light; there was no light at all.

LOVE'S PROGRESS

I

The possibles we dare!
O rare propinquity! —
I have considered and found
A mouth I cannot leave.
The great gods arch my bones.

II

The long veins of the vine
Journey around a tree;
Light strides the rose;
A woman's naked in water,
And I know where she is.

III

True, she can think a bird
Until it broods in her eyes.
Love me, my violence,
Light of my spirit, light
Beyond the look of love.

IV

It's midnight on the mouse,
The rabbit, and the wren;
A log sings in its flame.
Father, I'm far from home,
And I have gone nowhere.

V

The close dark hugs me hard,
And all the birds are stone.
I fear for my own joy;
I fear myself in the field,
For I would drown in fire.

ELEGY

I

Should every creature be as I have been,
There would be reason for essential sin;
I have myself an inner weight of woe
That God himself can scarcely bear.

II

Each fall by seasons to a separate fate:
Man unto man, you sheer heaven's gate;
I have myself an inner weight of woe
That Christ, securely bound, could bear.

III

Thus I; and should these reasons fly apart,
I know myself, my seasons, and I know:
I have myself one crumbling skin to show;
God could believe: I am here to fear.

IV

What you survived I shall believe: the Heat,
Scars, Tempests, Floods, the Motion of Man's Fate;
I bear one heart, and O! its weight of woe
That God that God leans down his heart to hear.

SYLVIA BERKMAN

WHO KILLED COCK ROBIN?

The hotel room was at the end of a long corridor, overlooking a narrow street. I went back, though it wasn't very late; I couldn't sit through the movie again. Any message? I asked as I stopped to get the key — telephone call or telegram? Oliver, Paul Oliver, room 86. The clerk turned his civil dim impersonal eyes on the empty cubicle I had already scanned. No, no message; no message of any kind for 86.

In the corridor I stopped a moment before my polished numerals; then I turned the key. It was strange, to be closed up in that wedge of space in a city I'd scarcely seen — Providence, Rhode Island. The room had the uncanny, suspended atmosphere of a room when you get up at night at last, not with any purpose or expectation, just in order not to lie stretched taut awake. Those are the moments, as you sit there smoking, when you seem to hear the naked machinery of time: intricate, unsleeping, irreversible, and dangerous. You look back at the pattern it has shaped through, or you have shaped through it, and you wonder if everything was meant to culminate in this last detail of the design, stamped in sharper and sharper repetition — until the whole instrument breaks.

What is the taste of knowledge? What fruit corresponds? Where do you bite into the rind to the adamant salt heart? In a hotel room, perhaps, locked in, anonymous, with no

75

companion but the crooked image of yourself the wall mirror reflects.

This time, how did it begin? First beginnings are lost, buried under a drift of gradual uncertainties falling like scattered snow. This time, how did it begin? She came home late as usual, long after her classes were through: I knew every minute of her schedule, every necessary move. I'd been working at the desk, correcting the last set of freshman themes. I was reminiscent, I was tender, stopping to watch New York turn blue and possible in twilight, starkness assuaged, distance muted, clothed for this moment in illusive grace. The papers were miscellaneous, an excercise in narrative, all absolutely predictable, the good students good and the bad students bad. As I read, while twilight graded into dusk, nine-tenths of me was poised alert listening for the sound of her key. Suddenly the strain and endless monologue inside — how could it happen? when did it begin? — fell away. Simplicity seemed wise and true: to go forward as she entered, draw her to the window, not even kiss her cheek, just stand there hand in hand letting estrangement dissolve without a word. Afterward, over a drink, it would be easy to say the few things we still needed to say.

Then in she flew, stripping off her clothes and diving into a change almost before the door had slammed. Committee meeting — the fourth that week. No time for a drink, no time for dinner. Please call a cab. It darts like streaking flame, the instant of reversal, unleashing hate, hate, hate, and icy hate. My hands began to tremble. I stood up behind the desk, pressing my fingers flat against the loose pages of a theme, reading, looking downward, in the childish semi-print the private schools turn out: « An Unforeseen Event. » My throat burned tight; I couldn't speak; and all the time my heart beat hate, hate, hate.

That silence is physical, the rigid clamp of silence under too much to be said. Every bone in my body felt choked. She moved capable and swift, lipstick renewed, powder blended, a run of the hairbrush over the hair. I waited, blindly following the first sentence of the theme under my hand: « It was a very beautiful morning when we started out for an unknown destination, at least to me. » She must have felt what I was feeling; it existed; she couldn't escape. Finally, she flicked me one of her looks: suave, impenetrable, uncomprehending, aloof. « I won't be back till late, » she said. « Don't bother to wait up. » That's Glenn; cold as coldest hell, cruel to every fingernail, and invariably polite.

I wanted to beat her head against the wall, crash books and furniture, rage, and make her rage. Words began to come, words rehearsed alone, clogging thick. Just then the telephone bell rang.

It was my department chairman, Dr. Sewall. Yes, I was delegate to the conference of teachers of Freshman English at Providence the next day. Yes... Oh, yes... I had of course heard of Josephine Robinson, active in public services and social charities. Yes, it was indeed very awkward, with the annual Brickett lecture scheduled for the twenty-third: it was most regrettable that Dr. Leander could not meet the engagement, for his sake also of course: at his age an operation could indeed prove dangerous. I did agree that a personal explanation of the matter might ensure success: I too hoped that Josephine Robinson would consent to act as substitute — I should of course be very careful to avoid that particular word. Thank you very much. Did my voice change during the conversation, when the door shut, when Glenn left?

I stood there, still holding the receiver, pounding with all the questions I had to contain. What did she want, of me, of herself, of both of us together? A convenient residence, with all expenses shared? A handy object to concentrate her cruelty upon, so she could glitter bright before a dazzled world? A token marriage, leaving her undistracted to drive on towards her own ambitious ends? Whatever she wanted, why couldn't she speak? Always the impervious good manners that lightning couldn't crack, always the cool deflection of your own violence, always the fixed determination to reach the place she intends to reach. And simultaneously, a curling underthread of admiration for Chairman Sewall mingled in — the crafty old department fox, to shove that mean commission off on me. I could see the exact evolution of his scheme, naked under his pompous idiom. Only the day before Josephine Robinson had made the papers again, for some act of importance I didn't bother to read. But I'd noticed the prominent photograph: crescent-shaped black eyes that grill you even from the printed page, eaglebeak like a scimitar, military chin, all cast in a mould of rock and steel. This was the monument I was to persuade.

— The night remains intact, broken off sharp. With morning, obligation predominates. The train must be taken, as scheduled: the conference, as scheduled, is convened. We come serious and respectable from our various institutions to assemble in debate. We are men of disciplined intellect. We must ponder and decide. Civilization totters; it must be steadied by our hand. We deal in ultimate values. The humane arts are in our charge. Words are the currency of truth. On words, on exactitude of communication, nations hang in balance; between freedom and tyranny, knowledge and delusion, in short between life and death. How many long papers do we recommend? What elementary texts?

And distance, denial, immutable estrangement, silence and frozen space? What currency applies there?

I was in no mood for this conference: everything pricked and scraped. I couldn't control my brain — it kept wheeling off along an independent course, or circling round one magnetizing point: Clayton the chairman, authority on eighteenth-century minor dramatists, elegant, sleek, composed, mild play of the ironic eyebrow, a slippery fish knowing exactly where to link his fins, already treated with deference by his enemies, rivals, and sycophants. Or Lucas the professional comedian, noisy, intrusive, deliberately gauche, rough big features flashing some private message to Clayton in hysterical secret code. I couldn't watch him; he embarrassed me. Not without malice, both of them, each according to his own technique. Clayton

the injection specialist, cordial hand clapped on your arm,
white teeth scintillating in an antiseptic smile as he drives
the needle straight into the festering nerve: « Finished the
thesis yet? » — quizzical eyebrow raised — « For God's sake,
Oliver, push it through. I've always felt you had something
original to offer if you'd only give yourself a break. » And
Lucas the captive bear capering when the rope is jerked:
« You're mixing up the genders. Glenn's the one. This is the
consort. Glenn aims at getting to run these United States.
Lady Macbeth with a political science degree. Very beautiful,
but very dangerous. » The wild glance roves to intercept
Clayton's glance as we all supply the artificial laugh. Or
Glenn's face would fuse in: perfect like perfect marble, slightly
long, fine pale coloring, long narrow eyes, grey with level
lashes, firm line of the jaw growing more pronounced. Is she
as absolute inside, sheer concentrated will, like the inmost
zone of cold blue ice? I'd wrestled with that thought so long
I'd worn it smooth, it glided off, it defeated me. Or again,
like an aimless insect flitting in and out, that crumpled little
creature in Josephine Robinson's big house.

She lives in the attractive part of the city, on the hill
where the university buildings are. I like the way some of
the streets there swing out leisurely and wide, and others veer
up sharp, with the irregular row of houses slanting along the
curb. From the terrace halfway up the hill, just above the
old white meetinghouse rising simple and demure, you over-
look the real city with its tangled traffic and silent river run-
ning slow. Big trees arch full along the broader streets — in
the morning light they send a leafy shadow pattern flickering.
Life seems more durable and honest here, viewed from the
outside at least.

Is it New York, is it metropolis? What engine impels
us to become what we never wished to be? We strive, through
desperation, nerves, and alcohol; we trust no one; we're spite-
ful, grudging, envious, the clever ones in secret, the rest in
clumsy ways; we're afraid, afraid that we'll be stripped, by
accident or design, to our ordinary, crucial rudiments — most

of all, afraid we'll fail. If you're recognized, for something, for anything — committee work, eighteenth-century dramatists, grotesque clowning — you've come in, you're safe. Other people have borne proof that you exist.

If not, do you collapse — like that broken-down little puppet at Josephine Robinson's? That's a beautiful room she has: tall windows ranked along one side, hundreds of books on shelves, a great mahogany table, two solid desks, brass implements at the fireplace, portraits of ancestors, crowds of roses in blue Chinese jars, and still offering a sense of retreat. Anyone could write anything, in a room like that; you could unfold into your own certainty. And he couldn't even produce one simple declarative sentence without revising half. He had thought, that is there had been a chance, that she could see me herself; but unfortunately she could not. He believed he had explained in our telephone conversation, when we had talked yesterday; he would be most unhappy if he had aroused false hope. She was of course extremely busy, that is to say, she was constantly engaged — today the board appointed by the governor to advise on the rehabilitation of state prisoners. It was not so much that he had forgotten her appointments, though that could happen alas, he was not always thoroughly informed: rather he had wondered, if her board meeting should run late, as now seemed probable, if he himself might not act as intercessor so to speak — casting now and again a look of inquiry through the horn-rimmed glasses which, with the neat white pompadour, gave him the look of a wizened boy. A supernumerary soul: the way he held himself when we sat down — elbows creased against his sides, skinny knees oblique — made you think he'd just been lifted from a suitcase and hadn't yet been shaken out. As a secretary I couldn't see how he kept his job. Perhaps it might be best to write the information down, as a precaution, just to be perfectly safe. Now — I needn't worry; he could promise to take my problem up that very night. He'd be certain to see her, he could count on that — prim lips closing back a smile while a look of covert gratification crept across his face. She'd told him just before she left there was a matter she particularly wished to speak to him about. He dared not offer encouragement; he could not venture to speak for his wife; but she was always interested in university groups because one struck the pliable intelligence. And we could both hope. If I'd telephone then tomorrow morning before noon? If I'd ask for Mr. Robinson.

I stared. This was *Mr.* Robinson; this droning little shuttlecock was *Mr.* Robinson. What did he do all day? What had he done all his life? Take messages for Josephine Robinson, getting them wrong unless he wrote them down, and probably even then? Drift about in the big library hung with her eaglebeaked ancestors muddling up her calendar of dates? And that subverted pride in his privileged relationship — he disgusted me, slithering on his belly through his worm's paradise gleaming and beaming through his spectacles. Yes, I'd be sure to telephone, yes. He had been very kind. Oh, no — not at all! It was a pleasure. I was most grateful; I did appreciate his help. I regretted too that I'd missed her of course; but this arrangement would serve very well. He was indeed most kind. Tomorrow morning then! Square on the walk as I left the house I met the Roman general herself: one concentrated look out of shrewd black seasoned eyes, then onward up her steps, like a huge pine tree stalking game. For sheer massive rockhewn power, grounded in the knowledge of power — not of beauty or intellect — you can't beat Josephine Robinson.

— Sudden, importunate in the hotel room, the telephone bell rings; the hooded instrument on the night table leaps alive; the hand stretched forward lingers a moment unsure: buoyant, convinced, retarded by disbelief; the mind throbs a rapid argument: it is, it must be, no, perhaps. The slow hand lifts the receiver; the civilized voice assumes control. Flat, distorted, crackling over the wire, the summoning voice responds; the surge of expectancy breaks on emptiness. Lucas the comedian, signalling through space, thrusting his presence into this solitary interval. The voice splutters and explodes, reduced to a garbled parody of what it wishes to convey. Lucas the buffoon, repetitive, insistent, babbling words that rise and ebb under variable stress: he has liquor, he had been waiting, Clayton had told him, Clayton had said, he had been waiting, sitting there waiting, he has liquor, Clayton had said, Clayton was caught, with the university nabobs, Clayton was busy, up on the hill. Clayton had just telephoned. Why not come over? — or could he come there.

Thanks, Lucas, 1 wish I could; but I'd better not try it I guess. It's pretty late. I don't know the city, just the beat around here. Thanks all the same, thanks a lot. Well... I wouldn't try it if I were you. The way you sound, you must have killed a bottle at least. If I were you I wouldn't try. After all it's pretty late. That's right, some other time. Sure I remember — I read the papers too. It wasn't yesterday; it was a couple of years ago. I don't know why. I don't know why a Harvard English professor would jump out of the window in a hotel. Nobody knows why. Don't try to figure it out. Seal off the brain. Okay... okay. See you in the morning with the brotherhood.

Midnight striking, as the silent receiver is set again into place.

And if the voice should come now, what would one answer? — if the voice should come. If picking up the receiver, here in the hotel room, one heard the imagined voice?

We are men of disciplined judgment, gathered in conference. We instruct the young; we assign papers and compile reading lists. We know, being stiffened by logic, that the wires will not vibrate; between city and city the still miles stretch. We know, through intellectual reason, we know, or we should learn, that the telephone in the hotel room is an obsolete furnishing.

Midnight closing: over, over, over, the clock-stroke of finality recessive on the air; the in-between passage marking off the present from the present moment that has been. What do you find in that channel of echoes? Pluck the fruit you must eat. What was, no longer is. Bite upon that.

Recover everything, remember all. Etch the knowledge clear. She didn't come back that night till late. I'd finished all the papers, packed my bag for the conference, rummaged out a supper in the kitchenette; and still she didn't come. Minute after minute slipped along the numerals of the electric clock. Time passing on a clock that doesn't tick seems more implacable and ominous. You can't watch it very long; you do something else — read the manufacturer's guarantee boxed in tiny letters on the pack of cigarettes, straighten the picture hanging crooked on the wall, pick up a magazine and put it down again. You sit immobilized, raking over the elements of your own bitterness. You haven't even an open adversary to confront: just deflection, estrangement; the daily, subtle instillation of betrayal through the alien voice and unresponsive flesh.

At last she came. I sat taut in the big chair, pressing my fingers steady against my knees. She said she hadn't expected to find me up; she was tired; she was going to bed. I watched her take the three pillows from the studio couch, set them methodically on the floor, fold the Indian spread end to end, then over again end to end, brushing back and forth before my chair. One corner of the spread flipped against my supper tray standing on the record cabinet: the coffee cup with its refuse of cigarette ash and dregs, the lump of butter softening, the sardine bits mashed into the corners of the opened tin. I might have put my dishes away, she said. « Listen, » I began. To talk, I had to catch her eye; but she moved too fast, she was inaccessible. « Glenn, » I said — it came out hoarse and low, pleading, making me enraged. I had to reach her, reach her, hold her eye transfixed, stare and stare until rankling accusation burned straight through the glacial depth. Words blocked heavy in my chest. I could only stare, bending nearer, nearer, focussing on her marble face. Then she flicked one of her swift contemptuous looks. All the banked-up anger rose, rushed, broke, spraying out through every limb. I lunged, I think I yelled.

I held her on the floor, pinning her shoulders hard. The

words tore free, beating, lashing down, dredging a sudden pathway through my ribs; I could breathe again. « There's more than one kind of murder, » I said — I do remember that, out of the incoherent swirl. Finally I noticed that her eyes were closed, she was white; I noticed that I was striking her head against the chair, for emphasis.

I hadn't hurt her. She was able to stand up. She wouldn't let me help. For hours after I sat smoking, raw, defiant, ashamed, yet elated too, and always with a frosty trickle of fear coursing deep, not because of what I'd done — I hadn't hurt her — but because I'd travelled to that violent place. Her face looked stern, remote, like ivory, under the thin light from the street lamp slanting through the window above the couch; the level lashes fringed down motionless. She might be asleep; she might not be asleep; she might have heard what I had said, she might not have heard. Whatever she did, or felt, or was, I'd never know.

In the morning she was polite and calm. She said she'd find a place uptown; she'd be gone when I returned.

Now the half-hour: four strokes forward, four strokes back. Put out the lights, shroud the hotel room in darkness, obscure the hooded telephone. Let all mortal creatures sleep as best they can: Lucas with his garments flung aside, deadened dreamless and inert; little Cock Robin up on the hill sheltering against his craggy monument. Who killed Cock Robin? Let him slumber forgotten drained of his blood; thrust the scratch of his bird-claw out of the mind. Let Lucas lie oblivious until the penetrating morning sun forced the jocular clown alive. Their midnight arrangements are their own.

This moment is yours. Search it deep. Here all recollected time and place converge, all memory concentrates. The shape of thought is whittled sharp to a single image burned upon the wakeful eyes: the still, defenceless figure on the floor, the dark stain blemishing the pallid face. Beneath this incandescent brand whatever else is felt, or has been felt, scatters to trivial ash.

If you could explain; if you could reach out and explain.

No action is isolate; you're enmeshed in multiplicity; the web tightens, galls, strangles; you plunge through, spinning wild. Or if you could explain that you can never totally explain. You can't translate the whole of any feeling into accurate words.

Midnight sounds different rung on different clocks: now the quarter-hour, poised like an incomplete question. Where was she now? Sitting, somewhere in a rented room, thinking, at midnight in New York? If you could reach out now, bridging distance; if the true voice could be conveyed.

Where was she in New York? Sitting, maybe, by a window, at hollow midnight, hearing the hour pass, staring into an unfamiliar street? She breathed, she was; she must realize, she must walk this passage too. Ending is not final; ending does not end. Time misspent in failure permeates the flesh. You can't tear out part of what you are without knowledge and pain.

Maybe, meeting the decision, she grew unsure; maybe the intertwining sinewy filaments that had been shaped held her fast. Maybe she was lying sleepless, the ivory mask discarded, the thin light slanting through the window upon the unprotected face. Let the one who should speak first be first to speak. Obliterate the burning image from the mind. It isn't too late. Telephone. Try. Maybe she'd still be there.

RICHARD EBERHART

THE DAY-BED

I

It is green, it is made of willow.
I am baffled: I cannot think about it.
An obsession of twenty seven years.
I am brutalized to look upon it.

The very form of love. Of time
The essence, which is memory.
The flash of light, and a long sleep.
This is the bed of day, and night.

No, but soft, but untold love
Arises. The very heart of love!
So long ago that suffering form
Slowly grew to death through pain,

Here on this very furniture.
It seems impossible. Time lies.
I do not see her lying there,
Great eyes, great gray-black hair.

I do not see that agonizing stare
That's deep through all my nights and days,
Substratum of the flying years;
The great pain without a cure.

II

Reality is a passing thing,
The Day-Bed lives, remains, reminds
Of the eternity of change
To this same, writing finger.

The emblem remains, bounteous gift,
The strange, pure gift of memory,
A blooded drench, a flushed presentiment;
And throngs and throngs of images.

Day-Bed of Life-in-Death,
That while my eyes shall change and see,
I look upon this furniture,
The not estranging imagery.

And summon up the love, and see
The very form and flesh of love
As it is with all mankind,
The loves long lost, the loves most near.

Who cursed the blood within the veins
Apparelling day with source of night
Shall dream upon a lovely dream
Though the deep heart choke, and fight.

III

It is green, it is made of willow.
Lithe winds of Spring wave over it.
It is a new time and a new day,
New flesh here springs in harmony,

Laughs and tumbles and is gay.
Is gay! Is lithe as winds of Spring
And bends to nature as a willow
Triumphing in its green, cool stay.

Two lovers here electing unity
Flaunt eclectic idols in the day,
Consuming the great world of sense,
And laughing in its careless sway.

They sway. They laugh. And leaping
Loosen the mind from iron prisons,
Celebrating speeds of instancy
In vernal cells of intimacy.

Green and willowy marriage time!
Time of the beliefless flesh!
Time of the charges of the ruddy blood,
Joy that is swift and free, pure joy.

IV

Other years and other foils
Requite the ancient mysteries,
Persuading of some subtle balance
Between the losing and the winning battles,

Here on this very furniture,
Day-Bed of Life-in-Death!
A child plays in boisterous industry,
Truth off the old bones of mating.

Embroiled in fate he does not know,
Smiling mischievous and saintly,
Evidently impossible to quell,
The very future in his active eye,

The willow Day-Bed of past time
That taught death in the substratum
Couches now the bliss of man,
A bright shape, a green new dream.

STANLEY KUNITZ

WHEN THE LIGHT FALLS

When the light falls, it falls on her
In whose rose-gilded chamber
A music strained through mind
Turns everything to measure.

The light that seeks her out
Finds answering light within,
And the two join hands and dance
On either side of her skin.

The lily and the swan
Attend her whiter pride,
While the courtly laurel kneels
To kiss his mantling bride.

Under each cherry-bough
She spreads her silken cloths
At the rumor of a wind,
To gather up her deaths,

For the petals of her heart
Are shaken in a night,
Whose ceremonial art
Is dying into light.

AMONG THE GODS

Within the grated dungeon of the eye
The old gods, shaggy with grey lichen, sit
Like fragments of the antique masonry
Of heaven, a patient thunder in their stare.

Huge blocks of language, all my quarried love,
They justify, and not in random poems,
But shapes of things interior to Time,
Hewn out of chaos when the Pure was plain.

Sister, my bride, who were both cloud and bird
When Zeus came down in a shower of sexual gold,
Listen! We make a world! I hear the sound
Of Matter pouring through eternal forms.

ANTHONY HECHT

OSTIA ANTICA

Given this light,
The departing thunderhead in its anger
Off to one side, and given
These ancient stones in their setting, themselves refreshed
And rendered strangely younger
By wetness alive with the wriggling brass of heaven,
Where is the spirit's part unwashed
Of all poor spite?

The cypress thrust,
Greened in the glass of air as never
Since the first greenness offered,
Not to desire our prayer: « To ghostly creatures,
Peace, and an end of fever
Till all this dust assemble, » but delivered
To their resistless lives and natures,
Rise as they must.

And the broken wall
Is only itself, deeply accepting
The sun's warmth to its bricks.
The puddles blink; a snail marches the Roman

Road of its own adopting.
The marble nymph is stripped to the flush of sex
As if in truth this timeless, human
Instant were all.

Is it the bird's
Voice, the delicious voice of water,
Addresses us on the splendid
Topic of love? And promises to youth
Still livelier forms and whiter?
Here are quick freshes, here is the body suspended
In its firm blessing, here the mouth
Finds out its words.

See, they arise
In the sign of ivy, the young males
To their strength, the meadows restored;
Concupiscence of eye, and the world's pride;
Of love, the naked skills.
At the pool's edge, the rippled image cleared,
That face set among leaves is glad,
Noble and wise.

What was begun,
The mastered force, breeds and is healing.
Pebbles and clover speak.
Each hanging waterdrop burns with a fierce
Bead of the sun's instilling.
But softly, beneath the flutesong and volatile shriek
Of birds, are to be heard discourse
Mother and son.

« If there were hushed
To us the images of earth, its poles
Hushed, and the waters of it,
And hushed the tumult of the flesh, even

93

The voice intrinsic of our souls,
Each tongue and token hushed and the long habit
Of thought, if that first light, the given
To us were hushed,

So that the washed
Object, fixed in the sun, were dumb,
And to the mind its brilliance
Were from beyond itself, and the mind were clear
As the unclouded dome
Wherein all things diminish, in that silence
Might we not confidently hear
God as he wished? »

Then from the grove
Suddenly falls a flight of bells.
A figure moves from the wood,
Darkly approaching at the hour of vespers
Along the ruined walls.
And bearing heavy articles of blood
And symbols of endurance, whispers,
« This is love. »

RICHARD WILBUR

LOVE CALLS US TO THE THINGS OF THIS WORLD

The eyes open to a cry of pulleys,
And spirited from sleep, the astounded soul
Hangs for a moment bodiless and simple
As false dawn.
          Outside the open window
The morning air is all awash with angels.

Some are in bed-sheets, some are in blouses,
Some are in smocks: but truly there they are.
Now they are rising together in calm swells
Of halcyon feeling, filling whatever they wear
With the deep joy of their impersonal breathing;

Now they are flying in place, conveying
The terrible speed of their omnipresence, moving
And staying like white water; and now of a sudden
They swoon down into so rapt a quiet
That nobody seems to be there.
                    The soul shrinks

From all that it is about to remember,
From the punctual rape of every blessed day,
And cries
          « Oh, let there be nothing on earth but laundry,

95

Nothing but rosy hands in the rising steam
And clear dances done in the sight of heaven. »

Yet, as the sun acknowledges
With a warm look the world's hunks and colors,
The soul descends once more in bitter love
To accept the waking body, saying now
In a changed voice as the man yawns and rises,

« *Bring them down from their ruddy gallows;*
Let there be clean linen for the backs of thieves;
Let lovers go fresh and sweet to be undone,
And the heaviest nuns walk in a pure floating
Of dark habits,
            keeping their difficult balance. »

FOR THE NEW RAILWAY STATION IN ROME

Those who said God is praised
By hurt pillars, who loved to see our brazen lust
Lie down in rubble, and our vaunting arches
Conduce to dust;

Those who with short shadows
Poked through the stubbled forum pondering on decline,
And would not take the sun standing at noon
For a good sign.

Those pilgrims of defeat
Who brought their injured wills as to a soldiers' home;
Dig them all up now, tell them there's something new
To see in Rome.

See, from the travertine
Face of the office block, the roof of the booking-hall

Sails out into the air beside the ruined
Servian Wall,

Echoing in its light
And cantilevered swoop of reinforced concrete
The broken profile of those stones, defeating
That defeat,

And straying the strummed mind,
By such a sudden chord as raised the town of Troy,
To where the least shard of the world sings out
In stubborn joy,

« What city is eternal
But that which prints itself within the groping head
Out of the blue unbroken reveries
Of the building dead?

What is our praise or pride
But to imagine excellence, and try to make it?
What does it say over the door of heaven
But homo fecit? »

SONNET

The winter deepening, the hay all in,
The barn fat with cattle, the apple-crop
Conveyed to market or the fragrant bin,
He thinks the time has come to make a stop,

And sinks half-grudging in his firelit seat,
Though with his heavy body's full consent,
In what would be the posture of defeat
But for that look of rigorous content.

Outside, the night dives down like one great crow
Against his cast-off clothing where it stands
Up to the knees in miles of hustled snow,

Flapping and jumping like a kind of fire,
And floating skyward its abandoned hands
In gestures of invincible desire.

PIAZZA DI SPAGNA

I can't forget
How she stood at the top of that long marble stair
Amazed, and then with a sleepy pirouette
Went dancing slowly down to the fountain-
quieted square;

Nothing upon her face
But some impersonal loneliness — not then a girl,
But as it were a reverie of the place,
A called-for falling glide and whirl;

As when a leaf, petal, or thin chip
Is drawn to the falls of a pool and, circling a moment
above it,

Rides on over the lip —
Perfectly beautiful, perfectly ignorant of it.

CAROLYN KIZER

THE FLOWER

Two, from a pit
Met, as they rose.
For strength, they offered each other their own bright blood
    to drink.
As cupped hands bumped in haste, there flashed some drops
    to soil.
Up sprang a rose.

« I used » he said,
« To sow and reap
In passionate haste, flinging the wild seed
Into the noon-hot trench, or where the unbroken, moon-cold
    ground
Lay cauled in sleep.

« But what I reaped
Was not a crop
Of anemones wildly roiling the contours of the hill.
No ocean of marigolds washed the soil in gold.
What struggled up

« Out of the loam
Was a giant mole
With onion eyes, who spoke: 'Be rich and wise, and dig below
Where coarse roots cut a worm to twins.' So I followed him
Into his hole.

« Into the night
I fell away.
Awash from wounds, I heard him scorning: 'Trail your seed!
Fall as it fell, in a shower of nothing. Lie in the dust you made.'
And so I lay.

« But later woke
And clambered out,
Not so weak as my wounds, meeting another struggler in the
    way.
We suffered, and were gentled, to give aid. Out of our surge
    to light
This flower sprouts. »

« I dreamed » she said,
« I was with child.
Something fathered a flower in my web of sleep, and then a
    dream
Within a dream told me I bore and buried it all in one grieving
    night.
So I woke, wild

« With loss, dug down
To find my fate.
In burrowing, matter and mould gave way. I fell far upon a
    grave.
Its marking shaft, that must have been the axle of the earth,
Impaled my heart.

« *With loamy eyes*
That ran, I read
Its epitaph, carved upside-down: 'Here lies
No dream of yours. Only the seed of weeds garlands this
  mourning.'
My wound was dead,

« *Deader than I,*
The lips a seam
Where no blood sprang. What caused my blood to flow so
  sweetly then,
After we climbed together, hand in brimming hand? »
She paused, to dream.

« *Listen!* » *he said.*
« *Summon your wits!*
What bright flare dies from the world if we pluck this flower?
Or if we pass on to our own ways again... »
But milk was streaming from her breast as she bent down
To nourish it.

COLUMNS AND CARYATIDS

I

The Wife:
« *I am Lot's pillar, caught in turning,*
Bellowing, resistant, burning
With brine. Fine robes laced with sand,
Solid, soon to be hollowed by tongues of kine. »

Solid, solitary salt-lick, she
Is soon to be shaped by wind, abstracted,
Smoothed to a sex-shape only.
Large and lonely in the plain,
Rain melting her slowly.

So proud shoulder dips with compliance
Never in life. God's alliance with weather
Eroding her to a spar, a general grief,
A cone, then an egg no bigger than a bead.

« I saw Sodom bleed, Gomorrah smoke.
Empty sockets are a joke of that final vision.
Tongueless, I taste my own salt, taste
God's chastisement and derision. »

II

The Mother:
« I am God's pillar, caught in raising
My arms like thighs, to brace the wall.
Caught by my own choice,
I willed myself to hold this ceiling.

« He froze me at the moment of decision.
Always I wished to bear weight,
Not in my belly where the seed would light.
That globe is great with stone.
But, over me, the weight of endless function,
My thick trunk set for stress,
My face, showing calmly through guano
No strain, my brain sloped by granite curls
To wedge the architrave.

« *The world is a womb.*
Neither I nor the foetus tire of our position.
My ear is near God, my temples to his temple.
I lift and I listen. I eat God's peace. »

III

The Lover:
« *I am your pillar that has fallen.*
And now, for centuries of rest
I will regard my breast, my calm hills,
My valley for the stars to travel. »

Stripped of all ornament she lies,
Looted alike by conquerors and technicians,
Her curling fingers for an emperor's flower,
Her trinkets in barbarian's museums.
They dust away, but she endures, and smiles,
Accepting ravage as the only tribute
That men can pay to gods, that they would dint them
To raise or decorate themselves, themselves are dinted,
The bruise upon the sense of generations.

So boys will turn from sleep and search the darkness,
Seeking the love their fathers have forgotten.
And they will dream of her who have not known her,
And ache, and ache for that lost limb forever.

BABETTE DEUTSCH

THE MOORS

They have giant
Knees; rough treasure
Spills over them.
No stone precious, but every blade and button
On fire with life: even the quakerish beads of bayberry,
And elderberry, darker than amethyst, holding,
Like hills at evening, dark in their winy grains.
And in pine plumes, wild grapevine, beachgrass, reaching
    stems — greens,
Various: jades, turquoise, the more sombre emeralds,
The green dozing in jasper.
As for hips of roses, there is coral, rosered, bloodred,
Prodigal as split pomegranates.
Of these live jewels, falling down and down,
There are none
At the cliff's foot.
Sand, bare even of a weedy bracelet, stretches
To receive the sea,
That comes slowly,
That comes powerfully,
With no gift but an embrace, where
Other riches drown.

PAUL ENGLE

FOR THE IOWA DEAD

I

Some left an office, cornfield, factory,
But these men left the study of mankind,
Glory and gloom of mortal history,
The wonder, madness, logic of the mind,
The live cell, atoms cunningly combined.
They closed their books, death closed their eyes, so we,
The lucky Iowa living, still could find
A future in our human liberty.

The wise and wicked past they came to study,
Right and wrong, life loved like light, but turned
Away from contemplation to the bloody
Present, and in appalling action learned
The old world's furious and deadly fact:
Murder for justice is a moral act.

II

Morning Sun, Stone City, Boone, What Cheer:
In the hysteria of history
These names for home rang in the homesick ear,

With the warm sound of friend and family,
Of Iowa, where winter cracks your skull,
Where summer floats on fields, green river flowing,
Where autumn stains your hand with walnut hull,
Spring shakes the land with a loud gust of growing.

But their true season was the one of dying.
Summer, autumn, winter, spring all ran
Into one flaming moment, doomed plane flying,
Sinking ship, exploding shell, edged knife:
For home is not birthplace, but the place a man
Dares a way of death, to keep a way of life.

III

Say that in the end their life was one
Quick autumn burning the leaves with their own blood,
Say that they fought so there might be the sun
Over their land, as they died in the mud.
Not from an abstract sense of wrong and right
But for the hill they fenced with aching arm
They went to the unwilled war — and wrote one night,
« It's a lousy land and a hell of a way to farm. »

Say that for those who came from corn and flock,
By inland rivers where the catfish hang
In the dark pool, and the moccasin hides its fang,
Where the warm milk is cooled in the old, gray crock,
It was a tough, hard, bitter death as they sprang
And poured their rich blood over the barren rock.

IV

Now in a later year
When sky on farm and town

Bleeds furious daylight down
On faces bleeding fear,
Let hope like a great blaze
Rise when we speak the name
Of those who died in flame.
Take pride in simple praise:

Brave, bitter, or afraid,
They won their appalling fight.
Eternal sun has laid
Its bending arm of light
Over their shoulder blade
And burned them into night.

V

Do not merge all of them as « honored dead, »
For they were individual men, one, one,
Their grave a foreign word on a map in red,
A name they saw in a book when child and son,
Or knew first when they hit that beach and ran it.
They only yearned to live in their own land,
To keep a toe-hold on a twisting planet
By job and sport and home and loving hand.

They hung their lives on the terrible wall of time
Up which, with face hoping for hope, we climb,
Face where accusing tears no longer fall,
While in their old rooms on the trophied wall
By rod, spiked shoe, girl's head, bent book, the dumb
Mirror waits the face that will not come.

VI

They fought the mighty fury of mass hate,
Uniform, party, group, replacing men,

The tribe abstracted to the absolute state,
Leaders like pigs locked in their filthy pen,
Man a mere number raised to the nth power.
Not only guns, the airman's faceless face,
Tanks, armies, ships, they fought in their doomed hour,
But all yet savage in the human race.

The brag of blood they fought, the brutal sneer
Of racial pride that mocks our mortal feature,
Good love of country heightened to great wrong.
Against that shame, they said for the world to hear:
We've had our human nature far too long
To go back, now, to being merely nature.

VII

Contrary century
Where men of plain good will
Must cry out — Enemy!
And teach their hands to kill,
Where earth explodes in space
Shamed with its human life,
Where live tears tear the face,
Where wound slashes the knife,

Where men of peace fought back
War-wanting men, and died
Attacking their attack:
As if on those old sands
The spear leapt from Christ's side
To cut the soldier's hands.

VIII

War was evil and they loathed the sight it
Gave to decent men, but worse than war

Was to know evil, and yet not to fight it.
They wanted life, but their own country more.
So learned the killing skill, its bloody ways,
Writing home, when heart and hand were numb:
Heaven and hell we have now in our days,
Earth and the simple living are to come.

So learned, and proved it by death's final scar,
That what we love is what, as men, we are:
Wonder of woman, child and friend, the least
Human good and glory that we try for.
God in the body of a thinking beast,
We are all things we hate, we love, we die for.

IX

Surely when Adam walked through the first trees
The Garden was astonished that a thing,
Upright, with glancing eyes, glad mouth, should tease
Innocent air with a live voice that could sing.
Surely when that first, mortal man had died
Death was astonished that he had a friend
To comfort when he came there terrified,
To give food, drink, on whom he could depend.

But surely death, like these men, is astonished
To find how much hard dying it has taken
To keep a country free, alive, unshaken,
Merely to keep a brutal world admonished
That there are always men willing to die
To keep a plain life, under an open sky.

X

War leapt at them — to its astonishment
These men who breathed peace like the common air

Fought back savage and magnificent.
They brought fear to the force that tried to scare.
Animal war they beat down till it whined.
They won that fight although they did not want it.
They beat that beast, as if in sleep the mind
Terrified the dream that came to haunt it.

They battered war by making war, war,
Defeated death, because their dying, dying,
Gave to their country more life, more, more.
Drenched with daylight where the sun dips, dips,
We hear their warning voices crying, crying:
World is a cave where the dark blood drips, drips.

XI

Now let our memory of these men make
No form in marble where an artist stood,
But lived-out, rounded rib-cage of a snake
Found perfect in the winter-ruined wood:
Image of nature beautiful in bone
Whose pure curve praises the abandoned breath,
No image like a stutter of bright stone,
But life-delighting shape denoting death.

Remember now their names and their hand's daring,
Whose eyes defied stiff death and left him staring.
Our future life is their memorial
And not bronze language bolted to a wall.
We praise their death by living, not by art,
By proving a free mind and loving heart.

XII

Casualty, calculated loss,
Dog tag, division, number, date,

The abstract death in triplicate:
From these big words what comes across
Is not men in their natural kindness,
But soldiers, sailors, pilots who,
By chart and luck in the flared night, flew
The bombers in their accurate blindness.

Our words corrupt reality.
The worn, quick syllable of war
Proves no blood, terror, agony.
The name of sorrow has no more
Night-weeping anguish than the look
Of petals dried in an old book.

XIII

Now in the century of clever knowledge
Where the trained mind measures true evidence,
Common sense is still the oldest college:
Wisdom is knowledge of our ignorance.
We trick the atom and teach birds to fly,
Make marvelous machines to make machines,
Cut with our cunning knives the living eye,
Tell the scared mind what each mad terror means.

Yet if these men returned and had their will,
Now, when dark earth through space-like-water dives,
In the great night of the future, they would still
Triangulate the star-drift of their lives
By those fixed points of home they died for: wives,
Table for bread, loved children laughing or ill.

111

WILLIAM ARROWSMITH

IN MEMORIAM

The favored nephew and the only heir
of an old aunt's estate worth nothing much —
this collapsing barn where I rummage now,
the old blistered house with the rotten elms
New England's dignity is dying of,
the inventory of an old maid's life,
old loves, old scraps, her college annual,
pressed flowers, letters, and last of all, her will —
her heir, hardly the role I would have chosen.
But heirs are not choosers; heirs are chosen.
She left me what she had. Let the heir take stock.

We shared the family nose, she and I,
and family resemblance makes a bond
when blood is none. This was my maiden aunt
who loved me and was kind; whose love was not
frustration for a son she could not have,
but love that gives the simple person up
in keepsakes and letters, knickknacks from Rome,
a snapshot of her horse, and tucked away
behind a drawer, a copy of her will,
the demon words scrawled in above my name
shyly and with love: memento mori.

I am the living heir of my dead aunt.
If lost hands rummage now, unsure of love,
in this Pandora's box of precious trash,
it was her will: what would stupid fingers know
unless they hurt, and hurting, came on hope?
She left me what she had: much hope, much hurt.
This photo shows her seated on the porch,
at thirty-eight, still alone, still alive,
starched in nurse's white, hurt eyes leached of love,
struggling to bless. Sweet ghost, who bless me now,
who left me love, make me worthy of your hope.

Somewhere a bell slams home, the windlass leaps
for the endless well and the long rope whirrs
to nowhere. This is the time of mourning
when honest heirs are honest with themselves
at last. We accept inheritance of love
if loss is real, or go with those who die
into the long home where all losses lie,
dead to the world and sixty years of life,
or more or less. It does not matter much,
nor matter who, if the tenure is such
the living heirs of love inherit that pride.

Think on time, dispassionate and cold,
when the self, hurt or lazy, crawled down its hole
to die, or sleep the livelong winter through.
Some call it hibernation, others hell,
but mockers call it death, which has no hope
and does not hurt. And so it was with her,
as once with me who mocked: the slow torpor
of the sleeping bear, alone, the lost ghost
who comes and goes in hope, untouchably.
Forgive me lesser love and touch me now.
Possess me of your love, courageous ghost.

WILLIAM STAFFORD

WITH MY CROWBAR KEY

I do tricks in order to know:
careless I dance,
then turn to see
the mark to turn God left for me.

Making my home in vertigo
I pray with my screams
and think with my hair
prehensile in the dark with fear.

When I hear the well bucket strike something soft
far down at noon,
then there's no place
far enough away to hide my face.

When I see my town over sights of a rifle,
and carved by light
from the lowering sun,
then my old friends darken one by one.

By step and step like a cat toward God
I dedicated walk,
but under the house
I realize the kitten's crouch.

114

And by night like this I turn and come
to this possible house
which I open, and see
myself at work with this crowbar key.

FOR THE GRAVE OF DANIEL BOONE

The farther he went the farther home grew.
Kentucky became another room;
the mansion arched over the Mississippi;
flowers were spread all over the floor.
He traced ahead a deepening home,
and better, with goldenrod:

Leaving the snakeskin of place after place,
going on — after the trees
the grass, a bird flying after a song.
Rifle so level, sighting so well
his picture freezes down to now,
a story-picture for children.

They go over the velvet falls
into the tapestry of his time,
heirs to the landscape, feeling no jar:
it is like evening; they are the quail
surrounding his fire, coming in for the kill;
their little feet move sacred sand.

Children, we live in a barb-wire time
but can follow the old hands back —
the ring in the light, the knuckle, the palm,
all the way to Daniel Boone,
hunting our own kind of deepening home.
From the land that was his I heft this rock.

Here on his grave I put it down.

115

ARCHIBALD MacLEISH

HOW THE RIVER NINFA RUNS THROUGH THE RUINED TOWN BENEATH THE LIME QUARRY

to remember Marguerite Caetani

Italy breaking her bones for bread
eating her stones

But the Nymph, O the Nymph in her crisp cresses
clattering over the cobbles on slippery
heels where the little palazzi were and the churches
ages ago, ages ago . . .

O but the Nymph in her cool cresses
jigging with midges in the slants of sun
nobody's shadow now, nobody's shadow . . .

chattering under the bridges nobody's shoes . . .

O but the Nymph in her crisp cresses
cracking her knuckles in time with a tune
nobody knows anymore now, nobody . . .

chuckling her fables
over and over again and then
when the dynamite kicks at the sky and the quarry . . .

116

Italy breaking her bones for bread
eating her stones

. . . shudders and tumbles . . .

O but the Nymph! — how she hushes and humbles
just for a heart's beat and is dumb . . .

. . . Nymph in the ruin of time . . .

                    and then laughs again.

KATHERINE GARRISON CHAPIN

THE CHINESE DEER

Through a colorless landscape on the last day of the year
We walked in the Zoo. The stream was a frozen line
Between black trees. Your hand slipped from mine
As you skipped down the path or hung on the iron
Fences, watching animals, who sniffed
At the wind for a taste of cold, as if it blew
From the steppes or the ragged Himalyas.
Hunched bison and goat ignored your questioning eyes,
Indifferent even to sparrows, pecking among grains
Or buzzards circling in the heavy sky.

ROBERT PENN WARREN

SHORT THOUGHTS FOR LONG NIGHTS

I. Nightmare of Mouse

It was there, but I said it couldn't be true in daylight.
It was there, but I said it was only a trick of starlight.
It was there, but I said to believe it would take a fool,
And I wasn't, so didn't — till teeth crunched on my skull.

II. Nightmare of Man

I assembled, marshalled, my data, deployed them expertly.
My induction was perfect, as far as induction may be.
But the formula failed in the test tube, despite all my skill,
For I'd thought of the death of my mother, and wept; and
weep still.

III. Human Nature

Even if you scotch it,
You'd still better watch it.

IV. Colloquy with Cockroach

I know I smell. But everyone does, somewhat.
I smell this way only because I crawl down the drain.
I've no slightest idea how you got the smell you've got.
No, I haven't time now — it might take you too long to
*   explain.*

V. Little Boy on Voyage

Little boy, little boy, standing on ship-shudder, wide eyes
*   staring*
At unease of ocean at sunset, and the distance long —
You've stared, little boy, at gray distance past hoping or
*   despairing,*
So come in for supper and sleep now; they, too, will help you
*   grow strong.*

VI. Obsession

Dawn draws on slow when dawn brings only dawn —
Only slow milk-wash on window, star paling, first wind-stir,
Sweat cold now on pillow before the alarm's burr,
And the old thought for the new day as day draws on.

VII. A Long Spoon

If afraid of water
Don't go to bed with the mermaid's daughter.

VIII. Joy

If you've never had it, discussion is perfectly fruitless,
And if you have, you can tell nobody about it.
To explain silence, you scarcely try to shout it.
Let the flute and drum be still, the trumpet toot-less.

IX. Theology

The old ape is blind — wipe the poor eyes with lace;
The hog is sick — catch his froth in a silver cup;
There is nameless blood on the sidewalk — kiss the place:
For if pain is not pleasing to God, what holds stars up?

X. Cricket, on Kitchen Floor, Enters History

History, shaped like white hen,
Walked in at kitchen door.
Beak clicked once on stone floor.
Out door walked hen then;
But will, no doubt, come again.

XI. Little Boy and General Principle

Don't cry, little boy, you see it is only natural
That little red trucks will break, whether plastic or tin,
And some other things, too. It's a general principle
That you'll have to learn soon, so you might, I guess, now
  begin.

XII. Grasshopper Tries to Break Solipsism

Sing summer, summer, sing summer summerlong—
For God is light, oh I love Him, love is my song.
I sing, for I must, for God, if I didn't, would weep,
And over all things, all night, His despair, like ice, creep.

NURSERY RHYME: WHY ARE YOUR EYES AS BIG AS SAUCERS?

« Why are your eyes as big as saucers — big as saucers? »
I said to the man in the gray flannel suit.
And he said: « I see facts that I can't refute —
Winners and losers,

Pickers and choosers,
Takers, refusers,
Users, abusers,
And my poor head, it spins, it spins like a top,
It spins and spins and it will not stop. »
Thus said the young man I happened to meet
Wearing his new gray flannel suit down the sunlit street.

« *Why do you shake like wind in the willows — wind in the*
  willows? »
I said to the man with the black knit tie.
And he said; « I see things before my eye —
Jolly good fellows,
Glad-handers of helloes,
Fat wind-bags and bellows,
Plumpers of pillows,
And God's sweet air is dust on my tongue,
For a man can't stand such things very long. »
Thus said the young man I happened to meet
Wearing gray flannel suit and black knit tie down the sunlit
  street.

« *Why is your face flour-white as a miller's — white as a*
  miller's? »
I said the man in the Brooks Brothers shirt.
And he said: « I see things that can't help but hurt —
Snitchers and squealers,
Healers and killers,
Pickers and stealers,
Ticklers and feelers,
And I go to prepare a place for you,
For this location will never do. »
Said the nice young man I happened to meet
Wearing gray flannel suit, knit tie, and Brooks Brothers shirt
  down the street.

EQUINOX ON MEDITERRANEAN BEACH

Sail-bellyer, exciter of boys, come bang
To smithereens doors, and see if I give a hang,

For I am sick of summer and the insane glitter
Of sea sun-bit, and wavelets that bicker and titter,

And the fat girls who hang out brown breasts like fruit over-
ripe,
And the thin ones drooped pale in rock-shadow, goose-pimpled
as tripe,

And the young men who pose on the headlands like ads for
Jantzen,
And the old who would do so much better to keep proper
pants on,

And all latin faeces one finds, like jewels, in the sand,
And the stare of the small, sweet octopus fondling your hand.

Come howl like a prophet the season's righteous anger,
And knock down our idols with crash, bang, or clangor,

Come blow the cat's fur sidewise, make dogs bark,
Blow the hen's tail feathers forward past the pink mark,

Snatch the laundry off the line, like youth, away,
Blow plastered hair off bald spot, lift toupee.

Come blow old women' skirts, bring Truth to light,
Though at their age morn's all the same as night.

Kick up the bay now, make a mess of it,
Fling spume on our sinful faces, like God's spit,

For now's the time pleasures, like peaches, get rotten, not riper,
And summer is over, and time we must pay the piper,

And be glad to do it, for man's not made for much pleasure,
Or even for joy, unless cut down to his measure.

Come swirl old picnic papers to very sky-height,
That the gulls will gabble in fury at breach of their air-right.

Come kick the garbage pail, and scatter garbage,
Let cat flee forth with fish-head, housewife rage,

For pain and pleasure balance in God's year —
Though whose is which is not your problem here,

Or perhaps not even God's. So bang, wind, batter,
While human hearts do the book-keeping in this matter.

JAMES WRIGHT

THE AVENGER

She — the woman whom I loved
Longer than her beauty lasted,
Loved as long as starlight moved
Carefully around the earth —
Lies behind me, old in death,
All her quiet patience wasted.

Now I walk beneath the night,
Having watched her die all day.
Rain veils soft the bedroom light
Where I held her in my arms.
What blind movers of the storms
Steal the living heart away?

Greek avengers used to cry
Of three women in the air.
Deaf to that religion, I
Leave my barren house and seek
Forces of my own to speak
Simple reasons for despair.

Waiting for the rain to fall,
Waiting for the air to slice
Lilies' heads along the wall;

125

Knowing soon enough the wind
Strikes the bee and rabbit blind,
Blows the sparrow out of eyes,

How should I begin to say
Everything I should have said?
Why should winter blow away
Fleshes bodied up in summer?
Hushed up like a silly rumor,
In the house my love is dead.

Had I caught her in the dark
Snarled in an alien lover's hair,
Murdered him, and left her stark
Wandering among the trees,
I could go to bed in peace,
Knowing I had done my share.

Had some human murderer
Beaten her to death alone,
Knowing I had done my share
Hunting him and cursing him,
I could let her face and name
Fade into a nub of stone.

She, however, loved me so,
I must seek her killers out.
I, who wonder where they go;
Follow faces through a door,
Slip along the river shore,
Leap, and echo every shout.

They who scatter down the rain,
Lop the lilies' heads away,
Spill a saucer, blow the pane
Open as I sit and stare,
Stitch a cobweb in the air,
Blind the rabbit, blind the bee:

What have I to do with such,
Whether they be here or gone?
Let them crumble at a touch
Continents, suck up the sea,
Level a blind mountain down;
Let me alone, let me alone.

AT THE EXECUTED MURDERER'S GRAVE

Reflective calm, you tangle, root and bone,
Fang, fist, and skull, that huddle down alone.
Sparrows above him, sneaking like police,
Peck at the lawn, the hedge, the careful trees.
Man's wild blood has no heart to overcome
Vengeance and summer and the lily's bloom.
Henceforth, so long as I myself shall live,
Earth will be torn, the mind be fugitive.
My shadow flees me over mattocked stone:
Father and citizen, I killed this man,
This man who killed another who might kill
Another who might slay another still
Till the tall shadows of mankind are cast
Bodiless on the empty stars at last.
Rage and destruction trouble me, and fade.
The casual flocks of sunbeam round my head
Flutter away to dusk, and I am dark,
Peering between the granites for his mark.
Slow hills away, the milch-cows pause and yawn,
Wondering when day will go, and man be gone:
That one man, angry at the heart's release,
This brutal pastoral, this unholy peace.

DAVID MADDEN

HURRY UP PLEASE IT'S TIME

I was ambling out of this art gallery on 53rd Street, a few blocks from the Mecca of modern art, and there she was. I had my hands crammed down into my pockets, one of them all the way to my knee (last summer on Fire Island I somehow managed to subconsciously culture a wart on my loose-cart-lidged knee cap, so I had punctured a hole in my left pants pocket, the better to scratch it with, so that I can be seen walking around Manhattan with a limp and a scratch, a limp and a scratch.) I was wearing a trench coat which made me feel like Humphrey Bogart when I passed a mirror. It was a chilly October evening and the pavement was wet from a gusty shower, which explains my presence in that particular museum. An autumn windy rain, a itchy wart and an hour of cubism...nothing could have depressed me more.

And there she was walking toward me from Sixth Avenue, cradling a miniature grandfather's clock in her arms, wearing a brown suede jacket and a green corduroy skirt, her tawny hair splattered back over her ears like a leprechaun.

It was by her ears that I recognized her after twenty years. I'm quite serious — she had the most exquisite ears I've ever seen. They were a sheer delight of form and contour, and the slightest glimpse of them, pink and wet, thrust me into a flood of remembrance so vivid, so nostalgic that as she passed me I *knew* it was Greta.

« Greta! Greta La Fonda! It's Dorish! » But she continued to walk with that lazy rhythm in her gait, a sort of list to the

128

left that rather disconcerted me. Of course, I could have been wrong, but not about those ears. Too many Sundays in the orphanage, when we were so bored to death we could sit together or lie on a divan together and contemplate an object for hours, had I examined her ears, with the sunlight bright as honey on them, or the cold stare of the winter light leaping up from the snow and sprawling over us in a dank room where we lay hidden from the others.

So I followed her slowly, planning what I would say to her now in this different time. She went down into the subway at Broadway and 50th. Just as she stepped down from the sidewalk, she slipped on the wet pavement and lost her balance. I was already at her elbow, so I caught her and set her aright with perfect co-ordination. But the turn of her head, the brilliant flash of recognition on her face did not come as I had anticipated. The only movement was a visible tightening of her arm grasp around the antique clock. I could hear it ticking, a sound like water dripping into a tin cup in an empty room...

And I remembered the Christmas morning when everyone but she and me and a few others had been taken into the homes of childless couples in the city for the weekend. Having grown tired of our uninteresting toys we had taken the dorm mother's clock from her dresser and had disassembled it piece by piece with quiet, whispering care, patience and engrossing fascination. And fantastically enough we almost effortlessly put it back together again — not because we feared old Miss Pruitt, which we did, but because we wanted to hear the sweet ticking again, its absence having frightened us a little. Just as we put the face back on, the alarm went off and Miss Pruitt pounced on us suddenly out of nowhere as if waiting for the signal of our doom. After that we always trembled when we passed her door, and the bald face of the clock mocked us from the black mahogany dresser.

As we waited for the dim yellow eye of the loping 7th Avenue Local to appear far down the track, I leaned with feigned nonchalance against the chicklet machine and gazed at the chewing gum wrappers and cigarette butts displayed below me like discarded years. I glanced now and then at

Greta who stood at the edge of the platform, so close to the edge and with such a look and posture of continued movement forward that I wanted to walk over and take her arm.

But the image of her suddenly stepping off in front of a subway with that tall clock in her arms struck me as ludicrous in the extreme. Yet she always had that look of being in one spot but just on the brink of stepping off into another. That sort of thing had captured my attention years ago so that when I was with her I did a great deal of looking at her with a kind of anticipation, though she never did anything extraordinary.

I looked at her now. She was very tall — willowy, I suppose, like a girl sketched by Dali, clock and all, only not in that rather humiliated, amoebic shape. Even at seven years old she had been unusually tall, five feet three of skin and bone, and three feet of light brown hair, her ears peeking through of course. She was much taller now, but there was the same thin face and sharp features with the very fragile mouth. Her lips were always very grave, except for her rare smiles which were frightening in the ferocity of their brilliance.

I followed her into the subway and sat down across from her. I hoped she would finally recognize me, but she continued to stare fixedly. So I sat there with my legs crossed, scratching my wart, waiting, remembering that day in another October, our last autumn together, when she was eight and I was nine, and we began to separate — or so I thought.

The orphanage was in Manhattan, squeezed in on both sides by brownstone apartment buildings. The back yards were no larger than family plots and some of them were rather humpy in those days. Greta was sick one week with the measles and so they wouldn't let me near her, but during the night I would slip up the drain pipe and in the window and we'd talk until she fell asleep of the things we'd do when she would be well again.

But during the chilly days I'd sit on one of those grassless humps under a scrawny, black, naked tree. From there I could see over the top of a rotten wooden fence. The odor of the wet wooden fence had a heady tang in the sharp air if you were bored and lonely enough to concentrate on it. Sometimes I talked nonsense into a rusty tin can just to hear my voice roar, like in a sea shell, with an almost adult richness and depth that made me feel even lonelier. I was looking for all kinds of designs, patterns, shapes of animals and humans in the various textures and surfaces the day I saw the window with the shade up and the lucid 4 o'clock sun splashed over it.

I could barely see the figures moving beyond the reflected glare. One of them came closer to the window. It was a girl about nineteen years old, wearing a blue sweater and a darker blue skirt. She stood a moment, arms akimbo with her back to the window, and moving through the dimness came a young man toward her, his red hair tousled, one hand scratching his head, the other in his pocket. He ambled as one who moves in casually to join a conversation. For a few moments he stood before her smiling, and took the hand out of the pocket and brought it up to rest gently on her shoulder, still mulling his hair. Suddenly she turned her face sideways, laughing with her eyes closed, and hugged his arm with both of hers, the sun holding the two in a golden sheen of warmth and brilliance.

And then he put his arms around her and held her a long time, swaying slightly, ruffling her long hair with one hand and running the other across her fanny. That struck me as peculiar behavior. I watched him fiddle around with her skirt and saw it slide down over her hips as he pulled her to him more tightly. And then he took her by the hand and led her away from sun-struck window and into the darkness of the room. I strained my eyes but could see only dark movement. Then a cloud obscured the sun's glare and I saw clearly through the cold window. They were both naked and playing some sort of game which I couldn't figure out even though I watched until it grew too dark to see.

I rushed back to the orphanage, climbed the drain pipe and pecked on the window that was beside Greta's bed. In an excited, rushing whisper, I told her what I had seen. But she looked at me with hurt confusion, as though I were playing a silly game with her. Yet she laughed at a few of the things I told her they had been doing, burying her face in the pillow to muffle the sound. I was a little peeved with her lack of enthusiasm for what I considered a mystery of human behavior quite enthralling to watch.

The next day she was released from the infirmary and we met at noon in the dining room. She appeared very excited now that we could be together again, but I ignored her and walked away. She ran after me and asked what the matter was and I told her that I had more interesting things to do than piddle around with a child. But she followed me to the fence and waited silently beside me, wondering what I was staring at. They were asleep on the bed with blankets over them, something I didn't find interesting enough to disclose to Greta as being my special secret.

But when the girl opened her eyes and sat up in bed and leaned over and put her mouth over his ear, I prodded Greta in the ribs and pointed at the window. She had to put on her hideous glasses to see. She was so awed by what transpired that she couldn't speak, while all I could do was laugh. That was the first time I ever saw her mouth show any expression besides that graveness and those rare smiles.

For two weeks we went every day to the fence and watched the boy and the girl in their ordinary activities as well as that one activity which so entranced us. Greta never spoke while that was happening but she called my attention to every little thing the boy did to or for the girl otherwise, like: tying her apron strings, zipping up her dress or handing her a cup of coffee as she stood gazing out the window, and once he even playfully combed her hair, and another time she sat by the window in her slip, painting her fingernails and he blew on them and then kissed her so hard that her head pressed against the window and her hair spread out like a fan.

In very small ways I found Greta imitating her. Like one time in art class in school at the orphanage, she colored her fingers with red paint and looked at me as though she expected me to blow them dry, but Miss Pruitt caught her and pulled her roughly to the sink and stood over her like the leaning tower of Pisa while Greta scrubbed them clean.

Then two weeks after we discovered them, we saw the thing that affected both Greta and the girl so profoundly. The girl was sitting by the window, her elbow on the sill and her head resting in her hand, running her finger listlessly over the glass with her other hand which also held a handkerchief. Her face was red from crying.

Suddenly, the door opened across the room. He came in wearing a straw hat and a happy-dan sort of suit. She ran to him and flung her arms around his neck but he pushed her away from him and after placing his hat over the bed post, began to put some clothes into a suit-case, while she cried and tried to put her hand on his arm. Shortly, he put his hat on again and with suitcase in hand started for the door. But she had locked it and was running across the room to the window when he caught her by the neck and struggled with her. She managed to raise the window slightly with her free hand and put the one holding the key through the opening. Greta was holding tightly to the rim of the fence, on the verge of tears. Then a loud, shrill scream split the air. He had slammed the window on her fingers and both the girl and Greta had screamed at the same instant.

I did not go back the next day. I had not only lost interest but Greta had asked me to let her go alone. She went back alone five days in a row, and I began to miss my playmate, so on the sixth day I followed her and quietly sat beside her. The girl was lying on the bed, motionless. After two hours she hadn't moved in the slightest and I brought this fact to Greta's attention, hoping she too would recognize the dull monotony of it all and come away to play jack-rocks with me. But she said blandly, « She hasn't moved for the last four days. »

« She's been lying there like that all this time? »

« Yes. She's asleep, dreaming of him. »
« She never gets up to eat or go out? »
« No. She just lies there asleep and never moves. »
« Well, why do you keep looking at her? »
« I don't know. » I jumped up and walked away in disgust.

A few days later, Miss Pruitt sent for me. A woman was there who was interested in adopting me. She was a fat woman with a black mustache. All the time she was talking to me I felt real panic. She looked me over and said yes, she'd take me.

I wasn't to leave for a few days yet but I had to find Greta and tell her. I found her sitting in the same position as the last time. A soft rain was falling and the sky was very dark and violet-colored though it was only three o'clock. Her hair glistened with the rain and her ears were pale. I could smell the strong odor of rot in the wooden fence. The girl lay on the bed the same as before, barely visible in the darkness of her room. Looking at her I completely forgot why I had come, because I was suddenly scared. Nobody sleeps that much and if they do they turn over once in a while or curl up. The dress she wore was the same as on that day when the boy slammed the window on her fingers and the door on her life.

I ran back to the orphanage and told Miss Pruitt what I had seen and what I thought about it. She immediately telephoned the police.

I returned to Greta because I didn't want her to see what would happen when the police came bursting through the door so I grabbed her by the wrist and pulled her away rather violently. She screamed, « You're hurting my fingers! » But I hadn't touched them.

The next day Greta returned to the fence and I followed. The room was empty. Everything was gone. I watched her cry. She wouldn't let me come near her.

I had often gotten into moods when I would reject her. Now that she was rejecting me, I felt the numbing sting of it and finally I rather cruelly yelled, « She's dead! Why don't you stop acting so crazy? »

But I didn't expect her answer, « She's not dead! She just went out to buy a clock so she can look at it while she waits for him. » I thought that was the craziest thing I'd ever heard in my life so I just turned around and got the hell away from her.

We didn't speak at all after that. I didn't even tell her I was going away. It was as though I wasn't around. She walked around with a blank expression on her face and her eyes staring. I couldn't stand to look at her but I had an awful lonely feeling not being able to talk to her.

A few weeks later the fat lady returned. She took me with her to New Jersey. She wasn't so bad after all. But when I was old enough I got the hell away from her.

Now Greta was a woman of twenty-eight and she was walking in front of me down a street of brownstone apartments with a clock in her arms, seemingly oblivious of everyone and everything, certainly of me. I tried in my mind the beginning of a conversation with her. « May I help you carry the clock, Greta? » « I was just taking it home to take it apart. Will you help me? Remember? » I couldn't imagine a likely flow of talk, and decided to delay speaking until she arrived at her destination.

Of course, her husband might have been nearby, thus calling for uncomfortable explanation, but for some inexplicable reason I felt that she was something of an old maid in corduroy. In my mind our conversation continued. « Yes, I was married but it didn't last long. He left me for another woman. » And I would soften the tension with, « I haven't married, myself. I'm married to my art. A woman is just a worry-wart for an artist like me. » Then she would laugh that completely shattering laugh of hers and I wouldn't be able to speak and the grandfather's clock would probably chime about then.

Then she slowed down at the corner building and climb-ed a short flight of steps. I was quickly at her elbow again, half expecting her to drop the black mahogany clock when she fumbled for her keys. « Please allow me to hold your burden while you find your keys, Miss. »

Not looking at me, she smiled rather uncomfortably, and began to rummage through some things in her pockets. She had her hand full of some sort of junk. As I watched her picking through it for her key, I noticed that on the fingers of one of her hands were fresh bruises and old scars. An object fell from her hands and she turned to catch it.

At the sight of the small rubber ball used in jack-rocks games bouncing slowly down the steps and rolling into the gutter, a nameless panic seized me and I looked around with the kind of fear one feels just prior to the clearer realization of the exact nature of the danger. My frightened glances re-vealed a familiar sight, unseen for twenty years. Across a vacant lot to the rear of the buildings on the next street over, I could see the miserably familiar drain-pipe and the window to the infirmary, and a few buildings down, the fence, the tree and the grassless mound of earth.

I half expected the clock to chime in my arms at that moment, but it had stopped ticking altogether, and Greta was ascending the steps again with the key in one hand and the ball in the other, bruised one. She looked up at me, full into my face and then she really saw me for the first time. Her eyes seemed almost to tremble but a slow smile moved across her lips. She reached out and softly laid the palm of her hand on my wrist, the fingers lightly touching the black mahogany.

« Hello, Greta. How have you been? »
« I've been asleep, dreaming of you. »
Maybe I'm a coward, but I just turned and leaned the clock against the door and walked quickly away.

W. H. AUDEN

ISCHIA

For Brian Howard

There is a time to admit how much the sword decides,
With flourishing horns to salute the conqueror,
Impassive, cloaked and great on
Horseback under his faffling flag.

Changes of heart should also occasion song, like his
Who, turning back from the crusaders' harbor, broke
With our aggressive habit
Once and for all and was the first

To see all penniless creatures as his siblings. But
At all times it is good to praise the shining earth,
Dear to us whether we choose our
Duty or do something horrible.

Dearest to each his birthplace; but to recall a green
Valley where mushrooms fatten in the summer nights
And silvered willows copy
The circumflexions of the stream

Is not my gladness to-day: I am presently moved
By sun-drenched Parthenopeia, my thanks are for you,

Ischia, to whom a fair wind has
Brought me rejoicing with dear friends

From gross productive cities. How well you correct
Our injured eyes, how gently you train us to see
      Things and men in perspective
   Under your uniform light.

Noble are the plans of the shirt-sleeved engineer,
But luck, you say, does more. What design could have washed
      With such delicate yellows
   And pinks and greens your fishing ports

That lean against ample Epomeo, holding on
To the rigid folds of her skirts? The boiling springs
      Which betray her secret fever
   Make limber the gout-stiffened joint

And improve the venereal act; your ambient peace
In any case is a cure for, ceasing to think
      Of a way to get on, we
   Learn to simply wander about

By twisting paths which at any moment reveal
Some vista as an absolute goal; eastward, perhaps,
      Suddenly there, Vesuvius,
   Looming across the bright bland bay

Like a massive family pudding, or, around
A southern point, sheer-sided Capri, who by herself
      Defends the cult of Pleasure,
   A jealous, sometimes a cruel, god.

Always with some cool space or shaded surface, too,
You offer a reason to sit down; tasting what bees
      From the blossoming chestnut
   Or short but shapely dark-haired men

From the aragonian grape distill, your amber wine,
Your coffee-colored honey, we believe that our
Lives are as welcome to us as
Loud explosions are to your saints.

Not that you lie about pain or pretend that a time
Of darkness and outcry will not come back; upon
Your quays, reminding the happy
Stranger that all is never well,

Sometimes a donkey breaks out into a choking wail
Of utter protest at what is the case, or his
Master sighs for a Brooklyn
Where shirts are silk and pants are new,

Far from tall Restituta's all-too-watchful eye,
Whose patronage, they say, is annually bought with blood.
That, blessed and formidable
Lady, we hope is not true; but, since

Nothing is free, whatever you charge shall be paid
That these days of exotic splendor may stand out
In each lifetime like marble
Mileposts in an alluvial land.

WALTER DE LA MARE

PRIDE

What shades are these that now oppress my heart
And hang a veil of night o'er burning day?
I see the sun through shadows; and his clouds,
Clothed in their mutable magnificence
Seem to some inward sorrow moving on.

What meaning has the beauty of the earth?
And this unageing sweetness of the spring?
Her trees that once, as if from a far dream,
Borrowed their shining simpleness; her flowers,
Blowing where nothing but the bleak snow was,
Like flames of crystal brightness in the fields?

Once I could gaze until these seemed to me
Only my soul's own splendour in disguise.
But now their inward beauty is lost and faded;
They are the haunts of alien voices now;
An alien Wonderment of light beams forth;
No more the secret reflex of my self.

AN ANGEL

Oh, now, Alexander's Angel,
Whither are thy pinions winnowing,
On what swift and timeless errand
Through the wilds of starry splendour
That to mortal eyes are merely
Points of radianse pricked in space?
Earthly minds can see thee solely
In the semblance of their bodies,
Winged with light thy locks of glory,
Streaming from thy brows gigantic,
Brows unmoved, and feet of crystal,
Heaven reflected in thy face!

C. DAY LEWIS

OUTSIDE AND IN

How pretty it looks, thought a passer-by —
That cyclamen on her windowsill:
Flowers flushed like the butterfly kisses of sleep that illumine
A child's alabaster cheek.
She who set it there must have warm hopes to bloom in,
So happy it looks, thought the passer-by,
On the newcomer's windowsill.

O passer-by, can you not feel my glances
Beating against the pane,
Fluttering like a moth shut off from the glades of musk
And the moonlit dances?
O passer-by, can you not see it plain?

She comes not to meet us, muttered the neighbours
Peering in from the stony street:
But look at her parlour, all lighted and spider-spruce!
How saucily wink the brasses!
So garnished a room never tokens a pure recluse.
Let us hope she'll bring, said the gossiping neighbours,
No scandal upon our street.

Ah, what do you know of the crippled heart, my neighbours,
That shrinks from the light and the press?
My winking brass, all the fine repetitive web

142

Of my house-bound labours —
Even I dare not know them for signals of distress.

A happy release, murmured the living
As they carried at last out into the world
Her body, light as a bird's that has died of hunger
Beneath some warped hedgerow:
Though it was her own doing if all humanity shunned her,
Yet a happy release to be done with living
An outcast from the world.

O living hearts, you are wrong once more. Unassuaged
Even now are my pangs, my fears.
I starved amid plenty. Death seemed no deliverance
To flesh that was caged,
O living hearts, in a ghost these fifty years.

KATHLEEN RAINE

SELF

Who am I, who
Speaks from the dust,
Who looks from the clay?

Who hears
For the mute stone,
For fragile water feels
With finger and bone?

Who for the forest breathes the evening,
Sees for the rose,
Who knows
What the bird sings?

Who am I, who for the sun fears
The demon dark,
In order holds
The void and violence within
Atom and chaos?

Who out of nothingness has gazed
On the beloved face?

EDITH SITWELL

THE SONG OF DIDO

My Sun of Death is to the deep reversedly
What the great Sun of heaven is to the height
In the violent heat
When Sirius comes to lie at the Sun's feet.
My Sun of Death is all depth, — heaven's sun
All height, and the air of the whole world lies between
Those suns.
    Now only the Dog sits by my bier
Where I lie flaming from my heart. The five dogs of the senses
Are no more hunting now.
For after the conflagration of the summer
Of youth, and its violent Suns,
My veins of life that seemed so high that the great rivers
Of Africa and Asia were but brooks to them,
Were quenched, and Time like fire
Had changed the bone to knotted rubies like the horizons
  of the light:
Beyond all summers lies the peony bud
In the veins,and the great paeons of the blood,
The empery of the rose.
Yet once I had thought my bed of love my bier the highest
Sun of heaven, the height where Sirius is flaming,
And then I thought it Death's Sun, and that there is no deep
Below... But now I know
That even the hunters in the heart and in the heaven,
At last must sleep!

ROY FULLER

FATHER AND CHILD

an observation of Frobenius

The fire burns low: the father reads,
But from the floor in all directions
The child, like a loop of wooden beads,
*   Strings her small noisy actions.*

He is distracted. 'Look', he says,
'There, go and play with these' — and passes
The flushed bright child the nearest toys,
*   Which are merely three burnt matches.*

The noise dies down: upon the floor
Now there is only the faintest whisper:
'I'll call this Hansel, this one here
*   Gretel and this one must be*

The Witch. And all goes well: the fire
Breaks up, the flames send moving
Shadows upon the walls and floor:
*   The room is quiet and loving.*

But suddenly he is startled by
A scream. She flies. He has to catch her.
'Father! Oh take the Witch away!
I am afraid to touch her'.

TO ALUN LEWIS

I found by chance in one of your letters, printed in a maga-
zine,
That you, who I never met, had praised my verses generously.
Touched by your casual words, preserved in such sad circum-
stance, I've been
Thinking about the war and you all this November day.

And now I've drawn the curtains on the rain and yellows
of the garden,
And come to the quiet fire to make some kind of pious return,
Although I know so well I do not have to ask your spirit
pardon
For war and threat of war that after three years' peace still
burn.

Because, like me, you were completely disillusioned: all you
wrote
Was to discover the closeness of individual men to men;
You would not have been shocked to find the other closeness
still remote:
Celebrating a sombre month in the midst of murder, I use
your pen.

Yes, we both tried, beyond our talents and our scope, to make
the times
Of parting, change and death live in our words. And now
I see
At last the superior grasp that made you in the end augment
your rhymes
By changing fear to what was feared, yourself to history.

THE MINOR VICTORIAN NOVELISTS

In time's salt stream their books have petrified.
The pages will not open: no one knows
What small clear vision glitters still inside
The complicated plot, the moral prose.

Only their lives are known, arranged for us
In patterns their creators did not seem:
The plot untidy and the style a fuzz,
The moral crude as someone else's dream.

HUGH MACDIARMID

MILK-WORT AND BOG COTTON

Cwa een like milk-wort and bog-cotton hair!
I love you, earth, in this mood best o' a'
When the shy spirit like a laich wind moves
And frae the lift nae shadow can fa'
Since there's nocht left to thraw a shadow there
Owre een like milk-wort and milk-white cotton hair.

Wad that nae leaf upon anither wheeled
A shadow either and nae root need dern
In sacrifice to let sic beauty be!
But deep surroondin' darkness I discern
Is aye the price o' licht. Wad licht revealed
Naething but you, and nicht nocht else concealed.

IN THE HEDGEBACK

It was a wild black nicht,
But i the hert o't we
Drave back the darkness wi a bleeze o licht,
Ferrer than een could see.
It was a wild black nicht,
But o the snell air we

Kept juist eneuch to hinder the heat
Meltin us utterly.
It was a wild black nicht,
But o the win's roar we
Kept juist eneuch to hear oor herts beat
Owre it triumphantly.
It was a wild black nicht,
But o the Earth we
Kept juist eneuch underneath us to ken
That a warl used to be.

THE WATERGAW

Ae weet forenicht i the yow-trummle
I sae yon antrin thing
A watergaw wi its chitterin licht
Ayont the on-ding;
An I thocht o the last wild look yye gied
Afore ye deed!

There was naw reek i the laverock's hoose
That nicht-an nane i mine;
But I hae thocht o that foolish licht
Ever sin syne;
An I think that mebbe at last I ken
What your look meant then.

GLOSSARY

cwa: come away   een: eyes   milk-wort: the bluebell   laich: low   lift: sky   dern: hide   sic: such   snell: bitter cold   weet: wet   you-trummle: ewe-tremble' [a cold spell after sheep shearing]   antrin: rare   watergaw: rainbow   chitterin: shivering   ayont: against   on-ding: down-pour   reek: smoke   loverock's-hoose: lark's-house.

LOUIS MACNEICE

THE CRASH LANDING

India at first sight. The Visitor is accompanied by four « familiars »
or voices in his head — The Uncle, the Nanny, the Missionary and the
Still Voice.

INDIA

Is is always a crash landing — when I come up to meet
you. With the red earth on my sandals and the brass jug on
my head my contradictory tongues and my millions of pairs
of hands. So noisy — and yet so silent. You don't know how
to talk to me — our meeting has been so abrupt — yet though
you have crashed, as you had to, not one of your bones is
broken.

THE VISITOR

No — not one of my bones — but my head's going round.
A moment ago I was living in the Twentieth Century but
where have I got to now? This is not what I think of as a
street, these are not what I call shops —

THE UNCLE

Holes in the wall, my boy — but for Heaven's sake mind
that cow! Haven't you heard they're sacred?

THE VISITOR

No... no... Might be all fancy dress — but it's too natural.
Or might be the Middle Ages. All this life in the streets —

151

cooking and stitching and hammering and tinkling and touting and — Yes, and the smells and the flies!

THE NANNY

The smell and the flies, Master Edward! You might catch anything in those bazaars.

THE VISITOR

And here comes a man leading a bear. And an old woman, concertina'd down on her hunkers, oscillating slowly forward, picking up dung. All so dirty, so rich, so manifold and so engrained. The Middle Ages — but not the ages of Europe.

THE STILL VOICE

Everything at ground level or over your head.

THE VISITOR

That's right. On this boy's head — pyramid of fruit, on the girl's — whole set of water-jars. And somewhere unseen — high, high above me — the muezzin. But squatting on the pavement a man mixing grated nut and lime and folding it up in a leaf — and taking his time about it — and pinning the leaf with a clove.

THE MISSIONARY

Chewing pan — that's a filthy habit too. Makes you spit red as if you had T. B.

THE VISITOR

And a naked man lying asleep and taking his time about it. And sprouting from under my feet the naked stump of an arm and twining itself up my legs the whine of a one-track voice —

THE UNCLE

Now, now, Eddie! You're only asking for trouble if you give those cripples an anna.

THE VISITOR

Uncle Howard, I left you in England. So why I've got
to tote you around in my head —

THE UNCLE

Want to know why? Back home you've had many a
laugh at the pukka sahib but now that you're out there your-
self, well, either you go fanti — which you won't — or ... Of
course, you blighter, of course I'm with you — in your head.

THE MISSIONARY

And so am I, young man. Remember that hookah I had
in my stall years ago? Well, there's an old boy — on the
charpoy over there — using one. And I bet he lit it with
cow-dung. Strange face, Hasn't he — but he's much stranger
inside. And if you'll take a tip from someone who knows —

THE VISITOR

Oh someone who knows my foot! I don't want any tips
from you vested interests, I want to forget all my own pre-
conceptions — everything I've heard and read. I want to
start from scratch, get my own impressions —

THE STILL VOICE

No one can start from scratch. Here comes a whole sub-
continent crowding upon you and here stand you, enmeshed
in your own background, your reactions not so different from
those of your Nanny or your Uncle —

THE NANNY

Bit like a picture book, isn't it? Remember when you got
that Arabian Nights for Christmas? And you wanted me to
make you a turban and —

THE MISSIONARY

Christmas! When one compares our festivals with those
of the Hindus or even the Muslims —

THE UNCLE

When one compares the white man's conception of play-
ing the game with ...er —

THE VISITOR

Oh when one compares anything with anything! India's
something new, I want to escape from comparisons. And
now that I'm here —

THE STILL VOICE

Look out!

THE VISITOR

Look out? Why?

THE STILL VOICE

You're *here*.

INDIA

Here in the middle of my great plain, my aggressively
featureless plain, my immutable imponderable interminable
plain — here there's no rise in the ground to be seen — no
shadows even for the sun is straight above you — here in
this desert that buzzes with people, here where the eye has
nowhere to rest and the restless hawk circles for ever.

THE STILL VOICE

For ever and ever and ever and ever —

INDIA

Here where you gaze beyond and beyond —

THE STILL VOICE

And beyond the beyond is only beyond —

INDIA

Here where the eyes of my babies like wet black prunes —

154

THE MISSIONARY

Here, here, here, young man; don't let India hypnotise you. It's a way she has but there's no future in it.

THE STILL VOICE

No future at all — or is it all the future?

THE NANNY

Now Master Edward, I've told you about that before. Don't moon so. It's unhealthy.

THE UNCLE

Nanny's quite right; don't let the place make you mystiical. Keep your eyes on the details, man.

THE VISITOR

The details —?

THE STILL VOICE

Look out; they're coming.

THE VISITOR

Who?

THE STILL VOICE

Either you can't see the trees for the wood or you can't see the wood for the trees.

INDIA

Nor can the wood see itself.

THE STILL VOICE

But here they come now — the trees — the details. Birnam Wood is not in it.

155

THE MISSIONARY

'And he looked up and said, I see men as trees, walking.'
I've often been reminded of that text in India. When you
meet these fellows with piles of brushwood on their heads —

THE STILL VOICE

Here they come now — from the dark side of the moon.

THE UNCLE

Here they come now; hand me my Nelson eye. And boy!
Boy! Fetch me a chota peg — no, make it a burra peg. And,
if anyone calls, I'm out.

THE VISITOR

If anyone calls...?

THE STILL VOICE

Look out, Eddie! And look in! You have two eyes but
you'd need a thousand. For here they come now and how
are you to see them? You'd need a thousand — and an inner
eye, too. In fact, Eddie, you need me.

THE VISITOR

On the dazzle of all these white clothes, it makes me
blink and —

INDIA

Here we come now, the men and women of India.

THE MASSES

In our dhotis and salvars and sherwanis and loincloths —
In our burqas and saris —
In our turbans and fezzes and lambskins and Gandhi
caps —
Riding in gharries, in ekkas, in tongas; palanquins, bul-
lock-carts, rickshaws —

With our mouths full of curries, of curds, of kebabs, bananas and brinjals, sweet peppers and spinach cakes, mangoes, chapattis —

INDIA

Or often with our mouths empty.

THE MASSES

Here we come now transplanting the paddy by hand, flailing a shirt on a rock in the dhobi ghat, flicking the fishlike shuttle across the loom by hand, nipping two leaves and a bud in the tea plantations —

Here we come now through creepered jungle, eroded loess and granite outcrop, through blood-red floods and eddies of alluvial dust —

From under our various roofs — flat mud, red tiles or palm-thatch —

Or the wooden roofs of Kashmir upon which in the spring the tulip and iris —

INDIA

Or from unden no roofs at all.

THE MASSES

Here we come, sannyasis and mullahs, banias and budmashes, sweepers and coolies —

INDIA

Here I come now with my cow-bells and conches, my chenars and my banyans, my charm and my touchiness.

THE STILL VOICE

With her inlaid marbles, her patterns of silver thread — chain stitch and cross stitch — and lucky designs on her threshold —

157

INDIA

With my musical instruments — veena and tanpura, sitar
and tabla and bamboo flute —

THE STILL VOICE

With her efflorescence of grace-notes, her topless towers
of wreathing and writhing sculpture, her intervolutions of
high metaphysics —

INDIA

Here I come now with my mantras and yantras and
mudras —

THE STILL VOICE

With her mosques and temples and sacred trees, her
stupas and chaityas and towers of silence —

INDIA

With my gods that dance in the rock, with my living
dancers timeless as they keep time —

THE STILL VOICE

With her mountains frozen in patience, her rivers on
which men built but the rivers moved elsewhere —

THE UNCLE

With her carrion crows and scavenger dogs, her rickety
children, her fevers —

INDIA

Here I come now in my squalor and my serenity.
With my vast riches and immemorial hunger.
The Gita in one hand and the Koran in the other —

THE STILL VOICE

Ambiguity; continuity; perpetuity.

INDIA

Here I am now. Take me or leave me.

STEPHEN SPENDER

TRAVELLING NORTHWARDS HOME

From the red peaks like roots dried up in air
Worn by gales and years to fruitless stone,
With sides parched gold by killing suns;

From heat twisting through white dust like snakes,
From skies hammering mountains and sea
Into one cracked and violet crystal.

To me travelling Northwards home, suddenly green
Blazed, from grass and barley fields
Along rivers where there were flowering trees;

And like a liquid trail of fire was the mile-long mildness
Which I had never looked at until this,
When being restored to me, it seemed visible happiness.

KATHLEEN RAINE

A SPARROW'S FLIGHT

To the ancestral spirits on both sides of the border.

> So seems the life of man, O King, as a sparrow's flight
> through the hall when you are sitting at meat in winter-tide,
> the fire on the hearth, the icy rain storm without. The spar-
> row flies in at one door and tarries for a moment in the light
> and heat of the hearth-fire, then flies forth into the darkness
> whence it came. So tarries for a moment the life of man in
> our sight, but what is before it, what after it. We know not.
>
> *Bede's account of the conversion of King
> Eadwine, by Paulinus, perhaps at Bamburgh
> Castle.*

1

Pure I was before the world began.
I was the violence of wind and wave,
I was the bird before bird ever sang.

I was never still,
I turned upon the axis of my joy,
I was the lonely dancer on the hill.

I was the rain upon the mountainside,
I was a rising mist,
I was the sea's unrest.

I wove the web of colour
Before the rainbow.
I was the intricacy of the flower
Before the leaf grew.

I was the buried ore,
The fossil forest;
I knew the roots of things.
Before death's kingdom
I passed through the grave.

Seven times my journey
Circles the universe
And I remain
Before the first day.

II

Let in the wind,
Let in the rain,
Let in the moor tonight.

The storm beats on my windowpane,
Night stands at my bed-foot,
Let in the fear,
Let in the pain,
Let in the trees that toss and groan,
Let in the north tonight.

Let in the nameless formless power
That beats upon my door,
Let in the ice, let in the snow,
The ban-shee howling on the moor,
The bracken-bush on the bleak hillside,
Let in the dead tonight.

The whistling ghost behind the dyke,
The dead that rot in mire,
Let in the thronging ancestors,
The unfulfilled desire,
Let in the wraith of the dead earl,
Let in the unborn tonight.

Let in the cold,
Let in the wet,
Let in the loneliness,
Let in the quick,
Let in the dead,
Let in the unfathomed skies.

Oh how virgin fingers weave
A covering for the void,
How can my fearful heart conceive
Gigantic solitude?
How can a house so small contain
A company so great?

Let in the dark,
Let in the dead,
Let in your love tonight.

Let in the snow that numbs the grave
Let in the acorn-trees,
The mountain stream and mountain stone,
Let in the bitter sea,
Let in the wild deer and the ram,
Let in the whitening bone.

Oh fearful is my virgin heart
And frail my virgin form,
And must I then take pity on
The raging of the storm
That rose up from the great abyss

Before the earth was made,
That pours the stars in cataracts,
And shakes this violent world?

Let in the fire,
Let in the power,
Let in the invading might.

Oh gentle must my fingers be
And pitiful my heart
Since I must bind in human form
A living power so great,
A living impulse great and wild
That cries about my house,
With all the violence of desire
Desiring this my peace.

Oh pitiful my heart must hold
The lonely stars at rest,
Have pity on the raven's cry
The torrent and the eagle's wing,
The icy water of the tarn
And on the biting blast.

Let in the wound,
Let in the pain,
Let in your child tonight.

III

The sleeper at the rowan's foot
Dreams the darkness of the root,
Dreams the flow that ascends the vein
And fills with world the dreamer's brain.

Wild tree, filled with wind and rain,
Day and night invade your dream,
Wild commotion of the air,

Unseen brightness of the sun,
Waters flowing underground
Rise in blood and flower and shoot,
And the burden is so great
Of the dark flow from without,
Of sun streaming from the sky
And the dead rising from the root
Of the world's desire to be
In this dreaming incarnate
That world has overflowed the trees.

Oh do not wake, oh do not wake
The sleeper in the rowan's shade.
Mountains rest within his thought,
Clouds are drifting in his brain,
Snows upon his eyelids fall,
Winds are piping in his song,
Night is gathered at his root,
Stars are blossoming in his crown,
Storm without finds peace within,
World is resting in his dream.

Lonely dreamer on the hill
I have dreamed a thousand years,
I have dreamed returning spring,
Earth's delight and golden sun.
I have dreamed the pheasant's eye,
The heather and the flashing burn,
For the world has flowed within,
And the world has filled my dream.
Dream has overflowed the tree.

World without presses so sore
Upon the roots and branches fine,
The dreamer can contain no more
And overflows in falling flowers,
Lets fall the bitter rowan fruit
Harsh as tears and bright as blood,

Berries that the wild birds eat
Till stripped of dream the sleeper lies,
Stripped of world the naked tree.

But on the hillside I have heard
The voice of the prophetic bird
That feeds upon the bitter fruit,
I have heard the blackbird sing
The wild music of the wind,
Utter the note the sun would cry,
Sing for the burn that flows away.

The dreamer in the rowan tree
As full of world as dream can hold;
As full of dream as tree can bear
Sends the bird singing in the air
As full of song as bird can sing,
As full of world as song can cry,
And yet the song is overflowed,
And pressing at the tree's deep root
Still underground is world, is world.

The invading dream must break the tree
So heavy is the weight of sky,
So violent the water's flow,
So vast the hills that would be born.
Beyond the utterance of bird
The mountain voice that would be sung,
The world of wild that would be man.

Make the dream and break the dream,
World that invades the rowan's root,
World that utters the bird's cry,
The river's spate is in the vein,
The song is rising from the heart,
The world is rising in the song,
The dream has overflowed the tree.

CHARLES TOMLINSON

POEM

I

Wakening with the window over fields,
To the coin-clear harness-jingle as a float
Clips by, and each succeeding hooffall, now remote,
Breaks clean and frost-sharp on the unstopped ear.

The hooves describe an arabesque on space,
A dotted line in sound that falls and rises
As the cart goes by, recedes, turns to retrace
Its way back through the unawakened village.

And space vibrates, enlarges with the sound;
Though space is soundless, yet creates
From very soundlessness a ground
To counterstress the lilting hooffall as it breaks.

II

Wakening to the burden of slow chimes...
The city air lifts, furred and crass,
On joists of steel and intersecting wires,
Piles fog against the window glass.

Space, grown narrow and confined
By all the walls that crowd it out,

166

Arrests and deadens each succeeding stroke
That country-space would, counterpointing flout.

And space grown small on each succeeding hill
Grants exodus to neither ear nor sight,
Awaits, in muffled, feckless ignorance
The frog, the locust-swarm, the blight.

THE LIGHT AND DARK

The sun is not for us. The dark subtends
The verticals of waste, the lost street-ends.
Moonlight defers day's rancours. The subfusc
Windows entertain new light: dissolving dusk
Grows angular once more and reinstates
The monumental architrave, the creaking gates.
The blood has its seasons, its molten course
Runs in time with sun and moon and stars,
Giving the true responses when the spring
Temperately creates an interim
Between the winter and the summer. As travellers know,
Exchanging hemispheres, when they anticipate:
'Summer follows spring', winter surprises them.
The sun is not for us. Our slow pulse-beats
Quicken as the ripening moon completes
Its rich progression to the full. Its light
Defines, does not obliterate the night
And in the union of light and dark
This mystique is confirmed: Life is the spark
Thrown off by grinding opposites, whose power
Relates the world of fearful symmetry with blood and flower.

DYLAN THOMAS

DO NOT GO GENTLE INTO THAT GOOD NIGHT

Do not go gentle into that good night,
Old age should burn and rave at close of day;
Rage, rage against the dying of the light.

Though wise men at the end know dark is right,
Because their words had forked no lightning they
Do not go gentle into that good night.

Good men, the last wave by, sighing how bright
Their frail deeds might have danced in a green bay,
Rage, rage against the dying of the light.

Wild men who caught and sang the sun in flight,
And learn, too late, they grieved it on its way,
Do not go gentle into that good night.

Grave men, near death, who see with blinding sight
Blind eyes could blaze like meteors and be gay,
Rage, rage against the dying of the light.

And you, my father, there on the sad height,
Curse, bless, me now with your fierce tears, I pray.
Do not go gentle into that good night.
Rage, rage against the dying of the light.

ROBERT GRAVES

THE DEVIL IS A PROTESTANT

As a child in London I was once covertly taken to High Mass by a nursemaid who had hitherto pretended to be Church of England. When my parents got wind of it they dismissed her on the spot and persuaded me that I had been given a foretaste of Hell. I cannot pretend that I became a secret Papist, intoxicated by the incense, the music, the antique ritual, and wept disconsolately for the wronged nursemaid; and that, by contrast, the matins celebrated next Sunday in our red-brick Evangelical church appeared inexpressibly drab and soulless. The truth is that what my parents disrespectfully called 'the mumbojumbo of Romanism' so dismayed and repelled me that I would have been quite willing to accept their interpretation as correct, even if I had not regarded the nursemaid as a thoroughly unprincipled person; and that a cradle-Protestant, even if he turns atheist and becomes converted to the elder faith, remains temperamentally a cradle-Protestant, however hard he may try to extirpate the heresy. Incense for me will always smell of brimstone; and this I heartily regret.

Having made my home in Mallorca for the last twenty-four years, I am of course long acclimatized to the Catholic atmosphere; so much that, when the U.S. aircraft carrier *Midway* put in at Palma the other day and I was invited by the local Spanish-Protestant parson, who lives a hole-and-corner life in a suburban catacomb, to interpret the sermons — Spanish-English, English-Spanish — at a 'Reunion of Solidarity', with the *Midway's* chaplain and choir, the un-Latin atmosphere dismayed and repelled me. Ah, the pitchpine pews, the puritanical communion-table, the plain brass cross, the wheezy harmonium (operated by a fish-like U.S. mess-steward), the dusty, turkey-red Protestant hassocks and the tattered copies of *Hymns Ancient and Modern!* Nevertheless, to be acclimatized is not to be indoctrinated. On my way home I paused outside a Catholic repository and gazed thoughtfully at a St Lucia wearing a gilt crown and carrying two glass eyes on a tray. St Lucia, who celebrates her feast on the shortest and dimmest day of the year (Old Style), helps Mallorquin girls embroider roses and palms and pansies on table linen for tourists, at two pesetas an hour. The heathen blinded her at Syracuse in the year 97 A.D., which made her the patron saint of needlewomen and gave her the power to cure ophthalmic distempers by the use of 'St Lucia's eyes'. These are small discs of nacre about the size of a little finger-nail, with a brown eye on one side and a spiral on the other: the artefact of a clever sea-snail. Lucia is a hard-working saint, like St Ivo, the only lawyer who was not a thief: *'Advocatus sed non latrunculus'* — emblems, a quill-pen, a briefcase, and a Madonna lily. Or St Isidore, who to dig is not ashamed. Or St Fiacre, who designs the optimistic flower pictures on seed-packets and makes the seeds actually grow to sample. Or St Piran, who came drifting from Ireland on a mill-stone, accompanied by his acolyte, a girl in disguise; landed at Zabulo in Cornwall; praised God; kindled a fire, banking it up with some lumps of ore, and lo! discovered tin.

To such saints a cradle-Protestant extends a certain humorous indulgence, Protestantism laying heavy emphasis on the social services; and this evening I felt warmly disposed towards the entire Catholic calendar, by way of protest against

Anglophile Mallorquins who sing *Onward, Christian Soldiers!*
in Spanish to a harmonium, and disregard even red-letter
saints. But what of crossgrained anchorites, who lived in
remote caves, like the egregious St Rule of Kylbrimont, or
on the tops of pillars sixty feet high, like St Simon Stylites?
Could I ever learn to love or honour these? St Simon kept
himself from a tumble not by faith, but by wearing an iron
dog-collar chained to a wooden pulpit which he also used
as a desk for writing unpleasant letters to the Byzantine
Emperor; and stood fast thirty-six years. And St Simon
Stylites Junior spent nearly seventy years on another pillar,
having cut his double-teeth up there...

The Catholics have a patron-saint for everyone, I reflect-
ed. St Simon Stylites for steeplejacks, no doubt. St Clement
for cap-makers — he made the first felt-block. St Crispin for
cobblers. St Dismas for reformed cutpurses. St Barbara for
cannoneers. St Joseph for carpenters, cuckolds and cross-
patches. The Spaniards call anyone they dislike a *tío*, mean-
ing an uncle, meaning a crosspatch uncle, meaning specifically
the Virgin's crosspatch uncle and husband, Tio Pepe, or
St Joseph. According to the gospel of *Pseudo Matthew* (once
canonical), St Joseph refused to humour the Virgin, who had
a *pica* for cherries, declaiming that the child in her womb
was none of his. 'And Joseph made answer in accent most
wild: I *will* pluck no cherries to give to chy child'! Every
Mallorgun knows that to refuse a woman with a *pica*, how-
ever illegitimate, is tantamount to child murder: a pregnant
woman can wander around the market from stall to stall
eating whatever fruit is in season, a cherry here, a strawberry
there, an apricot, a peach, and nobody will dare deny her
for fear of being called a *tío*. (Joseph Bonaparte being one
of the least popular Kings of Spain, his subjects called him
'Tío Pepe', acknowledging that he had a good taste in dry
sherry, or more frequently 'Pepe Botollas' denoting his taste
for an excess of it). Cap-makers, cobblers, cutpurses, can-
noneers, carpenters, cuckolds and crosspatches! And, of

course, St Mary Gipsy for courtesans. St Mary Gipsy felt impelled one day to go on a pilgrimage to the Holy Land. But the crew of the only ship bound for Acre warned her that she must pay her fare by sleeping with all of them in turn throughout the voyage. She accordingly made the supreme sacrifice, spending the rest of her life in patience and good works, and was eventually passed into Heaven by St Peter on the ground that 'she loved much'.

The early Fathers scorned the gods and dared deny that they existed; nevertheless for fear of causing an awkward religious vacuum, they invited the souls of defunct prophets, apostles, bishops, virgins and martyrs to take over these Olympian functions. Thus John the Baptist, who had been described as a 'burning and a shining light', supplanted Helius; John was Elias, and Elias had ascended to Heaven in a fiery chariot, and 'Elias' sounds like 'Helius'. St Lucia of Syracuse supplanted Artemis Lucia — Wolfish Artemis: she could see in the dark and was a goddess of healing. St Nicolas, whose feast introduced the mid-December Halcyon Days (Old Style), took over the temples and functions of Poseidon; this was his reward for boxing the ears of Arius, the originator of the Arian Heresy, at the Great Council of Nicaea. St Elmo (May 10), martyred at the naval base of Puteoli, replaced Castor and Pollux, to whom sailors had formerly appealed during storms at sea. The Nine Muses were ousted by the Holy Trinity. Hercules, the Porter of Heaven, yielded to St Peter...

In the scramble for Olympian functions, distribution seems sometimes to have been made at haphazard; but there was always a certain divine logic at work. For instance, one would have expected the patronage of bell-founders to have gone to one of the Typasas martyrs, whose tongues were cut out by Hunneric the Vandal when they refused to become Arians, and whose praise of God nevertheless continued to ring sweetly and articulately in the streets of Constantinople — Aeneas of Gaza the philosopher, Marcellinus, Procopius and Victor Tunnensis, three reputable historians, and Pope

Gregory the Great, all witnessed this miracle. Similarly one would have expected the patronage of pastry-cooks to be taken over by some such anchorite as Julian of Edessa (June 9), or Julian of Osroene (Oct. 18), as a reward for subsisting, year in, year out, on coarse grass and water from pools fouled by the stale of camels; though tempted every night with Apician visions of puffpastry, quince conserve and cream-cracknels. But no, the Saint of both bell-founders and pastry-cooks is St Agatha, martyred under Decius, whose persecutors hacked off her breasts and rolled her naked over live coals mixed with potsherds. Saints, as is well known, bear little emblems as distinguishing marks; St Laurence, a grid-iron; St Francis of the Tailors, a pair of shears; St Catalina Tomás (a peasant-girl who was baptized in our Parish church, and whose kitchen-sink I bought when her cottage was pulled down) a cone of fig-bread — and St Agatha of Catania, her two undraped breasts set side by side on a tray. The embarrassing objects have been claimed as bells by the bell-founders and as sugar-cakes topped with cherries by the pastry-cooks, but only because St Agatha is patroness of furnaces and because both bell-founders and pastry-cooks need to manage theirs with exceptional care. St Agatha's veil is carried in procession at Catania whenever Mount Etna is erupting and her 'letters' are a sure charm against burns.

Each pagan city or small town had kept a local deity or hero as a focus for its religious emotions, and Christian saints were called upon to fill these vacancies too, unless the former occupant cared to turn Christian, as did the goddess Brigit of Kildare, or the Blue Hag Annis of Leicester, or in the wilder parts of Italy, the gods Mercury and Venus. The chief difference between the saints and their pagan predecessors lay in the offerings they demanded — lighted candles instead of warm sacrificial blood, flowers instead of chopped fruit, wine and pearl-barley. Such well-tried phenomena as sweating and bleeding images, daylight visions, and miraculous interventions against drought and plague continued. Moreover, *ex voto* objects representing divinely healed parts of the human body, and the mass-produced figurines and religious charms which the Romans had exported all over the world remained in continuous use. The *Apocalypse of St John the Divine* did, indeed, perpetuate the Jewish ban on the sea as the corrupt home of the Sea-goddess Rahab, and the Assyrio-Phoenician architecture and furnishings of the Judgement Hall were not altered; but the atmosphere of Heaven became unmistakably Graeco-Roman.

According to cradle-Catholic gossip, to which I lend a fascinated ear, there is as much jealousy in Heaven as there ever was on Olympus. Peter and Paul are said to bicker for precedence on their common saint's day no less passionately than did Athene and Poseidon for the possession of Troezen or the Athenian acropolis; and even the patronage of syphilis is disputed — St Christopher brought the disease to Naples from America, but St Denis claims it as the 'French pox'. Namesakes are said to be a constant source of trouble, SS William of the Desert and William of Norwich accuse each other of sheep-stealing; and though John the Baptist and John the Evangelist continue to exchange beatific smiles, the Baptist scornfully rejects Evangelical Jacks and Johnnies — 'No sheep of mine', he growls; and quotes *Luke* i. 60: *'Not so: for he shall be called John'*.

As for the Anthony's... A mason working on the roof of Palma Cathedral once slipped from a scaffold and, as he fell, shouted 'Help, St Anthony!' An invisible hand arrested him in mid-air and a voice boomed: 'Which St Anthony?'.

'Of Padua!'

Catacrok!

He had guessed wrong! It was St Anthony the Abbot, whose temptations had left him as sour as a crab, and the mason hurtled another hundred feet to the flags below.

Greek gods and goddesses adopted a variety of local titles — the Virgin Artemis, for instance, could be Our Lady of Wild Things, Our Lady of the Lake, Huntress, Saviour, Spoil Winner, Strangled One, Assuager of Childbirth, Many-Breasted, Friend of Youth, Mistress of the Nets, Mistress of the Cedars, Wolfish, Light-Bringer, Persuader, Bear-Leader, Horse-Finder, and the like. But I do not recall that there was ever the same bitter rivalry between this Artemis and that, as is now presumed in Mallorca between the Black Virgin and the White. The Black Virgin of Lluch lives on the top of a mountain, among a collection of *ex voto* crutches, leg-braces, suspensory bandages, and other discarded orthopaedic contraptions. Occasionally she tours the Island, collecting money for the *Acción Católica*, the new Seminary, or similar causes; whereupon the witches of the red-light district of Palma raise thunderstorms to drench her devotees. She was appointed Patroness of the Island a century or two ago, because the monks of her monastery claimed that, soon after James I of Aragon drove out the infidel Moors, a bright light guided the shepherd boy Lucas to a cairn under which the image had taken refuge five centuries previously. Thus, though dated by art experts as not earlier than the close of the thirteenth century, the Black Virgin has been granted precedence of the lily-white 'Virgin of Good Health' who inspired James's expedition in 1229 and saved his fleet from shipwreck, and of whom the Palma women say: 'Only look at her; at once you feel better!' It is in troubled waters like these that the Devil fishes; and the Devil, the Catholics say, is a Protestant.

At times, it is claimed, even the Devil has nostalgic feelings about Heaven. A distinguished stranger once visited St Moling in his mediaeval Irish cell and announced himself as the Man of Tribulations.

'The Devil you are!' cried the astonished Moling. 'Does Christ come in purple and pomp rather than in the guise of a leper?'.

'The Devil I am!' he assented.

'What is your errand?' asked Moling politely. He was no gross inkpot-throwing Luther.

'I come for your blessing'.

'You have not deserved it, and besides, what good would it do you if I bestowed it?'.

'It would be like bathing in a tub of honey with my clothes on'.

'Be more explicit, pray!'.

'Though your blessing would not affect me inwardly, its good luck and virtue and bloom would be fragrant on me'.

'You might use it to deceive'.

'Then curse me properly!'.

'What good would that do? The venom and bitterness of the curse would merely scald my lips; for you are already beyond the reach of curses. Away with you, Satan! Leave me to my meditations. You shall be given neither blessing nor curse!'.

'I should dearly have liked a blessing. Can I not somehow earn it?'.

'Certainly; by service to God'.

'Alas, that is against my destiny'.

'Then by study of the Scriptures'.

'Your own studies have not been deeper or wider, and I am none the better for them'.

'Then by fasting'.

'I have fasted since Creation'.

'Then by genuflexions'.

'Impossible. My knees bend backwards'.

'Pray, excuse me', said Moling, reaching for his rosary. 'I fear I can do nothing for you'.

Thereupon the Devil recited his famous *Blessing Upon Moling, in Irish rhymed quatrains*:

> Golden sky the sun surrounding,
> Silver bowl replete with wine,
> Such is he, the prudent angel
> Of our King Divine.

> Fragrant branch, or gallon-measure
> Filled with honey to the brim,
> Precious stone of sovereign virtue,
> Who is true to Him;
>
> But who yields Him no obedience
> Sparrow in a trap is he,
> Sinking vessel, leaking goblet,
> Withered apple-tree.

Five more verses have been recorded in Whitley Stokes's *Felire Oingusso*, comparing Moling with a crystal vessel, a victorious race-horse, a holy shrine, a communion table, a clean golden chalice.

But the Devil must have been trying to seduce Moling by flattery. He has always been a perfectionist, even when sick, which is indeed what provoked his expulsion from Heaven: since no human soul, not even a Moling, came up to his mercilessly high standards, he had demanded that Saints should be abolished altogether. This could not be: the imperfect, all-too-human, easy-going world of cap-maker, cutpurse, cobbler, cuckold and courtesan needed saints to worship, gossip about, swear by, cultivate, laugh at. So he converted only the humourless Protestants to his view; and (here I come to the point) impressed his sneer on my infant features at the very font. Forgive me therefore, St Lucia — and you St William of the Desert — and you, St John the Baptist — and you, St Thomas the Doubter — in whose honour my four children celebrate their name days with rockets and candled cakes.

> Heaven is always early morning,
> Gold sun, silver olive-trees,
> Jewelled saints innumerable
> Kneeling on their knees.
>
> No more twilight, no more starlight
> Fog, nor sleet, nor hail, nor snow...

Were I a cradle-Catholic, or a flattering Devil, I could finish these stanzas, which swam prettily into my mind as I stood outside the Repository, and dedicate them jointly to you; but alas! I am neither, and to apologize for a congenital sneer is not to wipe it off one's face. I should be embarrassed by the honeyed blessing of a true saint (though true saints have been far more numerous than the Devil allows), nor am I destined to earn one. I do not fast, except when I become so engrossed in my studies that I forget to eat; and my knees bend neither forwards nor backwards. It is an unenviable situation.

THOM GUNN

APOCRYPHAL

Now Abraham lifted the blade and as he lifted
He saw in its shining a shining stranger walk.
Isaac lay motionless, counting already as object.
So Abraham turned, and watched the stranger climb
Up the hill, an angel, not God's but Abraham's angel
(He could not know this): the angel frowned, saying 'Hold!
Man of no faith.' And his frowning shadowed the world.

Now Abraham answered, his voice an indignant prophet's,
'My faith is so great that I kill my only son —'
And he pointed to Isaac swooning upon the hilltop,
Isaac, his neck self-offered to the sun,
Isaac, his eyes closed ignorant of fearing.
'So what is this mockery levelled against my faith
More strong than thought, more solid than life itself?'

The stranger pointed, his hand lay upon the valleys:
'Observe,' he said, 'the wild unquestioning course
Of that river, which knows in its rushing not men nor angels;
My frown, your wonder, as light as bouncing stones.
What is your greatest faith concerning that river?'
On its surface were tossed huge branches, a dead goat,
Which Abraham saw with his old clear eyes, but said:

179

'Imagine that river a mighty circling whirlpool,
So faith may turn its waters upon itself:
Imagine its level lowering until only,
Hard earth and cracks its solitary bequest,
A cloud of vapour floats to the straight horizon.
My faith is greater than matter, above the world,
My faith is essence which meets God outside space.'

Isaac had opened his eyes and gazed bewildered
Upon the stranger, his father, the dropped knife.
'Come,' said the angel, 'you too look on this river.
Do you believe it can dry at the fire of faith?'
'Why,' said the boy, 'it will flow, I suppose, for ever.
For it is in the nature of rivers to flow.
It is strong as itself. What force could be more strong?'

Now the angel turned to Abraham, and turning
Softened his voice a little and smiling said:
'Do not be angry, as he is of your begetting
So I am too, and a creature of your will.
His answer is mine, the strength of our two answers
Is yours against your own.' He strode away,
While Abraham walked with Isaac down the hill.

EXCURSION

Take me down with you to that white country
Where those fair ones bear you when we part at night.
Hide me in some portmanteau, when they claim you
Coming with Primavera faces, when they draw you
Through zones of falling snow, half-recognised streets
Empty but for a cat lurking to death,
In the yellow lamplight, in the yellow recognised light.

Tell them to strap it tight for the long journey
Lest, the one rope snapped, between I fall from the sleighing
Snow queen's carriage. Remember this, remember,
That however willingly you go with them
Past the starving peasants, the ice floes,
However gladly you hear the fragile call
To the play immaculate as soon as snow

Covered the lawn and sent the deer to hiding,
However cold she turns you as her presence
Revives that old splinter and her kiss
Charms your blood dark and thick too thick to tremble;
I shall be there and (snatching you) will defeat
This country, altered yet remembered, altered
For her minion of the future, altered to cheat.

The memory which desires all well-defined
To jingle through and recognise at once.
I shall know, little Kay, the way through the sad limbo,
I shall tear you from those cold perfect embraces,
Making away I shall churn the roads filthy, defile
The pallid grandeur with the rot it covers: my hand
Shall scorch black their grand bloodless faces.

ELIZABETH BOWEN

A DAY IN THE DARK

Coming into Moher over the bridge, you may see a terrace of houses by the river. They are to the left of the bridge, below it. Their narrow height and faded air of importance make them seem to mark the approach to some larger town. The six dwellings unite into one frontage, colour-washed apricot years ago. They face north. Their lower sash windows, front steps and fanlit front doors are screened by lime trees, making for privacy. There are area railings. Between them and the water runs a road with a parapet, which comes to its end opposite the last house.

On the other side of the bridge picturesquely rises a ruined castle — more likely to catch the tourist's eye. Woods, from which the river emerges, go back deeply behind the ruin: on clear days there is a backdrop of Irish-blue mountains. Otherwise, Moher has little to show. The little place prospers — a market town with a square, on a main road. The hotel is ample, cheerful, and does business. Moreover Moher is, and has been for ages, a milling town. Obsolete stone buildings follow you some way along the river valley as, having passed through Moher, you pursue your road. The flour-white modern mills, elsewhere, hum.

Round the square, shops and pubs are of many colours — in the main Moher looks like a chalk drawing. Not so the valley with its elusive lights.

You *could*, I can see, overlook my terrace of houses —
because of the castle, indifference or haste. I only do not
because I am looking out for them. For in No. 4 lived Miss
Banderry.

She was the last of a former milling family — last, that
is, but for the widowed niece, her pensioner. She owned the
terrace, drew rents also from property in another part of the
town, and had acquired, some miles out of Moher, a profitable
farm which she'd put to management. Had control of the family
mills been hers, they would not have been parted with — as
it was, she had had to contend with a hopeless brother: he it
was who had ended by selling out. Her demand for her share
of the money left him unable to meet personal debts: he was
found hanged from one of the old mill crossbeams. Miss Ban-
derry lived in retirement, the more thought of for being
seldom seen — now and then she would summon a Ford hack-
ney and drive to her farm in it, without warning. My uncle,
whose land adjoined on hers, had dealings with her, in the
main friendly — which was how they first fell into talk. She,
a formidable reader, took to sending him serious magazines,
reviews, pamphlets and so on, with marked passages on which
she would be dying to hear his views. This was her way of
harrying him. For my uncle, a winning, versatile and when
necessary inventive talker, fundamentally hated to tax his
brain. He took to evading meetings with her as far as possible.

So much I knew when I rang her doorbell.

It was July, a sunless warm afternoon, dead still. The ter-
race was heavy with limes in flower. Above, through the
branches, appeared the bridge with idlers who leaned on the
balustrade spying down upon me, or so I thought. I felt marked
by visiting this place — I was fifteen, and my every sensation
was acute in a way I recall, yet cannot recall. All six houses
were locked in childless silence. From under the parapet came
languidly the mesmeric sound of the weir, and, from a window
over my head, the wiry hopping of a bird in a cage. From the
shabby other doors of the terrace, No. 4's stood out, handsomely
though sombrely painted red. It opened.

I came to return a copy of *Blackwoods*. Also I carried a bunch of ungainly roses from my uncle's garden, and a request that he might borrow the thistle-cutter from Miss Banderry's farm for use on his land. One rose moulted petals on to her doorstep, then on to the linoleum in the hall. « Goodness! » complained the niece, who had let me in. « Those didn't travel well. Overblown, aren't they! » (I thought that applied to her.) « And I'll bet, » she said, « *he* never sent those! » She was not in her aunt's confidence, being treated more or less like a slave. Timed (they said) when she went errands into the town — she dare not stay talking, dare not so much as look into the hotel bar while the fun was on. For a woman said to be forty, this sounded mortifying. Widowed Nan, ready to be handsome, wore a cheated ravenous look. It was understood she would come into the money when the aunt died: she must contain herself till then. As for me — how dared she speak of my uncle with her bad breath?

Naturally he *had* never thought of the roses. He had commissioned me to be gallant for him any way I chose, and I would not do too badly with these, I'd thought, as I unstrangled them from the convolvulous in the flowerbed. They would need not only to flatter but to propitiate, for this copy of *Blackwoods* I brought back had buttery thumbmarks on its margins and on its cover a blistered circle where my uncle must have stood down his glass. « She'll be mad, » he prophesied. « Better say it was you. » So I sacrificed a hair ribbon to tie the roses. It rejoiced me to stand between him and trouble.

« Auntie's resting, » the niece warned me, and put me to wait. The narrow parlour looked out through thick lace on to the terrace, which was reflected in a looking-glass at the far end. Ugly though I could see honourable furniture, mahogany, had been crowded in. In the middle, a circular table wore a chenille cloth. This room felt respected though seldom entered — however, it was peopled in one way: generations of oil-painted portraits hung round the walls, photographs overflowed from bracket and ledge even on to the centre table. I was faced, wherever I turned, by one or another member of

A DAY IN THE DARK

the family which could only be the vanished Banderrys. There
was a marble clock, but it had stopped.

Footsteps halted heavily over the ceiling, but that was
all for I don't know how long. I began to wonder what those
Banderrys saw — lodging the magazine and roses on the table,
I went to inspect myself in the glass. A tall girl in a sketchy
cotton dress. Arms thin, no sign yet of a figure. Hair forward
over the shoulders in two plaits, like, said my uncle, a Red
Indian maiden's. Barbie was my name.

In memory, the moment before often outlives the awaited
moment. I recollect waiting for Miss Banderry — then, nothing
till she was with me in the room. I got over our handshake
without feeling. On to the massiveness of her bust was pinned
a diamond-studded enameled watch, depending from an enam-
eled bow: there was a tiny glitter as she drew breath. — « So
he sent *you*, did he? » She sat down, the better to take a look
at me. Her apart knees stretched the skirt of her dress. Her
choleric colouring and eyeballs made her appear angry, as
against which she favoured me with a racy indulgent smile, to
counteract the impression she knew she gave.

« I hear wonders of you, » said she, dealing the lie to me
like a card.

She sat in reach of the table. « My bouquet, eh? » She
grasped the bundle of roses, thorns and all, and took a long
voluptuous sniff at them, as though deceiving herself as to
their origin — showing me she knew how to play the game,
if I didn't — then shoved back the roses among the photo-
graphs and turned her eyes on the magazine, sharply. « I'm
sorry, I — » I began. In vain. All she gave was a rumbling
chuckle — she held up to me the copy of *Blackwoods* open at
the page with the most thumbmarks. « I'd know *those* any-
where! » She scrutinized the print for a line or two. « Did he
make head or tail of it? »

« He told me to tell you, he enjoyed it. » (I saw my uncle
dallying, stuffing himself with the buttered toast.) « With his
best thanks. »

« You're a little echo, » she said, not discontentedly.

185

I stared her out.

« Never mind, » she said. « He's a handsome fellow. »

I shifted my feet. She gave me a look.

She observed: « It's a pity to read at table. »

« He hasn't much other time, Miss Banderry. »

« Still, it's a poor compliment to you! »

She stung me into remarking: « He doesn't often. »

« Oh, I'm sure you're a great companion for him! »

It was as though she saw me casting myself down by my uncle's chair when he'd left the room, or watching the lassitude of his hand hanging caressing a dog's ear. With him I felt the tender bond of sex. Seven, eight weeks with him under his roof, among the copper beaches from spring to summer turning from pink to purple, and I was in love with him. Such things happen, I suppose. He was my mother's brother, but I had not known him when I was a child. Of his manhood I had had no warning. Naturally growing into love I was, like the grass growing into hay on his uncut lawns. There was not a danger till she spoke.

« He's glad of company now and then, » I said as stupidly as I could.

She plucked a petal from her black serge skirt.

« Well, » she said, « thank him for the thanks. And you for the nice little pleasure of this visit. — Then, there's nothing else? »

« My uncle wants — » I began.

« You don't surprise me, » said Miss Banderry. « Well, come on out with it. What this time? »

« If he could once more borrow the thistle-cutter...? »

« 'Once more!' And what will he be looking to do next year? Get his own mended? I suppose he'd hardly go to that length. »

His own, I knew, had been sold for scrap. He was sometimes looking for ready money. I said nothing.

« Looking to me to keep him out of jail? » (Law forbids one to suffer the growth of thistles.) « Time after time, it's the same story. It so happens, I haven't mine cut yet! »

« He'd be glad to lend you his jennet back, he says, to draw the cutter for you. »

« *That* brute! There'd be nothing for me to cut if it wasn't for what blows in off his dirty land. » With the flat of her fingers she pressed one eyeball, then the other, back into her head. She confessed, all at once almost plaintively: « I don't care to have machinary leave my farm. »

« Very well, » I said haughtily, « I'll tell him. »

She leaned back, rubbed her palms on her thighs. « No, wait — this you may tell my lord. Tell him I'm not sure, but I'll think it over. There might be a favourable answer, there might not. If my lord would like to know which, let him come himself. — That's a sweet little dress of yours, » she went on, examining me inside it, « But it's skimpy. He should do better than hide behind *those* skirts!

« I don't know what you mean, Miss Banderry. »

« He'd know. »

« Today, my uncle *was* busy. »

« I'm sure he was. Busy day after day. In my life, I've known only one other man anything like so busy as your uncle. And shall I tell you who that was? My poor brother. »

After all these years, that terrace focuses dread. I mislike any terrace facing a river. I suppose I would rather look upon it itself (as I must, whenever I cross that bridge) than be reminded of it by harmless others. True, only one house in it was Miss Banderry's, but the rest belong to her by complicity. An indelible stain is on that monotony — the extinct pink frontage, the road leading to nothing but those six doors which the lime trees, flower as they may, exist for nothing but to shelter. The monotony of the weir and the hopping bird. Within that terrace I was in one room only, and only once.

My conversation with Miss Banderry did not end where I leave off recording it. But at that point memory is torn across, as might be an intolerable page. The other half is missing. For that reason my portrait of her would be incomplete

if it *were* a portrait. She could be novelist's material, I daresay
— indeed novels, particularly the French and Irish (for Ireland
in some ways resembles France) are full of prototypes of her:
oversized women insultated in little provincial towns. Liter-
ature, once one knows it, drains away some of the shockingness
out of life. But when I met her I was unread, my susceptibil-
ities were virgin. I refuse to fill in her outline retrospectively:
I show you only what I saw at the time. Not what she was,
but what she did to me.

Her amorous hostility to my uncle — or was it hostility
making use of a farce? — unsheathed itself when she likened
him to the brother she drove to death.

When I speak of dread I mean dread, not guilt. That
afternoon, I went to Miss Banderry's for my uncle's sake, in
his place. It could be said, my gathering of foreboding had
to do with my relation with him — yet in that there was no
guilt anywhere, I could swear! I swear we did each other no
harm. I think he was held that summer, as I was, by the sense
that this was a summer like no other and which could never
again be. Soon I must grow up, he must grow old. Meanwhile
we played house together on the margin of a passion which
was impossible. My longing was for him, not for an embrace
— as for him, he was glad of companionship, as I'd truly told
her. He was a man tired by a lonely house till I joined him —
a schoolgirl between schools. All thought well of his hospitality
to me. Convention was our safeguard: could one have stronger?

I left No. 4 with ceremony. I was offered raspberry cordial,
Nan bore in the tray with the thimble glasses — educated by
going visiting with my uncle, I knew refusal would mark a
breach. When the glasses were emptied, Nan conducted me
out of the presence, to the hall door — she and I stopped
aimlessly on the steps. Across the river throve the vast new
mills, unabashed, and cars swished across the tree-hidden
bridge. The niece showed a reluctance to go in again — I think
the bird above must have been hers. She glanced behind her,

then, conspiratorially at me. « So now you'll be going to the hotel? »

« No. Why? »

« 'Why?' » she jibed. « Isn't he waiting for you? Anyway, that's where he is: in there. The car's outside. »

I said: « But I'm taking the bus home. »

« Now, why ever? »

« I said I would take the bus. I came in that way. »

« You're mad. What, with his car in the square? »

All I could say was: « When? »

« I slipped out just now, » said the niece, « since you want to know. To a shop, only. While you were chatting with Auntie. » She laughed, perhaps at her life, and impatiently gave me a push away. « Get on — wherever you're going to! Anybody would think you'd had bad news! »

Not till I was almost on the bridge did I hear No. 4's door shut.

I leaned on the balustrade, at the castle side. The river, coming towards me out of the distances of woods, washed the bastions and carried a paper boat — this, travelling at uncertain speed on the current, listed as it vanished under the bridge. I had not the heart to wonder how it would fare. Weeks ago, when first I came to my uncle's, here we had lingered, elbow to elbow, looking up-river through the green-hazed spring hush at the far off swan's nest, now deserted. Next I raised my eyes to the splendid battlements, kissed by the sky where they were broken.

From the bridge to the town rises a slow hill — shops and places of business come down to meet you, converting the road into a street. There are lamp posts, signboards, yard gates pasted with layers of bills, and you tread pavement. That day the approach to Moher, even the crimson valerian on stone walls, was filmed by imponderable white dust as though the flour-bags had been shaken. To me, this was the pallor of suspense. An all but empty theatre was the square, which, when I entered it at a corner, paused between afternoon and evening. In

189

the middle were parked cars, looking forgotten — my uncle's was nearest the hotel.

The hotel, glossy with green creeper, accounted for one end of the square. A cream porch, figuring the name in gold, framed the doorway — though I kept my back to that I expected at any moment to hear a shout as I searched for the independence of my bus. But where *that* should have waited, I found nothing. Nothing, at this bus end of the square, but a drip of grease on dust and a torn ticket. « She's gone out, if that's what you're looking for, » said a bystander. So there it went, carrying passengers I was not among to the scenes of safety, and away from me every hope of solitude. Out of reach was the savingness of a house empty. Out of reach, the windows down to the ground open upon the purple beeches and lazy hay, the dear weather of those rooms in and out of which flew butterflies, my cushions on the floor, my blue striped tea mug. Out of reach, the whole of the lenient meaning of my uncle's house, which most filled it when he was not there... I did not want to be bothered with him, I think.

« She went out on time today, more's the pity. »

Down hung my hair in two weighted ropes as I turned away.

Moher square is oblong. Down its length, on the two sides, people started to come to the shop doors in order to look at me in amazement. They knew who I was and where he was: what should *I* be wanting to catch the bus for? They speculated. For, for any extraordinary action there is a reason. All watched to see what I would do next — as though a sandal chafed me I bent down, spent some time loosening the strap. Then, as though I had never had any other thought, I started in the direction of the hotel.

At the same time, my uncle appeared in the porch. He tossed a cigarette away, put the hand in a pocket and stood there under the gold lettering. He was not a lord, only a landowner. Facing Moher, he was all carriage and colouring: he wore his life like he wore his coat — though, now he was finished with the hotel, a light hint of melancholy settled down on him. He was not looking for me until he saw me. We met at his car. He asked: « How was she, the old terror? »

« I don't know. »

« She didn't eat you? »

« No, » I said, shaking my head.

« Or send me another magazine? »

« No. Not this time. »

« Thank God. »

He opened the car door and touched my elbow, reminding me to get in.

RUTH PITTER

PERSEPHONE

There in the dark thou hast bestowed thy brightness,
Watching with me in divine hope and patience.
The high gods with their shining shame my dimness,
Age takes me soon and I am bowed before them,
Formless and squalid in death's filthy garment.
But thou, who art not dim beside the brightest,
Knowest my livery, for thou hast worn it:
In thy great mystery my magic cycle
Thou dost present, and in my cycle surely
Thy mystery I prove unto thy worship,
And from bare grain into the heavenly body
Arise, as in dread books is plainly written,
And by dread voices beyond death is spoken,
And by dread spirits to the soul is proven.
When the poor needy flesh is still a moment,
When the unquiet mind forsakes her clamour,
The awful whisper sighs through the quiet temple,
The inner oracle proclaims the triumph,
And lovely in eternal spring thou risest.

Now at the very heart of winter, earth
Seems dead; now all her lively streams stand still,
The wind's breath ceases, and the ashy snow

Whispering descends, and veils the stiffened clay.
Now the starved beast, coiled in his cave asleep,
Breathes at long intervals and longer, then
Shudders but once, as sleep unites with death.
Flowers are but memory; the ragged stem
Stands lifeless, and all hope lies in the root.
Frost strike no deeper! One inch more, farewell
Promise of resurrection, and farewell
Spring, and new beauty, and the precious seed,
The fruit of all; but roots are quiet in earth,
Feel not the pang of frost, but fast asleep
Await the rising, or unknowing die;
Leave them to heaven, to slay them or to spare.
Heaven is intent upon them: yonder Zeus
Gazes on earth, and everywhere sees death,
Hueless and naked stillness: by the rock
Frozen and senseless sees the Mother lie.
May pity move the gods? pity is man's,
Compunction towards the weaker from the weak;
The immortal mind who searches? but Zeus turns,
And upon Hermes looks, and nods command.
As the sea-swallow from the dizzy cliff
Launches her lightning wing, and shears the wind
With steely gleam, forth leapt the flying god,
Shot from Olympus like a meteor, fell
Through air, through cloud, and sank below the earth
As Hesper plunges underneath the sea.

But winter will recede: O not for ever
Sleeps the sown grain there in the grave; the earth
Is warmed, and it must upward. Let her hear,
Let her discern the summons; she has lain
Long for our sake under the heavy ground.
It is full time; the trumpet calls on her.
Far in the nether dark, it seemed her soul
Uttered a solitary note, a pearl
Of sound dropped in the subterranean sea

Of silence; and incredulous, her ear
She lent, and thirsted for the voice again.
She mistook not: in silence' lap now fell
Three liquid drops, as when the lonely bird
From her umbrageous oak salutes the night,
And for her prelude the soft trinity
Of sound lets fall. Amazed the goddess hears;
Hears her own spirit in the black abyss
Striking sweet echo from the awful dark.
A long, loud warble wakens: then a quick
And throbbing note recalls her late alarms:
Now like a bugle over all the dead
The full song mounts, and in her breast awakes
Knowledge again, and nobly marches forth
Triumph with all her banners, and the voice
Of vindicated honour soars from hell.
The divine hearts reclaims its heaven; at last
Of her long travail she is satisfied,
Knows herself victress: ay, and more than all,
Glories in wisdom heaped, in knowledge stored,
The golden granary of grief and pain.
All mystery lies open; now she sees
Clear through the core of being; now she knows
How the immortal gods are justified
And life is crowned for ever. Well mayest thou sing,
That to the lees hast drunk the dreadful cup
Of death, and found the elixir of life,
Queen of our fields and pattern of our fate!

Perfect in knowledge, beyond knowledge wise,
Proud of her victory, renewed by death,
By death enlightened and initiate,
She saw and loved: and Dis held forth his hand,
Proffering, with a look that almost seemed
Humble and yearning, the pale glimmering sphere,
The fair pomegranate, from whose golden rind
Burst the clear rubies' sacrificial gems,

Brighter than the soft flower on the same bough,
Whose rosy petals from the scarlet urn
Of the young fruit arising, proclaimed love
Victor of anguish; and the solemn leaves,
Pointed and dark, great wisdom's tribute paid.
She hungered and she thirsted; forthwith took
With human gratitude, celestial grace,
The orb that made her empress of the shades,
The fruit that slaked her longing, that assuaged
Her dearest need with an eternal wine,
And from the rock of sorrow struck for her
Sweet fountains filled for ever. Heavenly tears,
The overflow of that pure Helicon,
Bathed her immortal visage, brightening it
Even till the awful beauty blazed afar
Over the shadowy empire, from whose stones
The answering diamond shone, and scaly gold;
From whose dark woods the strange unvernal blooms
Gleamed a mysterious challenge to the mind,
And lambent-eyed and silent, the white owl
Fled forth illumined, like a lovely ghost.
The night put off her terror, and assumed
Sweetness, was secretly hospitable,
The cloak of sorrow, sorrow's remedy,
Darkly maternal and forgiving night!

But ancient earth awaits thee; rise and go.
The trees, that seem like heavenly presences,
Long for thee: send up to their mighty hearts
The wine of resurrection, crowning them
Each with his proper beauty: willow pale
With wealthy yellow for the thronging bees,
And sweet though barren silver: the broad oak
With cover that invites the nightingale,
The beech with all her young pellucid leaves,
The poplar with her incense, and the dark
Cedar, that scorns the winter, with new cones

Upright emerging from his level boughs.
Fair in their several kinds and purposes,
Nourish them all; for they are reverend,
Ancient, and earlier than gods or men.
Their legend is upon them; thou canst read;
Expound, and teach us how the thought emerged
From chaos, as from furnaces the coin
Stamped cleanly with the image of the king.

The Mother bowed herself, and from the earth
Mutely adored the proven deity;
No cherished babe, given back by fate reversed,
But all life crowned, and in full cycle raised
Up to an awful splendour, fate fulfilled.
Her babe had gone down to the dreadful grave
For ever; and the presence that returned,
The same and not the same, seeming to be
Death reconciled with immortality,
Awed and perplexed the mighty soul of earth,
Whose reason is divided: light and dark,
And life and death, and good and evil are
Parted to her, and now she knew them one.
Men saw the splendour bursting from the hill;
Near as they dared, they came, and at the foot
Of the blest valley pausing, there set up
Their altar, and adoring sacrificed:
The rumour flew, and now from far and near
Came all who might, and passed before the cave
Rejoicing, and laid down their offering there.

Goddess, among thy loves number these people,
Teach them the triumph of thy returning flowers,
And triumph's sister, the dark half of wisdom,
How to depart like flowers and to be nothing,
Loss that doth purchase all, love that embraceth
Night and the grave, all that such men call sorrow.

Night shall come down, but not upon the spirit:
Winter shall fall, but not the old despair:
Death take them, as by love he is permitted,
But forth again shall breathe them. See, great goddess,
A brightness flies in air, flashes and hovers:
It is my soul, that in the iron chariot
Plunged to the grave with thee, and shared in darkness
Thy long despair and anguish; heard the summons,
Awoke with thee to love, for love of wisdom
Wept with thee; then like to the star of morning
Swam above earth, and saw the high celestial
Pomp of eternal dayspring: now in gladness
And reassured for ever, in the purple
Air of the vernal eve, lo where she sings,
Her sad-hued plume reflecting the blue zenith
And red horizon, and her accents praising
Thee, and in thee the hierarchy of heaven.

ELIZABETH JENNINGS

TERESA OF AVILA

Spain. The wild dust, the whipped corn, earth easy for foot-
steps, shallow to starving seeds. High sky at night like
walls. Silences surrounding Avila.

She, teased by questions, aching for reassurance. Calm in con-
fession before incredulous priests. Then back — to the
pure illumination, the profound personal prayer, the four
waters.

Water from the well first, drawn up painfully. Clinking of
pails. Dry lips at the well-head. Parched grass bending.
And the dry heart too-waiting for prayer.

Then the water-wheel, turning smoothly. Somebody helping
unseen. A keen hand put out, gently sliding the wheel.
Then water and the aghast spirit refreshed and quenched.

Not this only. Other waters also, clear from a spring or a
pool. Pouring from a fountain like child's play — but the
child is elsewhere. And she, kneeling, cooling her spirit
at the water, comes nearer, nearer.

Then the entire cleansing, utterly from nowhere. No mind
ruffled it, no shadows slid across it. Her mind met it, her
will approved. And all beyonds, byways, backwaters, dry

198

words of old prayers were lost in it. The water was only itself.

And she knelt there, waited for shadows to cross the light which the water made, waited for familiar childhood illuminations (the lamp by the bed, the candle in church, sun beckoned by horizons) — but this light was none of these, was only how the water looked, how the will turned and was still. Even the image of light itself withdrew, and the dry dust on the winds of Spain outside her halted. Moments spread not into hours but stood still. No dove brought the tokens of peace. She was the peace that her prayer had promised. And the silences suffered no shadows.

PAUL WEST

KAMIKAZÉS
(A Selection of their Letters)

These knew of Dostoevsky the whole truth,
Answering his dark inquiry with a rare aplomb
As if a stony-deaf man witnessed a typhoon
He long had read about, and for his first time
Understood the blast of rain, the tousled homes
And then the long black wind. All of it dead
Silently and laying siege about his ears
While he yet listened with his memory, and wept,
Upheaval by vibration merely.
                                So these,
Who with philosophy, theirs or ours, to harden vows.
Invent their vastly silent letters of farewell,
Meet spleen with modesty and make assignment's
Pallid language all dolled-up like assignation's,
With no mention of hell. Making only cautionary
Tender mentions of the family, words like gold
And the constant pointless preoccupation with blossoms,
Lotus, cherry, pear. Twenty or so years old,
Acutely analytical, they doff their academic robes
For garlands of a frightful honour, and hear
Nervelessly their stated day arrive, take shape,
Then open fully into hohojiro song of praise,
The full anthem of white-headed birds reminding
How the letters, diaries, games with girls or cards
And even how completest purity must finish now.

« *Killed at sea near Kashimayo, 9th August, 1945,*
As the pilot of a specialized attack. » *Denied even*
Specialized obliteration. Yet that small box,
In which the clippings from his nails and hair
Are free to rattle, stays the true reminder;
Stays brave scruple of the family, lost face of Emperor.

VINEDRESSER

Even in her early ripeness, he had tasted
what was of grit in her, and without wondering
overmuch, spat out the stones. Too small they seemed
to pebble him with disenchantment, or be stars
in that long season of the sun. And so,
eyes narrowed from the heat, and brown his arm,
sailed on; made fable of their love, her beauty,
flaunting him as beast. And skewed his eyes
to laugh where bathing-hood and cape of red
lay crumpled by his door, the pip-strewn beach.

Until the blood began to falter in his arms,
missing the light; and few the uncut fruit, bosomed
no longer. The shingle-chink neared them,
numerously wide, a little noise outside their world,
which he let enter. For that, in time
would boulder down his door, infest his frames.
He then let slump his whitened sail, to deck him
finally for her. From whom he sourly took rights,
and shivered in the hail she was. Till he found argument
against his grapes, and took the road.

DUMB COUPLE ON A TRAIN

Say of your heart you only finger it
In colloquy with friends:
Say of your love you only speak of it

When complete love depends
No more on touch.

All platitudes turn into fresh
Endearments in your hands:
You cleave the muted silent light
With lucid, nimble wands,
Outlining such and such

Without explaining overmuch,

And clench your heart from those who'd finger it
Unheedingly, whose baffled eyes
Yet comprehend without a finger on it,
Something touching they can seize
Without upsetting overmuch

The sculping gesture of your colloquies.
They watch your hands, and dare not speak:
Hands, having accent, grammar, tease
Their hearts which, being meek,
Words can break with candid speech

And, without touching, touch too deep.

There are so few hands of such gentility
Which, in experience we see, or beyond
Illusion hold eloquent agility
Like these: hands of Mary burdened
Beyond human touch

For lovely and fatal occasions:
Manus Mariae, with transient aplomb,
Encompassing the child without the lesions
Romans made; then made to speak inside the tomb
Of nothing overmuch

Or deep, in human reach.

For interruption lacked a meaning there as here
Where what is purely silent goes untouched,
And being rich, deludes the interloper
Into hate of simple hearing which
Reveres no power of speech

And robs the uttered language of its proper
Diapason, relegating human speech
To something merely touching, within reach.

CAVE DRAWINGS

Dark statement ravenous for light,
Your primal hunger is of boar and bull,
Prodigious in arrested flight
From one dark age to darker still.

A temporary flare is all we portion
You of living light, though human blood
Re-fuels your primeval motion,
Witnessed unawares but understood.

And, peering, we decide that home
Is where the heart remembers having been
Its oldest version, while the tomb
Is a beginner's place, to wean

Mankind from long irrelevance,
And prove our bones inferiors of art,
Insipid tale which cannot sense
The spell these animals impart.

Black and dateless bridling flanks
Enlighten while the matches last:
We stay alive and ought to proffer thanks
For centuries our hooves by-passed:

For now another day corrodes another bomb;
Insensate fingers drum each crisis to a lull:
Dark statements lack their old aplomb,
Their calm inclusion of the beautiful,

And all our paths are shelterwards again.
A sudden light, as vast as flying bull or boar,
Assigns us to the cave again, where vain
Man's images deride his core.

PATRICK CREAGH

A FAMOUS MAN

to Sean O'Criadain

This is the house. Here he came to live
In his fortieth year. Already he had left behind
The shallows of his youth and coastal waters,
Cutting an icy path while those, wheeling, that followed,
Gathered rich fare from the mere galleys of his mind.
Here by his hearth they flocked to peck their quites
Or from under the broad lee of his benevolence
Board him with questions. Or watch the night out
Hoping to force a beach-head in his thought.
*   Even amongst his peers,*
Those few who like him were headlands rocked
With the roar and buffet of praise, he was familiar
Only on clearest days and afternoons of calm.
Then from the bay, from their warm beach and peace,
Others would scan his heights and aim to read
The legend of his rocks unrolled against the sea.

Here is the study — everything, you will notice,
Just as he left it. Where the rug is worn
He would tread every day his mill of indecision.
Unwelcome delegations from his past
Pestered him here, and he was seldom out
To a fatuous student adrift on a barge of words,
A lover too anxious for the heart's rebate,

205

Too ambitious to love, or a husband struck
In his vanity's heel by a reproach at random.
Here also he took all his scraps of shame,
Eyed them against the light, tried them with reasons,
And wrenched them into the true gestures of his time.

Upstairs, overlooking the garden... here is the bedroom
Where, as you know, in the last days of April,
After a long illness, patiently borne...
« I have always been afraid, » he used to say,
« Of dying counter to nature, being quenched
Just as, elsewhere,
The heart starts the hare of the new year. »
As it was he died like an abandoned hearth
Peacefully diminishing into ashes.

Nevertheless, he would keep on asking the time,
And what other people were doing about the house,
Probing the darkness with his thin, unsatisfied
    Blade of a voice.

SILENCES

I

In the room
Silence of hands at rest,
Of unopened books in wise repose
Binding on a spine of quiet
Hands dumbly waiting to resume,
Eyes that search the fire for another time.

Outside in
The November dusk, silence of old roofs,
Wise brows of ancient houses frowning under them,

Considering love as seen in the fumbling memory
And in the eyes' decline
And senses closed in the silence of the rain.

On the sill
Or above, imminent on the eaves
And clearer than any gazer's crystal eye,
The end and all of hope inferred
In the silence of a gathered
Water drop fattened to its fall.

II

Early, the first
Soft pace of morning the path
Barely prints the dust;
She enters diffidently dressed
As an old photograph.

Be subtle with her, time!
Be slow with her, alarm!

Patient with the thought that,
Awakened early, does not yet
Mould to the mind's frame, and cling;
And with love first entering
Uneasy, the imagined room,
Lest she depart the way she came.

Lest morning on the city's stones
Barefoot, bruise her ingenuous flesh,
Or the sun's lash
Lay bare her buttermilk-sweet bones.

III

Time is a fragment of
That fractured cadence of their peace
For lovers at the station, or by the dock:
Silence around them endless till
The next tick of the clock.

Later he will shed her leaf by leaf
In his America, and she'll
Shift under many passing feet, lie still
Only in damp hollows of regret
And helpless drifts.

But innocent of this,
Closed in their cuckoon of grief,
Numbly they press into that little space
Their hope of gentle ending.

IV

Time holds the pair
In brittle hands, the sisters
Indifferently with vacant stare
Receiving the clock flushed with its pressing message,
The fire with its faithful obstinacy of embers,
The door to the dark and narrow passage.

Crowded round them, eighty breakable years
Balance, as it were, on frail
Tables that would tilt and spill
Were an indiscreeter foot to fall.

Daylight over, firelight on the wane,
The mutter of knitting for a while is all
The talk tapped out between the two of them.
Then, even that laid down, they lean
Back amid the years that fill the room,
Fingering the silence like a wine-glass stem.

EPITHALAMIUM

Another mask laid by, perhaps the last;
Or changed at least, as it were from a man walking
Through an unfriendly town, blankly opposing
To its cold rectangular stone stare
His plastered wall, meticulous and frail,
Becoming a man at large in his own fields,
His feet bruising the grass, his eyeballs bruised
By a wind the supple grass lies down and laughs at;
Moving with men and sentient things, and brushed
By them in passing; seeing for the first time
Serenity in the sky, and not indifference.

But another secrecy foregone, another
Soliloquy muted, simplified at least
Into attempted speech, leaves him uncertain
What to lament and what to celebrate:
There was a certain calm on his savage island
Where, from time to time, others had come
With cheap and garish wares, trading beads.
None tried to settle there, or learn his language,
Or tried to plant, or toiled to make love wise.
But your sail the next morning still lay furled
In the crook of the bay: you came to colonize.

It was hard for him in the peopled days that followed,
Feeling your ploughshare scourge and turn his barren
Selfish hills to trellised terraces.
He was brute and ugly. Swathed in timid sleep
Vaguely his heart lay, but your pungent love
Pricked sense as when parched streets reek with rain,
Or, sleeping under the sky, as the head bursts
And senses scatter like seeds at the merest touch
Of an enquiring sun, or as the river
Cramped in ice all winter, budges at last
And moves into the containing bulk of summer.

It was nothing less than exile you ended,
An exile hard as glass, and he was held,

209

And might have been for ever, fugitive.
Enfranchised now, he cocks an eye at the sun,
Predicts inclement weather, gives not a damn,
Walks his own fields, leaves his own gates open,
Lets the cattle stray: a man residing in
Your love as his ancestral, his last home.
(Or perhaps his last but one, seeing we tread
Our aisle of days over the beckoning stone
That presses close on the faces of our dead).

PAUL VALÉRY

I.

Guidé par l'image que je veux que tu aies de moi;
Ou me voulant consoler, quand je rentrerai dans mon seul,
Par l'idée de t'avoir vaincu,
Devancé dans toi-même, prévu dans tes replis,
Opposé une part de ma force à la tienne toute,
Ton extrême puissance...

II.

O mes étranges personnages, — pourquoi ne seriez-vous pas
une poésie?
Toi, Présent... et vous Formes, et vous significations, Fonctions
et Phases et Trames.
Toi, acuité de la netteté et point; et toi l'informe, le latéral.
Cette espèce de re-création, que ne chanterait-elle pas?

211

Mais que d'exercices avant de se rompre à sa propre pensée!

Penser librement cette pensée, ces éclairs, ces moments séparés

— les penser en nature même.

Et après la recherche des éléments purs, les épouser, les être,

les faire enfin vivre et revivre...

ou:

Les faire enfin vivre et revivre...

en ligne finale.

ALBERT CAMUS

UN HOMME DE LETTRES

Vingt-sept années de prison ne font pas une intelligence conciliante. Une si longue claustration peut engendrer des valets ou des tueurs, et parfois, dans un même homme, les deux. Si l'âme est assez forte pour édifier, au coeur du bagne, une morale qui ne soit pas celle de la soumission, il s'agira la plupart du temps d'une morale de domination. Toute éthique de la solitude divinise la puissance. A ce titre, dans la mesure où, traité de façon atroce par la société, il y répondit d'atroce façon, Sade est exemplaire. L'écrivain, malgré quelques cris heureux et les louanges inconsidérées de nos contemporains, reste secondaire. Mais il est admiré aujourd'hui, avec tant d'ingénuité, pour des raisons où la littérature n'a rien à voir. Précisément, ces raisons nous intéressent.

On exalte en lui le philosophe aux fers, et le premier théoricien de la révolte absolue. Il pouvait l'être, en effet. Au fond des prisons, le rêve est sans limites, la réalité ne freine rien. L'intelligence dans les chaînes perd en lucidité ce qu'elle gagne en fureur. Sade n'a connu qu'une logique, celle des sentiments. Il n'a pas fondé une philosophie, mais poursuivi le rêve monstrueux d'un persécuté. Il se trouve seulement que ce rêve est prophétique. La revendication exaspérée de la liberté a mené Sade dans l'empire de la servitude. Sa soif démesurée d'une vie désormais interdite s'est assouvie, de fureur en fureur, en rêve de destruction universelle. Par ses contradictions au moins, Sade est notre contemporain. Suivons le dans ses négations sucessives.

Sade est-il athée? Il le dit, on le croit, avant la prison, dans le *Dialogue du prêtre et du moribond*; on hésite ensuite devant sa fureur de sacrilège. L'un de ses plus cruels personnages, Saint Fond, ne nie nullement Dieu. Il se borne à développer une théorie gnostique du méchant démiurge et à en tirer les conséquences qui conviennent. Saint Fond, dit-on, n'est pas Sade. Non, sans doute. Un personnage n'est jamais le romancier qui l'a créé. Il y a des chances, cependant, pour que le romancier soit tous ses personnages à la fois. Or, tous les athées de Sade supposent l'inexistence de Dieu pour cette raison claire que son existence supposerait chez lui indifférence, méchanceté ou cruauté. La plus grande oeuvre de Sade se termine sur une démonstration de la stupidité et de la haine divines. L'innocente Justine court sous l'orage et le criminel Noirceuil jure qu'il se convertira si elle est épargnée par la foudre céleste. La foudre poignarde Justine, Noirceuil triomphe, et le crime de l'homme continuera de répondre au crime divin. Il y a ainsi un pari libertin qui est à l'inverse du pari pascalien.

L'idée, au moins, que Sade se fait de Dieu est donc celle d'une divinité criminelle qui écrase l'homme et le nie. Que le meurtre soit un attribut divin se voit assez, selon lui, dans l'histoire des religions. Pourquoi l'homme serait-il alors vertueux? Le premier mouvement du prisonnier est de sauter dans la conséquence extrême. Si Dieu tue et nie l'homme, rien ne peut interdire qu'on nie et tue ses semblables. Ce défi crispé ne ressemble en rien à la négation tranquille qu'on trouve encore dans le dialogue de 1782. Il n'est ni tranquille, ni heureux, celui qui s'écrie: « Rien n'est à moi, rien n'est de moi », et qui conclut « Non, non, et la vertu et le vice, tout se confond dans le cercueil ». L'idée de Dieu est selon lui la seule chose « qu'il ne puisse pardonner à l'homme ». Le mot pardonner est déjà singulier chez ce professeur de tortures. Mais c'est à lui-même qu'il ne peut pardonner une idée que sa vue désespérée du monde, et sa condition de prisonnier, réfutent absolument. Une double révolte va désormais conduire le raisonnement de Sade: contre l'ordre du monde et contre lui-même. Comme ces deux révoltes sont contradictoires partout ailleurs que dans le coeur bouleversé d'un persécuté, son raisonnement ne cesse jamais d'être ambigu ou légitime, selon qu'on l'étudie dans la lumière de la logique ou dans celle de la compassion humaine.

Il niera donc l'homme et sa morale puisque Dieu les nie. Mais il niera Dieu en même temps qui lui servait de caution et de complice jusqu'ici. Au nom de quoi? Au nom de l'instinct le plus fort chez celui que la haine des hommes fait vivre entre les murs d'une prison: l'instinct sexuel. Qu'est cet instinct? D'une part, le cri même de la nature *, et d'autre part, l'élan aveugle qui exige la possession totale des êtres, au prix même de leur destruction. Sade niera Dieu au nom de la nature — et le matériel idéologique de son temps le fournit en discours mécanistes — et il fera de la nature une puissance de destruction. La nature, pour lui, c'est le sexe; sa logique le conduit dans un univers sans loi dont le seul maître sera l'énergie démesurée du désir. Là est son royaume enfiévré, où il trouve ses plus beaux cris: « Que sont toutes les créatures de la terre vis à vis d'un seul de nos désirs! » Le XVIIIème siècle se marque dans ce « nous » et le romantisme, plus fidèle à Sade que Sade lui-même, ne changera rien à son cri sinon la personne de ce pronom. Les longs raisonnements où les héros de Sade démontrent que la nature a besoin du crime, qu'il lui faut détruire pour créer, qu'on l'aide donc à créer dès l'instant où l'on détruit soi-même, ne visent qu'à fonder la liberté absolue du prisonnier Sade, trop injustement comprimé pour ne pas désirer l'explosion qui fera tout sauter. En cela, il s'oppose à son temps: la liberté qu'il réclame n'est pas celle des principes, mais des instincts.

Sade a rêvé sans doute d'une république universelle, dont il nous fait exposer le plan par un sage réformateur, Zalmé.

---

* Les grands criminels de Sade s'excusent de leurs crimes sur ce qu'ils sont pourvus d'appétits sexuels démesurés, contre lesquels ils ne peuvent rien.

Mais tout en lui contredit ce rêve pieux. Il n'est pas l'ami du genre humain, il hait les philantropes. L'égalité dont il parle parfois est une notion mathématique: l'équivalence des objets que sont les hommes, la terrible égalité des victimes. Celui qui pousse son désir jusqu'au bout, il lui faut tout dominer, son véritable accomplissement est dans la haine. La république de Sade ne choisit pas la liberté pour principe, mais le libertinage. « La Justice, — écrit ce singulier démocrate — n'a pas d'existence réelle. Elle est la divinité de toutes les passions ».

Rien de plus révélateur, à cet égard, que le fameux libelle, lu par Dolmancé dans la *Philosophie du Boudoir*, et qui porte un titre curieux: *Français, encore un effort pour être républicains.* Pierre Klossowski * a raison de le souligner, il s'agit dans ce libelle de démontrer aux révolutionnaires que leur république repose sur le meurtre du monarque de droit divin, et qu'en guillotinant Dieu et le roi, ils se sont interdit à jamais la proscription du crime et la censure des instincts malfaisants. La Monarchie, en même temps qu'un principe temporel, maintenait l'idée de Dieu qui fondait les lois. La République, elle, se tient debout toute seule et les moeurs doivent y être sans commandements. Il est pourtant douteux que Sade, comme le veut Klossowski, ait eu le sentiment profond d'un sacrilège et que cette horreur quasi religieuse l'ait conduit aux conséquences qu'il énonce. Bien plutôt tenait-il ses conséquences d'abord, et a-t-il aperçu ensuite l'argument propre à justifier la licence absolue des moeurs, qu'il voulait demander au gouvernement de son temps. La logique des passions renverse l'ordre traditionnel du raisonnement et place la conclusion avant les prémisses. Il suffit pour s'en convaincre d'apprécier l'admirable succession de sophismes par lesquels Sade, dans ce texte, justifie la calomnie, le vol et le meurtre, et demande qu'ils soient tolérés dans la cité nouvelle.

Pourtant, c'est alors que sa pensée est la plus profonde.

---

* *Sade, mon prochain.*

Il refuse, avec une clairvoyance exceptionnelle en son temps, l'alliance présomptueuse de la liberté et de la vertu. La liberté, surtout quand elle est le rêve du prisonnier, ne peut supporter de limites. Elle est le crime ou elle n'est plus la liberté. L'innocence ne peut se révolter sans cesser d'être l'innocence. Sur ce point essentiel, Sade n'à jamais varié. Cet homme qui n'a prêché que des contradictions ne retrouve une cohérence, et la plus absolue, qu'en ce qui concerne la peine capitale. Amateur d'exécutions raffinées, théoricien du crime sexuel, il n'a jamais pu supporter le crime légal. « Ma détention nationale, la guillotine sous les yeux, m'a fait cent fois plus de mal que ne m'en avaient fait toutes les Bastilles imaginables ». Dans cette horreur, il a puisé le courage d'être publiquement modéré pendant la Terreur et d'intervenir généreusement en faveur d'une belle-mère qui l'avait pourtant fait embastiller. Quelques années plus tard, Nodier devait résumer clairement, sans le savoir peut-être, la position obstinément défendue par Sade: « Tuer un homme dans le paroxysme d'une passion, cela se comprend. Le faire tuer par un autre, dans le calme d'une méditation sérieuse, et sous le prétexte d'un ministère honorable, cela ne se comprend pas ». On trouve ici l'amorce d'une idée qui sera développée encore par Sade: celui qui tue doit payer de sa personne. Sade, on le voit, est plus moral que nos contemporains.

Mais sa haine pour la peine de mort n'est d'abord que la haine d'hommes qui croient assez à leurs vertus, ou à celle de leur cause, pour oser punir alors même qu'ils sont criminels. On ne peut à la fois choisir le crime pour soi et le châtiment pour les autres. Il faut ouvrir les prisons ou faire la preuve, impossible, de sa vertu. A partir du moment où l'on accepte le meurtre, serait-ce une seule fois, il faut l'admettre universellement. Le criminel, qui agit selon la nature, ne peut, sans forfaiture, se mettre du côté de la loi. « Encore un effort pour être républicains » veut dire: « acceptez la liberté du crime, seule raisonnable, et entrez pour toujours en insurrection comme on entre dans la grâce ». La soumission totale au Mal débouche alors dans une horrible ascèse

217

qui devait épouvanter la république des lumières et de la
bonté naturelle. Celle-ci, dont la première émeute, par une
coincidence significative, avait brûlé le manuscrit des *Cent-
vingt journées de Sodome* ne pouvait manquer de dénoncer
cette liberté hérétique et de jeter à nouveau entre quatre murs
un partisan si compromettant. Elle lui donnait, du même
coup, l'affreuse occasion de pousser plus loin sa logique ré-
voltée.

La république universelle a pu être un rêve pour Sade,
jamais une tentation. En politique, sa vraie position est le
cynisme. Dans sa *Société des Amis du crime*, on se déclare
ostensiblement pour le gouvernement et ses lois, qu'on se dis-
pose pourtant à violer. Ainsi, les souteneurs votent pour
le député conservateur. Le projet que Sade médite suppose
pose la neutralité bienveillante de l'autorité. La républi-
que du crime ne peut être, provisoirement du moins, uni-
verselle. Elle doit faire mine d'obéir à la loi. Dans un monde
sans autre règle que celle du meurtre, sous le ciel du crime,
sur la terre du crime, au nom d'une criminelle nature, Sade
n'obéit plus, en realité, qu'à la loi inlassable du désir. Mais
désirer sans limites revient aussi à accepter d'être désiré sans
limites. La licence de détruire suppose qu'on puisse être soi-
même détruit. Il faudra donc lutter et dominer. La loi de
ce monde n'est rien d'autre que celle de la force; son moteur,
la volonté de puissance.

L'ami du crime respectera deux sortes de puissances, celle,
fondée sur le hasard de la naissance, qu'il trouve dans sa so-
ciété, et celle où se hisse l'opprimé, quand, à force de scélé-
ratesse, il parvient à égaler les grands seigneurs libertins dont
Sade fait ses héros ordinaires. Ce petit groupe de puissants,
ces initiés, savent qu'ils ont tous les droits. Qui doute, même
une seconde, de ce terrible privilège est aussitôt rejeté du trou-
peau, c'est à dire redevient victime. Il y a là une sorte de
« blanquisme » moral où un petit groupe d'hommes et de
femmes, parce qu'ils détiennent un étrange savoir, se placent
résolument au dessus d'une caste d'esclaves. Le seul problème,

pour eux, consiste à s'organiser pour exercer, dans leur plénitude, des droits qui ont l'étendue terrifiante du désir.

Ils ne peuvent espérer s'imposer à tout l'univers tant que l'univers n'aura pas accepté la loi du crime. Sade n'a même jamais cru que sa nation consentirait l'effort supplémentaire qui la ferait vraiment « républicaine ». Mais si le crime et le désir ne sont pas la loi de tout l'univers, s'ils ne règnent pas au moins sur un territoire défini, ils ne sont plus principe d'unité, mais ferments de conflits. Ils ne sont plus la loi et l'homme est livré à la dispersion et au hasard. Il faut donc créer de toutes pièces un monde qui soit à la mesure exacte de la nouvelle loi. L'exigence d'unité, déçue par la Création, se satisfait à toute force dans un microcosme. La loi de la puissance n'a jamais la patience d'attendre l'empire du monde. Il lui faut délimiter sans tarder le terrain où elle s'exerce et donner leur fonction métaphysique aux barbelés et aux miradors. C'est ainsi que la révolte est créatrice.

Chez Sade, elle crée des lieux clos, des châteaux à septuple enceinte, dont il est impossible de s'évader, où la société du désir et du crime fonctionne sans heurts, selon un règlement implacable. La révolte la plus débridée, la revendication totale de la liberté aboutit à l'asservissement. L'émancipation de l'homme s'achève pour Sade dans ces casemates de la débauche où une sorte de bureau politique du vice règle la vie et la mort d'hommes et de femmes entrés à tout jamais dans l'enfer de la nécessité. Son oeuvre abonde en descriptions de ces lieux privilégiés où, chaque fois, les libertins féodaux, démontrant aux victimes assemblées leur impuissance et leur servitude absolues, reprennent ce discours du duc de Blangis au petit peuple des *Cent-vingt journées de Sodome*: « Vous êtes déjà mortes au monde ».

Sade habitait de même la Tour de la Liberté, mais dans la Bastille. La révolte absolue s'enfouit avec lui dans une forteresse affreuse d'où personne, persécutés ni persécuteurs, ne peut sortir. Pour fonder sa liberté, il est obligé d'organiser la nécessité absolue. La liberté illimitée du désir est la négation de l'autre, et la suppression de la pitié. Il faut tuer le coeur, cette « faiblesse de l'esprit » ; le lieu clos et le règlement y pourvoiront. Le règlement, qui joue un rôle capital dans les châteaux fabuleux de Sade, consacre un univers de méfiance. Il aide à tout prévoir afin qu'une tendresse ou une pitié imprévue ne vienne déranger les plans du bon plaisir. Curieux plaisir, sans doute, qui s'exerce au commandement : « On se lèvera tous les jours à 10 heures du matin... » ! Mais il faut empêcher que la jouissance dégénère en attachement, il faut la mettre entre parenthèses et la durcir. Il faut encore que les objets de jouissance n'apparaissent jamais comme des personnes. Si l'homme est « une espèce de plante absolument matérielle », il ne peut être traité qu'en objet, et en objet d'expérience. Dans la république barbelée de Sade, il n'y a que des mécaniques et des mécaniciens. Le règlement, mode d'emploi de la machine, donne sa place à tout. Ces couvents infâmes ont leur règle, significativement copiée, parfois, sur celle des communautés religieuses. Le libertin se livrera ainsi à la confession publique. Mais l'indice change : « Si sa conduite est pure, il est blâmé ».

On voit que Sade, comme il est d'usage en son temps, bâtit aussi des sociétés idéales. Mais, à l'inverse de son temps, il codifie la méchanceté naturelle de l'homme. Il construit méticuleusement la cité de la puissance et de la haine, jusqu'à mettre en chiffres la liberté qu'il a conquise. Il résume alors sa philosophie dans la froide comptabilité du crime « Massacrés avant le Ier Mars : 10. Depuis le Ier Mars : 20. S'en retournent : 16. Total : 46 ». Précurseur sans doute, mais encore modeste, on le voit.

L'ogre Mirski, portrait idéal de l'homme libre et naturel, vit ainsi sur une île, cloîtré, selon le règlement, dans un château verrouillé. C'est ainsi qu'il faut être pour vivre librement et selon la nature. Si tout s'arrêtait là, Sade ne mériterait que l'intérêt qui s'attache aux précurseurs méconnus. Mais levé le pont-levis, il faut encore vivre dans le château. Aussi méticuleux que soit le règlement, il ne parvient à tout prévoir. Il peut détruire, non créer. Les maîtres de ces communautés torturées n'y trouveront pas la satisfaction qu'ils convoitent. Sade évoque souvent la « douce habitude du crime ». Rien ici qui ressemble, pourtant, à la douceur; mais plutôt une rage d'homme dans les fers. Il s'agit en effet de jouir. Et le maximum de jouissance coïncide avec le maximum de destruction. Posséder ce qu'on tue, s'accoupler avec la souffrance, voilà l'instant de la liberté totale vers lequel s'oriente toute l'organisation des châteaux. Mais dès l'instant où le crime sexuel supprime l'objet de volupté, il supprime la volupté, qui n'existe qu'au moment précis de la suppression. Il faut alors se soumettre un autre objet et le tuer à nouveau, un autre encore, et après lui l'infinité de tous les objets possibles. On obtient ainsi ces mornes accumulations de scènes érotiques et criminelles dont l'aspect figé, dans les romans de Sade, laisse paradoxalement au lecteur le souvenir d'une sorte de hideuse chasteté.

Que viendrait faire, dans cet univers, la jouissance, la grande joie fleurie des corps consentants et complices? Il s'agit d'une quête impossible pour échapper au désespoir et qui finit pourtant en désespoir, d'une course de la servitude à la servitude, et de la prison à la prison. Si la nature seule est vraie, si dans la nature, seuls le désir et la destruction sont vrais, alors, de destruction en destruction, le règne humain lui-même ne suffisant plus à la soif du sang, il faut courir à l'anéantissement universel. Il faut se faire, selon la formule de Sade, le bourreau de la nature. Mais cela même ne s'obtient pas si facilement. Quand la comptabilité est close, quand toutes les victimes ont été massacrées, les bourreaux restent face à face, dans le château solitaire. Quelque chose leur manque encore. Les corps torturés retournent, par leurs éléments, à la nature d'où renaîtra la vie. Le meurtre lui-même n'est pas achevé: « Le meurtre n'ôte que la première vie à l'individu que nous frappons; il faudrait pouvoir lui arracher la seconde... ». Sade médite l'attentat contre la création. « J'abhorre la nature... Je voudrais déranger ses plans, contrecarrer sa marche, arrêter la roue des astres, bouleverser les globes qui flottent dans l'espace, détruire ce qui la sert, protéger ce qui lui nuit, l'insulter en un mot dans ses oeuvres, et je n'y puis réussir ». Il a beau imaginer un mécanicien qui puisse pulvériser l'univers, il sait que, dans la poussière des globes, la vie continuera. L'attentat contre la création est impossible. On ne peut tout détruire, il y a toujours un reste. « Je n'y puis réussir... », cet univers implacable et glacé se détend soudain dans l'atroce mélancolie par laquelle, finalement, Sade nous touche quand il ne le voudrait pas. « Lorsque le crime de l'amour n'est plus à la mesure de notre intensité, nous pourrions peut-être attaquer le soleil, en priver l'univers ou nous en servir pour embraser le monde, ce serait des crimes, cela... ». Oui, ce serait des crimes, mais non le crime définitif. Il faut marcher encore; les bourreaux se mesurent du regard.

Ils sont seuls, et une seule loi les régit, la puissance. Puisqu'ils l'ont acceptée alors qu'ils étaient les maîtres, ils ne peuvent plus la récuser si elle se retourne contre eux. Toute puissance tend à être unique et solitaire, il faut encore tuer. A leur tour, les maîtres se déchireront. Sade aperçoit cette conséquence et ne recule pas. Un curieux stoicisme du vice vient éclairer un peu ces bas-fonds de la révolte. Il ne recherchera pas à rejoindre le monde de la tendresse et du compromis. Le pont-levis ne sera pas baissé, il acceptera l'anéantissement personnel. La force déchaînée du refus rejoint à son extrémité une acceptation inconditionnelle qui n'est pas sans grandeur. Le maître accepte à son tour d'être esclave, et peut-être le désire. « L'échafaud aussi serait pour moi le trône des voluptés ».

La plus grande destruction coincide alors avec la plus grande affirmation. Les maîtres se jettent les uns sur les autres et cette oeuvre érigée à la gloire du libertinage se trouve « parsemée de cadavres de libertins frappés au sommet de leur génie » *. Le plus puissant, qui survivra, sera le solitaire, l'*Unique*, dont Sade a entrepris la glorification, lui-même

---

* Maurice Blanchot, *Lautréamont et Sade*.

en définitive. Le voilà qui règne enfin, maître et dieu. Mais à l'instant de sa plus haute victoire, le rêve se dissipe. L'Unique se retourne vers le prisonnier dont les imaginations démesurées lui ont donné naissance; il se confond avec lui. Il est seul en effet, emprisonné dans une Bastille ensanglantée, toute entière bâtie autour d'une jouissance encore inapaisée, mais désormais sans objet. Il n'a triomphé qu'en rêve et ces dizaines de volumes, bourrés d'atrocités et de philosophie, résument une ascèse malheureuse, une tentative purement spirituelle de tuer l'âme, une marche hallucinante du non total au oui absolu, un consentement à la mort enfin, qui transfigure le meurtre de tout et de tous en suicide collectif.

On a exécuté Sade en effigie; il n'a tué de même qu'en imagination. Prométhée finit dans Onan. Il achèvera sa vie, toujours prisonnier, mais cette fois dans un asile, jouant des pièces sur une estrade de fortune, au milieu d'hallucinés. La satisfaction que l'ordre du monde ne lui donnait pas, le rêve et la création lui en ont fourni un équivalent dérisoire. L'écrivain n'a rien à se refuser. Pour lui, du moins, les limites s'écroulent et le désir peut aller jusqu'au bout. En ceci, Sade est l'homme de lettres parfait. Il a mis au dessus de tout « le crime moral auquel on parvient par écrit ». Son mérite, incontestable, est d'avoir illustré du premier coup, dans la clairvoyance malheureuse d'une rage accumulée, les conséquences extrêmes de sa révolte: la totalité close, le crime universel, l'aristocratie du cynisme et la volonté d'apocalypse. Ces conquêtes se retrouveront bien des années après lui. Mais les ayant réellement convoitées, il semble qu'il ait étouffé dans ses propres impasses, et qu'il se soit seulement délivré dans la littérature. Curieusement, c'est Sade qui a orienté la révolte sur les chemins de l'art où le romantisme l'engagera encore plus avant. Il sera de ces écrivains dont il dit que « la corruption est si dangereuse, si active, qu'ils n'ont pour but en imprimant leur affreux système que d'étendre au delà de leurs vies la somme de leurs crimes; ils n'en peuvent plus faire, mais leurs maudits écrits en feront commettre et cette douce idée qu'ils emportent au tombeau les console de l'obligation, où les met la mort, de renoncer à ce qui est ». Son œuvre révoltée témoigne ainsi de sa soif de survie. Même si l'immortalité qu'il convoite est celle de Caïn, il la convoite au moins, et témoigne malgré lui pour le plus pur de la révolte métaphysique.

Au reste, sa postérité même oblige à lui rendre hommage. Ses héritiers ne sont pas tous écrivains. Assurément, il a souffert et il est mort pour échauffer l'imagination des beaux quartiers et des cafés littéraires. Mais ce n'est pas tout. Le succès de Sade à notre époque ne s'explique pas autrement que par un rêve qui lui est commun avec la sensibilité contemporaine: la revendication de la liberté totale et la déshumanisation opérée à froid par l'intelligence. La réduction de l'homme à l'objet d'expérience, le règlement qui opère cette réduction et précise les rapports de la volonté de puissance et de l'homme objet, le champ clos de cette monstrueuse expérience, sont des leçons que les théoriciens de la puissance retrouveront, lorsqu'ils auront à organiser le temps des esclaves.

Deux siècles à l'avance, et sur une échelle réduite, Sade a exalté les sociétés totalitaires au nom de la liberté totale. Avec lui commencent réellement l'histoire et la tragédie contemporaines. Il a seulement cru qu'une société basée sur la liberté du crime devait aller avec la liberté des mœurs, comme si la servitude avait ses limites. Notre temps s'est borné à fondre curieusement son rêve de république universelle et sa technique d'avilissement. Finalement, ce qu'il haïssait le plus, le meurtre légal, a pris à son compte les découvertes qu'il voulait mettre au service du meurtre d'instinct. Le crime dont il voulait qu'il fût le fruit exceptionnel et délicieux du vice déchaîné, n'est plus aujourd'hui que la morne habitude d'une vertu devenue policière. Ce sont les surprises de la littérature.

PIERRE REVERDY

BONNE CHANCE

Avec du sang dans les rigoles
Et tant de soleil sous la peau
Tant de promesse au creux des ombres
Et de ciel entre les barreaux
Avec du plomb dans la prunelle
Et des rires dans les ruisseaux
Dans l'éther où grouillent les nombres
Le vent rageur dans les roseaux
La lumière sur les décombres
Et la nuit aux cils des rideaux
Un malheur que rien ne console
La douleur et ses oripeaux
Dans la poitrine nue d'un homme
Le splendide décor
Où le coeur joue son rôle faux
Quand la peur décharge ses ondes
Jusqu'à l'écume des naseaux

Cratères de l'oubli
Sève des étincelles
Tous ces volcans furieux
Qui se sont assoupis

La mémoire a perdu son pas de manivelle
Un nom qui n'a pas plus de chair qu'un numéro

Une voix sans timbre qui chante
Dans le vide où fondent les mots
La neige ne peut plus ni monter ni descendre
Parce qu'il n'y a plus ni de bas ni de haut

Et dans cet avenir lourd comme un soir sans lampes
    Aucun signe main
    Pas un froissement d'aile
    Rien
        Pas même un écho

ANTONIN ARTAUD

(1895 - † 1948)

L'ÉPERON MALICIEUX, LE DOUBLE-CHEVAL

(Autre *Enclume des Forces*)

Je me fais peut-être de la mort une idée excessivement fausse.

J'affirme — et je m'accroche à cette idée que la mort n'est pas hors du domaine de l'esprit, qu'elle est dans de certaines limites connaissable et approchable par une certaine sensibilité mentale. Tout ce qui dans l'ordre des choses écrites abandonne le domaine de la perception ordonnée et claire, tout ce qui vise à créer un renversement des apparences, à introduire un doute sur la position des images de l'esprit les unes par rapport aux autres, tout ce qui provoque la confusion sans détruire la force de la pensée jaillissante, tout ce qui renverse les rapports des choses en donnant à la pensée ainsi bouleversée un aspect encore plus grand de vérité et de violence, tout cela offre une issue à la mort, nous met en rapports avec des états plus affinés de l'esprit au sein desquels la mort s'exprime.

C'est pourquoi tous ceux qui rêvent sans regretter leurs rêves, sans emporter de ces plongées dans une inconscience féconde un sentiment d'atroce nostalgie sont des porcs. Le rêve est vrai. Tous les rêves sont vrais. J'ai le sentiment d'aspérités, de paysages comme sculptés, de morceaux de terre ondoyants recouverts d'une sorte de sable frais dont le sens veut dire: « regret, déception, abandon, rupture, quand nous reverrons-nous? » Rien qui ressemble à l'amour comme l'appel de certains paysages vus en rêve, comme l'encerclement de certaines collines, d'une sorte d'argile matérielle, dont la forme est comme moulée sur la pensée. Quand nous reverrons-nous? Quand le goût terreux de tes lèvres viendra-t-il à nouveau frôler l'anxiété de notre esprit? La terre est comme un tourbillon de lèvres mortelles. La vie creuse devant nous le gouffre de toutes les caresses qui ont manqué. Qu'avons-nous à faire auprès de nous de cet ange qui n'a pas su se montrer? Toutes nos sensations seront-elles à jamais intellectuelles, et nos rêves n'arriveront-ils pas à prendre feu sur une âme dont l'émotion nous aidera à mourir? Qu'est-ce que cette mort, où nous sommes à jamais seuls, où l'amour ne nous montre pas le chemin?

LETTRE À LA VOYANTE

Madame,

Vous habitez une chambre pauvre, mêlée à la vie. C'est en vain qu'on voudrait entendre le ciel murmurer dans vos vitres. Rien, ni votre aspect, ni l'air ne vous séparent de nous, mais on ne sait quelle puérilité plus profonde que l'expérience nous pousse à taillader sans fin et à éloigner votre figure, et jusqu'aux attaches de votre vie.

L'âme déchirée et salie, vous savez que je n'assieds devant vous qu'une ombre, mais je n'ai pas peur de ce terrible savoir. Je vous sais à tous les noeuds de moi-même et beaucoup plus proche de moi que ma mère. Et je suis comme nu devant vous. Nu, impudique et nu, droit et tel qu'une apparition de moi-même, mais sans honte, car pour votre oeil qui court vertigineusement dans mes fibres, le mal est vraiment sans péché.

Jamais je ne me suis trouvé si précis, si rejoint, si assuré même au delà du scrupule, au delà de toute malignité qui me vint des autres, ou de moi, et aussi si perspicace. Vous ajoutiez la pointe de feu, la pointe d'étoile au fil tremblant de mon hésitation. Ni jugé, ni *me* jugeant, entier sans rien faire, intégral sans m'y efforcer; sauf la vie, c'était le bonheur. Et enfin plus de crainte que ma langue, ma grande langue trop grosse, ma langue minuscule ne fourche, j'avais à peine besoin de remuer ma pensée.

Cependant, je pénétrai chez vous sans terreur, sans l'ombre de la plus ordinaire curiosité. Et cependant vous étiez la maîtresse et l'oracle, vous auriez pu m'apparaître comme l'âme même et le Dieu de mon épouvantable destinée. Pouvoir voir et me dire! Que rien de sale ou de secret ne soit noir, que tout l'enfoui se découvre, que le refoulé s'étale enfin à ce bel oeil étalé d'un juge absolument pur. De celui qui discerne et dispose mais qui ignore même qu'il vous puisse accabler.

La lumière parfaite et douce où l'on ne souffre plus de son âme, cependant infestée de mal. La lumière sans cruauté ni passion où ne se révèle plus qu'une seule atmosphère, l'atmosphère d'une pieuse et sereine, d'une précieuse fatalité. Oui, venant chez vous, Madame, je n'avais plus peur de ma mort. Mort ou vie, je ne voyais plus qu'un grand espace placide où se dissolvaient les ténèbres de mon destin. J'étais vraiment sauf, affranchi de toute misère, car même ma misère à venir m'était douce, si *par impossible* j'avais de la misère à redouter dans mon avenir.

Ma destinée ne m'était plus cette route couverte et qui ne peut plus guère recéler que le mal. J'avais vécu dans son appréhension éternelle, et à *distance*, je la sentais toute proche, et depuis toujours blottie en moi. Aucun remous violent ne bouleversait à l'avance mes fibres, j'avais déjà été trop atteint et bouleversé par le malheur. Mes fibres n'enregistraient plus qu'un immense bloc uniforme et doux. Et peu m'importait que s'ouvrissent devant moi les plus terribles portes, le terrible était déjà derrière moi. Et même mal, mon avenir prochain ne me touchait que comme une harmonieuse discorde, une suite de cimes retournées et rentrées, émoussées en moi. Vous ne pouviez m'annoncer, Madame, que l'aplanissement de ma vie.

Mais ce qui par-dessus tout me rassurait, ce n'était pas cette certitude profonde, attachée à ma chair, mais bien le sentiment de l'uniformité de toutes choses. Un magnifique absolu. J'avais sans doute appris à me rapprocher de la mort, et c'est pourquoi toutes choses, même les plus cruelles, ne m'apparaissaient plus que sous leur aspect d'équilibre, dans une parfaite indifférence de sens.

Mais il y avait encore autre chose. C'est que ce sens, indifférent quant à ses effets immédiats sur ma personne, était tout de même coloré en quelque chose de bien. Je venais à vous avec un optimisme intégral. Un optimisme qui n'était pas une pente d'esprit, mais qui venait de cette connaissance profonde de l'équilibre où toute ma vie était baignée. Ma vie à venir équilibrée par mon passé terrible, et qui s'introduisait sans cahot dans la mort. Je *savais* à l'avance ma mort comme l'achèvement d'une vie enfin plane, et plus douce que mes souvenirs les meilleurs. Et la réalité grossissait à vue d'oeil, s'amplifiait jusqu'à cette souveraine connaissance où la valeur de la vie présente se démonte sous les coups de l'éternité. Il ne se pouvait plus que l'éternité ne me vengeât de ce sacrifice acharné de moi-même, et auquel, moi, je ne participais pas. Et mon avenir immédiat, mon avenir à partir de cette minute où je pénétrais pour la première fois dans votre cercle, cet avenir appartenait aussi à la mort. Et vous, votre aspect me fut dès le premier instant favorable.

L'émotion de savoir était dominée par le sentiment de la mansuétude infinie de l'existence *. Rien de mauvais pour

---

* Je n'y peux rien. J'avais ce sentiment devant Eile. Le vie était bonne parce que cette voyante était là. La présence de cette femme m'était comme un opium, plus pur, plus léger, quoique moins *solide* que l'autre. Mais beaucoup plus profond, plus vaste et ouvrant d'autres arches dans les cellules de mon esprit. Cet état actif d'échanges spirituels, cette conflagration de mondes immédiats et minuscules, cette imminence de vies infinies dont cette femme m'ouvrait la perspective, m'indiquaient enfin une issue à la vie, et une raison d'être au monde. Car on ne peut accepter la Vie qu'à condition d'être *grand*, de se sentir à l'origine des

moi ne pouvait tomber de cet oeil bleu et fixe par lequel vous inspectiez mon destin.

Toute la vie me devenait ce bienheureux paysage où les rêves qui tournent se présentent à nous avec la face de notre moi. L'idée de la connaissance absolue se confondait avec l'idée de la similitude absolue de la vie et de ma conscience. Et je tirais de cette double similitude le sentiment d'une naissance toute proche, où vous étiez la mère indulgente et bonne, quoique divergente de mon destin. Rien ne m'apparaissait plus mystérieux, dans le fait de cette voyance anormale, où les gestes de mon existence passé et future se peignaient à vous avec leurs sens gros d'avertissements et de rapports. Je sentais mon esprit entré en communication avec le vôtre quant à la *figure* de ces avertissements.

Mais vous, enfin, Madame, qu'est-ce donc que cette vermine de feu qui se glisse tout à coup en vous, et par l'artifice de quelle inimaginable·atmosphère? car enfin vous *voyez,* et cependant le même espace étalé nous entoure.

L'horrible, Madame, est dans l'immobilité de ces murs, de ces choses, dans la familiarité des meubles qui vous entourent, des accessoires de votre divination, dans l'indifférence tranquille de la vie à laquelle vous participez comme moi.

---

phénomènes, tout au moins d'un certain nombre d'entre eux. Sans puissance d'expansion, sans une certaine domination sur les choses, la vie est indéfendable. Une seule chose est exaltante au monde: le contact avec les puissances de l'esprit. Cependant devant cette voyante un phénomène assez paradoxal se produit. Je n'éprouve plus le besoin d'être puissant, ni vaste, la séduction qu'elle exerce sur moi est plus violente que mon orgueil, une certaine curiosité momentanément me suffit. Je suis prêt à tout abdiquer devant elle: orgueil, volonté, intelligence. Intelligence surtout. Cette intelligence qui est toute ma fierté. Je ne parle pas bien entendu d'une certaine agilité logique de l'esprit, du pouvoir de penser vite et de créer de rapides schémas sur les marges de la mémoire. Je parle d'une pénétration souvent à longue échéance, qui n'a pas besoin de se matérialiser pour se satisfaire et qui indique des vues profondes de l'esprit. C'est sur la foi de cette pénétration au pied-bot et le plus souvent sans matière (et que *moi-même* je ne possède pas), que j'ai toujours demandé que l'on me fasse crédit, dût-on me faire crédit cent ans et se contenter le reste du temps de silence. Je sais dans quelles limbes retrouver cette femme. Je creuse un problème qui me rapproche de l'or, de toute matière subtile, un problème abstrait comme la douleur qui n'a pas de forme et qui tremble et se volatilise au contact des os.

Et vos vêtements, Madame, ces vêtements qui touchent *une personne qui voit.* Votre chair, toutes vos fonctions enfin. Je ne puis pas me faire à cette idée que vous soyez soumise aux conditions de l'Espace, du Temps, que les nécessités corporelles vous pèsent. Vous devez être beaucoup trop légère pour l'espace.

Et, d'autre part, vous m'apparaissiez si jolie, et d'une grâce tellement humaine, tellement de tous les jours. Jolie comme n'importe laquelle de ces femmes dont j'attends le pain et le spasme, et qu'elles me haussent vers un seuil corporel.

Aux yeux de mon esprit, vous êtes sans limites et sans bords, absolument, profondément incompréhensible. Car comment vous accommodez-vous de la vie, vous qui avez le don de la vue toute proche? Et cette longue route toute unie où votre âme comme un balancier se promène, et où moi, je lirais si bien l'avenir de ma mort.

Oui, il y a encore des hommes qui connaissent la distance d'un sentiment à un autre, qui savent créer des étages et des haltes à leur désirs, qui savent s'éloigner de leurs désirs et de leur âme, pour y rentrer ensuite faussement en vainqueurs. Et il y a ces penseurs qui encerclent péniblement leurs pensées, qui introduisent des faux-semblants dans leurs rêves, ces savants qui déterrent des lois avec de sinistres pirouettes!

Mais vous, honnie, méprisée, planante, vous mettez le feu à la vie. Et voici que la roue du Temps d'un seul coup s'enflamme à force de faire grincer les cieux.

Vous me prenez tout petit, balayé, rejeté, et tout aussi désespéré que vous-même, et vous me haussez, vous me retirez de ce lieu, de cet espace faux où vous ne daignez même plus faire le geste de vivre, puisque déjà vous avez atteint la membrane de votre repos. Et cet oeil, ce regard sur moi-même, cet unique regard désolé qui est toute mon existence, vous le magnifiez et le faites se retourner sur lui-même, et voici qu'un bourgeonnement lumineux fait de délices sans ombres, me ravive comme un vin mystérieux.

LETTRES

Paris, 30 novembre 1927

Cher ami

Vous ai-je dit que les séances de psychanalyse auxquelles j'avais fini par me prêter ont laissé en moi une empreinte inoubliable. Vous savez assez quelles répugnances surtout instinctives et nerveuses je manifestais quand je vous ai connu pour ce mode de traitement. Vous êtes parvenu à me faire changer d'avis, sinon du point de vue intellectuel, car il y a dans cette curiosité, dans cette pénétration de ma conscience par une intelligence étrangère une sorte de « prostitution », d'impudeur que je repousserai toujours, mais enfin du point de vue expérimental j'ai pu constater les bienfaits que j'en avais retirés et au besoin je me prêterai de nouveau à une tentative analogue mais du plus profond de ma vie je persiste à fuir la psychanalyse, je la fuirai toujours comme je fuirai toute tentative pour enserrer ma conscience dans des préceptes ou des formules, une organisation verbale quelconque. Je témoignerai malgré tout du changement qui de votre fait s'est produit en moi. Cependant et voici la raison pour laquelle je vous écris il y a autour de moi une tendance et chez vous particulièrement à me croire *guéri*, à penser que j'ai rejoint la vie de tout le monde et que mon cas cesse d'être justiciable de la médecine. Ce qui n'est pas. J'ai encore très besoin, j'ai fondamentalement besoin de quelqu'un comme vous pourvu que vous consentiez à réformer votre jugement sur mon compte. Je vois très bien la tendance que l'on a à croire que j'ai remonté la pente et que je suis dans une phase resplendissante de mon existence, que la destinée me favorise, me comble de ses dons, de ses bienfaits. Et tout en effet extérieurement semble le prouver. J'ai l'air béni des dieux tant au point de vue matériel qu'au point de vue moral et spirituel. Or il y a en moi quelque chose de pourri, il y a dans mon psychisme une sorte de vice fondamental qui m'empêche de jouir de ce que la destinée m'offre. Je vous dis cela pour que vous ne vous désintéressiez pas de moi et que vous croyiez que je continue à avoir besoin de votre secours. Ma lucidité est entière, plus aiguisée que jamais, c'est l'objet auquel l'appliquer qui me manque, la substance interne. C'est plus grave et plus pénible que vous ne croyez. Je voudrais dépasser ce point d'absence, d'inanité. Ce piétinement qui me rend infirme, inférieur à tous et à tout. Je n'ai pas de vie, je n'ai pas de vie ! ! ! Mon effervescence interne est morte. Voilà des années que je ne l'ai plus retrouvée, que je n'ai plus eu ce jaillissement qui me sauve. Cette spontanéité d'images porteuses du moi. Où ma personnalité se retrouve, fait le tour d'elle-même. Trouve sa densité, sa sonorité précieuse. Une langueur m'occupe uniquement l'esprit. Tout ce que je trouve comme images, idées, on dirait que je le trouve par raccroc, que ce n'est qu'un ressouvenir collé qui n'a que l'aspect de la vie neuve — et la qualité s'en *ressent*. Ce n'est pas une imagination, une impression. C'est le fait que je ne suis plus moi-même, que mon moi authentique dort. Je vais vers mes images. Je les arrache par touffes lentes, elles ne viennent pas à moi, ne s'imposent plus à moi. Dans ces conditions, je n'ai plus de critère. Ces images dont l'authenticité fait la valeur, elles n'ont plus de valeur, n'étant que des effigies, des reflets de pensées antérieurement ruminées, ou ruminées par d'autres, non actuellement, et personnellement *pensées*. Comprenez-moi. Ce n'est même pas une questiont de qualité d'images, de quantité de pensées. C'est une question de *vivacité* fulgurante, de vérité, de réalité. Il n'y a plus de vie. La vie n'accompagne pas, n'illumine pas ce que je pense. Je dis LA VIE. Je ne dis pas une couleur de vie. Je dis la vie vraie, l'illumination essentiellement: l'être, le brasillement initial où s'enflamme toute pensée, — ce noyau. Je sens mon noyau mort. Et je souffre. Je souffre à chacune de mes expirations spirituelles, je souffre de leur absence, de la virtualité dans laquelle passent immanquablement toutes mes pensées, dans laquelle s'absorbe et se retourne, MA PENSÉE. Toujours le même mal. Je n'arrive pas à *penser*. Comprenez-vous ce creux, cet intense et durable néant. Cette végétation. Comme affreusement je végète. Je ne puis ni avancer ni reculer. Je suis fixé, localisé autour d'un point toujours le même et que tous mes livres traduisent. Mais mes livres je les ai laissés maintenant derrière moi. Je n'arrive pas à les dépasser. Car pour les dépasser il faudrait d'abord *vivre*. Et je m'obstine à ne pas vivre. J'ai essayé de vous faire comprendre comment. C'est que ma pensée ne se développe plus ni dans l'espace, ni dans le temps. Je ne suis rien. Je n'ai pas de moimême. Car en face de quoi que ce soit, conception ou circonstance, je ne pense rien. Ma pensée ne me propose rien. C'est en vain que je cherche. Et ni du côté intellectuel, ni du côté affectif ou purement imaginaire je n'ai rien. Je suis sans aucune espèce de réserve. Sans aucune espèce de possibilité.

Je n'ai pas lieu de chercher d'images. Je SAIS que je ne trouverai jamais mes images. Qu'il ne s'élèvera rien en moi qui atteigne le degré de dureté mentale, de constriction interne où mon moi se rencontrerait, se retrouverait. Tant que je ne retrouverai pas ma fulguration personnelle, une intensité de vision, une *étendue* de conceptions nées dans la facilité, je veux dire nées et non provoquées et faites de toutes pièces, toutes mes oeuvres seront sujettes à caution, car elles seront nées dans des conditions fausses et telles que tout homme les ignore, sauf moi. Tout ce que j'écris n'est pas créé, ne participe pas à la création, a la face d'un pis aller, c'est fait non de bric et de broc, mais sans nécessité, et toujours à défaut d'autre chose. Je vous jure, cher ami, que c'est grave, que c'est très grave. Je végète dans la pire des fainéantises morales. Je ne travaille jamais. Ce qui sort de moi est tiré comme au hasard. Et je pourrais écrire ou dire ou penser tout autre chose que ce que je dis ou pense et qui me représenterait tout aussi bien. C'est-à-dire tout aussi mal. C'est-à-dire pas du tout. Je ne suis pas là. Je ne suis plus là, à jamais. C'est grave parce qu'il ne s'agit pas du travail gratuit de l'écriture, ou des images pour les images, il s'agit de l'absolue pensée, c'est-à-dire de la vie. La même vacuité m'occupe au sujet de n'importe quelle circonstance de la vie. Toujours l'histoire des lettres à Rivière. Je sais bien que j'emmerde tout le monde, que je n'intéresse personne, mais comment faire puisque je vis. A moins de *mourir* il n'y a pas d'issue. Mourrai-je, ou vous m'ayant compris, et sachant *le peu que vaut* ma vie actuelle qui fait illusion à tant de gens, trouverez-vous un moyen médical de me tirer de là.

A vous. Votre ami

ARTAUD.

P. S. — Je vous remercie des pilules mais depuis 15 jours elles sont dévorées. Or à Cannes j'en aurai besoin pour 3 semaines. Il m'en faudrait bien une quarantaine de bonnes car comme vous le pensez je suis retombé rudement dans le laud. Hélas ! ! !

17 février 1932. Jeudi matin.

Cher Monsieur,

J'ai été surpris et émerveillé de la façon dont vous *deviniez* mon état, dont vous repériez avec précision et une folle justesse les troubles profonds, désarmants, démoralisants dont je suis depuis si longtemps affligé et je vous enviais en même temps la façon synthétique que vous aviez de les présenter, sous leur angle vrai, les ayant *sentis* tels qu'ils se présentent et à leur place, faculté dont je suis éminemment privé.

Si donc je vous écris c'est simplement dans l'anxiété d'avoir oublié *tout de même* un fait caractéristique et qui vous permettrait de voir encore plus profond et plus clair dans mon abominable état. État abominablement cruel et que je n'ai en réalité pas de mots pour caractériser pour la raison que je ne puis rien voir ni déceler de net en moi dans l'incertitude où je suis touchant justement, et quel que soit mon état,

1° mes perceptions et observations intérieures,

2° l'efficacité des moyens qui me sont donnés pour les cerner et les représenter.

Si l'esprit est atteint il l'est naturellement dans tous les cas et à tous les degrés.

Rien ne m'est d'ailleurs odieux et pénible, rien n'est plus angoissant pour moi que le doute émis sur la réalité et sur la nature des phénomènes que j'accuse.

On me voit quelquefois trop brillant dans l'expression de mes insuffisances, de ma déficience profonde et de l'impuissance que j'accuse, pour croire qu'elle ne soit pas imaginaire et forgée de toutes pièces.

On ne met pas en doute la réalité de mes troubles subjectifs et de l'état de douleur où je plonge, on met en doute son objectivité et surtout *sa portée*.

Or et je n'insisterai jamais assez là-dessus, mon état subit des fluctuations infinies qui va du pire à un mieux être relatif. Dans ces états de mieux être je redeviens quelque peu capable de penser, *de sentir* et d'écrire et croyez bien entre autres choses que je ne me serais pas attelé à une lettre comme celle-ci si je n'étais quelque peu *rentré* en moi, de même qu'en général on ne se rend pas compte qu'aux moments où je parle et décris mon mal' c'est qu'il a en partie disparu.

Tout ceci est élémentaire et ce n'est pas pour vous que je le dis bien entendu mais il me faut en général y insister inlassablement.

J'ai été comme je vous l'ai dit beaucoup plus malade que je ne me trouve actuellement, en proie à des sortes d'écrasements et d'écartèlements affolants de la conscience, vraiment *dérouté* quant à mes perceptions les plus élémentaires, incapable de rien rassembler, de rien collecter en moi et encore moins de rien traduire puisque rien ne pouvait être conservé.

Psychiquement c'était la débâcle comme dans le domaine physiologique c'est la débâcle quand l'estomac ou les intestins ne peuvent plus rien conserver. Et physiquement je me trouvais sous le coup d'un écrasement insensé, écartelé entre une sensation de vide nerveux absolu et de compression, magnétique, de torride pesanteur portée aux extrêmes elle aussi.

Entre cette double, cette multiple sensation, l'esprit qui ne pouvait s'appliquer à rien se voyait également dépouillé de la continuité de sa vie intérieure, au point que les images qui naissaient au moment où le subconscient les enchaîne et va automatiquement leur donner forme, ces images, ces représentations, ces formes *s'amusaient* elles aussi à tantaliser l'esprit en se résorbant et en se détraquant avant terme, affolant la pensée qui voulait les saisir.

La *ligne* de mon état est actuellement la même avec une simple différence d'intensité et de degré. Et avec en plus ce fait que, alors que je me suis cru, quand ces maux, ces phénomènes singuliers ont commencé, complètement sombré, j'ai pu tout de même me rendre compte que j'étais parfois capable de quelque chose et la tantalisation est maintenant plus forte quand je ne parviens pas à m'exprimer.

Cet état donc d'écrasement et de compression physique toujours le même réapparaissant avec une intensité diminuée (fassent les dieux que certains états torrides que je connais bien ne reviennent plus jamais), doublé en outre par une sensation d'éloignement physique de moi-même comme si j'allais ne plus commander à mes membres, à mes réflexes, à mes réaction mécaniques les plus spontanées, cela joint à une autre sensation de dureté et d'horrible fatigue physique de la langue quand je parle, *l'effort de la pensée* retentissant toujours physiquement sur l'ensemble de ma musculature, et le bégaiement dont je souffre à des degrés variables et qui parfois disparaît tout à fait me fatiguant énormément (j'ai noté depuis ma plus tendre enfance (6 à 8 ans) ces périodes de bégaiement et d'horrible contraction physique des nerfs faciaux et de la langue, succédant à des périodes de calme et de facilité parfaite), tout cela donc se compliquant de troubles psychiques correspondants et qui n'ont apparu *avec éclat* que vers l'âge de 19 ans.

Il y a une certaine sensation de vide dans les nerfs faciaux, mais un vide actif si j'ose dire et qui physiquement se traduisait par une sorte d'aimantation vertigineuse du devant de la figure. Ce ne sont pas des images et il faudrait prendre cela presque au pied de la lettre. Car ce vertige physique était horriblement angoissant et cette sensation que je décris est apparue à son paroxysme deux ou trois ans après le début de mon mal. Cette sensation était remplacée quelquefois par une sorte de spasme moral, une angoisse virulente qui me roulait comme dans une vague de détraquement, qui, où que je fusse, me donnait envie non pas de pleurer mais de sangloter en tremblant, de hurler de désespoir. Depuis longtemps heureusement tout ceci n'est plus revenu et il reste maintenant un certain nombre de douleurs physiques errantes ou localisées, une profonde obnubilation de la conscience qui s'empare de moi par périodes, m'enlève mes représentations intérieures et mes idées, me prive du bénéfice du système intellectuel que je me suis fait.

Je souffre maintenant surtout

1° intellectuellement d'une part,

2° sentimentalement et affectivement de l'autre.

1° L'automatisme de l'esprit étant détruit dans sa continuité je ne puis plus penser que fragmentairement. Si je pense, la majeure partie des réserves de termes et du vocabulaire que je me suis personnellement constitué est inutilisable, étant rouillée et *oubliée* quelque part, mais le terme apparu, la pensée profonde cède, le contact est brutalement coupé, l'affectivité nerveuse profonde ne répond plus à la pensée, l'automatisme est désorganisé, et *cela pour les fois où je pense* ! ! ! Si je ne pense pas il est bien inutile de faire appel à mon vocabulaire particulier. Or soit que quelqu'un me sollicite, soit que moi-même je constate mon vide et que je m'efforce d'y faire naître de la pensée, le drame commence, le drame intellectuel où je suis perpétuellement vaincu.

Car il me paraît impossible que je n'aie pas quelque chose à dire, en outre je sais que dans tel ou tel sens j'ai eu jadis une manière à moi de penser, des conceptions me sont confusément apparues mais malheur à moi si je tente de les élucider, de concrétiser quelque chose. J'ai, me semble-t-il, oublié jusqu'à la *manière de penser*. Oui, c'est la notion de ce vide intellectuel particulier que je voudrais *éclairer* une fois pour toutes. Il me paraît la caractéristique éminente de mon état. C'est la chose que nul ne peut se vanter de partager aver moi, de posséder en même temps que moi, cela, cet *oubli* des formes de la pensée. C'est cela qui est caractéristique. Et à travers les formes de la pensée, oubli également de soi-même, des formes de sa sensibilité intellectuelle, ou morale, sensibilité en face des idées. Il ne s'agit de rien moins dans ces états-là que d'oublier le contenu intellectuel de l'esprit, d'avoir rompu le contact avec toutes les évidences qui sont à la base de la pensée.

2° Et le désarroi sentimental ou affectif auquel je faisais allusion tout à l'heure est étroitement lié à cette fuite, et à cette catastrophe par le haut, car on comprend bien que l'élément destructeur qui déminéralise l'esprit et lui ôte ses évidences ne se préoccupe pas de savoir si l'esprit gardera ses ennuis pour son usage personnel ou s'il les appliquera à quelque chose de plus impersonnel qui dans d'autres circonstances aurait pu servir à l'établissement d'une oeuvre quelconque, *d'un produit!* On ne saura jamais au fond ce qui fait que l'esprit se décide pour la création. Les mêmes pensées, les mêmes tendances volontaires pourraient ne servir après tout qu'à gonfler le moi, à le nourrir plus étroitement, à augmenter sa densité intérieure et tant pis pour les oeuvres et pour la création, puisque psychiquement le résultat est le même, mais en ce qui me concerne, cet obscurcissement, ce sarclage des parties hautes de la conscience et de la pensée vaut malheureusement pour toutes les circonstances de la vie, si intellectuellement mon cerveau est devenu inopérant, ne peut plus servir, les moments pendant lesquels ce vide m'occupe, me remplit d'angoisse et d'ennui, me fait sentir ma vie perdue, inutilisable, ont une valeur sentimentale eux aussi, ils se traduisent pour l'âme par une coloration du néant, par une affectivité toute noire bien faite à l'image de moi, mais cette affectivité d'autre part c'est son défaut de résonnances, c'est sa coagulation ...

Cher docteur et ami

C'est à toute votre science de vieux médecin que je m'adresse. Par principe, en général, *je ne crois pas à la science*, le savoir m'ennuie, et je crois que les vrais savants sont ceux qui toute leur vie ignorèrent leur science et ne s'en souviendront malheureusement que de l'autre côté du tombeau, le vrai savoir est une affaire musculaire nerveuse, il ne dit mot, mais fait à point nommé le geste simple qu'il faut et qui sauve les choses, lesquelles ne furent *jamais* entre les mains des initiés maïs de quelques humbles ignares qui étaient par hasard des hommes de bonne volonté.

Vous connaissant donc, c'est au médecin qui a vu des milliers de malades et a su faire entrer en jeu cet élément inconnu des médecins et de la médecine :

quel élément ?

quelque chose en moi allait dire la pitié, mais ce n'est pas cela, il y a dans ce mot une absence de commisération qui n'est pas votre fait,

la pitié semble venir du riche, du pourvu qui ne souffre pas et donne par hasard, parfois, comme le Boudha muni de toutes les magnificences spirituelles, ou comme le christ non couronné d'épines et qui en réalité ne la porta pas, cette couronne de barbelés, mais *s'enfuit avant* qu'elle ne lui fût imposée, qui donne donc, ce pourvu, au pauvre, un tremblement, une commotion fuyante, alors que celui qui souffrit comme le pauvre quelque chose d'unique et s'en souvient lui donne une commisération, un quelque chose de pris sur sa propre misère et qui jamais ne pensa qu'elle fut au-dessus de lui; je crois qu'il y a, dans l'occulte de vous-même, comme le ressouvenir d'une morsure forte, d'une de ces atteintes d'avant être que l'opium a cautérisée, que l'opium seul peut cautériser. Et comment?

Car l'opium en réalité qu'est-ce que c'est?

On regarde ce suc noir, vireux, qui, moi, m'a toujours fait penser à ces terribles flaques que l'on voit gicler des cercueils; et d'aucuns disent que c'est la vie, que c'est le principe de la vie lui-même qui est contenu dans cette liqueur noire, cette espèce d'inclassable, multiforme et, à mon sens, *hybride* suintement qui tient de l'évasion, de la contrainte, de l'étreinte, de l'effusion, de l'amplification, de la multiplication, de la confusion, de l'obtusion, de la clarté, de la légèreté, de la pesanteur, de l'opacité, de la minceur, de l'épaisseur, de la lévitation, de la stratification, de la masse, du poids, parce qu'il n'est pas venu d'une idée pure, désintéressée, détachée, mais intéressée, goulue, attachée, salace, lubrique et érotique de la vie, et non d'une idée fracassante, héroïque du moi corporel de l'homme et de son devenir.

Je crois que l'opium actuel, le suc connu noir de ce qu'on appelle le pavot, est la destitution d'une ancienne, *extirpante* puissance,

dont l'homme n'a plus voulu,

et ceux qui étaient fatigués de la liqueur séminale et des retournements érotiques du moi dans la liqueur du crime premier se sont rejetés vers l'opium comme vers une autre salacité.

C'est pourquoi l'opium guérit de la salacité sexuelle par le kieff qui est une autre manière de tirer profit des bains vireux de l'antique salacité humaine et c'est ce que j'y déteste.

Je n'y ai cherché, je n'y pense encore que pour y trouver

la guérison de certaines douleurs subtiles que la médecine
physiologique ne peut pas voir,
et qui sont l'entrée de la râpe noire, l'entrée de la friction
des exigences noires sur la voie de la plus hautaine sublimité.
Je veux dire que l'homme tend en haut vers l'holocauste de
la grandeur et que c'est là, sur la route de ces élévations
comme automatiques *internes,*
que le mal, le mal de n'être pas encore, de n'en être pas ar-
rivé là, s'accroche et exige corps et ce corps, qui guérit l'effort
ante-natal et comme sanguin-viscéral de la grandeur, celui
qui a déjà rué, l'homme, qui dans des efforts, des efforts de
transe, a frappé, a recueilli dans le coup de la frappe haute
des gouttes de l'impossible liqueur qui guérit qui n'est pas
encore monté.
Mais l'opium présent n'est plus le reste de la goutte noire.
Lui aussi a été mélangé.
Vous êtes le seul médecin à savoir quelque chose de cela
parce que vous avez senti cela avec un reste de coeur lacéré
qu'un autre médecin n'a pas.
Mais que voulez-vous que les législateurs de la drogue voient
le problème sous cet aspect.
A vous.

ANTONIN ARTAUD

P. S. Rien ne s'explique que par les effusions de la transe du
dos derrière le théâtre et la poésie. Mais qui veut vivre sur
ce plan? Personne.

Car qui veut concevoir que le théâtre ou la poésie soient une
chose ou un objet, qui veut admettre qu'il n'y ait pas d'état,
et que pour désigner ce qui est théâtre ou poésie arrive
quelque chose comme un corps ou personnage encore incréé
(mettons), mais déjà *volonté,* et qui tient lieu et place *d'état,*
la psychologie étant évincée.
Et à sa place une vivification d'insolites réalités.
Bien.

Mais qu'est-ce que je veux dire au juste?

Je veux dire que ce qui est le théâtre et la poésie est à mes yeux le minimum de la réalité, que ces espèces de chambres de chauffe, que j'appelle des effusions de transes du dos humain
derrière le théâtre et la poésie
sont comme des énergies en attente par delà ce qui à mes yeux est le seul écran et le seul crible valable du réel,
et qu'un réel qui, avant d'atteindre la réalité,
ne passe pas par le soubresaut
du plan surélevé du théâtre
et de celui de la poésie,
est un réel alors de *défécation* fait pour et par des lâches,
pensé depuis toujours par les lâches
inextirpables de la vie,
les atomes crochus des lâches inextirpables de la vie.
Mais qu'est-ce que cela vient faire avec l'opium?
Cela vient de ce que l'opium est un sursaut de la force invétérée première,
il y a opium
quand la force latente, bousculant son propre corps, monte en haut, d'un élan,
ou plutôt,
faisant cymbale des 2 mamelles de son souffle opposite,
se plaque comme sur soi-même de tout le tour du gond grinçant de la masse de son poids propre, qui,
(mais quelles limites le poids de la force invétérée latente, a-t-il
que celles, pourrait-on dire, de l'infini?)
Or si l'infini *temporel* peut être admis,
celui spatial n'est pas concevable,
et évoquer l'infini d'un effort.

Et il se plaque, cet opium, il fait le geste qu'on appellerait dans une certaine philosophie de monter,
comme une solennelle, rétractile douleur.
(Mémoire pincée de l'état de besoin quand il n'est plus là,)

Mais tout cela est bien spécieux, bien menu, bien particulier, bien sophistique presque pour une aussi palpitante et redoutable question.

Je veux dire que l'opium est le résidu corporel d'un état d'en haut qui a été gagné un jour par des hommes dans les transes et dans le sang, et que pour le comprendre il ne faut pas évoquer la sublimité psychologique et poétique ordinaire, mais celle d'un état caveau, une espèce d'échappée foncière sur les charniers génésiques du plan où s'échafaude inlassablement la matière, lequel est hors être et ne l'a jamais supporté.

Or ce plan, hirsute peut-être, héroïque en tout cas, est celui de la vie même. Et l'homme n'a jamais souffert que d'en avoir délaissé la suffocante peut-être, mais merveilleuse intensité. La perpétuelle *irascibilité*.

Au premier temps, avec l'opium, on veut tout casser, prendre des villes, partir en guerre contre des idées aussi immenses que terminées, cet état est demeuré longtemps confus en moi, mais un jour il s'est éclairé,

je me suis aperçu que l'opium me soulevait *vers* quelque chose, *contre* quelque chose contre quoi je n'étais pas prêt,

l'idée d'un vide épouvantable à boucher,

pour le boucher

il faudrait *travailler*,

travailler d'une certaine manière,

or il est dit que l'opium fait kieffer,

et bien vite la lâcheté humaine *revient*, qui incite à ne rien faire, à ne pas penser,

à ne pas penser, mais à se laisser aller aux soi-disant vérités nouvelles, aux soi-disant réalités étoffées que l'opium *bien incubé* apporte.

Alors on ne fait rien. On se laisse aller.

Il y a dans l'opium les scènes de la bisaïeule, je veux dire que l'opium laisse des séquelles pendant des jours, des semaines, des mois, alors que les autres toxiques s'oublient.

La liqueur séminale vient de la douleur, est un soutirage de la douleur des génies.

NOTE. — L'ÉPERON MALICIEUX, LE DOUBLE CHEVAL, se situe approximativement en 1926, l'ENCLUME DES FORCES ayant paru dans la RÉVOLUTION SURRÉALISTE le 15 juin 1926.

La LETTRE A LA VOYANTE a paru dans la RÉVOLUTION SURRÉALISTE le 1er décembre 1926. Elle était dédiée à André Breton.

La lettre datée 30 novembre 1927 est adressée au Docteur Allendy.

La lettre datée 17 février 1932 était destinée à Monsieur Soulié de Morant. Elle est inachevée et ne lui a pas été envoyée.

La lettre commençant par *Cher docteur et ami* était destinée au Docteur Achille Delmas, médecin de la Maison de Santé d'Ivry. Elle se situe aux environs du mois de mai 1947.

ANDRÉ DU BOUCHET

CLARTÉ

Avant que le jour sonne

comme le linge étendu qui s'allume avant l'apparition du soleil et glace le bois visible, feu blanc, en flambant sur la barrière come une couche de neige,

on sort de la tête, champ de massacre.

La terre étale retournée par le soc. Soulevée jusqu'au ciel par une rame de fer bleu. On respire dans une forge.

Tuerie des arbres. Regards défaits. Labours frais. Linge des arbres tordus se dissipant dans le ciel qu'on ne voit pas.

AVANT

Une vague de vent roule dans le ciel
l'oeil les cailloux pris dans le vent
doigts gourds dans les labours du vent
le champ bouge
les branches de la façade se défont
la paroi noire
qui crève

un rêve dont on sort
le coq du bocal carde l'air
hommes fouaillés
suffoquant
vivant comme on dort dans une rage de vent
en nage
roués par le vent

ceux qui font l'or

et de l'autre côté le bleu éclatant.

ON RESPIRE

Le matin taillé à coups de serpe. Une rame bleue s'enfonce dans la terre, charrue dans les lézardes. L'air est trop vaste pour que la guerre respire. La serre pourrit entre les branches avec les haillons de l'autre orage. L'air est un million de maisons neuves.

MARÉE

La maison ouverte flambe. Les croisées se détachent à leur tour, puis fondent.
La souche fichée dans le pré, flambe.
Le feu effleure les poteaux des barbelés, la terre qui roule.
Les rocs blancs tintent sous le pas. Le talon étouffé sous la tache sombre, écrasant les tisons.
Une fois passé le seuil de bois, le vent recommence à tonner, à tourner le cahier rond.

ÉQUERRE

Dans l'air mince où l'herbe se rétracte
comme un fil de verre
le ruisseau dort dans le sillon
grand os de seiche
plus qu'un oeil
le nuage cesse
terre frottée
froissée

rape d'ombre.

ANDRÉ MALRAUX

SUR *LE PAYS D'ORIGINE* *

... Comme Laclos avait mis la psychologie au service d'une mythologie, Stendhal avait fait de la sienne le moyen de la vaste création poétique accordée à tout ce qui l'avait séparé de lui-même. Ducroo (1) ne partage pas le goût de Beyle pour les mathématiques. Les décors le touchent peu: Milan moins que le souvenir de Stendhal, Florence moins que celui de Larbaud. Pour atteindre une vérité dont il ne préconçoit rien, il ne dispose que de l'observation de la comédie (Sa vérité serait: « ce qui reste », la comédie écartée). Et cette comédie n'est pas celle de Beyle.

Dans la théorie que celui-ci s'efforce d'élaborer au temps du *Journal*, l'homme est « à découvrir », comme la nature, mystère provisoire; mais la nature est obscure par sa complexité. L'homme l'est par son mensonge; ses moyens sont des ruses; le psychologue doit découvrir ce qu'il cache, plus que ce qu'il ignore. Inséparable de la vie de société, ce que ne sont ni Barnabooth ni Ducroo, il est l'homme traditionnel des moralistes français, qui semble obscur parce qu'il dissimule ses secrets. Le spectacle de la vie est comédie, il n'est pas énigme.

---

* Fragment de la Préface à l'édition française de l'ouvrage.
(1) Le personnage principal du livre.

Ducroo sait que l'élucidation de l'homme ne coïncide pas avec la révélation de ses secrets; que l'homme ne s'inventorie pas, que la sincérité est une « tendance ». Dans la comédie qu'il observe, il accorde au mensonge un faible rôle; les valeurs sociales lui sont étrangères, l'ambition et la vanité le retiennent peu. Les hommes n'y sont pas des imposteurs avides de grands rôles, mais des délirants avides de rôles tout court, et la surprise est qu'un si grand nombre de ces rôles soient insolites — que la comédie ne soit pas orientée.

Cette surprise tour à tour inquiète et émerveillée, Eddy Du Perron la doit-il à sa naissance à Java? Que celle-ci ait puissamment agi sur le dialogue qu'il entretient avec lui-même, il l'affirme; qu'elle n'ait pas moins agi sur sa relation avec le monde, tout son livre le suggère. Non qu'il écrive le livre de l'homme qui change de civilisation. Livre que nul n'a écrit, et dont T.E. Lawrence disait que nul ne peut l'écrire: « On cesse d'être Anglais, et on ne devient pas Arabe ». Sans doute, à devenir Arabe, perdrait-on les moyens d'exprimer comment on fut Anglais. Des quelques récits de conversions qui ont exprimé la foi trouvée, lesquels ont exprimé la foi perdue? Arabe, Lawrence n'eût hanté personne... C'est d'être aussi étranger à la confrontation qu'à la métamorphose et à la conversion, c'est de ne jamais devenir tout-à-fait Européen, n'ayant jamais été Javanais, qui donne quelquefois à Ducroo son accent de Candide désincarné.

Car il n'y a aucun exotisme dans ce livre — pas même celui de l'Europe. Son pittoresque, qui est grand, n'est pas relié au décor de l'« ailleurs », où la littérature a trouvé de faciles effets et une si efficace poésie. Java n'est pas un décor: c'est ce qui entoure son enfance — celle d'un fils de planteur antillais ou cochinchinois, non celle de Kim. Le prestige qu' exerçait hier encore l'Orient venait de ce qu'il était donné comme un tout, le marché avec le temple et le souk avec les Mille et une Nuits. Le temple n'existe pas pour ce petit garçon élevé dans des propriétés isolées. L'épopée non plus: bien que Du Perron ait parlé le soudanais mieux que le français (qu'il parlait sans accent) il s'intéressa tard à l'histoire des royaumes de Java, et n'avait pas vu le Boroboudour quand parut *Le Pays d'Origine*. Il grandit dans ce que les Hollandais appelaient les Indes et les Français les Isles: la rivière qui charrie les arbres morts, la propriété dans la chaleur, le village et les servantes indigènes...

C'est trop peu pour être Java, trop pour n'être rien. Ces servantes ont leurs légendes; la mère de Ducroo emploie leurs masseuses, consulte leurs devineresses. Le seule barrière est sociale. Rien de ce qui, dans les empires coloniaux, maintient d'ordinaire l'Occident: nationalisme, foi, ou vraie culture. Cet enfant n'est ni en exil, ni entre deux mondes inconciliables, mais entre deux mondes qu'il sera bientôt stupéfait de trouver semblables, alors que tout devrait les opposer.

L'Europe, absente par tout ce qui la fait Europe, est cependant présente par les incidences si puissantes sur les enfants: récits des grandes personnes et parenthèses « qui ne vous regardent pas», , photos du théâtre où nous n'irons pas parce qu'il a brûlé, et du Casino où nous irons dès que nous serons rentrés en Hollande. Et les livres! L'Europe, c'est d'abord le pays de d'Artagnan. Une vieille maison de famille, avec des chats... Son décor surprenant sera vite épuisé, comme celui de New-York l'est par nous — comme tout décor auquel l'histoire et l'art n'apportent pas la vraie vie des pierres. Après quoi, Ducroo trouvera des intellectuels. Mais déjà les personnages de Balzac savaient qu'il faut venir à Paris pour trouver d'Arthez dans sa mansarde et Canalis dans sa loge...

La liaison fut faite par les extravagants. On peut penser que Du Perron les a mis en lumière; ce n'est pas certain. Il avait du farfelu un goût très vif, dans lequel son refus de tout préjugé social rejoignait son amour de la poésie. Il aimait les satyriques français, le *Francion*, de début du XVII⁰ siècle, la littérature dont le *Songe de Pantagruel* et Callot semblent l'illustration; aux temps fortunés, il s'en était fait relier des recueils personnels de pages arrachées « parce qu' elles devaient être ensemble ». Auteurs et images se rejoignaient dans un monde semblable à celui des intermèdes de féeries où les balais et les fourneaux turlupinent les servantes sous le rire énorme des potirons. Le tout, naturel et familier: allant de soi. A un personnage à grelots l'accrochant au coin de la rue pour lui dire « Je suis cheval!» il eût assurément répondu: « — Excusez-moi de ne pas m'en être aperçu plus tôt: je suis si distrait... ». Fort lucide, au demeurant. Nullement étonné de voir la tireuse de cartes belge succéder à la sorcière javanaise, mais à mille lieues de Gozzi possédé par ses farfadets. Il observe extravagants et normaux du même petit oeil noir pénétrant et étonné: ils recèlent pour lui la même vérité. L'une des clefs du *Pays d'Origine* est qu'il n'y existe aucune norme. Les extravagants y sont les notes d'une octave parmi les autres... On peut imaginer Ducroo, lié à eux, regardant comme l'Ingénu les hommes de la loi d'Orient et ceux de la loi d'Occident. Non. Il est dans un constant détachement d'un monde d'apparences — liberté si profonde que le récit, nullement indifférent, du suicide de son père pourrait se terminer par la réponse de Liszt à qui l'on vient d'annoncer avec les plus grandes précautions la mort de Wagner: « Pourquoi pas?... ». Du Perron attachait grande importance à la justesse du ton. Peut-être le sien, dans sa langue, (et sans nul doute dans ses lettres en français) ne lui semblait-il tout-à-fait juste que lorsque sous la précision du trait, le « pourquoi pas » se devine comme un imperceptible écho...

Mais ce livre sans normes n'est pas sans valeurs. Et ces valeurs (celles du livre: l'homme était la générosité même, et de ceux que nous fûmes quelques-uns à aimer) sont révélatrices parce qu'elles ne sont fondées sur rien. Ducroo est indifférent au christianisme, aux religions de l'Asie, à l'humanisme traditionnel, à toute métaphysique. Ses connaissances intellectuelles (ses connaissances littéraires sont beaucoup plus étendues) touchent trois cultures européennes, mais commencent à Montaigne: ce qui précède l'ennuie. Il doit d'ailleurs à la seule littérature ces valeurs, dont beaucoup sont celles de son maître Stendhal, celles de la plupart des intellectuels de son temps; et dont il serait instructif d'établir la carte pendant qu'il en est temps encore, afin de savoir pourquoi, bien qu'on fasse de la bonne littérature avec de mauvais sentiments, on ne fait que de la qualité humaine avec la vraie littérature...

Mais que Ducroo peigne les gens de Java ou ceux de Grouhy, ces valeurs n'ordonnent jamais sa peinture. (Pensons au rôle que jouent celles de Conrad, de Kipling). Il saisit les êtres par d'autres voies. Si épisodiques que soient ses Javanais, ils convainquent; ce n'est pas courant. Pourtant, la lecture achevée, on cherche à préciser par quoi ils sont Javanais. Y a-t-il des Javanais? Il y a des Européens — insolites. Y aurait-il donc des hommes « partout les mêmes etc... », une structure mentale unique costumée de civilisations? Elle n'est pas moins absente du livre, que l'individu fondamental, de Ducroo. C'est, au contraire, par le fait d'être costumés que tous les hommes se ressemblent — unis avant tout par l'identité de leurs folies différentes. Les amours de la petite baboue rejoignent la passion héraldique du père. Souvenons-nous du portrait de la grand'mère: « Elle ressemblait à son père, et l'on dit que je lui ressemble... ».

Son introspection, qui est constante, ne cherche aucune clef de l'homme; elle poursuit la connaissance de sa singularité. Ce que l'homme cache ne l'obsède pas: sans morale préconçue et sans hypocrisie, Ducroo accepte aisément ce qu'il découvre. Son dédoublement tient à des prises de conscience différentes parce que successives, à des retours sur lui-même (il note évidemment le journal après coup: le présent immédiat lui est souvent ennemi); et surtout à la maladresse avec laquelle le Ducroo quotidien comme Dominique et Barnabooth obéit à son double nourri des grands livres. D'où, beaucoup plus qu'irritation ou honte, l'étonnement du cavalier de cheval-jupon devant la passivité, voire l'indépendance, de sa monture.

N'oublions pas que l'introspection désintéressée nait lorsque la confession disparaît. Le péché de bêtise contre la raison, la «lo-gique», puis la lucidité, prend la place des autres. (Ducroo sera plus indulgent que Dominique). Curieux retour de l'humilité: la revendication désespérée de Rousseau succède à la superbe du cardinal de Retz. Mais le christianisme donnait au « Pourquoi? » fondamental une réponse immédiate. A la connaissance de la Faute, l'Europe tente de substituer la découverte de la Loi. Beyle sera moins assuré de l'existence d'une telle loi à soixante ans qu'à vingt; et l'introspection littéraire prendra de plus en plus conscience de sa qualité propre, de ce qu'elle doit au ton, à la saveur de l'intelligence, au jugement caché sous l'analyse, à tout ce qui distingue le *Journal* de Gide d'un document psychanalytique. Beyle avait tenu le sien afin d'apprendre, lorsqu'il le relirait, comment il s'était trompé; et cru qu'il écrivait ses souvenirs pour ordonner, dans quelques chambres tristes la rêverie où flottait le parfum de sa jeunesse italienne. A porter sur le passé et non sur le présent, à devenir désintéressée, l'introspection trouvait un pouvoir mystérieux. En un temps où le roman commençait à poursuivre l'illusion de la vie, l'introspection du passé donnait l'illusion du souvenir (le mot tient d'elle son accent nostalgique) mais le souvenir était en train de changer de nature. Il suffit de comparer les *Souvenirs d'Egotisme* aux mémoires du XVIème et du XVIIème siècle, à Montluc, à d'Aubigné, à Retz, à Saint-Simon, pour voir que l'analyse suscitait de nouveaux moyens de poésie. Or, comme l'examen de conscience renforce la présence du dieu qui l'ordonne, l'introspection peut étendre subtilement au monde l'irréalité qu'elle pourchasse en l'homme. Que l'admirateur de Molière et de Napoléon observe Dominique avec ironie, ne suffit pas pour que Beyle devienne son égal; ni même son semblable. Il se dégage du second sans atteindre le premier. Le réel incertain et le cours de rivière dans lequel il se reflète, s'accordent dans la même instabilité; il cesse d'être le vrai, comme il cessa de l'être dans les grandes religions. Et comme dans les grandes religions, apparaît un autre monde — celui qui n'est pas soumis au cahos des apparences. Sa vérité, qui n'a rien à voir avec le vérifiable, et tout avec l'adhésion, n'est pas sous les apparences, mais au-delà. Il est le vrai monde, comme l'éternel pour l'Egyptien; et le réel est apparence, illusion ou vanité, comme il le fut pour tout l'Orient et l'est encore pour l'Inde. Qu'il compense, qu'il justifie, est secondaire. (De même la vraie foi commence au-delà de tout ce qui n'est pas elle). Il naît quand le réel cesse d'être contrainte, pour devenir moyen d'expression de ce qu'il ne peut contraindre. Il n'en apporte pas la clef, mais il en apporte le Fin. Il appelle de curieux états psychiques, l'euphorie dans laquelle Casanova écrit et Stendhal dicte la *Chartreuse* en cinquante-deux jours dans laquelle la comédie devient féerie, et la jeunesse de Beyle, Henri Brulard ou l'entrée des Français à Milan.

A l'autre pôle, celui de l'introspection haletante de Dostoievski, la comédie s'appelle « le vaudeville du diable ». Et la lucidité n'est pas davantage seule à lutter contre elle: à la voix du souterrain, et sans doute au jaillissement le plus sombre et le plus constant de son génie, Dostoievski oppose la nuit hors du temps où Aliocha se débat, en parlant aux enfants, contre les implacables questions d'Ivan. « Aimez les oiseaux et toutes les bêtes vivantes... ».

La nuit, non la réponse: la création. Non pas l'histoire de Lear, mais la lande; l'histoire de Macbeth, mais le corridor sans fin et la forêt de Dunsinane. Ce qui, de l'oeuvre d'art, ne peut être ramené au résumé, ni au contenu, ni à la prédication. Comme les anciennes civilisations appelaient des mondes sacrés qui n'étaient pas toujours des paradis, l'homme-marionnette appelle sourdement, sous la voix du montreur haussée jusqu'à la lucidité, la voix séculaire dont le lointain écho fait du journal de Beyle, *la Chartreuse de Parme* de Stendhal.

De Rousseau à Proust, l'introspection suscite en littérature un passé délivré que celle-ci n'avait jamais connu, et en égale la pénétrante mélodie au buccin des figures exemplaires. (Proust n'aime pas Claudel, Beyle n'aime pas Chateaubriand). De *Henri Brulard* et *des Souvenirs d'Egotisme* à toute *la Chartreuse de Parme*, Stendhal fait écho à la cantilène sur laquelle la mort brisa les *Rêveries*: « Aujourd'hui, jour de Pâques fleuries, il y a précisément cinquante ans de ma première connaissance avec Madame de Warens... ». L'homme désaccordé se ressaisit dans l'accord musical qui sépare à la fois *Henri Brulard* de *Cécile*, et *la Chartreuse de Parme*, d'*Adolphe*. Ce parfum de violettes aussi mortes que les roses d'Ispahan, qui monte de la triste ville encore appelée Parme, est-ce le souvenir de Fabrice et de Mosca, celui même de la Sanseverina, ou celui de tout un opéra dont chaque mesure chante son unique héroïne, la vie devenue jeunesse? Paradis de passé transfiguré, que le vent qui se lève sur les palais du fleuve éventrés par la guerre porte encore, avec son tourbillon de poussière, vers la Venise de Shakespeare...

L'accord musical du *Pays d'Origine* est celui du réel avec le romanesque de l'imaginaire. Un romanesque non orienté, où la vanité, le prestige, ont peu de place: qui serait la fantaisie si la fantaisie ne se séparait du réel comme le chant se sépare des paroles dans l'opéra-comique. Ici, Fantasio est réellement aussi « le monsieur qui passe », et le monsieur qui passe est aussi Fantasio. On voit sans peine le relief que la constante recherche psychologique peut apporter à une telle optique, relief parent de celui que la psychologie de Stendhal apporte à sa rêverie. D'autant plus que cette recherche n'est pas orientée non plus, et fait de toute vie une aventure, non par les évènements dont elle est faite, mais par sa nature même, au sein d'une énigme universelle qui semble participer à ce ballet. D'où une relation entre l'auteur, son personnage et ses personnages, tour à tour irritée et attendrie, qui fait penser à celle de Cervantès avec don Quichotte, et exprime constamment l'absurde, (en un temps où cette expression n'a pas encore fait fortune) sur le ton inattendu de la complicité. Folie du monde ce romanesque, que Ducroo chaque jour pêche à la ligne en lui-même, en est aussi l'essence. Si précis que soit son passé javanais, il est une interrogation poétique à quoi répond, dans le présent, l'interrogation quotidienne du journal, même la plus concrète, la plus pressante, et qui donne aux meilleures parties de ce livre inégal la complexe cohérence de la création. Aux Champs-Elysées, don Quichotte cite Valéry à Cervantès: « La littérature, profession délirante... » et lui affirme qu'entre employer sa vie à chercher Dulcinée, et l'employer à raconter des histoires, la différence n'est pas si grande; à quoi Cervantès répond que c'est bien possible, mais qu'elle s'appelle *don Quichotte*.

YVES DE BAYSER

AVEC CE MATIN

I

Avec ce matin ensemencé de nuits
Et les multiples yeux du songe
Les pas fauchés et liés
Avec ce monde couvant ses brumes jaunes
Puissant est mon sommeil au pôle des moissons
Joyeuse l'inquiétude. Matin
Ne ferme pas les yeux de mon sommeil
Je te confie les neiges

Ombre des perles violentes
Amour
Fleuris les froides raies de tes odeurs joyeuses
Ligne rude et brisée à l'endroit de l'éclat
Poussière

Je te confie l'azur aux cimes de ce deuil.

II

On connaît la terre à la folie du froid
A l'haleine de l'animal de l'espace
Au visage renié

La rose lui réplique.
Dis que tu es le cœur ô bouche
La terre effleurée.

III

Ici gît le sommeil. Un chasseur le précède. Mort que la terre repousse. Les oiseaux le profanent. Chanson aveugle. L'air appelle à beaux cris le second soleil, ses oiseaux tombés, ses yeux nus. Dans la gorge lointaine on a ravi le cœur, et dans le ciel si bas la famine du feu.

IV

Tu nommes la terre le diamant de jadis. Toi et moi nous venons des pierres dispersées. Les étoiles apprirent le chemin. Devine-les, si près de la terre dérobée, où les chemins se réfugient, gravés dans le ventre, effacés sur les fronts; où le ciel tombe sans aucune lumière. Donne-leur l'apparence, comme au dieu sur le sentier, le coursier naissant, la colline éternelle. Donne les yeux en friche, les yeux curieux de larmes, les mains apprivoisées. Je creuserai ton corps où les oiseaux sont lourds. Que tu es bien dans le paysage séduit, entre les disparus et les agiles, pour la parole rare, ô nuit abandonnée même des murs.

HENRI MICHAUX

VACANCES

SOUS LE NUAGE CIRCULAIRE

J'étais en haute montagne, face à la Zugspitz. Un nuage s'arrêta audessus de moi, qui marchais lentement. Je m'arrêtai aussi. Nous nous arrêtames. Les arbres étaient arbustes sans plus. Les herbes d'été, très siliceuses, fortes et dures, sans peine soutenaient le papier que j'avais tiré de ma poche. Il semblait que le nuage était posé sur un espace audessus de moi comme le papier sur les tiges inflexibles.

Cependant que, tête en arrière, je le considerais, il rappela en mon fond quelque chose, l'objet que j'avais le plus vu, ou c'était lui qui me voyait, car il était — lorsqu'il apparaissait — toujours à la verticale, immense, circulaire, et, en mon enfance venait chaque nuit, semblant profiter que j'étais jeune, inexperimenté, sans personne, pour m'appuyer.

Car, malgré toute sa puissance, sa façon de faire fi de tout, il ne pouvait paraitre que de nuit, lorsque les distractions de la journée passée je coulais à fond. Alors il venait, droit sur moi.

Je ne bougeais plus. Lui non plus, ne bougeait plus. Tout à coup (est-ce qu'il laissait tomber ou se préparait à laisser tomber quelque chose?) je savais que si je ne me réveillais à l'instant même, je n'existais plus. Il me detruisait complêtement.

Sans doute, j'arrivais à me réveiller et très vite, ma vie en dépendant, malgré la fascination, malgré la torpeur... mais j'aurais pu une fois n'être pas assez vite.

Et puis petit à petit, avec l'age, devenant habile, fuyant les émotions, (les émotions tôt ou tard conduisant au face à face), mes nuits se sont faites désertes.

Cependant, sans avoir songé à tout cela, j'étais sous le nuage d'en face la Zugspitz, j'étais en grande sueur et comme dans l'attente d'un immense drame à venir, un drame que je connaissais, que je reconnaissais... lorsque les vents contradictoires qui le retenaient sur place, ayant changé légèrement, emportèrent, et bougrement vite, le nuage qui m'avait tenu fasciné et suant comme sous un fardeau considérable.

RENCONTRE

Un chien me rencontra près du lac. Il m'appela. Je ne le connaissais pas. Je n'avais rien pour lui. Je lui répondis par de bonnes paroles. Il me suivit. Il gratta mon imperméable de ses pattes. Je devins silencieux. Il pleuvait. Par ce temps même un loup, est transi. J'allongeai le pas. La distance entre nous grandit, tandis que de côté et d'autre il furetait. Au dela d'un carrefour, je me trouvai seul. Il m'avait abandonné.

Je rentrai lire. Parfois entre les pages le proche passé me revenait vivement à la memoire. C'était court, comme avait été la rencontre. Une heure passa. J'entendis un gémissement. Très faible. Je connaissais ce gémissement. J'ouvris la porte. Il était là, couché, la tête entre ses pattes, la confiance dans sa tête. Et derechef, faute de biscuit, de bonnes paroles. Il ne paraissait pas désirer entrer dans la chambre. Nous étions dans l'annexe. Il n'était que je sache à personne habitant l'annexe. Venait-il du village?

Porte fermée (il faisait froid dans le couloir), j'avais des repentirs. Et si je l'adoptais? Mais ne suis-je pas un chien moi-même et cherchant on ne sait quoi?

Deux heures après, je sors pour aller diner. Il est là. La

confiance est là devant ma porte, la confiance, éternel maillon de toute chaine. Voilà donc ce que stupidement j'ai fait. Mes bonnes paroles, il les a prises pour un acte d'adoption. Je ne dis plus rien. Nous descendons les degrés de l'escalier. Il pleut. C'est bien ça: il croit à une convention, comme si je l'avais déja signée. Je me dirige vers la salle de restaurant. Soit, je laisse au sort le soin de décider. J'ouvre la porte. Largement. Tiens, il n'a pas suivi. La porte nous sépare. Je reviens sur mes pas. Il y aurait lâcheté à me tirer d'affaire et d'hésitation grâce à une porte que moi je sais ouvrir et non lui. Je le cherche. Il n'est pas dans l'entrée. La cuisine l'aura interceptée. J'y vais, tout à coup commandé par notre étrange alliance. Il n'y est pas. On ne l'a pas vu. On ne le connait pas. Ni au bureau, ni dans l'hotel on ne le connait. Je me tais. Ce que j'ai dit a paru étrange. On me questionne. Je réponds évasivement. Moi même, je me questionne. Enfin ce chien, pourquoi se voulait-il près de moi, sans plus? Une erreur de sa part? Ou que voulait-signifier?

VACANCES

Devant ma chambre auvergnate, il passe souvent des vaches. A côté est une autre chambre, occupée par des voix. Des voix pleines d'assurance. Des voix qui ont passé par le Conservatoire. Sur un vieux répertoire, elles se sont usées. Elles aiment encore à y faire de la gymnastique. Dehors, il pleut. Sans arrêt. Sans arrêt, les chanteurs puisent dans le puit de l'Operette et de l'Opera Comique parfois même du cafcons, à grands seaux grinçants des airs d'autrefois qu'ils croient réjouissants. Parfois une femme se lève et sort. Une voix toulousaine fait alors défaut. Bientôt c'est le retour, et des duos tantôt avec ténor, tantôt avec baryton reprennent avec vigueur.

La montagne en face en a fait et en a subi du gigantesque. Autrefois elle renversait ses terrains comme rien. Maintenant elle est toute calme, incapable d'une secousse à renverser un bébé. Les estivants en profitent.

Les groissiers d'à côté continuent, en despotes, l'occupation de l'espace aux sons. Ils malaxent leur nougat d'Occidental. Parfois ils s'arrêtent un peu, attendant un nouvel afflux de souvenirs vocaux.

On entend alors, venant d'un tout petit bassin naturel aux rares, mourantes vagues, alimenté par un torrent grand comme une orvet, un « chut » d'une extrême retenue, suivi d'un souffle plus discret encore, plus effacé, modulé diversement, selon la grosseur du caillou rencontré, selon l'ampleur du creux formé par les racines d'un saule ou d'un vieil osier. Il y a un instant d'arrêt, et le souffle infime s'éteint, pendant que l'eau revenue couvre le vide avec le son tamisé d'une indicible satisfaction. Pas un homme, pas un être n'aurait pareille délicatesse pour inviter à se taire, et à retrouver dans les délices, la merveilleuse musique de base. Mais *vain* est le signe, complêtement vain. Le Conservatoire a bouché les oreilles.

ECHTE UNGARISCHE BLUTIGELS

... et toujours je revenais dans cette Neuhaustrasse, où dans une vitrine de pharmacien ces êtres qu'on voyait mal, qu'on eût pu prendre pour des serpents, s'ils n'avaient été si plats et rubanés, vivaient d'une vie à part et tout à fait étrange dans le soir éclairé de cette ville trop gaie, où des hommes habillés drôlement, se rassemblaient sur des bancs, par grandes tablées, dans des cafés comme Versailles, pour boire de la bière.

Mais indifférentes aux hommes qui passaient, aux autos, aux nocturnes plaisirs en commun qui à cette heure se préparaient, ces sangsues — car c'en était — séparées par le verre du bocal de l'agitation citadine, séparées par leur organisme fou de sang de la jouissance par la bière, restaient fixées aux parois transparentes.

Les unes dansaient mollement, les autres, la plupart, sans bouger, serrées comme lézards, se livraient au repos et à la méditation ou rêvaient d'un corps blanc, grand comme un étang, mais rouge dès qu'on en a percé la peau, si rouge, si délicieux, si fortifiant.

Est-ce qu'aucune ne suce jamais le sang d'une autre, match à qui sucera le plus vite, à qui sucera à fond, à qui sucera jusqu'à l'étourdissement, à qui sucera à mort? Je ne sais. Je ne sais jamais rien de ce que je voudrais savoir.

Tranquille était leur danse souple, façon feuille flottante de sagittaire, sauf en trois ou quatre, jamais plus, qui folles de vitesse soulevant la tête à la manière d'un serpent naja, puis l'abaissant, la relevant encore, vite, vite, follement, prodigieusement vite, paraissaient, dans une perpetuelle, mysterieuse prosternation, adresser humbles et vaines prières à leur dieu indifférent qui les oubliait dans la vitrine de cette strasse aseptique.

Elan extraordinaire, rapidité extraordinaire, dévotions extraordinaires. Petit était le bocal, mais grave comme une Collegiale.

Parfois une du groupe des tranquilles, tout à coup, lâchant le petit mur de verre, décollait prestement, filait en souplesse comme une anguille n'a jamais filé, ni surtout pas un phoque, ni une loutre n'a ondulé, montrant en éclairs les rayures jaunes et vertes de son dos nerveux de panthère admirablement lisse (l'autre face est de couleur unie) et glissait, ruban dangereux et passionné dans le lac du petit bocal mal éclairé. Une vague envie me venait... mais je ne suis pas un cheval. D'ailleurs, je ne m'étais pas rendu si loin, à des centaines de lieues de chez moi, pour rester le nez à la vitre d'une boutique de pharmacien. Je m'en détachai donc, me hâtant dans la direction de la brasserie que l'on m'avait specialement recommandé de visiter, où, dans de grandes salles boisées pour le rebondissement des rires et des propos joyeux, l'atmosphère étant chaude, et dense la joie d'être ensemble et comme frères, la bière, à tous commune, étendait son pouvoir et son volume dans les corps humains qui ne sont pas infinis. Il y avait de continuelles allées et venues. La musique tombant de l'estrade se répandait, chaud champignon de sons, voguait entre les oreilles satisfaites, orgues sur la plénitude des vessies.

Moi, cependant, ne goûtant pas la boisson qu'est-ce que je faisais là? Le temps de me faire la leçon et j'étais parti, marchant à grandes enjambées vers le bocal de mystère de la Neuhausstrasse, derrière la vitrine aux médicaments, savamment éclairée, mais pas autant que je l'aurais voulu, ni qu'il l'aurait fallu, et je me collais le visage à la vitre froide de l'autre coté de laquelle le désir et l'attention me portait tumultueusement.

Quelle femme à portée de main, ou seulement à portée de regard ondulera jamais, en quelque lieu que ce soit, si nerveuse, si merveilleuse, si totalement incompréhensible?

CHASSE DANS UNE GARE

C'était à la gare St. Lazare. Un moineau cherchait vainement en ce jour de Pâques à attraper un virevoltant insecte que je ne pus, à cette distance, identifier, et que, sans la chasse de l'oiseau et sans de ci delà un rajon de soleil, je n'aurais jamais apercu.

Le grand voleteur poursuivait le tout petit qui feintait, chutait, se retournait, se relevait et soudain lui moucheronnait le dos. Alors le passereau ulcéré s'arrêtait, se perchait sur l'ornement ridicule d'un montant de fer mille neuf cent, en basculant follement sa tête ébouriffée qui ne craint pas les vertiges auriculaires.

Mais un insecte ne va pas loin, même dans la liberté. Un rayon décroché dans une éclaircie subite le demasquait. Le moineau, l'espoir revenu, le reprenait en chasse, plongeait, filait, virait, toujours trop fort, brutalement pour l'insecte qui, lui, fait ça très glissando, et sans perdre la tête, qu'il a pourtant si petite qu'elle échappe à ma vue. La poursuite continue, éveillée sans doute par la faim matinale. Cette fois, on va l'attraper le petit, quand sur son rail inflexible, le rapide du Cherbourg entrant en gare à cinquante kilomètres à l'heure, soulève providentiellement l'insecte, le derobant à son poursuivant surpris, tandis que doucement prenant de la vitesse, mon train m'emporte fatigué, mais décidement allègre vers les vacances, la vie sauve, les vacances encore une fois.

LES PLATEAUX DE LA BALANCE

Je vais à la mer hors saisons pour être seul, mais il fait froid, trop froid. Il s'ensuit un bourdonnement insupportable dans ma tête, le bourdonnement du problème que j'agite « si je reste, ou si je vais m'en aller ».

Les voix de la nature se mêlent en mille murmures à mon embarras.

Voilà pourquoi mes voyages sont si fatiguants. Sur les deux plateaux de la balance, les poids sont constamment changés, déplacés, replacés, déplacés, replacés, si bien que je vois venir le soir comme si j'avais dans la journée, soulevé des tombereaux ou poussé aux roues. Quels tombereaux? Quelles roues? Est-ce que je sais, moi? ...et je m'abats sur le lit, anéanti.

Cependant les poids changent encore de plateau, mais doucement, à partir de ce moment, doucement. Je les retrouverai, arrêtés, le lendemain « dans l'ordre » de la fatalité.

A demain, donc .....

DIRECTION: INDES

Toujours hésitant, avant d'aller aux Indes pour la deuxième fois, je m'entretiens constamment avec moi-même, me poussant tantôt à y aller, tantôt à n'y aller pas, et m'en faisant un monde, pays somme toute nouveau, où n'est plus mon ami, où son fils gêne du père, comme d'un enfant d'autrefois, un enfant lourd, arrière, enténébré, me va gêner aussi.

En attendant, je vis un jour avec le « oui », le lendemain avec le « non » — avec l'argent du voyage, hélas jamais — et j'y envoie des gens.

Tous ceux que je vois flaner, je les envoie là-bas, je les y pousse. Je les assoiffe de l'Inde et ils ne savent plus comment vivre, s'ils n'y volent au plus vite.

S'il n'en est pas parti un plus grand nombre, c'est que le formidable aimant de l'Hindoustan n'agit pas également sur tous. Tous, néanmoins seront poussés et je les rendrai envoutés et anxieux, comme moi, pour l'Inde que je ne verrai peut-être jamais plus.

Il est vrai aussi que j'ai peur, ou aversion, ou malaise, car il y a partout — et je ne dois pas l'oublier, — en quelque pays ou l'on pénètre une sorte de tension superficielle qu'il faut forcer. Désagréable! désagréable! Vous avancez et la résistance est là, contre vous, ne cédant pas, comme le public d'un bar, où vient d'entrer un buveur d'eau ou un pasteur.

J'ai pourtant tellement besoin de voyager. Ah, si je pouvais vivre en télésiège, toujours avançant, toujours en de nouveaux pays, progressant sur des espaces de grand silence.

LA NUIT VENUE, DANS AVILA

... et j'entrai dans un merveilleux irréel. En effet, Avila, où j'étais arrivé dans le soir, à cette heure tardive, sous un ciel bourré d'étoiles, comme un dessin de fou, pur plateau hautement fortifié, était composé de quatre absurdités.

D'abord, elle était entourée de tous côtés par la mer. Une mer de lait. Sans doute, des faits dans ma mémoire entrent en rebellion, se mettent à discuter. La mer, en ces lieux! N'empêche, la mer est là, entourant de tous côtés la noble ville, fermé de rempart, où je marche dans les hauteurs.

Les bruits de la ville sortent et ne reviennent pas, l'abîme autour les garde.

Deuxième absurdité. Par moments, d'une sorte de baie

qu'on devine viennent des croassements de grenouille. Des grenouilles dans la mer!

Troisième absurdité. Au loin, la grande barrière de glace de l'Antarctique.

Quatrième absurdité. Entre sept et neuf heures du soir, vingt mille perroquets paraissent, habillés en hommes et un plus grand nombre en femmes, jacassent, puis disparaissent tous ensemble dans les pierres.

Passé dix heures, vous avez l'Antarctique pour vous seul. Vous pouvez en profiter jusqu'au lendemain. Mais la cuisine épaisse comme du goudron que vous venez d'avaler vous blige à regagner l'hotel et à soigner votre ventre comme un enfant. Les bonnes paroles ne suffisent pas. Il faut le rentrer.

Non, on ne peut faire cela. Déjà on revient sur ses pas. Il serait fou de se détacher du spectacle inoui (dont on ne veut savoir l'explication, si explication il y a) qui — sait-on jamais? — pourrait n'avoir pas de lendemain.

L'air est pur et glacé, immobile, destiné a la contemplation et parfaitement sec.

Sur la tête, le ciel d'Arabie, le ciel qui fit les astronomes de la Chaldée, un ciel où toutes les étoiles qu'on peut voir à l'oeil nu sont là, là au dessus des ramparts de cette ville haute, de cette ville sans vis à vis, de cette ville-plateau qui — pas d'autre issue — vous projette sur Dieu.

Le matin, cartes consultées, on s'apercevra que se sont les crètes enneigées de Monts Gredos, un des plus beaux spectacles qui soient.

Ah, toutes ces villes basses de par le monde, où l'on vit enfoui dans les autres, dans les échos et les rebondissements continuels des paroles vaines, dix mille fois marié, traversé, retenu, piegé! De toutes, celle-ci en un soir ne dégageait, me lavait, me débarrassait, guérissant la vieille plaie. Je respirais, je montais. Je vivais en hauteur sur cet autel admirable, unique, où d'autres en d'autres temps, sachant y faire (y répondre) eussent offert un sensationnel sacrifice.

Moi-même ne devais-je pas...? Mais qui choisir comme offrande? Je voyais seulement un mulet et trois ânes, qui par les ruelles se dirigeaient vers la grande porte des muletiers. Le ciel accepterait-il un âne en offrande? Douteux! Et je ne vois pas de vaches. Car si même la surface qui s'étale au pied de notre plateau n'est pas la mer, elle est, sauf un jardinet ou deux entr'aperçus dans la brume basse du soir, elle est un désert. Donc, pas de vaches. Quelques chèvres. Pas assez, pour la dalle immense du sacrifice.

Restent les vierges, offrande de choix, en tous temps. Mais des vierges bavardes, qui vont au cinéma, qui sont allées au cinéma, qui ne rêvent que d'aller au cinéma voir des garçons langoureux aux baisers fondus et gluants...

Mieux, à n'importe quel dieu offrir le silence, le silence à présent total, monastériel dans l'air froid sous mille étoiles, face à l'antarctique.

Le silence.

NOTRE PAUVRE REINE

Etrange est notre sol, étrange est notre air. Il nous retire notre chaleur. Il nous retire nos couleurs. L'eau qui nous permet de vivre. Nous fait lentement mourir.

Nos maisons sont petites, nos pièces sont des armoires. Les étrangers se demandent comment nous pouvons y loger. Que répondre? C'est le logement qui nous convient, je suppose.

Nous arrivons jamais à nous sentir grands. Le vent est là. Dès que nous mettons le pied dehors, il est là, le vent qui griffe nos âmes. Il n'excite pas. Seulement il retire les forces. Défaut qui va s'ajouter à nos autres défauts.

Ici, se place l'histoire de notre reine. Nous avions pensé nous sauver de notre misérable condition, en ayant nous aussi une reine, une reine de rêve, exempte de nos maux. Miracle: Trouvée, elle accepta. L'intronisation se fit dans la ferveur, dans des fêtes sur l'eau, dans l'odeur d'anguille fumée, gratuite ce jour là par ordre de la Reine et abondant et le peuple était heureux. Peut-être y eut-il exagérations, à cause de l'odeur du poisson qui est tenace, qui tenait toute la ville jusqu'à la robe du couronnement et ne s'en alla pas d'une semaine entière. Sur grand place, une couronne, une énorme couronne et telle que, se trouvant dessous, par milliers il y avait encore de la place. Comme les pauvres en grandeur, nout étions heureux de cette royauté.

Et puis du temps a passé. Un temps pas tres considérable et puis c'est arrivé. Comment est-ce arrivé? Comment cela a-t-il pû se faire, et ne l'a-t-on pas pû empêcher? Enfin, il fallut s'écraser contre le mur: La Reine avait contracté notre mal. Terrible le grossissement. Atroce la prolifération. Mais nous n'avons rien dit.

D'autres peuples ont eu plus de chance avec leur reine. Ici tout est difficile. Nous ne sommes pas un peuple de ténors.

Mais telle qu'elle nous l'aimons notre grosse, laide reine.

YVES BONNEFOY

HUIT POÈMES

LE JARDIN

Tu cesses de venir dans ce jardin,
Les chemins de l'argent, de l'étain s'effacent,
Les herbes signifient ton visage mort.

Il ne t'importe plus que soient cachés
Sous la pierre l'église obscure, dans les arbres
Le visage aveuglé d'un plus rouge soleil,

Il te suffit
De mourir longuement comme en sommeil,
Tu n'aimes même plus la nuit que tu épouses.

L'ARBRE

L'oiseau qui s'est dépris d'être Phénix
S'est retiré dans l'arbre pour mourir.
Il s'est enveloppé de la nuit de blessure,
Il ne sent pas l'épée qui pénètre son coeur.

Comme l'huile a vieilli et noirci dans les lampes,
Comme tant de chemins que nous étions, perdus,
Il fait un lent retour à la matière d'arbre.

Il sera bien un jour,
Il saura bien un jour être la bête morte,
L'absence au col tranché que dévore le sang.

Il tombera dans l'herbe, ayant trouvé
Dans l'herbe le profond de toute vérité,
Le goût du sang battra de vagues son rivage.

LE SOL

Tu te coucheras sur la terre simple,
De qui tenais-tu qu'elle t'appartînt?

Du ciel inchangé l'errante lumière
Recommencera l'éternel matin.

Tu croiras renaître aux heures profondes
Du feu renoncé, du feu mal éteint.

Mais l'ange viendra, de ses mains de cendre,
Apaiser les feux du monde enfantin.

VENERANDA

Il vient, et c'est vieillir. Parce qu'il te regarde,
Il regarde sa mort qui se déclare en toi.
Il aime que ce bien que tu es le menace,
Regarde-le dormir sous tes grands arbres froids.

Il a confiance, il dort. Arbre de peu d'alarme
Que soit ton coeur anxieux de ne l'éveiller pas
— Arbre où viendra le nom et l'oeuvre de la flamme
Sur l'échafaud d'un corps qui ne tremblera pas.

LE VISAGE

Aube, fille des larmes, rétablis
La chambre dans sa paix de chose grise
Et le coeur dans son ordre. Tant de nuit
Demandait à ce feu qu'il décline et s'achève,
Il nous faut bien veiller près du visage mort.
A peine a-t-il changé... Le navire des lampes
Entrera-t-il au port qu'il avait demandé,
Sur les tables d'ici la flamme faite cendre
Grandira-t-elle ailleurs dans une autre clarté?
Toi viens, soulève, prends ce visage de cire,
Regarde-le rougir de l'or du faible jour.

LES GUETTEURS

Il y avait un couloir au fond du jardin,
Je rêvais que j'allais dans ce couloir,
La mort venait avec ses fleurs hautes flétries,
Je rêvais que je lui prenais ce bouquet noir.

Il y avait une étagère dans ma chambre,
J'entrais au soir,
Et je voyais deux femmes racornies
Crier debout sur le bois peint de noir.

Il y avait un escalier et je rêvais
Qu'au milieu de la nuit un chien hurlait
Dans cet espace de nul chien et je voyais
Un horrible chien blanc sortir de l'ombre.

LE PONT DE FER

Il y a sans doute toujours au bout d'une longue rue
Ou je marchais enfant, une mare d'huile,
Un rectangle de lourde mort sous le ciel noir.

Depuis la poésie
A séparé ses eaux des autres eaux,
Nulle beauté nulle couleur ne la retiennent,
Elle s'angoisse pour du fer et de la nuit.
Elle nourrit

Un long chagrin de rive morte, un pont de fer
Jeté vers l'autre rive encore plus nocturne
Est sa seule mémoire et son seul vrai amour.

LE RAVIN

Tu sauras qu'un oiseau a chanté, plus haut
Que tout arbre réel, plus simplement
Que toute voix dans nos tristes ramures,
Et tu demanderas de quitter le port
De ces arbres d'ici, de pierre ou cendre.
Tu marcheras,
Tes pas seront de boue et nuit, de terre obscure,
Et lui taira son chant de rive en rive, étant
La passion qui t'enchaîne et qui te perd.

ANDRÉ DHÔTEL

LES NUITS DE MALMONT

Jacques Tudais occupait depuis quelques mois un emploi d'ingénieur chimiste à l'usine de carrelages d'Aigly. Il s'accommoda très bien de la vie un peu ennuyeuse du bourg, ayant passé la plus grande part de sa jeunesse dans sa famille à Bermont, qui est une ville à peine plus grande et guère plus animée qu'Aigly. Il employa ses loisirs à des parties de chasse ou de pêche, et son plus grand plaisir fut de parcourir les environs sur sa moto pendant les longues soirées d'été. Parfois il s'arrêtait dans une auberge, à la buvette d'une gare, ou bien il allait au cinéma de Bermont et il rentrait assez tard. Une nuit, en revenant au bourg, comme il longeait la route qui contourne Seneux, il aperçut les lumières d'une fête au fond du val où est bâti le village. Il se détourna de son chemin pour aller flâner sur la place de Seneux parmi les gens qui circulaient devant les boutiques vivement éclairées.

Quand on sort de la campagne obscure pour pénétrer dans l'enceinte d'une fête paysanne, on n'est pas surpris par une agitation qui contraste avec le calme environnant. Bien au contraire c'est le silence qui vous étreint. Il semble que les lumières, les voix, le crépitement rare du tir, la musique du bal n'arriveront jamais à rompre la puissance de la nuit qui tombe des étoiles et s'avance dans les ruelles, les jardins et les champs proches. Jacques avait rangé sa machine contre le mur de l'école. Il s'avança du côté du bal.

Il n'avait pas le désir de danser. Il regarda un moment les couples qui allaient et venaient sur le gazon. Comme il détournait les yeux, il aperçut une jeune fille assise sur un petit mur, à la limite du terrain de bal. Une des lampes du pourtour éclairait sa robe et sa chevelure. Jacques devina qu'elle était belle.

La danse finissait. Une autre allait commencer. Un jeune homme vint inviter la fille qui refusa. Deux autres se présentèrent auprès desquels elle s'excusa de nouveau. Jacques se dit qu'il ne risquait rien de l'inviter lui-même pour la danse suivante. Ce serait une occasion de la voir de plus près. A sa surprise elle accepta.

Son visage avait une beauté singulière, non pas des traits parfaits mais une gentillesse timide et insouciante, comme une clarté. Jacques la conduisit au milieu du bal avant de prendre sa main pour la faire danser. Il lui dit quelques mots, expliquant qu'il était un étranger et qu'il se trouvait tout à fait par hasard sur ce bal. Elle lui apprit qu'elle-même venait d'un pays voisin, mais elle se tut quand il lui demanda où elle habitait. A la fin de la danse elle déclara qu'elle devait s'en aller. Il était bientôt minuit, et elle avait promis à sa mère de rentrer tôt.

— Vous êtes seule? s'étonna Jacques.

Après avoir salué son cavalier, elle se dirigea vers l'école où elle avait rangé son vélomoteur. Jacques s'avança de nouveau vers elle.

— Je puis vous accompagner sur ma moto..., avec votre permission, dit-il. Si vous allez loin, c'est peut-être mieux.

— Pas très loin, répondit-elle. Non, ne venez pas, je vous en prie.

Elle enfourcha sa machine et s'éloigna. Jacques vit la petite lumière se perdre dans la côte. Il entendit aussitôt deux jeunes gens qui riaient entre eux.

— Méfie-toi des filles de Malmont, disait l'un.

Jacques ne sut si c'était de la jeune fille qu'il parlait. Il regagna Aigly. Les semaines suivantes, il s'informa des fêtes qui se donnaient dans les environs et ne manqua pas d'aller faire un tour sur chacun des bals le dimanche soir et même parfois le lundi et le mardi, quand les fêtes se prolongeaient. Il visita ainsi Charbeuil, Perarges, Saint-Loup. Un dimanche il retrouva la jeune fille à Perarges. Elle se tenait, comme elle l'avait fait à Seneux, un peu à l'écart du bal, et elle refusait les invitations. Cette fois elle n'accepta pas la sienne. Aussitôt qu'elle se fut excusée, elle s'éloigna. Pourtant elle lui avait répondu sur un ton charmant. Jacques éprouva un serrement de coeur. Il se jura de la retrouver encore et de la presser de questions.

Il la revit de façon inattendue vers la fin de juillet dans une rue d'Aigly. Elle sortait d'un magasin où il s'apprêtait à entrer. Il voulut l'aborder, mais elle lui jeta un regard sauvage et cria: « Allez-vous-en! » d'une voix altérée et mauvaise. Son visage paraissait encore plus beau qu'il ne l'était à la lueur des quinquets, mais ce regard, cette voix démentaient à tel point la bonté profonde qu'il avait éprouvée venant d'elle, lors de leurs rencontres précédentes, qu'il demeura incapable de proférer un mot. Depuis ce jour il ne cessa de penser à elle.

Il décida de surveiller pendant toutes ses heures de liberté la place et les rues avoisinantes. Les commerces sont groupés au centre d'Aigly et il ne pouvait manquer d'apercevoir celle qu'il cherchait. Il la rencontra un soir à la nuit tombée. Elle entrait dans une épicerie-buvette qui restait ouverte très tard. Cette fois elle lui répondit avec la plus grande douceur. Elle était pressée, lui dit-elle. Non elle n'allait plus sur les bals. Il y avait du travail à la maison. Jacques l'accompagna jusqu'à l'angle de la place. Soudain elle dit: « Laissez-moi ». Il s'écarta d'elle, puis il se ravisa. Il la prit dans ses bras et lui donna un baiser. Elle-même lui avait doucement offert ses lèvres. Aussitôt elle se sauva et gagna une petite ruelle.

Elle n'habitait pas Aigly, il en était sûr. Jacques interrogea les commerçants, qui lui firent des réponses ambigues: « Une étrangère, une passante... » Il semblait qu'on ne voulût pas parler d'elle. Pourtant, si elle faisait ses provisions à Aigly, elle ne devait pas venir de très loin. Le surlendemain il la rencontra chez le boulanger, juste à midi. Elle le traîta cette fois avec mépris et même une sorte de haine et lui tourna le dos. Il la poursuivit.

— Ne comprenez-vous pas..., dit-il.

— C'est vous qui ne comprenez pas, vous qui ne savez pas, répondit-elle avec violence.

— Si vous avez quelque ennui, je suis prêt à le partager. Pourquoi, maintenant...

— Allez-vous-en!

Vers le milieu du mois d'août il la surprit de nouveau. C'était dans l'après-midi du samedi. Au lieu d'aller vers elle, il la suivit de loin. Il faisait un temps chaud et pénible. Le bourg était désert. Elle gagna la rue de la Couture et fut bientôt dans la campagne. Elle prit un sentier vers la gauche. Alors il courut et la rejoignit.

Le sentier montait une côte rapide. En haut de la côte s'élevaient les maisons d'un hameau que Jacques avait déjà aperçu en passant sur la route. On y accédait d'ordinaire par un chemin qu'il n'avait jamais eu l'occasion de suivre.

— C'est là que vous allez, dit-il.

Elle s'était tournée, quand elle avait entendu ses pas. Ses regards étaient brillants d'orgueil et péniblement durs et perfides. Elle répondit sur un ton railleur :

— Je vais à Malmont, c'est sûr.

— Je n'ai jamais entendu ce nom, observa Jacques trop heureux d'avoir pu engager l'entretien.

— On dit Bel Air le plus souvent, mais c'est Malmont. Allez-vous-en !

Il assura qu'il était décidé à l'accompagner, quelle que fût son opposition :

— Je désire...

Elle l'interrompit :

— Si vous voulez. Mais vous n'êtes pas au bout de vos peines.

— Que pensez-vous qui puisse arriver?

Elle reprit sa marche. Il lui emboita le pas. Le sentier franchissait une légère butte avant d'aboutir à l'extrêmité en impasse de la petite rue du hameau. Sur un terrain très inégal s'élevaient quatre maisons assez grandes. Deux d'entre elles comportaient grange et communs, mais une seule présentait l'animation d'une ferme avec ses volailles et des porcs qui reniflaient au seuil de la cour. Du haut de la butte on apercevait aussi la pente abrupte sur le canal et plus loin que les maisons c'était un plateau avec des cultures coupées de buissons. Malgré l'élévation du lieu on sentait l'odeur des herbes de marécages, et il y avait des nuées de moustiques.

Entre la butte et la rue se dressait un grand orme qui était mort pour moitié. Une pie était perchée sur l'une des branches mortes. Comme Jacques et la jeune fille passaient devant l'arbre, on entendit un coup de feu et la pie tomba.

— C'est Bertache, dit la jeune fille.

— Il aurait pu aussi bien blesser un de nous deux, d'où il était placé, dit Jacques.

— Cela lui est égal. Un accident, qu'est-ce que cela peut faire?

Bertache, un homme d'une cinquantaine d'années, vint ramasser la pie sans faire attention aux nouveaux venus, puis il jeta l'oiseau dans les jambes de Jacques.

— Ce sont ses plaisanteries, dit la jeune fille.

Jacques commençait à trouver le lieu bizarre.

— Allez-vous-en! ajouta-t-elle sur un ton de défi.

Cela le décida à persévérer. Ils arrivèrent au seuil de la première maison qui était comme une ferme désaffectée. Une femme parut.

— Qui est-ce que tu nous ramènes? s'écria-t-elle.

— Ce monsieur a voulu me suivre.

— Te suivre! Qu'il entre! Nous allons nous expliquer.

Sur cette invitation, Jacques pénétra dans une cuisine sombre et assez bien tenue.

— Vous n'êtes pas le premier, dit la femme. Mais je ne donnerai pas ma fille à n'importe qui.

— Je ne pensais pas... murmura Jacques.

— Vous pensiez plutôt à vous amuser et à la séduire. Il n'en est pas question. Vous l'épouserez si vous avez une situation convenable. Qu'est-ce que vous faites dans la vie?

— Je ne comprends pas..., protesta Jacques. Je venais simplement pour... Je ne sais pas..., mais peut-être...

— C'est entendu. D'abord il faut que vous connaissiez nos habitudes, trancha la mère.

Elle déclara qu'elle appartenait à la famille Demart et que depuis la mort de son mari, il y avait entre elle et les Vortoux (ceux qui tenaient la ferme en activité), une haine qui n'était pas près de s'éteindre. En descendant sur le canal on rencontrait une villa que Jacques n'avait pas pu voir. Cette villa, bâtie par un vieux cousin commun aux Demart et aux Vortoux, avait été léguée à M. Demart mais cette déclaration d'héritage coincidant avec la mort de ce dernier, les Vortoux s'étaient opposés à ce qu'elle passât à la veuve. On plaidait depuis cinq ans. En outre les Vortoux avaient juré que leur fille habiterait cette maison et qu'elle se marierait avant Violette.

— Violette, ma fille, trouvera à se marier quand elle voudra, vous m'entendez? Mais je tiens à ce que mon gendre habite la maison là bas, au nez des Vortoux. C'est ma première condition. Que faites-vous dans la vie?

Jacques se trouvait désorienté. Au lieu de répondre, il regarda la jeune fille qui se tenait debout près de l'évier, nullement honteuse des déclarations de sa mère. Son visage exprimait l'insolence et elle avait une telle attitude que son corps semblait brûler de passion. Ainsi on l'appelait Violette, et quand il l'avait rencontrée sur les bals et aussi à l'épicerie buvette tout en elle était douceur et pureté. Il n'avait pu rêver cela et il ne comprenait pas le vulgaire cynisme qu'elle affectait aujourd'hui.

— C'est vous qui avez exigé de venir jusqu'ici, dit Violette. J'ai pourtant cherché à me débarrasser de vous. Mais vous me guettiez sans cesse.

— Je veux bien vous débarrasser de moi, dit Jacques. J'ai eu tort c'est sûr.

— Vous débarrasser, s'écria la mère. Et vous pensez qu'on peut presser une jeune fille avec insistance et l'envoyer promener par simple caprice?

— Un traquenard, murmura Jacques.

Il fit mine de s'en aller. Alors Bertache entra sans prévenir dans la cuisine. Il avait son fusil sur l'épaule. Il saisit aussitôt le jeune homme par le bras.

— Je dois vous expliquer, monsieur, que je suis l'allié de Mme Demart. La semaine dernière elle a eu la bonté d'empoisonner le chien de la mère Jecros, qui est une ancienne fiancée à moi, et qui m'a éconduit autrefois, mais qui ne s'est jamais mariée vous m'entendez bien, parce que je ne l'ai pas voulu. Plus tard elle a réfléchi que je n'étais pas un si mauvais parti, mais c'était trop tard.

— On se demande comment on peut rester dans ce pays, s'écria Jacques, la mère Jecros et vous tous.

— Vous ne connaissez pas Malmont, jeune homme, reprit Bertache. Nous détestons ce pays, mais nous y sommes attachés. On ne peut pas s'en aller de Malmont, me comprenez-vous?

— Vous me dégoûtez tout simplement. Adieu, dit Jacques.

L'homme lui serra le poignet avec plus de force.

— Vous irez à vos affaires quand on vous le permettra. Personne ne vous a forcé à venir ici. Alors, écoutez-moi bien...

Violette demeurait toute raidie. Les épaules rejetées en arrière, elle paraissait se réjouir profondément de cette scène.

— Ici, reprit Bertache, c'est un pays où le soleil brûle les plantes, où viennent les mauvais orages avec la grêle, et les brouillards qui réduisent tout en eau. Mais nous aimons notre vie mauvaise. Enragés! Nous vivons tous dans la rage. Vous savez que dans la maison que vous habiterez avec Violette, il y a un nid de frelons.

— Je n'habiterai jamais, dit Jacques.

— Un nid de frelons, poursuivit l'homme. Trois seulement peuvent donner la mort. Il n'y a pas chez nous un insecte qui ne soit plus méchant qu'ailleurs. Vous tâcherez de vous débarrasser de ce nid. Mais vous ferez encore attention au lait que vous boirez, parce qu'il faut bien aller chercher le lait chez les Vortoux, qui nous en donnent volontiers avec l'espoir de nous empoisonner un jour. Il vous faut avoir des chats. Vous faites boire un chat avant vous. Trois sont déjà morts chez moi, et quatre dans cette maison.

Jacques résolut de le laisser parler et de fuir dès qu'il le pourrait. C'était simplement une bande de fous. Il regarda encore le visage de Violette. Il fut surpris par l'éclat de ses yeux. En depit de leur orgueil, ils restaient très beaux et rayonnaient d'une pensée insaisissable. Que pouvait-il y avoir de merveilleux dans une fille qui ne s'était refusée que pour en venir à un vulgaire marché où entraient en jeu les histoires les plus laides?

— Vous voulez partir? dit Bertache. Mais partez, bon petit jeune homme. Nous saurons vous retrouver. Informez-vous bien. Vous nous croyez ordinaires et insensés. Vous ne connaissez pas encore Malmont. Il y a eu des batailles ici pendant la guerre. Certains sont morts en combattant dans leurs champs contre tout espoir. C'est par miracle que nous avons il avait affaire. Mais justement cela n'était pas possible parce que la jeune fille avait joué l'innocente avec un naturel incroyable.

Le premier dimanche de septembre il revit Violette sur un bal éloigné. Dès qu'il l'aperçut il s'écarta, mais par un hasard elle-même prenait au même instant le parti de quitter le bal et il la croisa devant une boutique. Elle s'inclina légèrement, sourit et passa. C'était un sourire sincère comme un sourire d'enfant. Rien que de l'avoir vue et de s'en souvenir, il passa trois jours de bonheur paisible. Il comprit qu'aucune raison ne pouvait le détacher de cette jeune fille, quelle qu'elle fût. Il fallait attendre que la passion s'éteignît. Cependant il s'obstinait à chercher ce que signifiait une telle alternance de douceur lumineuse et de méchanceté stupide et avare. Cette question le hanta beaucoup plus que la vague angoisse qu'il avait conçue à propos des accidents qui le menaçaient, aux dires de la buraliste. Il passait tous ses moments de liberté à marcher au hasard dans la campagne. Souvent il imaginait que Violette apparaîtrait au tournant d'un buisson, qu'elle se jetterait dans ses bras, qu'ils partiraient ensemble loin de Malmont. Simple folie, se disait-il.

Les jours devenaient plus courts, mais la chaleur se prolongeait encore très longtemps dans la nuit. Un de ces soirs tout emplis de la grâce des pommiers mûrissants que l'ombre et le clair de lune mêlés envahissaient, il prit le sentier de Malmont.

Dans le hameau, tout était désert et silencieux. Pas de lumière dans les maisons. Les chiens devaient dormir. On entendait simplement un bruit de chaines dans l'écurie des Vortoux. Jacques s'approcha d'une porte, puis d'une autre. Il ne perçut pas un murmure. A cette heure peu tardive ce profond silence était inexplicable. Il contourna la maison de Violette. Il chercha à s'en approcher par le jardin, mais il s'embarrassa dans un tel fouillis de ronces qu'il dut s'éloigner. Il se retrouva au bord de la pente qui descend au canal, près d'un treillage. Il vit des ombres se dessiner dans l'herbe haute de chaque côté du treillage. Il s'avança. Quelqu'un parlait:

— Clémence, ma chère Clémence, ton père le disait toujours, ces poires de notre verger sont un miracle. Déjà mûres survécu. Mais nous ne cesserons jamais de nous quereller, et nous ne laisserons personne se moquer de nous.

Jacques sut à peine comment il sortit et dévala le sentier. Au moment où il quittait la maison la mère s'était élancée derrière lui et avait crié:

— Nous sommes des misérables, mais vous nous rendrez raison.

Il crut entendre Violette répéter en écho: « Nous sommes des misérables ».

Il ne respira que lorsqu'il fut sur la place d'Aigly. Le lendemain et les jours suivants il réfléchit à son aventure, et il parvint à obtenir de la buraliste quelques renseignements sur Malmont:

— Vous avez courtisé l'une des deux filles de Malmont? s'exclama la dame. Vous n'êtes peut-être guère enclin à l'epouser, si vous avez visité Malmont. Mais sachez que ces gens ne vous laisseront jamais en paix.

— Ils peuvent faire ce qu'ils voudront, déclara Jacques.

— Ils feront ce qu'ils voudront. Ils vous tueront peut-être. Il y a déjà eu quelques accidents aux environs du hameau depuis une vingtaine d'années. La mère Delmart et sa fille Violette ont mis un feu autrefois à Aigly. Rien ne les arrête.

— On laisse ces fous en liberté?

La vieille buraliste soupira.

— Personne n'y peut rien, dit-elle. Ils sont capables aussi de travailler, de rendre service. En tout cas la moindre affaire s'envenime dans leur pays. A Aigly on n'est pas tendre non plus, mais il n'y a pas de comparaison. Gardez-vous bien, monsieur.

Jacques avait résolu de ne jamais plus songer ni à Malmont ni à la fille. Il coupa court aux histoires que Mme Delmart chercha à mettre en jeu auprès de sa famille à Bermont, et même auprès du directeur de l'usine. Vers la fin du mois d'août, comme il revenait d'une course en moto avant la tombée du jour, il essuya un coup de feu. Il porta plainte vainement à la gendarmerie. Aucune preuve, et personne ne voulait entreprendre une enquête inextricable. Il en résulta que Jacques éprouva un véritable dégoût pour la région d'Aigly et songea à trouver un emploi à Bermont. Sa famille cependant lui donnait tort. Il aurait dû comprendre tout de suite à qui au début de septembre, dorées et sans une tache. Ce sont les premières que je te donne.

— Il faut en garder pour toi, Emmeline. Tu ne gardes rien pour toi. Je t'ai choisi un beau coq pour la fête d'Aigly. Je te le préparerai. Tu n'as guère le temps. Toujours à travailler dans les champs avec Violette.

— Mais cette maison du canal, pourquoi ne la veux-tu pas pour Sylvie et son mari plus tard? La nôtre est bien assez grande. Les histoires d'héritage ne signifient rien.

— Vortoux me disait tout à l'heure...

Oui c'étaient la mère Demart et la Vortoux. Il y avait dans leurs voix ce même charme qui animait les paroles de Violette, lorsqu'il avait rencontré la jeune fille sur le bal de Seneux. Dans le calme de la nuit ces mots de paix avaient une force bouleversante. Jacques ne parvenait pas à croire.

— Oui, Vortoux va mieux. Il dort. Combien de nuits, Emmeline, as-tu passées avec moi pour le veiller!

— Tu es venue soigner Violette, toi aussi l'an dernier.

Puis elles rappelèrent des souvenirs, mais c'étaient toujours des souvenirs d'évènements nocturnes et de veillées. Elles parlèrent du mois passé où tous les gens du hameau allaient pêcher à la lanterne dans le canal. On revenait vers minuit, et on chantait à mi-voix. Et dans les années anciennes c'étaient des parties de chasse au sanglier, les bals, les longs retours sur les routes, où l'on bavardait sans fin, et quand on se taisait on priait en regardant les étoiles.

— Lorsque Violette sera mariée, on fera encore de belles promenades, et il y aura des fêtes.

— Sylvie se mariera avant elle, je l'espère, disait la mère Demart. Violette est encore bien jeune.

A Jacques il sembla que tout était sens dessus dessous. Il avait le sentiment d'une vérité criante et qu'il ne saisirait jamais. Il se fraya un chemin dans les herbes pour s'éloigner des deux femmes. Peut-être allait-il rencontrer Violette. Il y avait dans l'air un repos plein de fraîcheur qui donnait une vie nouvelle aux moindres fibres du corps. La nuit était si tempérée, si dénuée de vent et de bruit, qu'il semblait qu'on n'aurait plus jamais besoin de dormir. Jacques s'avança au hasard, d'abord soucieux de ne pas rompre le silence et de se cacher. Il remarqua un bosquet qui était dans la pente audessus du canal, un peu plus haut que la maison en litige dont il voyait briller le toit d'ardoises. Il pensa gagner le bosquet, puis cette maison. Comme il parvenait à la lisière du bouquet d'arbres il entendit un froissement de feuilles. Il eut tout juste le temps de s'écarter. Il vit sortir du couvert deux jeunes filles. L'une c'était Violette et l'autre sans doute Sylvie. Elles parlèrent. Des voix inoubliables. Celle de Violette était encore la plus pure. Violette disait :

— Je voudrais le revoir. Mais comment le revoir? S'il savait que je suis toute à lui...

— Tu le reverras, disait Sylvie.

Jacques n'osa pas les suivre. Il les vit regagner la maison. Puis il descendit vers le canal, comme en proie à un rêve. En passant près d'un buisson il entendit un chant. C'était peut-être Bertache qui chantait seul. Les accents étaient âpres et discordants parfois, mais ils se perdaient dans un appel si plein d'espoir que la nuit étoilée soudain apparaissait infinie, telle qu'elle était vraiment. Jacques passa la nuit entière à errer. Que signifiait tout cela? Rien de plus inattendu ni de plus banal. Il suivit le chemin de halage, remonta sur le plateau, se perdit dans les champs. A l'aube il fut le premier passant de la rue de la Couture. Il alla acheter un paquet de cigarettes chez sa buraliste. Il lui dit :

— Les gens de Malmont ... je crois qu'ils ont fait la paix. Cette nuit...

La dame eut un air horrifié :

— Jamais ils ne feront la paix, vous m'entendez. Jamais...

— Cette nuit... reprit Jacques.

— Toutes les nuits, aux veillées d'hiver, dans les étés, par le beau temps ou par l'orage, toutes les nuits ils font la paix. Et au matin cela recommence. Ah! ne vous y fiez pas.

Jacques était trop désorienté pour prolonger la discussion. Il regagna sa chambre, puis se rendit à son travail. Un mois plus tard on apprenait son mariage avec Violette. L'affaire se traîta, dit-on, grâce à un échange de paroles malsonnantes. Il y eut dix fois menace de rupture de part et d'autre. La famille de Jacques s'exaspéra. Cependant, chaque soir, quel que fût le temps, les deux fiancés se retrouvèrent sur la route ou sur un bal, et ils eurent des moments de bonheur qu'on ne peut imaginer.

Jacques habita avec Violette la maison de la mère De-
mart en attendant d'emménager dans celle de la pente, en
dépit des Vortoux. Les gens lui disaient, les siens lui disaient :
« Soit, il te fallait la fille. Au moins filez, allez habiter le plus
loin possible. Ne restez pas dans cet enfer ». Mais les nuits de
Malmont demeurent merveilleusement incomparables et qui
pourrait jamais s'en détacher ?

WALLACE FOWLIE

EXERCICES

*Une idée naît en moi et une parcelle de ma force pourrit.
Je me trouve diminué par ce qui m'exalte.*

*Un étudiant me confie ce soir qu'il n'a jamais été heureux,
que son souvenir le plus ancien est un sens de culpabilité, une
angoisse infuse qui lui tient lieu de tout. Il a vécu par et pour
l'expérience de la fatalité.*

*Ce n'est pas systématiquement que j'ai écrit mes meilleu-
res pages. Ce qui est systématique est au fond assez ridicule.
La puissance du hasard et de l'absurde apparaît dans les pas-
sages les mieux réussis.*

*Tout amour dans ma propre vie personnelle et tout amour
que l'on m'a raconté, où Dieu n'est pas, est quelque chose
d'affreux. N'aimer que l'enveloppe charnelle d'une âme pro-
voque tôt ou tard la pire des catastrophes, la plus amère des
déceptions.*

*Je vis à la merci des silences. Silences de quelques amis
qui me connaissent ou qui croient me connaître et qui justi-
fient mon existence en louant l'intégrité de ma foi et en taisant
les graves erreurs de mes pensées et de mes actes.*

Même dans ses oeuvres les plus sobres et dépouillées (Celles qu'on prend dans ses bras), *le style de Montherlant est remarquablement dru et fort. C'est une combinaison de voix adolescente et de voix mâle. La voix de quelqu'un qui croit au sérieux de la vie. Par ce style si énergique, cette oeuvre est justifiée.*

Gide, le grand professeur du désir et donc l'auteur le plus délirant pour les adolescents. A-t-il jamais dit non à un désir? Comme c'est étrange de découvrir dans chaque désir les exigences d'une vie!

Le mépris peut-il être une passion? On dirait que oui pour Montherlant.

L'homme n'est pas seulement la somme de ses actes. Il est aussi tout ce qu'il aurait pu être, tout ce qu'il aurait pu devenir. Comme cette pensée s'applique exactement à l'écrivain!

Seules les vertus acquises m'intéressent et m'émeuvent. J'ai une aversion innée pour tout ce qui est naturel, pour tout ce qui est vertu native. L'histoire secrète des vertus acquises d'un homme serait un roman passionnant.

Ma mémoire s'est désencombrée de tous les souvenirs futiles, de toutes les déceptions absolues.

La littérature ne nous accueille jamais d'un sourire humain.

Dans ma robuste solitude américaine, je pense parfois à l'atelier montmartrois de Picasso, rue Ravignan, aux soirées de La Plume, au théâtre des Noctambules, à certain bistrot du boulevard Saint Michel, au vers qui résume une époque: « *nous nous sommes rencontrés dans un caveau maudit.* »

Le vin, moyen d'oublier ou de vaincre? Non! le vin n'apporte aucune solution et il pèse lourd sur l'âme.

L'audace de Baudelaire, je ne cesse d'y revenir. C'est l'audace d'une conscience d'homme dans toute sa rigueur. Qui a combattu autant que Baudelaire contre le néant de la vie, contre la promesse de la mort?

La littérature, piège fatal. Devant Filippo Argenti, au cercle des coléreux (iracondi), Dante subit la contagion du mal. La colère du poète vivant est bien plus douloureuse à voir que celle du damné.

Baudelaire a bien senti que la mort est moins tragique que l'attente de la mort.

Les mots tombent dans un cimetière quotidien. Seul le concetto, seule la métaphore artificielle reste et consacre de nouveau la vigueur de la langue.

La philosophie s'arrête lorsqu'il est question du salut de l'homme. La croix fait pâlir Athènes.

La vie mondaine est l'abîme où nous perdons toute pureté d'âme et de corps. Impossible de prolonger la solitude. Notre corruption la plus profonde est celle que nous n'appelons jamais corruption.

La conversation: abîme et piège. J'en sors toujours avec la convinction que mes instincts ont été rongés.

INGEBORG BACHMANN

LIEDER VON EINER INSEL

Schattenfrüchte fallen von den Wänden,
Mondlicht tüncht das Haus, und Asche
erkalteter Krater trägt der Meerwind herein.

In den Umarmungen schöner Knaben
schlafen wir und entfernen
die Nägel, dein Fleisch
besinnt sich auf meins,
es war mir schon zugetan,
als sich die Schiffe
vom Land lösten und Kreuze
mit unsrer sterblichen Last
Mastendienst taten.

Nun sind die Richtstätten leer,
sie suchen und finden uns nicht.

* * *

Wenn du auferstehst,
wenn ich aufersteh,
ist kein Stein vor dem Tor,
liegt kein Boot auf dem Meer.

Morgen rollen die Fässer
sonntäglichen Wellen entgegen,
wir kommen auf gesalbten
Sohlen zum Strand, waschen
die Trauben und stampfen
die Ernte zu Wein,
morgen am Strand.

Wenn du auferstehst,
wenn ich aufersteh,
hängt der Henker am Tor,
sinkt der Hammer ins Meer.

* * *

« Einmal muss dass Fest ja kommen!
Heiliger Antonius, weil du gelitten hast,
heiliger Leonhard, weil du gelitten hast,
heiliger Vitus, weil du gelitten hast.»

Platz unsren Bitten, Platz den Betern,
Platz der Musik und der Freude.
Wir haben Einfalt gelernt,
wir singen im Chor der Zikaden,
wir essen und trinken,
die mageren Katzen
streichen um unseren Tisch,
bis die Abendmesse beginnt,
halt ich dich an der Hand
mit den Augen,
und ein feierlich mutiges Herz
opfert dir seine Wünsche.

Honig und Nüsse den Kindern,
volle Netze den Fischern,
Fruchtbarkeit den Gärten,
Mond dem Vulkan, Mond dem Vulkan!

Unsre Funken setzten über die Grenzen,
über die Nacht schlugen Raketen
ein Rad, auf dunklen Flössen
entfernt sich die Prozession und räumt
der Vorwelt die Zeit ein,
den schleichenden Echsen,
der schlemmenden Pflanze,
dem fiebernden Fisch,
den Orgien des Winds und der Lust
des Bergs, wo ein frommer
Stern sich verirrt, ihm auf die Brust
schlägt und zerstäubt.

Jetzt seid standhaft, törichte Heilige,
sagt dem Festland, dass die Krater nicht ruhn!
Heiliger Rochus, dass du gelitten hast,
o dass du gelitten hast, heiliger Franz.

* * *

Wenn einer fortgeht, muss er den Hut
mit den Muscheln, die er sommerüber
gesammelt hat, ins Meer werfen
und fahren mit wehendem Haar,
er muss den Tisch, den er seiner Liebe
deckte, ins Meer stürzen,
er muss den Rest des Weins,
der im Glas blieb, ins Meer schütten,
er muss den Fischen sein Brot geben
und einen Tropfen Blut ins Meer mischen,
er muss sein Messer gut in die Wellen treiben
und seinen Schuh versenken,
Herz, Anker und Kreuz,
und fahren mit wehendem Haar!
Dann wird er wiederkommen.
Wann?
    Frag nicht.

* * *

Es ist Feuer unter der Erde,
und das Feuer ist rein,

es ist Feuer unter der Erde
und flüssiger Stein,

es ist ein Strom unter der Erde,
der strömt in uns ein,

es ist ein Strom unter der Erde,
der sengt das Gebein,

es kommt ein grosses Feuer,
es kommt ein Strom über die Erde.

Wir werden Zeugen sein.

NEBELLAND

Im Winter ist meine Geliebte
unter den Tieren des Waldes.
Dass ich vor Morgen zurückmuss,
weiss die Füchsin und lacht.
Wie die Wolken erzittern! Und mir
auf den Schneekragen fällt
eine Lage von brüchigem Eis.

Im Winter ist meine Geliebte
ein Baum unter Bäumen und lädt
die glückverlassenen Krähen
ein in ihr schönes Geäst. Sie weiss,
dass der Wind, wenn es dämmert,
ihr starres, mit Reif besetztes
Abendkleid hebt und mich heimjagt.

Im Winter ist meine Geliebte
unter den Fischen und stumm.
Hörig den Wassern, die der Strich
ihrer Flossen von innen bewegt,
steh ich am Ufer und seh,
bis mich Schollen vertreiben,
wie sie taucht und sich wendet.

Und wieder vom Jagdruf des Vogels
getroffen, der seine Schwingen
über mir steift, stürz ich
auf offenem Feld: sie entfiedert
die Hühner und wirft mir ein weisses
Schlüsselbein zu. Ich nehm's
um den Hals und geh fort
durch den bitteren Flaum.

Treulos ist meine Geliebte,
ich weiss, sie schwebt manchmal
auf hohen Schuhn nach der Stadt,
sie küsst in den Bars mit dem Strohhalm
die Gläser tief auf den Mund,
und es kommen ihr Worte für alle.
Doch diese Sprache verstehe ich nicht.

Nebelland hab ich gesehen,
Nebelherz hab ich gegessen.

HEINRICH BÖLL

ABSCHIED VON IRLAND

Der Abschied fiel schwer, gerade deshalb, weil alles darauf hinzudeuten schien, dass er notwendig sei: kalt war es geworden, das Geld verbraucht, neues versprochen, aber noch nicht angekommen, und in der Pension (der billigsten, die wir in der Abendzeitung hatten finden können), waren die Fussböden so schief, dass wir kopfabwärts in unendliche Tiefen abzusinken schienen; auf einer sanft geneigten Rutschbahn glitten wir durch das Niemandsland zwischen Traum und Erinnerung, fuhren durch Dublin, bedroht von den Abgründen des Bettes, das mitten im Zimmer stand, umbrandet vom Lärm und vom Neonlicht der Dorset Street; wir hielten uns aneinander fest; die Seufzer der Kinder aus den Betten an der Wand klangen wie Hilferufe von einem Ufer, das unerreichbar war.

Das ganze Inventar des Nationalmuseums, in das wir nach jedem abschlägigen Bescheid des Schalterbeamten zurückgegangen waren, wurde in diesem Niemandsland zwischen Traum und Erinnerung überdeutlich und starr wie die Requisiten eines Panoptikums, wie auf der Geisterbahn im Märchenwald fuhren wir kopfabwärts dahin: St Brigids Schuh leuchtete silbern und zart aus der Dunkelheit, grosse schwarze Kreuze trösteten und drohten, Freiheitskämpfer in rührenden grünen Uniformen, in Wickelgamaschen und rötlichen Baretts zeigten uns ihre Schusswunden, ihre Ausweise, lasen uns mit kindlicher Stimme Abschiedbriefe vor: « Liebe Mary, Irlands

Freiheit...»; ein Kochtopf aus dem dreizehnten Jahrhundert
schwamm an uns vorüber, eine Kanu aus vorgeschichtlicher
Zeit; goldener Schmuck lächelte, keltische Fibeln, aus Gold,
Kupfer und Silber waren wie unzählige Kommas auf einer
unsichtbaren Wäscheleine aufgereiht; wir fuhren durchs Tor
in Trinity College ein, aber unbewohnt war diese grosse graue
Stätte, nur ein blasses Mädchen sass weinend auf der Treppe
zur Biblitohek, hielt seinen giftgrünen Hut in der Hand, trau-
erte um einen Liebsten oder weinte ihm nach; Lärm und
Neonlicht von der Dorset Street herauf rauschten an uns vor-
über wie die Zeit, die für Augenblicke Geschichte wurde:
Denkmäler wurden an uns vorbeigeschoben, oder wir an ihnen:
Männer aus Bronze, ernst, mit Schwertern, Federkielen, Zei-
chenrollen, Zügeln, Zirkeln in der Hand; Frauen mit strenger
Brust zupften an Leiern, blickte mit süsstraurigen Augen in
viele Jahrhunderte irischer Geschichte zurück; unendlich lan-
ge Kolonnen dunkelblau gekleideter Mädchen standen Spa-
lier, mit Hurlingschlägern in der Hand, stumm waren sie,
ernst, und wir fürchteten, sie würden ihre Schläger wie Keu-
len erheben; engumschlungen rutschten wir weiter; alles, was
wir besichtigt hatten, besichtigte jetzt uns: Löwen brüllten
uns an, turnende Gibbons kreuzten unsere Bahn, wir fuhren
den langen Hals der Giraffe hinauf, hinunter, und der Leguan
mit seinen toten Augen warf uns seine uralte Hässlichkeit
vor; das dunkle Wasser des Liffey gurgelte grün und schmut-
zig an uns vorüber, fette Möven kreischten, ein Klumpen
Butter — «zweihundert Jahre alt, im Moor in Mayo gefun-
den» — schwebte vorbei wie der Klumpen Gold, den Hans
im Glück verschmäht hatte; ein Polizist zeigte uns lächelnd
sein Rainfall-Book, vierzig Tage hintereinander hatte er O
geschrieben, eine ganze Kolonne von Eiern; das blasse Mäd-
chen mit dem grünen Hut in der Hand weinte immer noch
auf der Treppe zur Bibliothek.

Schwarz wurden die Wasser des Liffey, trugen als Treib-
gut Geschichte ins Meer: Urkunden, deren Siegel wie Senk-
bleie nach unten hingen, gewichtig von Siegellack, Holz-
schwerter, Kanonen aus Pappe, Leiern und Stühle, Betten und
Schränke, Tintenfässer Mumien, deren Bandagen sich gelöst
hatten und dunkel, wie Palmwedel flatternd, sich durchs Was-
ser bewegten; ein Schaffner kurbelte aus seiner Fahrschein-

mühle eine lange Papierlocke heraus, und auf den Stufen der Bank von Irland sass eine alte Frau und zählte Eindollarscheine, und zweimal, dreimal, viermal kam der Schalterbeamte der Hauptpost und sagte mit bekümmerter Miene hinter seinem Gitter hervor: « Sorry ».

Unzählige Kerzen brannten vor der Statue der rothaarigen Sünderin Magdalena; ein Haifischwirbel schwamm an uns vorüber, einem Windsack glich er, schwankte, die Knorpelgelenke brachen auseinander, und die Wirbelknochen rollten wie Serviettenringe einzeln in die Nacht und verschwanden; siebenhundert O' Malleys marschierten an uns vorüber, braunhaarige, weisshaarige, rothaarige, sangen ein Preislied auf ihren Klan.

Wir flüsterten uns Trostworte zu, hielten uns aneinander fest, fuhren durch Parks und Alleen, durch die Schluchten Connemaras, durch die Berge von Kerry, die Moore von Mayo, zwanzig, dreissig Meilen weit, fürchteten immer, dem Saurier zu begegnen, aber wir begegneten nur dem Kino, das mitten in Connemara, mitten in Kerry, mitten in Mayo stand: aus Beton wars, die Fenster waren mit dicker grüner Farbe beschmiert und drinnen schnurrte der Vorführapparat wie ein bösses gefangenes Tier, schnurrte die Monroe, den Tracy, die Lollobrigida an die Wand; auf grünen Schattenbahnen, immer noch den Saurier fürchtend, fuhren wir zwischen unendlich langen Mauern dahin, so weit von den Seufzern unserer Kinder entfernt, kehrten in die Dubliner Vororte zurück, an Palmen, Oleander vorbei, durch Rhododendronwälder, kopfabwärts; immer grösser wurden die Häuser, höher die Bäume, immer breiter die Kluft zwischen uns und den seufzenden Kindern; die Vorgärten wuchsen, bis sie so gross waren, dass wir die Häuser nicht mehr sehen konnten, und wir fuhren rascher in das zarte Grün unendlich grosser Wiesen ein.

Der Abschied fiel schwer, obwohl die rauhe Stimme der Wirtin am Morgen im Klirren des Tageslichts das Treibgut der Träume wie Gerümpel zusammenfegte, und obwohl das tak - tak - tak vom vorüberfahrenden Omnibus aus uns erschreckte: so täuschend ähnlich war das Geräusch dem eines schiessenden Maschinengewehrs, dass es uns wie ein Vorsignal zur Revolution erschien, aber Dublin dachte nicht an Revolution, es dachte an Frühstück, an Pferderennen, Gebet und belichtetes Zelluloid. Die rauhstimmige Wirtin rief uns zum Frühstück, herzlicher Tee floss; rauchend sass die Wirtin im Morgenrock bei uns, erzählte von Stimmen, die sie nachts quälten: Stimme eines ertrunkenen Bruders, der nachts nach ihr rief, Stimme der verstorbenen Mutter, die an die Gelübde der ersten Heiligen Kommunion erinnerte, Stimme des verstorbenen Mannes, der vor Whisky warnte: Trio von Stimmen, im dunklen Hinterzimmer gehört, wo sie den ganzen Tag über mit Flasche, Schwermut und Morgenrock allein war. « Der Psychiater », sagte sie plötzlich leise, « behauptet, dass die Stimmen aus der Flasche kommen, aber ich hab ihm gesagt, er soll nichts gegen meine Stimmen sagen, denn schliesslich lebt er davon. Sie » sagte sie mit plötzlich veränderter Stimme, « Sie hätten nicht Lust mein Haus zu kaufen, ich lasse es Ihnen billig ».

« Nein, danke », sagte ich.

« Schade », kopfschüttelnd ging sie in ihr dunkles Hinterzimmer zurück, mit Flasche, Schwermut und Morgenrock.

Vom « Sorry » des Schalterbeamten erschlagen, kehrten wir ins Nationalmuseum zurück, gingen von dort in die Gemäldegalerie, stiegen noch einmal in die dunkle Gruft zu den Mumien hinab, die ein ländlicher Besucher dort mit « kippered herrings » verglich; letzte Pennies gaben wir für Kerzen aus, die vor bunten Heiligenbildern rasch verbrannten, gingen zu Stephens Green hinaus, fütterten Enten, sassen im Sonnenschein, hörten zu, wie die Gewinnchancen für « Purpurwolke » standen; sie standen gut. Mittags um zwölf kamen viele Dubliner aus der Messe, verteilten sich in die Grafton Street. Unsere Hoffnung auf das « Yes » des Schalterbeamten blieb unerfüllt; sein « Sorry; war immer trübseliger geworden, fast — so schien es mir — hätte er eigenmächtig in die Kasse gegriffen und uns ein Darlehen des Postministers gegeben, seine Hände jedenfalls zuckten zur Schublade hin, seufzend nahm er sie leer auf die Marmortheke zurück.

Zum Glück lud das Mädchen mit dem grünen Hut uns zum Tee ein, stiftete den Kindern Bonbons, stellte neue Kerzen auf, vor dem richtigen Heiligenbild: St. Antonius, und als wir noch einmal zur Post gingen, strahlte das Lächeln des

Schalterbeamten uns durch die ganze Halle hindurch bis zum Eingang entgegen. Fröhlich leckte er sich die Finger, zählte die Scheine auf die Marmorplatte, triumphierend: eins, zwei, vielmal, in ganz kleinen Noten gab er uns das Geld, weil das Zählen ihm soviel Spass machte, und silbern sangen die Münzen über den Marmor hin; das Mädchen mit dem grünen Hut lächelte: hatte sie nicht die Kerzen vor dem richtigen Heiligen aufgestellt?

Der Abschied fiel schwer; die langen Reihen der dunkelblau gekleideten Mädchen, mit Hurlingschlägern in der Hand, hatten alles Drohende verloren, die Löwen brüllten nicht mehr, nur der Leguan warf uns immer noch mit toten Augen seine uralte Hässlichkeit vor.

Musikautomaten dröhnten, Schaffner kurbelten lange Papierwolken aus ihren Fahrscheinmühlen, Dampfer tuteten, leichter Wind kam von der See, viele, viele Fässer Bier wurden in dunkle Schiffsbäuche gehievt; sogar die Denkmäler lächelten: die Dunkelheit des Traumes war von Federkiel, Zügel, Leier und Schwert genommen, und nur alte Abendzeitungen waren es, die im Liffey dem Meer zuschwammen. In der neuen Abendzeitung waren drei Leserbriefe abgedruckt, die Nelsons Sturz forderten; siebenundreissig Häuser wurden zum Verkauf angeboten, eins nur wurde gesucht, und in einem Nest in Kerry hatte dank der Rührigkeit des örtlichen Festivalkomitees ein wirkliches Festival stattgefunden: Wettbewerbe hatte es gegeben in Sacklaufen, Eselsreiten, Rudern und im Langsamfahren für Fahrräder, und die Siegerin im Sacklaufen hatte dem Pressephotographen zugelächelt: sie zeigte uns in der Abendzeitüng ihr hübsches Gesicht und ihre schlechten Zähne.

Die letzten Stunden verbrachten wir auf dem schrägen Fussboden des Pensionszimmers, spielten Karten wie auf einem Dach; Stühle und Tisch gab es nicht im Zimer, zwischen Gepäckstücken sitzend, bei offenem Fenster, die Teetassen neben uns auf dem Boden, jagten wir Herz-Bube und Pik-As durch das Spalier ihrer Artgenossen, umbrandet von heiterem Lärm der Dorset-Street; während die Wirtin mit Flasche, Schwermut und Morgenrock im Hinterzimmer blieb, schaute das Zimmermädchen lächelnd unserem Spiel zu.

«Das war wieder einmal ein netter Bursche», sagte der

Taxichauffeur, der uns zum Bahnhof fuhr, « ein reizender Kerl ».

« Wer? » fragte ich.

« Dieser Tag », sagte er, « war das nicht ein Prachtbürschchen? » Ich stimmte ihm zu, während ich ihn bezahlte, blickte ich nach oben, die schwarze Front eines Hauses hinauf: eben stellte eine junge Frau einen orangefarbenen Milchtopf auf auf die Fensterbank hinaus. Sie lächelte mir zu, und ich lächelte zurück.

GÜNTER GRASS

DER KUCKUCK

*Ein Kiefernwald. Der Querschnitt des sich in der Bühnen-
mitte erhebenden Hügels zeigt eine Fallgrube. Bollin bedeckt
die Grube mit Zweigen. Sobald er damit fertig ist, läuft er
zur linken Bühnenseite und verändert mit einigen Griffen seine
Kleidung, als wolle er sein zukünftiges Opfer mimen.*

BOLLIN: Ich weiss von nichts! — Ich komme daher! — Ich
denke an nichts Böses! — Ich komme daher, weiss von
nichts und denke an etwas Angenehmes. (*Er nähert sich
der Fallgrube*) Meine Augen heften sich auf den Boden.
Meine Sinne sind hellwach. Misstrauen bewegt meine
Seele! (*Er steht vor der Fallgrube, hebt schon das eine
Bein, um den verhängnisvollen Schritt zu machen*) Wenn
jemand daherkäme, der nicht ich wäre, der von nichts
wüsste, an nichts Böses denken würde, im Gegenteil, an
etwas Angenehmes. Trotz hellwacher Sinne und dienstlich
misstrauischer Seele, er täte diesen Schritt — den ich nicht
mache. Natürlich nicht! Vielleicht noch dieses Zweiglein
so herum und hier die Spuren meiner Ordnungsliebe be-
seitigt. (*Er ändert noch etwas an der Anordnung der
Zweige und betrachtet sodann befriedigt sein Werk*) Man
könnte sich da rein verlieben. Es verlockt zu gefährlichen
Gedankengängen, zieht mich fast in den Abgrund, zöge
mich ganz gewiss, — wenn nicht die Pflicht Bollin zu-
rückhielte und mit der wohlbekannten Stimme riefe: Noch

nicht, Bollin, noch nicht. Dein Werk hat erst begonnen! *(Er springt über die Grube, hüpft zwischen den Bäumen umher und ruft nach links)*: Kuckuck, Kuckuck, — Kuckuck...

STIMME: Kuckuck!

BOLLIN: Kuckuck!

STIMME: Kuckuck, — Kuckuck!

(Von links kommt der bärtige, Pfeife rauchende Förster).

BOLLIN: Kuckuck!

FÖRSTER: Kuckuck! *(Er nähert sich der Grube, steht kurz davor, betrachtet misstrauisch den Boden, will sich schon bücken...)*.

BOLLIN: Kuckuck, Kuckuck, Kuckuck! *(Der Förster richtet sich auf, will dem Kuckucksruf nach und fällt, Flinte und Jagdbeutel verlierend, in die Grube. Bollin springt hinter dem Baum hervor, reibt sich fröhlich die Hände, hängt sich Flinte und Jagdbeutel um und blickt in die Grube)* Kuckuck!

FÖRSTER *(an der ausgegangenen Pfeife ziehend)*: Bollin?

BOLLIN: Kuckuck!

FÖRSTER: Zieht nicht mehr! *(Er klopft die Pfeife aus)* Ob Sie Bollin sind, will ich wissen.

BOLLIN: Mit grossem B und zwei L.

FÖRSTER: Wie ich mir gedacht habe. — Wo ist denn nur? *(Er sucht in seinen Taschen, Bollin öffnet den Jagdbeutel)*.

BOLLIN: Wenn der Herr sein Büchlein suchen und den dazugehörigen Bleistift? — Bitte schön! *(Er reicht beides in die Grube)*.

FÖRSTER *(schreibend)*: Mit B und zwei L. Wohnhaft?

BOLLIN: Schreiben Sie, er zieht gerade um.

FÖRSTER: Im Umzug begriffen. — Warum?

BOLLIN: Luftveränderung.

FÖRSTER: Aus Gesundheitsgründen?

BOLLIN: Erraten, die Grosstadt hat mein Wohlbefinden untergraben.

FÖRSTER: Und jetzt untergraben Sie die Sicherheit meines Reviers.

BOLLIN: Kuckuck!

FÖRSTER: Warum tun Sie das?

BOLLIN: Kuckuck!

FÖRSTER: Antworten Sie, Bollin! Meine zwei Forsteleven sind seit drei Wochen überfällig, und Förster Platzmann aus Melchow ist auch verschwunden.

BOLLIN: Spurlos?

FÖRSTER: Spurlos.

BOLLIN: Hm. Er wird doch nicht etwa im Himmel sein?

FÖRSTER: Wahrscheinlich.

BOLLIN: Er was ein frommer Mann, es wäre nur gerecht, wenn nun da oben sein Plätzchen wäre.

FÖRSTER: Zu früh, Bollin, bedenken Sie, fünfunddreissig Jahre, das ist doch kein Alter!

BOLLIN: Dort oben wird er Gelegenheit haben, die Hundertjahrgrenze nicht nur zu erreichen, nein, sogar zu überschreiten. Ein ruhiger Lebensabend ist ihm gewiss.

FÖRSTER: Sein Platz war hier! Spielen Sie nicht Schicksal, das kommt Ihnen nicht zu. Ich weiss zwar nicht, was Sie gelernt haben, aber von der Forstwirtschaft haben Sie keine Ahnung.

BOLLIN: Ich mag keine Förster!

FÖRSTER: Niemand zwang Sie, die Stadt zu verlassen.

BOLLIN: Ich halte sie für überflüssig!

FÖRSTER: Oho! Und die Waldfrevler, die Wilddiebe, die Brandstifter, Harzzapfer, Wilddiebe, immer wieder die Wilddiebe?

BOLLIN: Gibt es nur, weil es Förster gibt.

FÖRSTER: Das muss ich vermerken. Gibt es nur...

BOLLIN: Es ist vernünftig von Ihnen, diesen Satz zu notieren. Ich habe lange darüber nachgedacht.

FÖRSTER: Paperlapapp, intellektuelles Geschwafel. Sie sind ein Idealist, ein unverbesserlicher Weltverbesserer, ein Revoluzzer, ein Umstürzler. Destruktiv, pessimistisch bis auf die Knochen, ein Nihilist wie er im Buche steht, — aber was tut das Bürschchen, es masst sich Urteile an! Ohne Förster gebe es keine... Ist ja lächerlich. Dabei bin ich überzeugt, Sie können kein Kaninchen von einem Schaukelpferd unterscheiden.

BOLLIN: Warum sollte ich auch unterscheiden?

FÖRSTER: Der Orientierung wegen, auch um zu lernen, zu bewerten, um sich ein Bild zu machen. Ein allumfassendes, lückenloses Wissen hat noch niemandem geschadet.

— Ja, können Sie mir überhaupt sagen, wie diese Bäume sich nennen, zwischen denen Sie herumirren und pflichtbewussten Förstern auflauern?

BOLLIN: Bäume? Sagen Sie Bäume? Wo denn?

FÖRSTER: Lassen Sie mich heraus, und ich erkläre Ihnen den Baumbestand.

BOLLIN: Das liegt kaum in meiner Absicht. Wozu hätte ich diese Arbeit geleistet? Ich habe Schwielen an den Händen. Mein Hemd ist verschwitzt und klebt. Und Sie? Sie laufen grün und überflüssig durch die Gegend, wollen mich dann um meinen sauer verdienten Lohn bringen, — ein Ausbeuter sind Sie, ein Leuteschinder!

FÖRSTER: Unsinn, Bollin, niemand will Ihnen etwas. Meine Arbeiter werden das Loch wieder zuschippen, Sie werden straffrei bleiben, das verspreche ich feierlich — und ausserdem wird etwas für Ihre Bildung getan. Ich werde Sie in die Geheimnisse des Waldes einweihen.

BOLLIN: Was wäre damit gewonnen?

FÖRSTER: Aha, daher weht der Wind! Er verachtet die Natur!

BOLLIN: Aber woher denn! Ganz im Gegenteil. Passen Sie auf: Kuckuck!

FÖRSTER: Selbst einen so einfachen Vogelruf können Sie nicht nachahmen. Hier, die Mundstellung: Kuckuck!

BOLLIN: Sag ich ja. Kuckuck!

FÖRSTER: Falsch! Kuckuck!

BOLLIN: Kuckuck, Kuckuck! Kuckuck!

FÖRSTER: Ich gebe es auf. Sie lernen es nie.

BOLLIN: Immerhin sind Sie auf meinen Kuckuck hereingefallen. Kuckuck! (*Er springt über die Grube und holt hinter den Bäumen eine Schaufel hervor*) Darf ich jetzt vielleicht eine bescheidene Frage stellen?

FÖRSTER: Nur zu. Keine falsche Scham! Solange der Mensch Fragen stellt, ist in ihm noch Hoffnung und guter Wille. Was wollen Sie wissen, Bollin? Gut, die Bäume finden nicht Ihr Interesse. Vielleicht etwas über unsere einheimische Vogelwelt oder die Waldameisen oder die Borkenkäfer? — Na?

BOLLIN: Wissen Sie, was eine Schaufel ist?

FÖRSTER (*nach einer Pause*): Fangen Sie an, ich habe abgeschlossen.

BOLLIN: Kein Spaten, eine Schaufel?

FÖRSTER: Nun los doch! Zeigen Sie dem alten Forschbach, was man mit einer Schaufel alles machen.

BOLLIN: Och, so viel ist das ja nun auch wieder nicht. — Immer dasselbe: Kuckuck, Kuckuck und so weiter!

FÖRSTER: Einerlei, ich bin gespannt. Welcher Förster kann sich das leisten, so unter seinen Bäumen zu liegen.

BOLLIN: Den Bäumen ist das gleich.

FÖRSTER: Oh nein, da bin ich ganz sicher. Ein rechter Wald weiss seinen Hüter zu schätzen.

BOLLIN: Alles Einbildung, Förstergeschwätz! — Ich habe mir so einen Stamm mal genau angeguckt. — Die machen sich nichts aus uns!

FÖRSTER (*selbstgefällig*): Meine Kiefern kennen mich!

BOLLIN: Real bleiben, Forschbach, wir wollen die Tatsache doch nicht verkennen. Wer bezahlt Sie? Das Holz oder die Forstverwaltung?

FÖRSTER: Es haben mir beide ihren Lohn gegeben.

BOLLIN: Ah, keine blasse Ahnung von der Natur, — und das nennt sich Förster.

FÖRSTER: Auf jeden Fall kann ich den Ruf eines Kuckucks beträchtlich besser nachahmen als Sie — und mein Revier kenn ich in- und auswendig.

BOLLIN: Und jetzt dürfen Sie nich sogar das Grünzeug von unten angucken. (*Er lacht höhnisch*).

FÖRSTER: Fangen wir an!

BOLLIN: Noch einen Wunsch?

FÖRSTER: Meine Pfeife ist ausgegangen. Beim Sturz muss ich meinen Jagdbeutel verloren haben.

BOLLIN: Ja — höre ich richtig? Sie wollen doch nicht etwa hier mitten im Wald?

FÖRSTER: Nur ein Pfeifchen noch.

BOLLIN: Ich habe da vorhin so ein Schild gesehen, da stand was drauf von verboten und so.

FÖRSTER: Das gilt nur für Spaziergänger und Beerensammler.

BOLLIN: Na schön, ist ja nicht mein Wald! Wenn Sie mir versprechen, vorsichtig zu sein. (*Es zieht ein Feuerzeug aus dem Jagdbeutel und wirft es in die Grube*) Also, auf Ihre Verantwortung! (*Der Förster zündet die Pfeife an und raucht*).

FÖRSTER (*nach kurzer Pause*): Bollin?

BOLLIN: Hm?

FÖRSTER: Meine Flinte?

BOLLIN: Macht sich ganz gut hier oben.

FÖRSTER: Sie liegt doch nicht etwa im Sand?

BOLLIN: Im Gegenteil, sie hängt an einem Ast.

FÖRSTER: Kann ich sie haben?

BOLLIN: Die Flinte?

FÖRSTER: Sie ist ja nicht geladen.

BOLLIN: Nee, Forschbach, das geht zu weit.

FÖRSTER: Auch wenn sie nicht geladen ist.

BOLLIN: Flinte ist Flinte!

FÖRSTER: Sie können ja nachsehen, kein Schuss drinnen.

BOLLIN: Ich sag ja, ob geladen oder nicht, es geht mir ums Prinzip.

FÖRSTER: Vielleicht dieses Mal eine kleine Ausnahme.

BOLLIN: Ich hör ja gar nicht mehr hin. Da könnte jeder kommen und nach seiner Flinte jammern. Solche Methoden wollen wir überhaupt nicht erst einführen.

FÖRSTER: Ich hätte sie so gerne im Arm.

BOLLIN: Sentimentalitäten sind das!

FÖRSTER: Fast zwanzig Jahre hat sie mich nun begleitet.

BOLLIN: Dann wird es aber höchste Zeit, dass ihr euch mal trennt.

FÖRSTER: Wir hängen doch so aneinander.

BOLLIN: Genau das mein ich! Normalerweise nennt man das Hörigkeit. Schluss damit! Flinte bleibt oben, Forschbach unten...

FÖRSTER: Zwanzig Jahre!

BOLLIN: Trennungsstrich wird gezogen. Man soll nicht so am Irdischen kleben. Frei sei der Mensch, ohne Ballast!

FÖRSTER: Aber die Flinte...

BOLLIN: Können Sie ja doch nicht mitnehmen. — Na schön, ich mache jetzt erst mal 'ne Schicht. So bis an die Binde ungefähr, und dann lang ich sie runter. — Zufrieden nun?

FÖRSTER: Danke, Bollin, danke und — Weidmannsheil!

BOLLIN (*zur Schaufel greifend*): Sagen wir lieber Petri heil!

FÖRSTER (*lächelnd*): Ach so, wegen der Regenwürmer.

(*Bollin beginnt, Erde in die Grube zu schütten. — Von links kommen Jannemann und Sprotte. Sie tragen mit*

Blaubeeren gefüllte Körbe und stellen sich an den Rand der Grube).

JANNEMANN: Kennste den?

SPROTTE: Klar doch, das is der olle Forschbach. *(Der Förster springt auf, Bollin stützt sich auf die Schaufel).*

JANNEMANN: Nu wird der auch eingelocht!

SPROTTE: Wurde auch langsam Zeit. — Willste paar Blaubeeren haben, Opa? *(Sie wirft einige Beeren in die Grube).*

FÖRSTER: Bollin, jagen Sie die Gören weg! Sie haben keinen Sammelschein.

BOLLIN: Na, wenn schon!

FÖRSTER: Das regt mich auf und nimmt mir die Stimmung.

BOLLIN: Habt ihr gehört, Kinder? Der Forschbach will seine Ruhe haben.

SPROTTE: Bah, uns hat er ja auch nicht in Ruhe gelassen.

JANNEMANN: Immer den wilden Mann markiert und mit den Augen jerollt, als wenn er direktemank aussem Märchen abstammt und wir wären unjefähr so was wie Hänsel und Gretel.

FÖRSTER: Ich appelliere an Ihr Anstandsgefühl. Schaffen Sie die Kinder fort!

BOLLIN: Nun geht schon! — Ihr könnt ja wiederkommen, wenn es hier fertig ist, und stampfen helfen.

SPROTTE: Ich will aber zugucken!

JANNEMANN: Sieht man doch nicht alle Tage, so was.

SPROTTE: Du, Opa Forschbach, auf'm Erbsberg machense Brennholz.

JANNEMANN: Und im Jäschkental sindse auch.

SPROTTE: Mit'm Handwagen.

JANNEMANN: Aber da war nich nur Gestrüpp drinnen, da war noch was drunter.

SPROTTE: Was Braunes mit'm ganz kurzen Schwanz...

JANNEMANN: ...und langen Ohren.

FÖRSTER: Bollin?

BOLLIN: Nun ist genug, lasst ihn in Ruhe!

SPROTTE: Ach was, so was interessiert ihn doch, da is er immer schon hinterher gewesen.

JANNEMANN: Und det Schönste hätten wir fast vergessen: Überm Schwedensprung qualmt es!

SPROTTE: Da hat einer aus Versehen 'n Streichholz fallen jelassen.

BOLLIN: Ihr müsst ihm nicht solche Geschichten erzählen. Das tut ihm weh.

SPROTTE: Und mir, was hatter mit mir gemacht? — Jannemann, erzähl du dem Onkel, wie er mich vorgekriecht hat neulich.

JANNEMANN: Na ja, paar überjezogen hatter ihr.

FÖRSTER: Weil sie in der Schonung waren.

SPROTTE: Was heisst hier Schonung? Meinen Sie vielleicht, meine Mutter sagt da was, wenn ich Schonung zu ihr sag? (*Sie zeigt auf die Körbe*) Hier, das willse sehen, und nich Schonung!

FÖRSTER: Diese Stadtkinder! Das wächst auf zwischen Häusern und geht, wenn es hoch kommt, einmal im Jahr in den Zoo.

SPROTTE: Und da können wir nun auch nich mehr hin, weil se uns evakuiert haben.

JANNEMANN: Ich wär viel lieber bei uns geblieben.

SPROTTE: Nich mal Löwen gibt's hier!

JANNEMANN: Oder 'n Pavian oder 'n anständiges Känguruh aus Australien.

FÖRSTER: Bollin?

BOLLIN: Was soll's denn sein?

SPROTTE: Warum schaufelste nich, Onkel?

JANNEMANN: Ich würd' da nich lange überlegen.

BOLLIN: Ruhe! — Was ist, Forschbach?

FÖRSTER: Sie haben doch meine beiden Eleven und den Platzmann unter die Erde gebracht...

BOLLIN: Kuckuck — und weg war er!

FÖRSTER: Genau so wird es gewesen sein. Haben die ihre Ruhe dabei gehabt, frage ich Sie, oder, oder...

BOLLIN: Wunderbar still ging es zu. Der Platzmann ist sogar eingeschlafen, als man noch mehr als die Hälfte von ihm sah.

FÖRSTER: Und die Eleven?

BOLLIN: Gott ja, zuerst ein bisschen unruhig, weil sie noch so jung waren und dachten wunder, was sie versäumen könnten, — aber dann haben sie sich zusammengenommen. War richtig feierlich, wie in der Kirche.

FÖRSTER (*laut*): So, feierlich, Kirche, warum ich nicht? Warum dieser Lärm, diese Stimmen? (*Ruhiger*) Ich bitte Sie,

Bollin: Nur die Schaufel will ich hören, den guten märkischen Sand, vielleicht dann und wann einen Vogel und den Wind in den Kiefern.

Sprotte: Siehste, Kiefern hat er gesagt. — Nich wahr, Opa Forschbach, sind doch welche?

Förster: Meine Kiefern!

Sprotte: Er sagt immer Fichten.

Förster: Diese Kinder, was lernen sie nur in den Stadtschulen?

Jannemann: Auf jeden Fall handelt es sich um Nadelbäume.

Förster: Ist das nicht furchtbar, Bollin? Diese Unwissenheit? Aber sie machen sich ja wohl auch nichts aus unserer wunderbaren Natur.

Bollin: Gott, dass das Nadelbäume sind, hab ich auch inzwischen gemerkt.

Förster (bitter): Nadelbäume! — Das ist die grosse Familie. Ein Spross davon, zum Beispiel die Fichte...

Jannemann: Gibt es also doch.

Förster: Gewiss, Kinder, doch nicht bei uns. Die Fichte kommt fast nur in bergigen Ländern vor. Sie hat spitze, vierkantige Nadeln und hängende Zapfen. Das Holz der Fichte wird für Brennzwecke, aber auch für billige Möbel verwandt. Das Harz der Fichte wird gesammelt, und Terpentin wird aus ihr gewonnen.

Jannemann: Is ja interessant, was, Sprotte?

Sprotte: Schon möglich, aber das sind Kiefern hier!

Förster: Langsam, langsam! Davon reden wir später. Erst besprechen wir die Fichte zu Ende. Was sagte ich?

Jannemann: Terpentin.

Förster: Richtig! Auch Zellulose, Holzwolle, Fichtennadelextrakt...

Sprotte: Auch Öl?

Förster: Gut, mein Kind! Und in die Badewanne tut man, na?

Sprotte: Wir haben keine.

Förster: Der Herr Bollin vielleicht?

Bollin: Ich würde sagen Fichtennadelsalz.

Förster: Gut, sehr gut. Sie sind mir der rechte Schlauberger. Ich habe das Gefühl, Sie verstehen mehr von der Natur, als Sie sich und mir eingestehen wollen.

BOLLIN: Was denn, reiner Zufall, dass ich da auf dem laufen-
den war. Kauf mir manchmal 'ne kleine Packung, weil
das mein Hobby ist, Körperpflege.

SPROTTE: Und nun mal was von die Kiefer!

JANNEMANN: Klar doch, immer reden se nur von Fichten.

SPROTTE: Haste gehört, Opa Forschbach? Der Jannemann will
auch über die Kiefern hören.

FÖRSTER: Mir scheint, wir müssen wohl oder übel noch etwas
Geduld haben. Die Kinder... (*Bollin gibt mit einer gross-
zügigen Handbewegung seine Einwilligung*) Los, lauft!
Der Herr Bollin hat nichts dagegen. Sammelt einige Kie-
fernzapfen und werft sie herunter.

JANNEMANN: Schon dabei! (*Er sammelt schnell und wirft in
die Grube*).

FÖRSTER: Genug, mehr als genug!

SPROTTE: Da können Sie ja doch nix sehen, in dem Loch da.

JANNEMANN: Wird sich noch die Augen verderben.

SPROTTE: Jetzt guckt er mit'm Feuerzeug.

FÖRSTER: Es ist wirklich kein Büchsenlicht hier unten.

SPROTTE: Sollst ja auch nicht schiessen, sondern erzählen.
Kannste das nicht aussem Gedächtnis machen?

JANNEMANN: Wie du dir das vorstellst. Er will es doch an-
schaulich bringen. Soll er mal raufkommen für'n Moment.

SPROTTE (*zu Bollin*): Du, Onkel, mal raufkommen soll er!

BOLLIN: Ist das auch Ihr Wunsch, Forschbach? Wollen Sie
jetzt die Gören benutzen, nur um noch einmal frische
Luft zu schnappen?

FÖRSTER: Nichts liegt mir ferner. Ich habe schon lange ab-
geschlossen. Nur der Wissensdurst der Kinder — sie wol-
len die kleinen Geheimnisse des Waldes erklärt bekom-
men.

BOLLIN: Geht das denn nicht von unten?

SPROTTE: Is doch zu dunkel, Onkel. Siehste das nich?

JANNEMANN: Nachher geht er ja wieder in'n Keller.

BOLLIN: Die Dingsda, die Fichten hat er auch von unten
erklärt.

SPROTTE: Begreif doch, wenn es hier keine hat und der Jan-
nemann nich glauben wollte, dass es hier keine gibt und
nur inne Berge.

JANNEMANN: Auf jeden Fall hat mir das eingeleuchtet, wie
er das so gesagt hat.

FÖRSTER: Ich will Sie gewiss nicht überreden. Aber vielleicht sollte man doch den Kindern ein wenig die Augen öffnen. In der Stadt ergibt sich wohl kaum eine solch günstige Gelegenheit, unsere heimatlichen Nadelbäume kennenzulernen.

JANNEMANN: Wir haben jedes Jahr 'nen Weihnachtsbaum.

SPROTTE: Wir nich. Meine Mutter sagt immer: Die nadeln zu sehr, und dann sind meistens noch Ostern welche im Teppich, und das Gerippe von dem Baum steht auf'm Balkon rum.

FÖRSTER: Nun, was sagen Sie jetzt?

BOLLIN: Kommen Sie rauf für 'ne Sekunde! (*Er reicht ihm die Hand und zieht ihn aus der Fallgrube. Der Förster klopft sich den Sand vom Rock, Sprotte hilft ihm dabei*).

SPROTTE: Klopp auch, Jannemann!

JANNEMANN: Wird ja nachher doch wieder dreckig.

FÖRSTER: Jaja, der gute märkische Sand! Und seht ihr, mit diesem Sand wollen wir anfangen. Nur auf solch einem Boden wächst unsere Kiefer.

JANNEMANN: Warum?

FÖRSTER: Sie ist genügsam, ein echter Preusse. Kein Edelholz, gewiss, aber doch ein wichtiger Nutzbaum. Die Kiefer hat eine Pfahlwurzel und lässt sich ähnlich verwenden wie die Fichte.

JANNEMANN: Aber nich im Gebirge.

FÖRSTER: Doch, in verwandter Form. In höheren europäischen Gebirgsgegenden, nahe der Baumgrenze, wächst die Knieholzkiefer, auch Zwergkiefer, Legföhre oder Latsche genannt.

JANNEMANN: Zwergkiefer is doll!

SPROTTE: Wieso denn Zwerg?

FÖRSTER: Nun, in jenen Regionen herrschen ganz andere Witterungsverhältnisse, da hält sich kein solch hoher, schlanker Baum. Deshalb ist die Knieholzkiefer?

SPROTTE: Knieholzkiefer! (*Der Förster nimmt den Jagdbeutel*).

FÖRSTER: Auch Zwergkiefer? (*Er nimmt die Flinte von einem Ast*).

SPROTTE und JANNEMANN: Zwergkiefer!

FÖRSTER: Legföhre oder Latsche? (*Sie entfernen sich ohne Bollin*).

SPROTTE und JANNEMANN: Legföhre oder Latsche!

FÖRSTER: ...klein geblieben und erscheint uns buschförmig und verkrüppelt. Sagen wir es noch einmal. Deshalb ist die...?

SPROTTE und JANNEMANN: Knieholzkiefer!

FÖRSTER: Auch Zwergkiefer (*Sie gehen ab*).

SPROTTE und JANNEMANN: Zwergkiefer!

FÖRSTER: Legföhre oder Latsche?

SPROTTE und JANNEMANN: Legföhre oder Latsche klein geblieben.

(*Bollin blickt ihnen nach, spuckt dann in die Hand und beginnt, die Grube wieder zuzuschaufeln. Fern erschallt mehrmals der Kuckucksruf*).

BOLLIN (*sich auf die Schaufel stützend*): Kuckuck, Kuckuck!

(*Nachdem er vergeblich eine Zeitlang auf die Antwort des Kuckucks gewartet hat, schaufelt er weiter*).

UWE JOHNSON

BESONDERS DIE KLEINEN PROPHETEN

Jehova war der Herr, der das Meer und das Trockene gemacht hat, und die Juden waren sein Volk, er schloss einen Vertrag mit ihnen. Der ging über die menschlichen Kräfte, von Zeit zu Zeit geriet er in Vergessenheit. Dann erweckte Jehova einen Vorbedachten und Auserwählten in seinem Volke zum Propheten, der sollte dem König mit seinen Grossen und ihren Untertanen sagen wie der Herr es meine. Jesaja lebte im Unglück mit seinen Reden, Jeremia kam in die Kloake zu sitzen. Die Seele des Propheten ist empfindlich und wissend und zweiflerisch um die Stimme des Herrn zu hören und das Unglück zu erfahren.

Als die Bosheit und Sünde der Stadt Ninive vor Jehova gekommen waren, geriet er in Zorn wegen seines Gesetzes. Er berief Jona (den Sohn Amitthais, von Gath-Hahepher) und beauftragte ihn mit dem Ausrufen seines grossen Ärgers und mit der Verkündung des nahen Untergangs in den Strassen von Ninive.

Da wollte Jona nach Tharsis fliehen. Die gelehrte Forschung dieser Hinsicht meint dass diese Stadt vielleicht in Südspanien vermutet werden könne und hält eine unvergleichliche Entfernung für jedenfalls wahrscheinlich. Als das Schiff aus dem Hafen von Joppe gelaufen war, warf Jehova einen gewaltigen Wind auf das Meer, und es entstand ein gewaltiger Sturm auf dem Meere, so dass das Schiff zu scheitern drohte. Die Besatzung warf das Los über den Schuldigen, und das Los fiel auf Jona. Da er es selbst für das beste hielt, warfen sie ihn ins Meer, und das Meer stand ab von seinem Wüten. Und Jehova entbot einen grossen Fisch, der verschlang Jona, und Jona sang drei Tage und drei Nächte im Bauch des Fisches zu Jehova seinem Herrn. Dann spie der Fisch ihn ans Land, und Jona ging nach Ninive.

Ninive war eine über alle Massen grosse Stadt und nur in drei Tagereisen zu durchqueren. Und Jona ging in die Stadt hinein eine Tagereise weit; dann predigte er: Noch vierzig Tage, und Ninive ist zerstört!, und die Leute von Ninive erkannten Gott in seinem grossen Ärger. Sie riefen ein schlimmes Fasten aus und kleideten sich in ihre Trauergewänder. Und der König von Ninive bedeckte sich mit dem Trauergewand und setzte sich in die Asche. Der König befahl: Menschen und Vieh sollen nichts geniessen, sie sollen nicht weiden noch Wasser trinken. Sie sollen sich in Trauer hüllen: Menschen und Vieh, und mit Macht zu Gott rufen, und sollen ein jeder sich bekehren von seinem bösen Wandel und von dem Frevel, der an seinen Händen ist. Wer weiss, vielleicht gereut es Gott doch noch. Als Gott nun diese Dinge alle sah, die sie tun wollten, gereute ihn das angedrohte Unheil, und er tat es nicht.

Das verdross Jona sehr, und er ging zornig weg. Er baute eine Hütte östlich der Stadt und sass darunter, bis er sehe wie es der Stadt ergehen werde. Und zum dritten Male redete Jehova mit ihm: Ist es recht dass du hier sitzest und lieber sterben möchtest als noch weiter leben. Aber Jona antwortete das sei recht, denn warum habe er nach Tharsis fliehen wollen? Weil du nie tust wie du gesagt hast und wie es gerecht ist nach deinem Gesetz! Und der Herr entbot einen Rizinus, dessen Saft als castor oil gehandelt wird anderswo in der Welt; der wuchs über Jona empor um seinem Haupte Schatten zu geben und ihm so seinen Unmut zu nehmen. Über diesen Rizinus freute Jona sich sehr. Am folgenden Morgen entbot Jehova einen Wurm, der stach den Rizinus, so dass er verdorrte. Und der Herr setzte Jona zu mit schwülem Wind und grosser Hitze. Da wünschte Jona sich den Tod. Der Herr aber sprach zu Jona: Ist es recht dass du so zürnest um des Rizinus willen? Jona antwortete: Das Leben ist mir verleidet. Da sagte Jehova sein Herr: Dich jammert des Rizinus, um den du keine Mühe hattest, der gross gewachsen ist und verdorben von einem Morgen zum anderen. Warum jammert dich nicht der grossen Stadt Ninive, in der über hundertundzwanzigtausend Menschen sind, die zwischen links und rechts noch nicht unterscheiden können, dazu die Menge Vieh?

Und Jona blieb sitzen im Angesicht der sündigen Stadt Ninive und wartete auf ihren Untergang länger als vierzig mal vierzig Tage? Und Jona ging aus dem Leben in den Tod, der ihm lieber war? Und Jona stand auf und führte ein Leben in Ninive? Wer weiss.

STORIA D'AMORE

DI

GIORGIO BASSANI

> Enfin, des années entières s'étant
> passées, le temps et l'absence ra-
> lentirent sa douleur et éteignirent
> sa passion.
>
> LA PRINCESSE DE CLÈVES

I

Finché visse, Débora Abeti ricordò sempre il breve periodo di tempo che aveva preceduto il parto. Ogni volta che ci ripensava, si commuoveva. Eppure, quei giorni non erano certo stati densi di avvenimenti e di sensazioni. Era vissuta per un mese stesa in un letto, in fondo a un corridoio. Da una finestra che dava nel giardino della Maternità, i suoi occhi si posavano sulle foglie lustre di pioggia di una grande magnolia. Era aprile: ma faceva già caldo, e la finestra restava aperta tutto il giorno. Poi, verso la fine, aveva perduto interesse anche per le foglie nere, come unte, della magnolia. I dolori l'assalirono con molto ritardo; non capiva né sentiva piú in modo normale. Si era ridotta ad essere una cosa molto gonfia e insensibile (la calma che la circondava era pari a quella che aveva dentro...) abbandonata in fondo a una corsia. Non mangiava quasi piú nulla, ma il professore, per via dell'aria sciroccale che le rendeva faticosa la respirazione, diceva che era meglio cosí.

II

Poi, dopo il parto, il tempo era ricominciato a passare.

In principio, pensando a David (talvolta la feriva il ricordo della sua faccia annoiata e scontenta: non le rivolgeva quasi mai la parola, rimaneva tutto il giorno steso sul letto a leggere romanzi francesi...) Débora era tornata a stare nella

317

camera ammobiliata dove era vissuta con lui gli ultimi sei mesi. Ma poi, a poco a poco, anche perché il pensiero del bambino la spaventava (le mancava il latte, David non s'era fatto piú vedere, ormai quei pochi soldi stavano per finire...), ella si era rassegnata all'idea di tornare a casa, dalla madre. Cosí, nell'estate di quello stesso anno, Débora Abeti era ricomparsa in via Salinguerra. Aveva rivisto la viuzza tortuosa e deserta, i muriccioli irti di pezzi di vetro che la fiancheggiavano, le sue casupole corrose, l'erba che spunta tra i sassi del fondo stradale. Aveva infine rivisto la bassa cameraccia dal pavimento di legno polveroso e dai due letti di ferro affiancati dove aveva passato la prima giovinezza.

Il piano della stanza che un tempo, forse, era stata una cantina o il magazzino di un carbonaio, non era allo stesso livello della strada, bensí un poco piú basso. Nonostante ciò, per accedervi bisognava salire una rampa di scale esterna, e scenderne una interna. Erano come i lati, nascosti l'uno all'altro, di un triangolo la cui base era data dai fondi ugualmente umidi e oscuri del portico, da una parte, e della camera, dall'altra; e il vertice, dal pianerottolo e dalla porta. Quest'ultima, che dal lato del portico si apriva su una parete la cui ampiezza si perdeva nel buio (la scala, protetta da una sottile e rugginosa ringhiera continuava a salire verso i piani superiori), da quello della stanza risultava quasi al livello del soffitto. Appena Débora entrò, vide di lassú sua madre che aveva alzato il capo dal cucito. Nei suoi occhi non c'era stupore, soltanto un'interrogazione pungente. Ella scese gli scalini adagio, le andò incontro, infine si chinò a baciarla sulla guancia. E il bacio, proprio come se Débora fosse rientrata dopo un'assenza di poche ore, fu tranquillamente restituito.

C'era ora la questione del battesimo. Débora rammentava che i primi giorni dopo il parto, mentre ancora si trovava alla Maternità, in lei il pensiero del battesimo del bambino si era scontrato, improvviso e fulmineo, con quello di David. David! Dopo l'intervallo degli ultimi mesi di gravidanza, durante i quali la sua indifferenza per ogni cosa era andata aumentando progressivamente fino all'insensibilità assoluta degli ultimi giorni, quella era stata la prima volta che lei era ritornata a ricordarsene, a soffrirne. Il suo era stato, ed era, un amore fatto di sgomento e di devozione, un amore che accettava tutto, disposto a tutto: per questo — sorrideva amaramente — soltanto per questo aveva voluto aspettare. Ma ora — soggiungeva — perché avrebbe dovuto continuare ad aver scrupoli? A che pro? Finalmente si decise a confidarsi con la madre.

« Sei matta? », esclamò costei, facendosi un rapido segno di croce.

Quindi cominciò a parlare. Parlava con una libertà e una sicurezza (non era mai stata cosí espansiva, cosí sollecita) che meravigliavano la figlia. La sera stessa il bimbo, al quale fu imposto il nome di Ireneo, venne portato in chiesa. Recandovisi, le due donne avevano camminato in fretta, come se si sentissero inseguite. Tornarono invece adagio, improvvisamente stanchissime, senza scambiare una parola.

La madre taceva, Débora pure. Ambedue erano grate l'una all'altra di un riserbo che le tratteneva dal tornare su un periodo di tempo che per ragioni diverse era stato cosí doloroso per tutte e due. La testa china sul cucito, accanto alla finestra, esse si tenevano compagnia, si facevano coraggio. Insomma era nata tra loro una strana, silenziosa amicizia, un mutuo desiderio d'appoggio che per esprimersi non aveva bisogno di nessuna parola. Tutte e due sapevano bene di che si trattava. Era un patto che poteva durare soltanto cosí, evitando di parlarne.

Ma la piú forte tuttavia era sempre Débora. Talvolta la madre non resisteva, azzardava uno scherzo, un'allusione velata. E se capitava, come quasi sempre capitava, che la figlia mostrasse di non capire, di non risentirsene, la madre provava per lei un moto di tenerezza che era veramente materna, e che prima d'allora non aveva mai provato. Rialzava il capo, s'incantava a guardarla. « Poveretta », diceva tra sé, « com'è dimagrita! ». Eppure era proprio in quel viso cosí affilato che ella si ritrovava, finalmente si riconosceva. Débora non assomigliava piú a *lui*, soltanto a *lui*. Non c'era piú nulla, in

Débora, della subdola dolcezza di suo padre, il meccanico di paese (il paese dove lei era nata) dal quale l'aveva avuta vent'anni prima. «Gli uomini sono tutti uguali»; «l'uomo è cacciatore»: era in frasi sentenziose o proverbi come questi, di cui si rammentava magari con un sorriso, che ella cercava sollievo, consolazione. David, quel figlio di signori, anzi di «signoroni», era come *lui*. Con la fantasia, ella lo rivestiva della tuta azzurra del suo uomo; gli imprestava i suoi capelli unti e arruffati, le sue labbra grosse, i suoi gesti pieni di pigrizia. Gli uomini erano tutti uguali, tutti cosí. Anche la società paesana che tanti anni prima, quand'era rimasta incinta, l'aveva rifiutata, scacciata, costretta ad emigrare in città, dava a poco a poco il suo volto crudele a quell'altra società cittadina, borghese, che, servitasi di sua figlia, l'aveva poi respinta «come una scarpa vecchia». Madre e figlia — pensava — esse avevano sofferto gli stessi dolori, si erano consumate alle stesse ansie, avevano subíto le stesse ingiustizie. Non c'era piú niente che le dividesse: ecco perché i loro volti ormai potevano assomigliarsi. Da questi pensieri la vecchia ricavava una strana allegria, la invadeva una specie di febbre. Una sera prese per mano la figlia e la condusse davanti allo specchio dell'armadio.

«Vedi, vedi?», diceva con voce soffocata.

E restarono a lungo a guardare attraverso lo specchio appannato (nella stanza non si udiva che il soffio della lampada a carburo) i loro visi accostati.

Naturalmente le cose non andavano sempre cosí lisce; non sempre Débora era tranquilla, disposta ad ascoltare senza ribattere. Una sera, per esempio, la vecchia si era messa a raccontare la propria storia. Alla fine, quasi a conclusione, ella pronunciò una frase che ebbe il potere di far scattare in piedi Débora.

«Se i suoi parenti avessero voluto», aveva detto sospirando, «lui m'avrebbe sposato».

Stesa sul letto, il volto nascosto nelle mani, Débora ripeteva mentalmente queste parole, riudiva il sospiro pieno di rammarico che le aveva accompagnate. Non piangeva, no. E alla madre che le era corsa dietro, e ansimante stava china su di lei, ella non seppe mostrare che un viso asciutto, uno sguardo pieno di disprezzo e di noia.

Del resto le sue insofferenze erano rare (quel volto impassibile, che non tradiva la presenza di nessun pensiero tormentoso, divideva pur sempre l'animo della madre tra sentimenti opposti di compiacenza e d'invidia), e se l'assalivano, l'assalivano senza preavviso, come raffiche tempestose in un giorno di bonaccia. Una volta, sentendo la madre chiamarla col suo nome, le si rivoltò contro con un riso cattivo. «Débora! E perché non Cunegonda, Genoveffa? Col calendario sotto mano, potevi trovare anche di meglio». Ma la vecchia non rispose. Sorrideva. Lo scatto della figlia la riportava a cose lontane, che ella sola poteva comprendere. «Débora», ripeté tra sé piú volte. Pensava al suo uomo. Ella era venuta a stare in città; e lui, ogni domenica, faceva sessanta chilometri in bicicletta. Trenta andare e trenta tornare. Sedeva lí, dove ora sedeve Débora. Le pareva ancora di vederlo: con la sua tuta, i suoi capelli spettinati... Finché una notte, tornando al paese, era stato sorpreso a mezza strada dalla pioggia, e si era ammalato di pleurite. D'allora in poi non l'aveva piú visto. Era andato a stare in un paese del Veneto, un paese di montagna, dove aveva preso moglie e avuto figli. Se i parenti avessero voluto, lui l'avrebbe sposata. Che ne sapeva, cosa poteva capirne Débora? Lei sola poteva specchiarsi nella figlia, capire per tutte e due.

Compatire la figlia, comprenderla, perdonarla: per lei era un modo di sentirsi davvero madre, per la prima volta in condizione di superiorità. Soprattutto per questa ragione le era stato cosí facile non rimproverarla di ciò che aveva fatto. Talvolta Débora smetteva di lavorare; i suoi occhi cercavano la finestra, si perdevano oltre i vetri. E allora era con gioia, una gioia cosí piena da non accorgersi di esser crudele, che la vecchia si metteva a parlare di David e del bambino. Non bisognava disperare — diceva. Il passato era passato, e, poiché il bambino c'era, bisognava tenerselo. Del resto chissà: non era figlio d'un signore?

E fu veramente soltanto in grazia di quest'ultima frase, che la madre aveva detto pensando a ben altro (no, da lui non sarebbe mai andata: se per la strada avesse veduto comparire di lontano un cappottone di falsa pelliccia blu, o un impermeabile stretto alla vita; se David, passandole accanto, le avesse sfiorato il gomito, ella avrebbe continuato a camminare abbassando la faccia, sicura di non esser stata riconosciuta...) soltanto in grazia di quella frase Débora ricordò con vivezza David, rivide il suo lungo viso di cavallo triste. Non gli avrebbe chiesto un soldo, non l'avrebbe seccato. Cosa avrebbe potuto dirgli, scrivergli? Ricordava la barba d'otto giorni che si era lasciato crescere. In quella stanza faceva un caldo! Egli stava continuamente a letto, sudava, leggeva romanzi francesi.

Soltanto allora, dopo aver teso le sue labbra disseccate in un riso felice (ella rideva a chissà quali ricordi, a chissà quali sogni: e Débora, distolti gli occhi dalla finestra, li posava con pietà su quel povero viso consunto), soltanto allora la vecchia sembrava tornata tranquilla. Dopo cena, le due donne restavano sedute a lungo, senza sparecchiare, coi gomiti puntati sul tavolo e il mento appoggiato nel cavo delle mani. La prima a coricarsi era sempre Débora. Ma l'altro letto, di fianco a quello dove Débora e il bambino già dormivano (la lampada a carburo posta nel centro del tavolo spandeva attorno una bianca luce vacillante), spesso rimaneva intatto fino a notte inoltrata.

III

Via Salinguerra è una stradetta serpeggiante che comincia da un piazzale terroso, frutto di un'antica demolizione, e termina ai piedi dei bastioni comunali, ai margini della campagna. Percorrendola, specie nell'ultimo tratto, si ha l'impressione di trovarsi ben oltre la cinta delle mura. Di certi viottoli della campagna suburbana, questa via, a parte l'aspetto, ha anche l'odore. Odore di letame, di terra arata, di stalla. Lo stesso silenzio che vi domina (le campane delle chiese di F., ascoltate da qui verso sera, hanno un suono diverso, come sperduto) è un silenzio che ha qualcosa di agreste. In realtà, sebbene ci si trovi ancora dentro il perimetro delle mura cittadine, si può dire che la campagna cominci da qui, dai grandi orti che si stendono oltre i rossi muretti che fiancheggiano dai due lati la strada, e di cui pochi in città, pur conoscendone l'esistenza, sospettano l'estensione. Muggiti di buoi, gracidii di rane, odore d'erba e di strame, e, la sera, il lontano scampanío dell'Angelus. Suono e odori arrivavano anche laggiú, in fondo al pozzo dove le due donne badavano a cucire stoffe militari per conto di una sartoria specializzata. Esse tenevano la testa china sul lavoro, e non l'alzavano che per scambiare qualche parola, o per guardare i rari passanti : ombre fugaci che esse scorgevano di sotto in sú, scarpe strascicate sui ciottoli, occhi indifferenti, abbagliati dalla luce meridiana. Alle loro spalle, in cima alla scala, sospesa sopra il vano della porta a un braccio di lamiera flessibile, pendeva una campanella. Una lunga corda, la cui estremità usciva da un foro del portone di strada, la collegava con l'esterno. E questa corda, che un soffio di vento bastava a fare oscillare, pareva invitare ad aggrapparvisi, ad imprimervi strappi violenti. Sopra la porticina di legno non verniciato (quattro assi inchiodate alla meglio : delle teste e delle punte dei chiodi non perfettamente ribattute nel legno le due donne si servivano per appendervi qualche indumento, qualche straccio), ogni tanto la campanella dava in scosse frenetiche. E se dall'esterno tornava un suono flebile, lontano, dentro la stanza il silenzio era lacerato da uno squillo improvviso, acutissimo. Sedute di fronte alla finestra, sopra due scalcagnati seggioloni di paglia, ogni volta madre e figlia trasalivano con violenza, si volgevano di scatto indietro.

Talora la vecchia alzava il capo, accennava a cominciare un discorso. Batteva le palpebre, tossiva, ma poi, sfiduciata, lasciava cadere la frase. Seguiva un riso secco, che pretendeva d'essere misterioso, carico di promesse, ed era soltanto angosciato. « Se tu volessi, se tu mi ascoltassi, quante cose potrei dirti ». In quel riso, in quella tosse, in quel vano agitarsi, c'era questo ed altro : desiderio d'abbandono e insieme orgoglio dispettoso, forse un ultimo resto di vanità femminile...

Cosí se Débora, come faceva quasi sempre, non raccoglieva l'invito, il suo senile bisogno di parlare, di riempire con qualcosa il vuoto delle loro vite, le si risolveva di dentro in un monotono e fitto balbettio di parole volute dire e non pronunciate, di nomi — Débora, Ireneo, David — che, come una preghiera, aveva il potere di calmarla, di farla tornare la povera vecchia rassegnata che in fondo era. Allora pensava a Débora in modo diverso, pensava che la figlia era giovane, che avrebbe potuto ancora maritarsi. E quando Oreste Benetti, che aveva in via Salinguerra una bottega di legatore di libri, cominciò, la sera dopo cena, a far loro qualche visita, fu lei la prima, forse, a comprendere che queste visite erano fatte in omaggio alla figlia. Ella andava e veniva per la stanza, non diceva mai nulla. Dal viso si sarebbe detta una suocera bonaria e discreta sí, ma ben consapevole del valore dei propri diritti e del peso delle proprie responsabilità.

Débora sosteneva la conversazione con una specie di calma sommissione. Guardava la grossa testa dell'ospite, una testa che pareva troppo pesante per quel piccolo corpo seduto; guardava le sue lunghe mani nodose, intrecciate sulla tovaglia. Quanto al legatore, egli ricordava volentieri alle due donne gli anni passati. Rammentava a Débora che l'aveva veduta bambina, « alta cosí ». Capitava in bottega, si alzava in punta di piedi per arrivare con gli occhi all'altezza del banco e chiedergli in regalo ritagli di carta colorata. Egli parlava ad ambedue, pareva che mettesse una certa cura nel dare ai suoi discorsi un tono impersonale; ma gli occhi, mentre parlava, li volgeva assai piú spesso verso Débora che verso la madre. Il consenso e l'attenzione egli li cercava soprattutto nel volto di lei; ed ella gli rispondeva con una amabilità contegnosa, una compostezza, da cui ricavava un piacere mai provato prima d'allora. Senza che se ne accorgesse, ella si atteggiava nel modo che era piú gradito al Benetti.

Egli era molto compreso di sé; pure, era continuamente in caccia di prestigio. Una volta (una delle poche), che si rivolse direttamente alla vecchia, fu per ricordarle l'anno in cui ella era venuta a stare in città. Era stato un anno — rammentava — di freddo eccezionale. I cumuli di neve sporca erano rimasti ai lati delle vie fino ai primi d'aprile. La temperatura s'era talmente abbassata che perfino il Po aveva gelato. « Perfino il Po. Vi dico: una vera Siberia! ». Gli pareva ancora di vederla, diceva, la grande distesa ghiacciata. Tra gli argini, l'acqua aveva smesso di scorrere. Rammentava lo spettacolo straordinario del fiume, gli argini coperti di neve, le case ai piedi degli argini mezzo sepolte sotto la neve. Verso sera, i barrocciani che risiedevano nei paesi di là dal Po, tornavano da F. coi carri vuoti. Dalle segherie che lavorano in mezzo ai boschi delle due rive, avevano trasportato in città quintali e quintali di legna da ardere. Alcuni, forse per scommessa, guidavano i loro carri, invece che per il ponte di ferro, attraverso l'immensa lastra gelata. Avanzavano lentamente, qualche metro davanti ai cavalli, tenendo le redini dietro la schiena, raccolte in un pugno. Con l'altro pugno, perché gli zoccoli non slittassero sul ghiaccio, spargevano segatura. Intanto fischiavano, emettevano grida gutturali. Un modo come un altro — soggiungeva Oreste — per riscaldarsi e per far coraggio a sé e alle bestie.

Parlando del Po, egli assumeva lo stesso tono rispettoso di quando parlava delle persone e delle cose della religione. Orfano dall'infanzia ed educato in Seminario, aveva conservato per i preti, per i preti in genere, una venerazione quasi figliale.

« Ricordo che quel famoso inverno », disse una sera, « il povero Don Castelli ci conduceva quasi ogni sabato pomeriggio a vedere il Po. Appena fuori porta, si rompeva le righe e si camminava ognuno per nostro conto, come Dio consigliava. Quattordici chilometri a piedi: non era il giro dell'orto. Don Castelli, poveretto, sebbene tirasse il fiato coi denti, era sempre davanti a tutti. Non voleva mai che si prendesse il tram, nemmeno al ritorno. Diceva che camminare fa bene alla salute, conserva l'appetito. A me », e intanto guardava sorridendo Débora, le strizzava l'occhio allegramente, tra il faceto e il paterno « a me mi teneva sempre vicino, mi voleva bene come un padre ».

«Dovevo avere la bambina», disse a questo punto la vecchia. «In città mi sentivo persa, non sapevo leggere né scrivere, e, se non fosse stato per lei» — intanto accennava col mento a Débora — «sarei scappata via, tornata al paese. Ma come potevo fare? Voi sapete, Oreste, com'è la gente di campagna».

«Un freddo così, dopo d'allora, non ci fu che nel diciassette», confermò Oreste: e rimase pensieroso. Poi, con un lampo improvviso negli occhi:

«Ma no», soggiunse, «anzi. Per quello che ne so io, nel diciassette il freddo fu molto meno intenso. Faceva un caldo, da noi sul Carso! Certe cose è meglio domandarle alla gente che marcava visita, a certi imboscati di comune conoscenza» (sottolineava con ironia queste ultime parole) «che il fronte lo vedevano soltanto in cartolina».

Raccogliendo l'allusione, la vecchia si irrigidí. Ma poi, pensando al suo uomo che era stato riformato e non aveva fatto la guerra, si ritrovò, di lí a poco, a fantasticare intorno a lui, intorno a se stessa, intorno a tante cose che sarebbero potute essere e non erano state. Se i parenti non si fossero opposti, se egli non si fosse ammalato, certo l'avrebbe sposata. Nel '19 si era trasferito in un paese dell'alto Veneto, sopra Trento, dove si era ammogliato. Moglie e figli: chissà se si rammentava di lei. Anch'egli, ormai, doveva avere i capelli tutti grigi; forse, chissà, si era dimenticato perfino del suo dialetto.

«Vigliacco, vigliacco...»: mentre il viso si addolciva, si inteneriva, le labbra non cessavano di muoversi.

«Vigliacco, vigliacco, vigliacco...», ripeteva a non finire.

Il vecchio insulto, dopo tanti anni, si era trasformato in un bisbiglio senza significato, in una giaculatoria da beghina.

Stabilite certe distanze, Oreste poteva tornare a mostrarsi cavalleresco, a comportarsi con finezza, come del resto gli comandava la sua natura. Si era fatto da sé, e ne era fiero. Aveva avuto una giovinezza triste, le cui uniche isole felici restavano, tra pochi altri, i ricordi delle passeggiate invernali fatte coi compagni di collegio. Poi era venuto il lavoro, il mestiere, il suo mestiere. «Noi artigiani», diceva, come se dichiarasse un titolo nobiliare. Débora l'ascoltava con attenzione. Ed egli le era grato che ella sedesse lí, davanti a lui, cosí silenziosa, cosí composta, cosí attenta a rispondere femminilmente al suo desiderio.

Egli continuava a parlare fino a tardi (parlava di tutto: di religione, di storia, di prezzi, perfino di politica...). Nei primi tempi, senza smettere d'ascoltarlo, Débora faceva oscillare con la punta del piede la culla dove il bambino dormiva. Piú avanti, col passare degli anni (cresceva gracile: verso i cinque anni aveva avuto una lunga malattia infettiva che lo lasciò poi sempre di salute malferma e forse influí sul suo incerto carattere), ella si alzava ogni tanto dalla seggiola, si accostava al lettino, e restava china sul ragazzo, con la mano posata sulla sua fronte.

IV

Nell'estate del '28 — Débora compiva giusto trent'anni — una sera che come al solito sedevano tutti e tre attorno alla lampada, il Benetti chiese a Débora se acconsentiva a sposarlo. La sua domanda (egli aveva parlato con grande semplicità) non era stata preannunciata da nessun atteggiamento particolare. Anche se vagamente attesa, essa era venuta improvvisa. Débora lo guardò. «Chissà quanti anni ha», pensava. «Forse quarantacinque, forse cinquanta, forse piú...». Le pareva di vederlo per la prima volta. Soltanto ora s'accorgeva di quegli umidi occhi nerissimi, di quella fronte bianca e alta, chiusa tutta attorno da un arco di capelli color grigio ferro, tagliati corti a spazzola secondo un gusto un po' militare. Ad un tratto fu presa da un senso di imbarazzo. Voleva dire qualcosa, e non sapeva che. In cerca d'aiuto, si volse allora verso la madre; ma la bocca di costei, che già si torceva in una smorfia patetica, non fece che aumentare la sua confusione. «Che ti piglia?», le disse in dialetto. Si sentiva torcere lo stomaco dal disgusto, accecare dall'ira.

Si alzò di scatto, fece di corsa la rampa interna, uscí sbattendo la porta. Dalla camera la udirono scendere adagio, gradino per gradino (come se, affranta, si appoggiasse alla ringhiera) la scala esterna. Infine raggiunse la strada, e subito alzò gli occhi al cielo. Era un bellissimo stellato. Sola, in distanza, si udiva la musica di una banda. Dalle imposte di una casetta di fronte filtrava un tenue chiarore di luce elettrica. Débora appoggiò le spalle al muro, vi aderí con tutta la schiena, e intanto guardava in alto, al cielo pieno di stelle. Attraverso il muro udiva la voce di Oreste. Egli parlava quietamente alla madre: la sua voce, il suono della sua voce (non riusciva a distinguere le parole) la persuadeva alla calma, la invitava dolcemente a rientrare.

Quando riapparve, era soltanto un po' pallida. Il Benetti e la madre, che per tutto quel tempo non si erano levati dalle loro seggiole, la guardavano dal basso, mentre ella scendeva le scale, col viso di chi attende una risposta. Débora si strinse leggermente nelle spalle. Che avrebbe potuto dire? Andò a sedersi di nuovo al suo posto; e per quella sera, come, del resto, anche per le altre che seguirono, nessuno tornò piú sull'argomento.

In realtà il Benetti dimostrò subito di non nutrire dubbi eccessivi circa il tenore di una risposta a cui Débora si era rifiutata (cosí pensava, e lasciava intendere di pensare) soltanto per timidezza. Per lui, Débora aveva già detto di sí, ormai erano fidanzati.

«Bisogna esser ragionevoli», diceva, «bisogna star quieti e tirare avanti».

E dicendo ciò, il suo viso contento contrastava col tono triste e rassegnato della voce. La sua bontà, la sua generosità (non era poco: innamorarsi di una ragazza che aveva avuto un figlio con un ebreo!) lo riempivano d'orgoglio. Riguardo a David, sebbene lasciasse capire che gli era ben noto chi fosse il padre di Ireneo, tuttavia evitò sempre di parlarne. Egli era un cattolico molto osservante, e il suo sentimento per Débora (ciò, d'altra parte, testimoniava della serietà delle sue intenzioni...) aveva sempre avuto qualcosa di religioso. Un dovere, una missione; egli aveva sempre provato, fin da principio, il bisogno di sentirsi disposto a perdonarla, ad assorverla di un grande peccato.

In fondo in fondo, non era troppo sicuro di sê. No, non nominò mai David (aveva la cavalleria e la gentilezza istintive di certi piccoli militari); e se tentava di legarla a sé con argomenti che le apparissero piú grandi delle loro persone (vent'anni di differenza: se ne rendeva ben conto!...), era proprio perché temeva che Débora potesse tornare sopra una decisione che egli considerava già presa. Certo, nei suoi discorsi l'idea della redenzione attraverso il matrimonio era sempre implicita, suggerita, mai espressa a chiare parole. Gli bastava ogni tanto alludere al passato di Débora, alla sua giovinezza inquieta, randagia, alla necessità di riscattarsene con una maturità migliore, con una vita dignitosa e serena. Era quanto egli le avrebbe dato, ciò che le offriva. « Bisogna esser ragionevoli, star quieti e tirare avanti ». Lui solo, doveva convincersene, era in grado di guidarla. Il passato era passato: eppure, per esser diversi, per guarirne, bisognava pensarvi continuamente. Seduto al tavolo, tra le due donne, egli riconduceva i loro pensieri sempre là, dove sapeva che risiedeva la sua forza. Allusioni, accenni, niente altro. Di quella storia, che col passare del tempo appariva sempre piú irreale e scandalosa, bisognava, anche se non era bene parlarne, non dimenticarsi mai.

Ma stavano cosí all'erta, avevano i nervi tanto tesi, che bastava nulla perché andassero oltre la misura. Dopo, restavano per un pezzo turbati, si tenevano il broncio.

Una volta, per esempio, Oreste disse che si sentiva veramente come il padre di Ireneo. Si era lasciato trasportare, si era abbandonato un po' troppo.

« Ma come, non sei lo zio Oreste? », esclamò a questo punto Ireneo, che aveva già otto anni, e aveva preso l'abitudine, ogni sera prima di coricarsi, di farsi correggere i compiti da lui.

Il legatore si volse di scatto verso il bambino. La sua confusione dava a Débora un senso molto preciso, assai gradito, della propria importanza. Mentre egli si affannava a rispondere, ella e la madre si scambiavano rapide occhiate di intelligenza.

Con tutto che non fossero piú dei ragazzi, sebbene si conoscessero da tanti anni, il loro fu un fidanzamento lungo; e certo, se nell'inverno successivo la vecchia non fosse morta improvvisamente, lo sarebbe stato anche di piú. Comunque, dopo quella sera famosa, Oreste era stato prodigo d'attenzioni e di regali. Sebbene avesse fatto capire che dopo le nozze sarebbero andati a stare tutti e tre assieme in una casa nuova (un villino fuori porta, ancora in costruzione, per il quale era in trattative), fece montare l'impianto della luce elettrica, acquistò alcuni mobili, una cucina economica di ghisa, un quadro, utensili da cucina, ecc. Era innamorato. Se la sposava, la sposava perché l'amava. Prima, non aveva mai pensato a nessuna donna. Indugiava volentieri sui suoi atti, sui suoi pensieri. Li gustava adagio, ne ricavava una profonda, egoistica felicità. Se ne era privato per tanti anni: tutta la giovinezza, gran parte della maturità! Aveva ogni diritto di pretendere che le cose non fossero fatte in fretta, che tutto si svolgesse con le dovute regole.

Arrivava ogni sera alla stessa ora, alle nove e mezza in punto. La scena era sempre la stessa. Una scampanellata vigorosa dalla strada, passi che salivano le scale, la sua voce gioconda che gridava dalla soglia:

« Buona sera, mie signore ».

Egli entrava canticchiando tra i denti, ma s'interrompeva subito, con una piccola tosse educata. Non c'erano varianti, da anni. Eppure, nonostante ciò, se l'arrivo del legatore non mancava mai di far trattenere il fiato alla vecchia, se esso riusciva sempre a suscitare sulle sue labbra stirate un rapido, indulgente sorriso da mezzana, Débora non si lasciava piú prendere dalla sorda ira di un tempo. Era la sua volta, ormai, di pensare: « povera mamma, com'è dimagrita, com'è invecchiata! ». Presto, lo sentiva, ella se ne sarebbe andata, per sempre.

D'altronde erano passati tanti anni — si diceva —, tutto era ormai cosí diverso, che gli stracci appesi ai chiodi della porta, quando ondeggiavano lievemente rispondendo ai sobbalzi della campanella sovrastante (il piccolo battacchio continuava ancora per poco a oscillare in silenzio), non avrebbero potuto destare, in lei, che confronti sempre più vaghi, sempre più sbiaditi. Non avevano avuto nemmeno il tempo di avvicinarsi alla scala per andare incontro all'ospite, non si erano ancora alzate dalle seggiole, che già di lassù, dal pianerottolo, la nota voce canticchiava:

«Buo-na se-ra, mi-e signo-re», sull'aria del *Barbiere*. Seguiva la tosse, entrava l'allegria del piccolo uomo dai capelli grigi, la dolce allegria militare del legatore Oreste Benetti.

Erano passati tanti anni, lei stessa era così mutata: perché, pur potendo, avrebbe dovuto perdersi a ricordare?

Certo, quando una scampanellata altrettanto vigorosa significava che David, chiuso nel suo cappottone di falsa pelliccia blu, battendo i piedi sui ciottoli per l'impazienza e per il freddo (mai aveva voluto entrare, mai aveva voluto conoscere sua madre...), l'aspettava come d'accordo giù in istrada: allora le rimaneva appena un momento per infilarsi il soprabito, darsi un poco di cipria, aggiustarsi i capelli davanti allo specchio. Un attimo: ma bastava perché nello specchio, piccola e lucida di capelli tirati sulla nuca (la luce da tergo la faceva sembrare quasi calva), ella vedesse apparire e sparire, svelta svelta dietro le spalle, la testa grigia di sua madre.

«Che vuoi, cosa cerchi?», urlava. «Sai cosa ho da dirti? Ne ho abbastanza di te e di questa vita».

Usciva sbattendo la porta, a David non piaceva attendere.

V

Ancora fremente, aggrappata al suo braccio, si lasciava portare. Di solito risalivano via Salinguerra. Arrivati in fondo alla strada e saliti sui bastioni (da una parte si vedevano i lumi della città, dall'altra si stendeva la campagna immersa nel buio), prendevano per il sentiero che, tra una doppia fila di alberi di grosso fusto, tigli quercie e castagni, segue tutto attorno lo sviluppo delle mura. Camminavano in fretta, senza scambiare una parola. A quell'epoca David progettava di laurearsi al piú presto. Si era riconciliato con la famiglia (per potersene staccare piú tardi — diceva — a migliori condizioni), perció aveva ripreso, erano le sue parole, a «fare un po' d'attenzione». Fare attenzione significava non farsi vedere con lei: era necessario, doveva capirlo. A ció lui si adattava per il bene di tutti e due, non per altro. Lungo quel sentiero, al cinema della periferia dove erano diretti, non li avrebbe visti nessuno, nessuno della buona società alla quale apparteneva la sua famiglia. Del resto, non era piú bello cosí? L'amore, per essere amore, aveva bisogno di quei contrasti, di quei sotterfugi...

Aveva *ripreso* a fare attenzione. Perché c'era stato un periodo di tempo anteriore a quello (nell'estate dell'anno precedente) in cui David non temeva affatto di fare attenzione. Allora, a quell'epoca davvero favolosa, davvero incredibile (la portava nei migliori cinema, si sedevano di pieno giorno nei caffè del centro), sembrava proprio che egli volesse troncarla col suo passato. Studi, amici, famiglia; egli *doveva* finirla con tutti e con tutto («non mi sei rimasta che te», sospirava), con una vita che, a suo dire, non gli faceva che schifo. I pomeriggi, molto spesso, li passavano lí sui bastioni, sdraiati nell'erba come due zingari. Dormivano abbracciati, scoperti agli sguardi di tutti. Talvolta David si alzava, si accostava a un gruppo di giovinastri intenti, in circolo, a giocare d'azzardo sotto l'ombra di un albero. E mentre egli, seduto, gettava con stanchezza le carte, ella restava in piedi dietro di lui, chinandosi ogni tanto per dargli qualche consiglio. In piedi dietro le sue spalle, quasi a proteggerlo, a vegliarlo... La città era lí, a poche centinaia di metri di distanza, addormentata nel sole sotto i suoi tetti rossi, dietro le persiane accostate.

Al cinema, la sera, non andavano che di rado; spesso — ricordava Débora — tornavano sui bastioni. L'aria era calda, coppie d'innamorati passavano bisbigliando. E anch'essi, piú tardi, aspettando il fresco, si incamminavano lentamente. Ogni tanto da un lato del sentiero si apriva un piazzale erboso. La luna, specchiandovisi, faceva sí che le panchine di cemento (le poche ancora vuote...), splendessero laggiú, sul limite estremo del prato, come per luce propria. La luna trasformava tutto. Perfino le cartacce sporche, che allontanate di giorno col piede destavano covi immondi di mosche, la notte, sparse qua e là nell'erba, brillavano intensamente. L'aria era dolce, profumata; qualunque oggetto diventava prezioso. Perché ogni cosa, ora, appariva tanto diversa? Il sentiero, lungo il quale si affrettavano, era bensí il medesimo, ma erano bastati pochi mesi, il volgere d'una stagione, perché, da amico e ospitale (il luogo del loro primo e migliore amore) fosse diventato ostile, addirittura sinistro. La nebbia che cominciava a salire dai canali della campagna sottostante aveva già invaso i piazzali, li aveva tramutati in golfi di tenebre paurosi allo sguardo, dove le panchine, viscide d'umidità, erano disertate da tutti. E se allora David, mentre camminavano adagio, l'uno a fianco dell'altro, neppure la sfiorava; se ogni tanto, sentendo il suo sguardo, si volgeva a sorriderle con tristezza: adesso (erano bastati cosí pochi mesi perché egli cessasse di amarla!), adesso egli la teneva stretta ad un braccio, non la guardava, la sospingeva dove lei non voleva andare. Tutto era mutato, dentro e fuori di loro, tutto si era spento. E se ella si fosse ribellata, se gli fosse sfuggita? Improvvise, quasi in risposta, le luci al neon del sobborgo splendevano azzurre e rosse sulla sua testa. Era tardi, per resistere. n antro caldo e fumoso (spinta alle spalle, ella vi scivolava dentro) si apriva davanti e lei con la lentezza di uno sbadiglio.

Ma appena entrata (la sala era lunga e bassa, stretta poco meno d'un corridoio), subito i nervi le si distendevano. Sulla platea stipata, punteggiata di sigarette, il ronzío della macchina da proiezione aveva per lei, non sapeva perché, qualcosa di rassicurante. Nonostante tutto, i film le piacevano. Di solito erano belle storie, bellissime storie d'amore. Ragazze povere che al termine di lunghe peripezie venivano «impalmate» dal signore ricco e fatale, dal concertista celebre travestito da studente, dal principe in incognito. In tutti i casi la virtú, la bellezza (la bellezza: ma talvolta un cuore ardente e disinteressato, un aspetto simpatico, bastavano a compensare qualche difetto del viso e della persona), erano la contropartita che veniva offerta al prestigio del nome e della fortuna, alla superiorità dell'educazione e del livello sociale. Ogni tanto ella volgeva gli occhi verso David. Egli si era levato il cappello e il cappotto. Nella penombra, ella ne distingueva il collo alto e sottile, il profilo scontento, come assonnato, i capelli ondulati, lucidi di brillantina. Allungava una mano per cercare la sua, e David lasciava fare. Talvolta si girava a rispondere al suo sguardo: pareva tranquillo, innamorato anche lui. Ma poi, bruscamente, respingeva la mano, si scostava con tutta la persona. «Che caldo», lo sentiva sbuffare; «non si respira».

Intimorita, ella non insisteva. Riportava gli occhi sullo schermo, e presto, affascinata dal film, dimenticava ogni cosa. Dimenticava perfino David che, deluso di non sentir piú la mano dalle dita gonfie e screpolate cercare la sua (deluso, magari, di non poterla scacciar via di nuovo), stava rannicchiato nella sua poltrona come se temesse che lei lo toccasse. Coi suoi abiti stretti alla vita, con quei suoi gesti lenti e staccati, David era lassú, sullo schermo, angelo, dio; e lei, confusa nella platea, si accontentava di guardarlo, di adorarlo da lontano. Il film la prendeva talmente, che piú tardi, mentre con gli altri uscivano dal cinema, se David, facendo a un tratto la voce carezzevole, le proponeva di accompagnarla a casa rifacendo il sentiero dei bastioni («la strada, tanto, si allunga di poco...»), allora essa trasaliva, il risveglio era sempre brusco e amaro. Il momento temuto — e fors'anche oscuramente desiderato —; il passo necessario che, per quanto conteso alla fantasia, ciò nondimeno aveva determinato fino ad allora il fondo d'angoscia dei suoi pensieri: l'inevitabile le era sopra, ella non poteva sottrarvisi. Cercava scuse («non mi sento bene, lo sai...»), inventava divieti («è tardi, la mamma mi aspetta per mezzanotte»), invocava ostacoli («fa freddo, sarà tutto bagnato...»): cercava di resistere in qualche modo. Davanti alla porta del cinema una vecchietta, soffiando in un suo fornello, badava ad arrostire castagne sulla bragia. Non gli piacevano le caldarroste? — ella gli chiedeva. Lasciasse almeno che la piazzetta si vuotasse, qualcuno avrebbe potuto vederli.

Cercava di non cedere, di guadagnar tempo. Come sarebbe stato meglio, ora che la nebbia infittiva, incamminarsi lentamente verso casa. Nessuno avrebbe potuto vederli, nemmeno se fossero passati per il centro, nemmeno se fossero scesi giú per Corso G. La nebbia stava aumentando talmente, che i globi dei lampioni non si scorgevano quasi piú. Avrebbero attraversato la città (la nebbia si posava sulle labbra, sulle ciglia...) invisibili agli altri come due fantasmi. A causa dei marciapiedi umidi, avrebbero camminato adagio, stretti l'uno all'altro come due fidanzati veri e propri. David le avrebbe parlato di sé, dei suoi studi, dei suoi progetti per il futuro. Magari le avrebbe parlato del film: era cosí intelligente (anche se, forse, un po' troppo aspro), cosí acuto nei giudizi... Oppure sarebbero entrati in qualche caffè, vi si sarebbero seduti. David avrebbe ordinato due bicchierini (per lui grappa, per lei anisetta): e mentre sorbivano adagio il liquore, ella si sarebbe sentita felice. Non avrebbe pensato a nulla: forse al letto, al sonno vicino... Potersi fidare di David, non aver piú bisogno nemmeno dei suoi baci per esser certa del suo amore! Ma invece cedeva. E alcuni soldati, che erano rimasti a fumare davanti all'ingresso del cinema, vedendoli allontanarsi in direzione dei bastioni, cominciavano a ridere, uscivano in fischi, in urla, in lazzi osceni. Affrettare il passo non serviva. Le voci dei soldati, che la distanza rendeva piú acute, la inseguivano nel buio, la cercavano nella schiena, la facevano rabbrividire.

Al primo buio, al primo prato, era rovesciata nell'erba. Col mento appoggiato alla spalla di lui, gli occhi spalancati, ella si lasciava andare.

Dopo, era la prima a rialzarsi. E se da ultimo era stata presa da una improvvisa, acre voglia di lotta (David non reagiva mai: la sua lunga schiena si torceva e s'allentava, sfinita), la furia che a un certo punto l'aveva indotta a strapparlo via

335

da sé, subito dopo aveva dato luogo in lei a una sorta di
paura. Si affannava a rassettare gli abiti di David ancora
prima che i suoi. Egli le pareva lontano, ormai perduto per
sempre. Ormai aveva fretta di sbarazzarsi di lei: ella lo sen-
tiva. Ma nello stesso tempo comprendeva che nell'impazienza
di David risiedeva piú che mai la ragione di quel suo amore
che si nutriva di adorazione e basta, un amore che per esi-
stere non aveva bisogno di altro premio. Non aveva nulla da
rimproverargli: né a lui, né a se stessa. Non sapeva, forse,
come la serata sarebbe andata a finire? Tutto era sempre an-
che troppo chiaro, fin da principio. Eppure, non era mai riu-
scita a resistere, mai aveva trovato la forza per dir di no.

Si avviavano. Se David avesse detto qualcosa, se si fosse
curato di riempire in qualche modo quel silenzio che li allon-
tanava sempre piú l'uno dall'altro! Freddo, distratto, ormai
egli non avrebbe detto che cose cattive. D'allora in poi, qua-
lunque cosa le fosse venuta da lui, certo non avrebbe potuto
che ferirla. Tuttavia lo provocava: niente poteva esser peggio
di quel vuoto, di quel deserto di ghiaccio su cui camminavano.
Si serviva di ingenue astuzie. Chiedeva, ad esempio:

« Come si chiama, la tua mamma? ».

E poiché David non rispondeva, rispondeva lei per lui.
« Teresa », sillabava con pronuncia artificiosa, volutamente
puerile. Non era divertente che lei gli facesse domande simili,
che fosse lei a rispondere a se stessa? Era la sua bambina, la
sua povera bambina senza difesa.

« E Marina », riprendeva, « come si chiama tua sorella
Marina? ».

Scoppiava a ridere. Poi ripeteva: « Ma-ri-na », con appli-
cazione esagerata, da piccola scolara attenta a non sbagliare.

Sbadigliava, accelerava il passo: sí, David ormai aveva
fretta di liberarsi di lei. A quell'ora, nonostante ciò, egli ama-
va dilungarsi in discorsi pieni di cose elevate, poetiche. Par-
lava volentieri di sé, pareva ispirato, mutava perfino la voce.
Il timbro di questa, gli argomenti dei suoi monologhi, s'ac-
cordavano stranamente al senso di vaga leggerezza che li fa-
ceva camminare spediti lungo il sentiero indurito dal gelo.

Egli raccontava di una sua relazione con una signorina della migliore società. Ne descriveva i lineamenti (era bionda, con gli occhi azzurri, l'aria delicata), ne vantava i gusti raffinati, le abitudini mondane. I loro rapporti, i loro contrasti (egli riferiva interi dialoghi), si svolgevano sempre al centro di mondi meravigliosi e proibiti: un ballo al Circolo T., dove l'aveva vista la prima volta, una rappresentazione di gala al Comunale, l'ultima caccia alla volpe. Si trattava di una relazione difficile, forse avversata dalle rispettive famiglie (ma soprattutto, a quanto le era dato di indovinare, da quella di lei...), una relazione comunque «di testa», dove i sensi, insomma «la cosa» che avevan fatto poco prima, sul prato, non c'entrava per nulla: una storia molto simile — ella pensava — a quelle dei film che tanto le piacevano. Scendevano dai bastioni, imboccavano via Salinguerra. E se fino a quel momento ella era rimasta ad ascoltare in sillenzio, quasi senza respirare, quando s'accorgeva, dai profili delle case e dai fanali, che erano ormai arrivati, ciò le metteva addosso una specie di febbre, una agitazione tutta nervosa. Si sentiva piccola, senza attrattive, certo irritante nella sua improvvisa vivacità. Odiava tutto di se stessa; quel suo soprabito striminzito e liso, quella sua corona di capelli arruffati, inumiditi dalla nebbia (avrebbero avuto bisogno di un po' di parrucchiere...), quelle sue mani volgari, deformate dal lavoro e dai geloni. Non si faceva illusioni, s'era vista allo specchio. Cosí com'era, non *poteva* aver fortuna, la sua sorte era già segnata. E allora, sempre piú febbrile ed eccessiva, si dava a recitare la parte della vecchia amica a cui son permesse tutte le domande, in grado di dare i consigli piú scabrosi. Godeva a nascondersi, a dissimulare la realtà del suo sentimento. Non era questo, d'altronde, ciò che David voleva? Ella si doveva comportare come se tra loro non ci fosse nulla, come se nulla, nemmeno mezz'ora prima, fosse mai successo. Ciò era quanto egli pretendeva da lei. Ma non era a quest'unico prezzo, dopo tutto, che il suo amore per David sarebbe potuto tornare bello, ideale e contrastato come quello di David per la signorina del Circolo T.?

Godeva e soffriva. Provocato, David continuava a parlare. Le sue parole erano leggere, gelate, le parole di uno che ha soddisfatto il suo desiderio. Il disgusto che lo prendeva notando le mani di lei aggrappate al suo braccio («mani da cuoca», forse pensava con disprezzo; «possibile che non cerchi di nasconderle un poco?») gli dava fretta e crudeltà sempre maggiori. Appena presa la laurea, sarebbe andato via (arrivati davanti al portone, entrati nel portico, ella lo sentiva allontanarsi, sottrarsi al bacio di commiato), forse in America, comunque solo. Solo, sicuro, perché lui, naturalmente, non si sarebbe mai sposato.

«La donna che mi ama deve ficcarselo bene in testa. Patti chiari e amicizia lunga».

Nemmeno la signorina di cui era tanto innamorato?

«No certo; e poi non è vero che io sia *tanto* innamorato. Ad ogni modo figúrati» soggiungeva egli con enfasi, ma con un'ombra di incertezza nella voce, «figúrati se potrei adattarmi a marcire per tutta la vita in questo buco di provincia!» Ed ella annuiva nel buio.

Ma certe volte (e se ne rammaricava piú tardi, a letto, quando per il tic-tac della sveglia posta sulla credenza, e per l'ansimare che la madre faceva dormendo, non riusciva a prender sonno) certe volte le veniva da ridere. Gli chiedeva:

«E se restassi incinta?»

Sapeva bene che questa domanda avrebbe costretto David a dire chissà quali assurdità. Comunque, lo avrebbe indotto a non andar via subito, a prolungare i suoi confusi monologhi per altri cinque minuti almeno. Certo, a questo proposito David non aveva mai detto che cose assurde: sempre, fino da allora. Eppure... eppure sarebbe rimasto ancora: un momento, qualche minuto. Forse, prima d'andarsene, egli l'avrebbe baciata. In fondo non era mai stato che un bambino, un bambino viziato. Se alle volte poteva essere un po' cattivo, non ne aveva colpa, non se ne accorgeva.

VI

Chi non ricorda l'inverno del '29? Per trovarne uno simile bisognava rifarsi al 1898, quando il Po aveva gelato, o al '17. Cosí almeno affermava Oreste Benetti. Cominciò a nevicare verso Natale, e continuò neve e neve fino all'Epifania. Ma la temperatura non era ancor rigida, tutt'altro. Anzi, appunto nei giorni attorno all'Epifania, ci fu un breve intervallo di sole, di tepore quasi primaverile, e la neve già si scioglieva. Dal letto (aveva dovuto mettercisi ai primi freddi, a causa di un'influenza: ed ora, oltre a una brutta tosse, le era rimasta una piccola febbre oscillante), la vecchia ascoltava lo sciacquío che le biciclette facevano passando. Però non c'era da fidarsi. Con la sera, saliva dalla campagna un mare di nebbia tiepida, pesante come pioggia. E quando Oreste arrivava, doveva, tanto era fradicio, appendere il cappotto lassú, ai chiodi della porta.

Scendeva gli scalini, si sedeva come al solito da un lato del tavolo. Tema dei suoi discorsi era quasi sempre Ireneo. A ottobre, all'inizio dell'anno scolastico, il ragazzo era stato ammesso come internista al Seminario dove lui, Oreste Benetti (ne era sempre stato il rilegatore di fiducia) contava molte aderenze. Ci andava molto spesso; ne tornava giusto ora. Uno scolaro un po' fiacco, un po' svogliato: questo gli aveva detto di Ireneo Don Bonora, il prefetto che era succeduto al suo caro Don Castelli. «Ma c'è tempo», soggiungeva Oreste; «nel latino, le basi sono tutto. E quel Don Bonora...» — e stringeva le labbra in modo significativo. Quindi passava a parlare della stagione. Alzava gli occhi al soffitto, fiutava l'aria con diffidenza. «Non ne siamo fuori», diceva, «il peggio deve ancora venire». Stesa sul letto, la vecchia ascoltava come sempre senza fiatare. Si limitava a corrugare la fronte, a sorridere sotto le coperte che teneva tese fino all'altezza della bocca.

Come sempre, Oreste aveva ragione. La stretta piú forte del freddo doveva ancora venire. Infatti, all'inizio della terza settimana di gennaio, il cielo di nuovo si chiuse, la temperatura si abbassò, e, insieme con un vento impetuoso di tramontana, si abbatté sulla città una straordinaria nevicata. Vento e neve: pareva di essere chissà dove. In qualche punto, dove l'aria aveva fatto mulinello, la neve aveva raggiunto un metro e mezzo d'altezza. Per le strade, i passanti procedevano in fila indiana lungo le anguste trincee che le squadre di spalatori ingaggiati dal Comune tenevano sgombre a fatica. Sui bastioni comparvero sciatori in perfetta tenuta alpina; furono perfino organizzate delle gare; e via Salinguerra, di solito cosí deserta e silenziosa, divenne per l'occasione piena di movimento e di colore. Attratta dal nuovo spettacolo che si svolgeva sui bastioni, tutta la città passava di lí.

Improvvisamente, col ritorno della neve e del freddo, lo stato della vecchia si aggravò. Di là dai vetri, da cui la luce naturale filtrava ormai cosí scarsa da render necessario l'uso della corrente elettrica fin dal mattino, si scorgeva la neve cadere a vortice, fitta, sulla melma rappresa della via. Si trattava di polmonite, dichiarò il medico, e, date le condizioni generali e l'età della malata, c'era poco o nulla da sperare.

La vecchia tendeva l'orecchio. La città era in festa. Via Salinguerra risuonava di grida allegre, di passi precipitati, di motori e di sirene d'automobili... Che succedeva? Ma ogni voce, ogni suono, le giungeva tuttavia come da una grande distanza.

«Non ci sento bene», si lamentava, «non ci sento piú».

«Nevica» rispondeva piano Débora, seduta di fianco al letto; «è per questo che ti sembra cosí».

Anche la stanza era piena di gente. Dietro il prete e il chierico — Oreste non s'era dimenticato di mandare per loro — era entrata una piccola folla di donnette del vicinato. Il prete se ne era andato, ma esse erano rimaste. Con gli scialli neri in testa, sgranando rosari e portando ogni tanto i fazzoletti agli occhi, si erano raccolte sotto la finestra dove Débora e la madre avevano cucito panni militari per tanti anni. Oreste, in piedi al centro della stanza, tra il gruppo delle donne (in confuso controluce) e il letto, teneva le mani giunte. Le sue labbra si muovevano rapide, sicure.

Non era *per questo*, per la neve, che ogni suono veniva da cosí lontano, come fasciato d'ovatta. Ella — rideva tra sé la vecchia — sapeva bene perché. Inutile mentirle. «Il peggio deve ancora venire», aveva detto Oreste. Ma questa volta Oreste si sbagliava. Il peggio, lei non l'avrebbe visto, se ne sarebbe andata prima. Aveva ragione anche lei, questa volta. Quanto a Débora, ella si sarebbe sposata. Cosa c'era di piú bello del matrimonio? — E mentre moriva, la bocca, tesa nello sforzo del rantolo, le tremava agli angoli per un sorriso che voleva apparire, e forse finalmente era, di felicità.

Ad un tratto Oreste si mosse, venne avanti, si chinò sul capezzale. Gli occhi aperti della vecchia non vedevano piú nulla: ella aveva cessato di respirare. Leggera ed esatta, la sua mano calò sugli occhi, abbassò le palpebre, raccolse le braccia in croce sul petto. La sua sveltezza, la sua sicurezza (ora la mano era passata ad aggiustare le coperte...) affascinavano Débora. Quindi egli si ritirò, riguadagnò il centro della stanza.

Débora non si muoveva. Rimasta sola accanto al letto, ella fissava il profilo di cera della mdre. Ne osservava i particolari con attenzione caparbia, quasi con avidità, mentre sentiva invadersi da uno strano senso di liberazione. Per tanti anni avevano lavorato assieme, accanto alla finestra, evitando di guardarsi. Ora era diverso. Le palpebre abbassate, il naso profilato, le labbra socchiuse a quel vago, assurdo sorriso felice: tutto, nel volto della morta, le riusciva nuovo e sorprendente, e insieme come ritrovato. Intanto qualcosa, un antico nodo di rancore e di riserbo (se piangeva, piangeva per questo) si scioglieva dentro il suo petto.

Levò il viso dalle palme.

«Vorrei restare sola. Anche voi, Oreste, andatevene anche voi».

«Sí cara, sí cara...».

Nei suoi occhi arrossati, nella sua voce, c'era un tono nuovo di freddezza, un comando. Oreste non l'aveva mai vista cosí. Fu con un'ombra di soggezione, quasi di timore, che egli distolse gli sguardi dai suoi. Le vicine si avviavano già su per le scale. Ultimo del gruppo, anch'egli raggiunse il pianerottolo, infine chiuse la porta dietro di sé.

Seduta di fianco al letto, col gomito puntato nella coltre e la guancia appoggiata alla mano, Débora rimase sola. Pensava alla madre, a se stessa, alla loro storia. E a poco a poco l'immaginazione la portava in un'altra stanza simile in tutto a questa dove ora si trovava, la stanza dove, al principio di una lontana primavera, ella era andata a vivere insieme con David. Come in questa, c'erano due letti affiancati, il catino in un angolo, la specchiera appannata, un cassettone... L'unica differenza (a parte la temperatura: sotto i tetti, col progredire della stagione, il caldo s'era fatto soffocante), era data dalla finestra: qui bassa, al livello della strada; là alta, aperta sulla distesa dei tetti, la campagna, e, nello sfondo, le colline di B*. Per il resto tutto era uguale, tutto si ripeteva. Vedeva se stessa accanto a un altro letto, col gomito puntato nella coltre e la guancia appoggiata alla mano, intenta, nei lunghi pomeriggi estivi, a vegliare un altro corpo, quello di David. Egli dormiva. Ma così lento era il suo respiro, così pallida la lunga mascella sotto una barba di molti giorni, che alle volte, presa dall'angoscia, lei lo scuoteva ad un braccio. «Cosa?», borbottava egli, svegliandosi a mezzo. Si agitava nel letto (un romanzo cadeva con un tonfo sul pavimento), il pigiama sul dorso appariva intriso di sudore, ricadeva a dormire.

La stanza, ricordava, era all'ultimo piano di un grande casamento popolare: un'ex-caserma, che in città chiamavano il Palazzone. Un giorno, nel periodo che più le era parso lontano, ormai perduto, David le aveva proposto di andarvi a stare con lui. Aveva deciso — diceva — di rompere definitivamente i rapporti con la famiglia, di farsi una vita nuova. Perché aveva voluto spinger le cose fino a quel punto? Non aveva mai capito: sempre, fin dal principio, le era stato difficile capire ciò che pensava, prevedere ciò che avrebbe fatto. Comunque, allora, non si era chiesta nulla, non aveva esitato un momento. Uscita una sera in compagnia di David, non era più tornata, ecco tutto. Qualche giorno dopo, aveva fatto sapere alla madre dove si trovava. Non ne aveva avuto risposta. Ma allora, chi pensava al domani? Neppure David sembrava pensarvi. La parola « perché?» era insorta in lei molto piú tardi, quando, dopo il parto, era tornata a vivere lassú, e la solitudine la spaventava. La finestra altissima (un abbaíno, piú che una finestra: dapprima, l'idea di vivere in un granaio era piaciuta a David, pareva divertirlo...), le permetteva di spingere lo sguardo molto lontano, oltre la nera massa degli alberi del Parco, oltre gli ultimi tetti della città. Di là, dalla campagna, saliva il buio che avrebbe ben presto occupato la stanza. « Perché, perché?... ». Il bambino, posato sul letto, piangeva. Ella si staccava dal davanzale, si sedeva sul letto, gli dava il seno. Poi si sdraiava accanto a lui. Il sonno veniva cosí col buio e il gridío monotono delle rane. Soltanto allora (non prima: la gravidanza era stata per lei un periodo fuori del tempo, di cui si ricordava come ci si ricorda d'un sogno), ella aveva compreso che tutto, ormai, era finito davvero.

Ma David — insisteva —: chi era, cosa voleva? Non si era mai chiesta nulla, non aveva mai capito. Studiava Legge (uno studente invecchiato, in ritardo con gli esami e con la laurea: passava i pomeriggi steso sul letto, un po' a leggere un po' a dormire...), e faceva vita comune con lei. « Cosa fa suo marito? », le aveva chiesto la moglie di un infermiere dell'Ospedale Maggiore che abitava, col marito e quattro figli, in una camera al piano di sotto. « È disoccupato; ma presto entrerà in zuccherificio », aveva risposto lei. Non era ciò che egli le diceva? Bastava che David parlasse — e sapeva parlare! Tutto allora diventava facile, possibile, credibile. Il matrimonio? Pura formalità. Del resto, se ci teneva tanto, l'anno venturo al piú tardi avrebbero sistemato ogni cosa in Municipio. Chissà che per allora i suoi genitori... Sarebbe diventata sua moglie; « la mia signora », aggiungeva sorridendo. Frattanto, era come se lo fosse.

Il Parco, che aveva al centro un chiosco di gelati, non distava dal Palazzone che un centinaio di metri. La sera, dopo cena, scendevano le scale. Si tenevano per mano: e ad ogni gradino di quelle scale interminabili (ad ogni piano, quattro famiglie: d'oltre i muri, suoni di grammofoni, voci, rumori di stoviglie...), ella sentiva crescere la noia e la stanchezza di David. Pure tra il fogliame tenebroso del Parco, la lampada ad acetilene del chiosco dei gelati splendeva di lontano, viva e minuscola come un faro. Vedendola, le si affrettavano incontro. Ed era stata una sera di quelle, mentre camminavano diretti verso quel punto di luce, che ella aveva trovato il coraggio di dirgli del suo stato. « Sai, credo proprio che avrò un bambino », o qualcosa di simile. Doveva pur dirglielo. David non era parso sorpreso, non replicò nulla. « Limone o cioccolata? », le aveva chiesto con gentilezza, quando s'erano fermati col petto contro il banco di zinco. Mentre egli sorbiva il suo gelato (sceglieva sempre un misto di crema e panna), la guardava da capo a piedi, triste. Ella, come al solito, aveva scelto cioccolata. Ma quella sera, una delle ultime, non era arrivata alla fine del gelato. « Non ti sembra che faccia un caldo insopportabile? », aveva detto a un tratto David. « A Cortina, di sera, bisogna mettere i maglioni ». La sua famiglia si era trasferita a Cortina fin dai primi di luglio. Abitavano all'Hôtel Faloria, una costruzione grande come un castello, in mezzo a un bosco d'abeti e di larici...

« Chi era David, cosa voleva? Perché, perché?... ». La domanda non trovava risposta, non l'avrebbe trovata mai. Del resto era tardi. Qualcuno, forse Oreste, bussava ai vetri. Bisognava alzarsi, andargli ad aprire.

VII

Infatti era Oreste.

Chiusa la porta dietro di sé, e raggiunto il gruppo delle vicine che erano rimaste a parlare sulla soglia del portone, Oreste si era unito al crocchio delle donne finché queste — al termine d'una buona mezz'ora — non si furono tutte disperse. Rimasto solo, aveva preso a camminare in su e in giú, davanti alla casa, senza sapere a che santo votarsi. In lui si urtavano due sentimenti opposti, due necessità contrastanti. Da una parte gli premeva allontanarsi almeno per qualche ora, per correre a chiudere bottega e per provvedere a tutto ciò che imponeva, purtroppo, la morte della vecchia (essa si era aggravata improvvisamente, e nessuno, nemmeno lui, aveva avuto tempo e cuore, in quei due ultimi giorni, per prepararsi al peggio). Ma Débora era sola, e il pensiero di lei bastava a trattenerlo. Piú volte, chinandosi, aveva tentato di guardare nella stanza attraverso il vetro appannato. Accanto alla sagoma bianca del letto, aveva distinto una piccola figura nera e curva. Dunque, per tutto quel tempo, Débora non si era mossa. « Cosa fa? », borbottava ogni tanto tra sé con impazienza affettuosa, già da marito. Scendevano le prime ombre della sera; aveva smesso di nevicare, ma il freddo mordeva. Attorno, dalle finestre delle case, trapelavano interni di cucine, di tinelli illuminati. Bisognava spicciarsi, concludere qualcosa. Finalmente, dopo che si fu chinato un'ultima volta a scrutare nella stanza, e, per il buio, non vi ebbe scorto piú nulla, egli si decise a battere sul vetro con le nocche delle dita. Stette quindi in ascolto, col cuore che gli batteva. E non appena gli parve di udire il passo di Débora su per la scala interna, fu svelto a infilare il portone e a trovarsi in cima al pianerottolo ancora prima che Débora aprisse la porta.

Subito, al primo sguardo, egli si accorse di aver ripreso il sopravvento. Col dorso appoggiato allo stipite della porta, Débora lo guardava in silenzio, abbandonando gli occhi nei suoi. Tutto, nel suo atteggiamento, chiedeva protezione.

« Dio santo, non vorrete mica passare tutta la notte cosí », disse egli sottovoce, ma quasi con ruvidezza.

Poi, sempre bisbigliando, e senza varcare la soglia, cominciò a esporle il suo piano. Lui doveva correr via, a chiudere bottega, e non sarebbe stato di ritorno (c'era qualche altra piccola cosa da sistemare) che tra due ore. Però, prima d'andarsene, sarebbe passato da una delle vicine, da certa Bedini, che già gli si era offerta, per chiederle di venire. « A far che? Diamine, a farvi compagnia, magari un po' di cena ». Comunque — aggiunse subito, perché Débora, alla parola *cena,* aveva cominciato a scuotere il capo in segno di diniego — comunque la vecchia Bedini, non fosse che per pregare insieme con lei, era bene che venisse. « Perciò, mi raccomando, non chiudete la porta », ammoní sorridendo. Quanto al resto, lei non doveva pensare a nulla. C'era lui apposta. « Fidatevi di me », disse, toccandole un braccio. Ad ogni modo — ripeté — sarebbe tornato al massimo per le nove. Intesi? E strettale la mano, sparí di corsa giú per la scala.

Oreste aveva ragione, ma la vecchia non era piú lí per accorgersene. La tenue luce rosa che l'indomani mattina si fece strada a fatica attraverso i vetri incrostati di ghiaccio (Débora si era distesa sul letto accanto, la Bedini si era appisolata su una seggiola, mentre Oreste, che aveva pregato per tutta notte, stava in piedi presso la finestra, scrutando il tempo), era una luce che veniva da un sole distante, perduto nel cielo d'un azzurro vago, nebbioso, un sole che non scaldava. Dalla sera del giorno precedente, da quando aveva smesso di nevicare, la temperatura era precipitata. In quel momento — calcolava Oreste mentre, col bavero del cappotto rialzato sulla nuca fitta di corti capelli d'argento, soffiava adagio nelle dita intirizzite — il termometro doveva segnare dieci, quindici, forse venti gradi sotto zero. Ciò — prevedeva — avrebbe stabilizzato la stagione. Per lungo tempo, per tutto gennaio e, forse, buona parte di febbraio, ci sarebbero stati freddi anche maggiori. Avrebbero avuto un inverno eccezionale, durante il quale i canali e i fiumi della campagna sarebbero gelati, le tubature dell'acqua potabile sarebbero scoppiate, un inverno paragonabile soltanto a quello del 1898...

I funerali si svolsero nel tardo pomeriggio dello stesso giorno. Dietro il carro di terza classe, che avanzava scorrevole sulla neve battuta, camminava, oltre al prete, il solo Oreste. Per suo consiglio (un consiglio che dal tono paterno, protettivo della voce, aveva tutta l'aria di valere per una decisione già presa...), Débora era rimasta a casa. Quanto a lui, l'antico seminarista prediletto dal povero Don Castelli, il vecchio soldato del Carso, a lui il freddo intenso infondeva energia, restituiva magicamente tutte le ore di sonno che aveva perdute. Le ruote del carro, alte e sottili, alzavano blocchi di neve compatta che, prima d'esser giunti alla sommità del giro, ricadevano senza rumore impolverando appena raggi e balestre. Egli camminava con gli occhi intenti ai solchi impressi nella neve dalle ruote, alle piccole frane di neve che si staccavano via via dai cerchi di ferro; e intanto il passo, che gli si regolava per istinto su quello del prete, ridava alla sua andatura un po' della volenterosa alacrità dell'ottimo soldato di fanteria che era stato da giovane.

Tornò che era già notte. E dalla strada, invece che battere ai vetri come nei giorni passati, preferí farsi precedere dalla solita scampanellata. Débora lo attendeva in piedi, in fondo alla scala. Durante la sua assenza, ella doveva aver dormito. Il suo viso, prima segnato profondamente dalla stanchezza, ora appariva fresco, riposato. Certo, s'era mutata d'abito. Egli sedette sotto la lampada, al suo vecchio posto. Di lí, mentre Débora si affaccendava attorno alla cucina economica, la osservava con compiacenza, con la gratitudine che era nei suoi occhi ogni volta che credeva di scoprire in una parola di lei, in un suo gesto, studio e desiderio di piacergli.

« Per questa notte », disse, « la Bedini verrà a dormire con voi. Bisogna che ci passi, piú tardi. Domani, andrò a parlare con Don Bonora, perché veda di lasciare che il ragazzo, almeno per qualche tempo, torni a dormire a casa. In seguito si vedrà ».

Era lui che decideva, ormai, che disponeva del suo futuro.

Dopo cena (sedevano l'uno di fronte all'altro come avevan fatto per quasi ogni sera durante tutti quegli anni), il discorso cadde sulla madre. Oreste parlò a lungo della sua vita, dei suoi meriti: con molta dolcezza e con molto tatto. Descrisse quindi il luogo del camposanto dove l'indomani l'avrebbero collocata. Era un posto bellissimo, assicurò, un posto da signori. Non ricordava quel portico di mattoni rossi, costruito di recente, che, partendo dalla Certosa e descrivendo un grande arco, arrivava quasi fin sotto i bastioni? Ebbene, sua madre sarebbe stata sepolta (« macché sepolta: la

terra, poveretta, nemmeno la sfiorerà...») sotto quel portico.
Un posto bellissimo, ripeté, esposto a mezzogiorno, col sole,
quindi, che ci batteva dall'alba al tramonto come in una
serra.

«Certo», aggiunse dopo una pausa, «i lóculi costano
cari»: ma subito, quasi a prevenire qualsiasi possibilità di
equivoco su questa frase, volle dire che lei, Débora, non do-
veva preoccuparsi per questo. «In tanti anni di lavoro, qual-
cosa, grazie a Dio, m'è pur riuscito di metterla da parte». E
dato che lei gli aveva fatto sperare... (qui ebbe un momento
di incertezza)... gli aveva fatto credere...; dato che ciò, pen-
sava, avrebbe reso contenta la sua povera mamma...: «insom-
ma, quello che è mio è tuo», concluse, guardandola fissa-
mente negli occhi e passando per la prima volta dal *voi* al *tu*.

Mentre parlava, si veniva inchinando leggermente sulla
seggiola, non senza galanteria. Alla fine si levò in piedi; e,
congedandosi in fretta, assicurò Débora — avevano tante altre
cose da dirsi — che sarebbe tornato a farle visita la mattina
seguente.

VIII

«Abbiamo tante altre cose da dirci»: questo affermava
esplicitamente Oreste ad ogni commiato, o, almeno, promet-
tevano in silenzio i suoi occhi seri, dolcissimi.

In realtà, a parlare era sempre lui. Quando non si trat-
tava di ricordi (la fanciullezza trascorsa in Seminario, la guer-
ra sul Carso, gliene fornivano i temi abituali), erano lunghi
discorsi intorno alla Religione, con particolare riguardo ai
compiti del clericato nella società e ai rapporti tra Papa e
Stato (il suo patriottismo, dopo la Conciliazione del febbraio
di quello stesso anno, si effondeva ormai liberamente nelle
manifestazioni di tenerezza sentimentale proprie d'un innamo-
rato alla fine corrisposto). Papa e Stato, ciascuno nella sua
sfera, dovevano esser liberi ma concordi. A questo proposito,
egli citava passi della Bibbia, del Vangelo, di Dante, nei quali
il suo sogno di perfetto accordo, di armonia universale, tro-

vava sostegno d'autorità. Anche la storia degli uomini, del resto, sembrava aver messo finalmente la testa a partito. Forse, con la primavera che già si annunziava, sarebbe cominciata l'èra della pace e della gioia, si sarebbe rinnovata la mitica età dell'oro. Gli occhi, mentre diceva queste cose, gli brillavano d'esultanza. Il villino fuori porta (quasi tutte le sere, dopo aver chiuso bottega, egli si recava in bicicletta sui lavori), non sarebbe stato pronto prima di maggio. Non aveva mai voluto accompagnare Débora a vederlo. Doveva essere una sorpresa, fino all'ultimo. Il luogo lo conosceva, vero? Era dalla parte opposta della città, nei pressi della stazione, in una zona tutta occupata da costruzioni recenti. Ogni villetta aveva attorno un palmo di terreno proprio, da coltivarsi a orto o a giardino. E intanto, mentre i lavori progredivano, egli se la prendeva col muratore, perché un muro scialbato di fresco trasudava macchie d'umidità; col carpentiere, per una serranda che non funzionava; coll'ingegnere, perché la data di consegna, a causa della cattiva organizzazione dell'impresa, aveva dovuto esser rimandata d'un mese... Ogni discorso finiva cosí, con l'immagine concreta di una felicità a lungo sognata, ma già in vista, già a portata di mano, da cui li separava uno spazio di tempo sempre minore. A maggio, al piú tardi, si sarebbero sposati.

Quanto a Débora, ella cercava di secondare il fidanzato con tutta la migliore volontà di partecipazione di cui era capace. Non c'era piú sua madre, è vero, con cui potesse scambiare a tempo opportuno il sorriso d'intelligenza che spesso le saliva alle labbra. Ma anche di ciò, a poco a poco, ella seppe fare a meno senza sforzo. La passione che ardeva negli occhi di Oreste era talmente sincera; era cosí caldo, affettuoso, accogliente il mondo suscitato dalla sua fantasia, che ella vi si abbandonava volentieri, comunque senza proteste. Tutta la luce, tutto il calore veniva da lui. Ella si limitava a lasciarsene illuminare e scaldare, come un pianeta che, spento, continua a vivere della vita che scende a lui dal sole a cui appartiene. L'età dell'oro, la felicità che gli occhi e le parole di Oreste le promettevano, ella non credeva, nel segreto del suo cuore, che le avrebbe viste mai, né che fossero possibili su questa terra. Eppure, sebbene non potesse illudersi, sebbene fosse consapevole dei guasti che il tempo e il dolore avevano lasciato dentro di lei, nonostante ciò sapeva confusamente che proprio a quelle promesse in cui non credeva, a quelle fantasie alle quali aderiva con tante intime riserve, proprio a quei sogni («ancora sogni — pensava —: alla mia età, e con un figliolo che è ormai un giovanotto!...») era ormai legata ogni sua ragione di esistere. Quali argomenti, d'altronde, avrebbe saputo opporre a quelli di Oreste? Se le fosse mancata la forza che le veniva di riflesso dalla fede illimitata che era in lui, con cosa l'avrebbe sostituita? Forse — e sorrideva — coi ricordi del passato? Egli era superiore a lei, in tutto. Ogni altro pensiero si formava in lei con difficoltà, lentamente. Ma quest'ultimo rifletteva un dato preciso, reale, della cui verità non dubitava mai, nemmeno in fondo alla coscienza. La certezza della propria inferiorità la riempiva sempre di piacere, di pace.

Venne maggio. Negli ultimi giorni la fretta di Oreste si era trasformata in ansia, in angoscia. Débora gli diceva sorridendo: «Se non vi conoscessi abbastanza, direi che siete diventato un altro uomo. Avete aspettato tanti anni, che una settimana di più non farà poi questo gran disastro». In realtà egli non era mutato, non c'era nessuno che se ne rendesse conto meglio di lei. Ella sapeva tutto, di lui. Sapeva bene che la ragione di quella sua smania improvvisa, apparentemente così in contrasto col suo carattere, era la stessa che lo aveva indotto ad aspettare per tanto tempo, ad accontentarsi per anni di una promessa nemmeno formulata a parole, ad acconsentire a qualunque dilazione. Allora come oggi, assai più forte di ogni possibile egoismo, in Oreste dominava il sentimento di incredulità di chi non osa sperare in una felicità troppo grande, della quale si sente indegno. Per questo egli aveva voluto che le nozze fossero celebrate con la maggiore solennità (subito dopo i due «sí» e la benedizione, l'organo esplose nella marcia nuziale di Mendelssohn). Il matrimonio rappresentava il difficile e tardivo coronamento della sua vita; un traguardo d'arrivo, oltre il quale era inutile, forse empio, spingere gli sguardi. Dopo, essi avrebbero camminato insieme, protetti dalla divina Provvidenza.

Gli anni che seguirono furono infatti anni tranquilli, felici. Anni di lavoro; e, se non proprio di ricchezza, certo di agiata prosperità. Comunque, di inverni come quello del '29 non se ne videro altri; e tanto meno ne vide Oreste, che morí presto, nella primavera del '38. Verso la fine d'ogni autunno, egli era solito soffermarsi davanti ai vetri delle finestre, studiando il tempo. Pensava che in quella casa nuova, dove non mancava nulla, dove c'era perfino l'impianto del calorifero, nessun inverno, per quanto rigido fosse, avrebbe potuto piú impensierirlo. Il futuro gli sorrideva. Dopo il matrimonio, Débora si era conformata subito alle sue abitudini devote, e aveva preso a frequentare assiduamente la chiesa. Ella si era ingrassata, imbellita. La ragazza magra, limata dall'ansia, che egli aveva conosciuto tanti anni prima, quando aveva cominciato a farsi vedere ogni sera in una certa stanza di via Salinguerra, si era trasformata col tempo in una bella donna tranquilla, un po' pingue, della pinguedine che sta bene alle donne pie. Tutto, anche questa tarda bellezza della moglie — di cui spesso, tra il serio e il faceto, egli si faceva un po' di merito — mostrava che il Signore aveva benedetto la loro unione.

IX.

« È stato felice », si diceva a volte Débora.

Ma subito, come se un'eco interna la deformasse, la voce diventava interrogativa, si distorceva in una domanda piena di dubbio, d'invidia dolorosa. « Sarà stato felice?... ».

Soltanto ora, ora che anch'egli non era piú che un ricordo, ella sapeva che no, qualcosa gli era sempre mancato. Per anni, per tutti gli anni del loro matrimonio, egli aveva desiderato un figlio, un figlio suo, e lei non aveva saputo darglielo.

Quanto doveva aver lottato, per non far capire e per non capire egli stesso; quanto doveva essersi consumato in quel desiderio nascosto! Ogni volta che Débora pensava a questo, le tornavano in mente le cure tenerissime, piú che paterne, che egli, sebbene non corrisposto, aveva sempre avuto per Ireneo. A tredici anni, appena uscito dal Seminario, l'aveva preso con sé, in bottega, dove, tra la macchina rifilatrice e la porta a vetri, gli aveva sistemato un piccolo banco tutto per lui. Gli aveva voluto insegnare il suo mestiere: e a lei (certe sere, dopo la Benedizione, si spingeva a piedi fino alla legatoria...), pareva ancora di vederlo, mentre, da dietro al suo banco, covava con occhi ardenti di zelo quel suo allievo che un nulla, pur che venisse di fuori, dal piazzale davanti alla bottega, bastava a distrarre. Le pareva ancora di vederlo e di udirlo: col torso grande e vigoroso, sproporzionato rispetto alla misura degli arti, che si ergeva sullo sgabello di là dal banco; con quelle sue mani nocchiute (alla sinistra spiccava la fede matrimoniale) che, anche quando gli occhi erano altrove, alzati insieme con la voce a salutare chi entrava, non smettevano un momento di lavorare. Quanto doveva essersi tormentato, se, non contento di ciò che aveva fatto e faceva per il ragazzo, a un certo punto aveva voluto che assumesse il suo nome! Il significato, la ragione vera d'ogni suo gesto le appariva chiaro soltanto ora, quando lui se n'era andato per sempre. Egli aveva sempre cercato di smentire se stesso, di soffocare dentro se stesso un altro bisogno, un altro desiderio.

Eppure — ella ne era certa — eppure egli non aveva mai disperato. Nel fondo piú segreto dell'anima sua, egli doveva esser stato sempre sicuro che Débora, un giorno o l'altro, gli sarebbe venuta incontro con la grande notizia. Presto, senza alcun dubbio, ella gli avrebbe dato un figlio che fosse veramente suo e non si levasse tra loro con la precoce, silenziosa, immotivata tristezza del ragazzo di quindici anni (era cresciuto d'intelligenza non molto viva: un ragazzo alto e magro, dalla lunga mascella di cavallo triste...) che, sebbene lui gli avesse dato il suo nome, il suo onorato nome di « onesto anche se modesto artigiano »; sebbene gli venisse insegnando il mestiere come l'avrebbe insegnato a un suo figlio carnale: nonostante ciò, non aveva mai voluto chiamarlo altro che «zio Oreste». Soltanto allora, e non prima, egli avrebbe potuto dire di non essersi ingannato quando, nel febbraio del '29, aveva predetto il ritorno dell'età dell'oro. In caso contrario... Ma la morte, cogliendolo di sorpresa, doveva aver spento, insieme con la sua vita, ogni principio di disperazione.

Queste erano state le uniche ombre — pensava Débora —, gli unici crucci che avessero turbato la serenità della loro vita.

UCCELLI

DI

UMBERTO SABA

PETTIROSSO

Trattenerti, volessi anche, non posso.

Vedi, amico del merlo, il pettirosso.
Quanto ha il simile in odio egli di quella
vicinanza par lieto. E tu li pensi
compagni inseparabili, che agli orli
di un boschetto sorpreso li sorprendi.
Ma un impeto gioioso al nero amico,
che una sua preda ha nel becco, l'invola.
Piega un ramo lontano, cui non nuoce,
se un po' ne oscilla, l'incarco; la bella
stagione, il cielo tutto suo l'inebbriano,
e la moglie nel nido. Come un tempo
il dolce figlio che di me nutrivo,
si sente ingordo libero feroce;

e là si sgola.

CIELO

La buona, la meravigliosa Lina
spalanca la finestra perché veda
il cielo immenso.

354

UCCELLI

Qui tranquillo a riposo, dove penso
che ho dato invano, che la fine approssima,
più mi piace quel cielo, quelle rondini,
quelle nubi. Non chiedo altro.

Fumare
la mia pipa in silenzio come un vecchio
lupo di mare.

UCCELLI

L'alata
genia che adoro — ce n'è al mondo tanta —
varia d'usi e costumi, ebbra di vita,
si sveglia e canta.

PIAZZA DELLE POSTE

Pianticelle con rossi fiori in cima
fanno l'ombretta all'aiuola di fresco
smossa. Colombi passeggiano in mezzo.

Uno lascia lo stormo e mi cammina,
che si lusinga di un'offerta, incontro.
Esita, si ritira; al volo pronto
sempre, e alla fuga; che dell'uomo — dice —
fido e non fido. — Anch'io. — Meno felice
di lui, nel chiuso
gli rispondo del cuore: Questa piazza,
cui giungevo affannato perché prima
abbia il mio augurio chi ben so l'attende,
la fontana che in vaga iride splende,
tra le pietre fiorita di gerani
ombrosa aiuola, ove di me deluso
ritorni in fretta, fece l'uomo all'uomo.

Pure è un triste bambino. E del suo dono
chi più diffida ha più ragione, io penso.

L'ORNITOLOGO PIETOSO

Raccolse un ornitologo pietoso
un espulso dal nido. Come l'ebbe
in mano vide ch'era un rosignuolo.

In salvo lo portò con il timore
gli mancasse per via. Gli fece, a un fondo
di fiasco, un nido; ritrovò quel gramo
l'imbeccata e il calore. Fu allevarlo
cura non lieve, ed il dispendio certo
di molte uova di formiche. E ai giorni
sereni, ai primi gorgheggi, l'esperto
in un boschetto libertà gli dava.
« Più — diceva al perduto, e lo guardava
a terra e in ramo cercarsi — il tuo g r a z i e
udrò sommesso ». E si sentì più solo.

IL FANCIULLO E L'AVERLA

S'innamorò un fanciullo d'un'averla.
Vago del nuovo — interessate udiva
di lei, dal cacciatore, meraviglie —
quante promesse fece per averla!

L'ebbe; e all'istante l'obliò. La trista,
nella sua gabbia alla finestra appesa,
piangeva sola e in silenzio, del cielo
lontano irraggiungibile alla vista.

Si ricordò di lei solo quel giorno
che, per noia o malvagio animo, volle
stringerla in pugno. La quasi rapace
gli fece male e s'involò. Quel giorno,

per quel male, l'amò senza ritorno.

QUEST'ANNO...

Quest'anno la partenza delle rondini
mi stringerà, per un pensiero, il cuore.

Poi stornelli faranno alto clamore
sugli alberi al ritrovo del viale
XX Settembre. Poi al lungo male
dell'inverno compagni avrò qui solo
quel pensiero, e sui tetti il bruno passero.

Alla mia solitudine le rondini
mancheranno, e ai miei dì tardi l'amore.

PASSERI

Saltellano sui tetti
passeri cinguettanti. Due si rubano
di becco il pane che ai leggeri sbriccioli,
che carpirti s'illudono al balcone.
Vanno a stormi a dormire...

                    Uccelli sono:
nella natura la sublimazione
del rettile.

MERLO

Esisteva quel mondo al quale in sogno
ritorno ancora; che in sogno mi scuote?
Certo esisteva. E n'erano gran parte
mia madre e un merlo.

Lei vedo appena. Più risalta il nero
e il giallo di chi lieto salutava
col suo canto (era questo il mio pensiero)
me, che l'udivo dalla via. Mia madre
sedeva, stanca, in cucina. Tritava
a lui solo (era questo il suo pensiero)
e alla mia cena la carne. Nessuna
vista o rumore così lo eccitava.

Tra un fanciullo ingabbiato e un insettivoro,
che i vermetti carpiva alla sua mano,
in quella casa, in quel mondo lontano
c'era un amore. C'era anche un equivoco.

ROSIGNUOLO

Dice il nostro maggiore
fratello, il rosignuolo:

Iddio, se ha fatto il mondo e se lo guarda,
non di te si compiace, uomo, che a un'esca
— ahi, troppo irrecusabile! — divide
noi che abbiamo la casa in siepe o in fronda.

Si tace. E, dopo una nota pietosa:

La voce — dice — più meravigliosa
del silenzio, è la mia. Dei pleniiuni
d'Aprile a tutti gli incanti si sposa.

Dice a te il tuo maggiore
fratello, il rosignuolo:

La dolcezza del mondo è una una una.
Solo a lei canto al lume della luna.

UCCELLI

NIETZSCHE

Intorno a una grandezza solitaria,
non volano gli uccelli, né quei vaghi
gli fanno, accanto, il nido. Altro non odi
che il silenzio, non vedi altro che l'aria.

NOTE. — *Uccelli.* Fanno parte di un libretto di versi, che s'intitola *Epigrafe,* e che, scritto nel 1947-48, uscirà probabilmente dopo la mia morte.
Pettirosso. L'amicizia del pettirosso per il merlo, come il suo odio per tutti gli altri pettirossi, è nota agli ornitologi. Vedi, oltre gli antichi, Alberto Bacchi della Lega, *Caccie e costumi degli uccelli silvani,* Città di Castello, 1892, pp. 197-198.
Cielo. Il primo verso è tolto da *Avevo* (Il Canzoniere, Einaudi 1948, pag. 578).
L'ornitologo pietoso. Gli uccelli, amorosissimi — come tutti sanno — della prole, espellono dal nido il piccolo che sia, o loro sembri essere, nato male o, comunque, difforme dagli altri. Ornitologi ed amatori si sono provati a rimettere gli infelici nel nido, ma ogni volta questi ne venivano ributtati. Alcuni pochi, allevati (come il rosignuolo della mia favoletta) dalla mano dell'uomo, riuscirono tuttavia a sopravvivere; né, tenuti in gabbia, si mostrarono per il canto, la longevità ecc., inferiori ai loro fratelli più fortunati. Aggiungo — come una semplice curiosità — che, scrivendo la favoletta, avevo un po' presente Leonardo, che comperava al mercato gli uccelli per rendere loro la libertà.
Rosignuolo. « Un'esca — Ahi, troppo irrecusabile! » —: un baco da crusca. Basta, a chi voglia prendere un rosignuolo, mettere un baco da crusca bene in vista dentro una gabbia a scatto, ai piedi dell'albero sul quale l'uccello canta. Questi, fiducioso per sua natura, vi entra quasi subito... Non c'è bisogno di aggiungere — almeno per i miei lettori — che si tratta di un'azione criminale, tanto più se commessa al tempo degli amori e dei nidi.

359

POESIE

DI
EUGENIO MONTALE

I

So che un raggio di sole (di Dio?) ancora
può incarnarsi se ai piedi della statua
di Lucrezia (una sera ella si scosse,
palpebrò) getti il volto contro il mio.

Qui nell'androne come sui trifogli;
qui sulle scale come là nel palco;
sempre nell'ombra: perché se tu sciogli
quel buio la mia rondine sia il falco.

II

Hai dato il mio nome a un albero? Non è poco;
pure non mi rassegno a restar ombra, o tronco,
di un abbandono nel suburbio. Io il tuo
l'ho dato a un fiume, a un lungo incendio, al crudo
gioco della mia sorte, alla fiducia
sovrumana con cui parlasti al rospo
uscito dalla fogna, senza orrore o pietà
o tripudio, al respiro di quel forte
e morbido tuo labbro che riesce,
nominando, a creare: rospo fiore erba scoglio —

quercia pronta a spiegarsi su di noi
quando la pioggia spollina i carnosi
petali del trifoglio e il fuoco cresce.

III

Se t'hanno assomigliato
alla volpe sarà per la falcata
prodigiosa, pel volo del tuo passo
che unisce e che divide, che sconvolge
e rinfranca il selciato (il tuo terrazzo,
le strade presso il Cottolengo, il prato,
l'albero che ha il mio nome ne vibravano
felici, umidi e vinti) — o forse solo
per l'onda luminosa che diffondi
dalle mandorle tenere degli occhi,
per l'astuzia dei tuoi pronti stupori,
per lo strazio
di piume lacerate che può dare
la tua mano d'infante in una stretta;
se t'hanno assomigliato
a un carnivoro biondo, al genio perfido
delle fratte (e perché non all'immondo
pesce che dà la scossa, alla torpedine?)
è forse perché i ciechi non ti videro
sulle scapole gracili le ali,
perché i ciechi non scorsero il presagio
della tua fronte incandescente, il solco
che vi ho graffiato a sangue, croce cresima
incantesimo jattura voto vale
perdizione e salvezza; se non seppero
crederti più che donnola o che donna,
con chi dividerò la mia scoperta,
dove seppellirò l'oro che porto,
dove la brace che in me stride se,
lasciandomi, ti volgi dalle scale?

IV

(Le processioni del '49)

Lampi d'afa sul punto del distacco,
livida ora annebbiata,
poi un alone anche peggiore, un bómbito
di ruote e di querele dalle prime
rampe della collina,
un rigúrgito, un tanfo acre che infetta
le zolle a noi devote

                  ... se non fosse
per quel tuo scarto in *vitro, sulla gora,*
entro una bolla di sapone e insetti.

Chi mente piú, chi geme? Fu il tuo istante
di sempre, dacché appari.
La tua virtú furiosamente angelica
ha scacciato col guanto i madonnari
pellegrini, Cibele e i Coribanti.

POESIE DELL'OROLOGIO

DI

CARLO LEVI

I.

Ruggito dei leoni nella notte
del profondo del tempo alla memoria,
gufi, Madonne, simboli, interrotte
vicende giustapposte e senza storia,

selve di case, uccelli, rami, grotte,
corti dei topi e di disfatta gloria,
ed occhi, e voci, e gesti, ed oro, e scoria,
verde ritorno delle età corrotte,

briganti al bosco, serpi alla mammella,
re veri e finti, ministri e pezzenti,
contadini alla vanga e vermi in sella,

compianto antico e funerario elogio,
coraggio, e fame, e uomini pazienti,
e Roma, e Italia: questo è l'Orologio.

II.

C'è chi muore perché l'amico è morto
o ha perso la ragione, oppur l'amante
o la moglie o la madre: a questi il viso
rode la lebbra o il cancro, e quello smorto
s'assottiglia pensandolo già ucciso;
ma già a nuove fanciulle il petto sboccia
ingenuo e gonfio, e avanzano gloriose
d'antichissimi sensi nuovamente
sentiti, in frotte per le strade; e piante
novelle già verdeggiano, e la roccia
grigia il muschio ricopre, e nuove rose
spuntan sui rami tra quelle sfiorite;
ed al posto dei morti un'altra gente
parla e respira, e contempla le cose
la prima volta, con occhio innocente.
Sui sepolcri e sull'ossa costruite
sono le case vestite di festa;
dal vecchio nido provandosi al volo
cadon gli uccelli nell'aria accogliente.
Tra rocce e foglie e tronchi e le infinite
ombre degli altri, certo d'esser solo
ti meravigli di trovare tante
orme di passi in vergine foresta.

Orme di passi in vergine foresta
suoni lontani nel silenzio, verdi
ore che il tempo incise ad una ad una
dentro i cerchi del legno fino a questa
dell'ultima corteccia che già imbruna,
e ch'è la tua, solitaria, spiando
vai stupefatto di tanto vigore
in sì mobili immagini perplesso
dove ti cerchi, ti trovi e disperdi.
Già dài nomi alle cose, come quando

erano fresche del loro fattore
nascosto tra le piante, e l'usignuolo
ascolti e il lupo; e già scopri riflesso
nell'acqua un viso che ti specchia, e amore
t'offre, e delude, liquido te stesso.
Quindi, se appare a un tratto un boscaiolo
che mena sciolto l'ascia, ti par sorto
da un altro mondo. Riconosci in quello
il tempo e gli altri, ed in ciascuno un messo
d'amore, anche nel ricino dal suolo
sorto in un'ora e già secco: fratello
lo chiami perso, e piangi, e in lui ti perdi
e vuoi morir perché l'amico è morto.

Non sempre scende un Dio dalla sua stella
(o, se pur scende, di rado egli è scorto)
ironico e bonario, a mostrar quale
sia vano affetto, dopo le budella
della balena, ogni cosa mortale.
Non sempre scende ad arrestare il gesto
o a serrare una bocca; allor seguiamo
il batter matematico del cuore
che segna un tempo ad ogni ora più corto
quanto è più presso al termine del testo.
Ma se tu esci dal triste richiamo
dell'orologio dal cuore d'insetto,
se ti rifiuti al seducente errore
d'una vicenda, se respingi l'amo
d'un solo senso delle cose, presto
ti apparirà che in ogni tempo stiamo
insieme, e quel che fu tuttavia resta
presente, anche nel vicolo, nel muro
diroccato alla luna, anche nel mesto
sguardo pieno di lacrime, nel ramo
spezzato in terra, come un senso oscuro:
lasciò l'amico che tu piangi morto
l'orme dei passi in vergine foresta.

III.

Passa il vento fra le case
e risveglia antichi suoni
tra balconi e cornicioni
come dentro una conchiglia.

Quel che passa qui rimase
una ferma meraviglia:
ogni tempo si assottiglia
in ruggito di leoni.

Ecco un giorno, ancora un giorno
ecco un secolo passato:
tutto il pianto fu versato
che ancor brilla fra le ciglia.

Quel che nasce, in suo ritorno,
in memoria si attorciglia:
spunta l'erba, ancor vermiglia
di altri soli, sul selciato.

IV.

Non sei nel libro, non nell'Orologio
non sei nel tempo smarrito
del bosco nero, ché forse
qui c'è solo il detrito
della memoria, e l'elogio,
senza rimedio, dell'ore trascorse.

V.

Resta in me, resta in me! Perché vuoi nascere?
dice la donna, e ti trattiene e spinge
a quella pianta ambigua, a quell'origine
che ti fa solo, e ti allontana e stringe.

VI.

Una strada, un balcone, un po' di gente
ferma a ascoltare la partita, il suono
della macchina espresso, ed una coppia
che si tengon per mano alla parete
coperta di cartelli — è sufficiente
gioia per oggi; è quel che mi compete
del mondo, che mi arriva, cosí, in dono.

Se tu fossi presente
divideremmo queste viste liete:
la mia gioia, per te, sarebbe doppia.

VII.

Coi grandi occhi trasparenti
neri, per vedere nell'ombra,
stai sotto la lampada e senti
il tempo vuoto che ti ingombra.

Nel tempo vuoto pazienti
misurando angelico l'inferno
al batter rosato dei cigli
di trina, tu, gufo reale.

Ma se apri araldico l'ale
alle sbarre dove ti impigli,
allora tu stringi gli artigli
in un pugno crudele e fraterno.

VIII.

Il vento muove le conchiglie, bianche
foglie secche del mare
e soffia strage e guerra sulle stanche
terre d'Europa amare.

Dopo sette anni di sangue e di guai
da quelle spiagge sole,
fatto ha di Roma, la guerra, Shangai
sotto un modesto sole.

Dopo l'asciutta storia di Firenze
e le tragedie vane
ritrovo l'ore fuor d'adolescenze,
solitarie, qui, e umane.

IX.

Come un uccello nell'aria che imbruna
sopra i campi violetti delle altane
veduto ho a volo queste storie vane
affidandomi al vento e alla fortuna.

NATALIA GINZBURG

VALENTINO

Abitavo con mio padre, mia madre e mio fratello in un piccolo alloggio del centro. Avevamo la vita dura e non si sapeva mai come pagare l'affitto. Mio padre era un maestro di scuola a riposo e mia madre dava lezioni di piano: bisognava aiutare un po' mia sorella ch'era sposata con un rappresentante di commercio e aveva tre figli e non ce la faceva a andare avanti; e bisognava mantenere mio fratello agli studi e mio padre credeva che sarebbe diventato un grand'uomo. Io andavo alle magistrali e nelle ore libere davo qualche ripetizione ai bambini della portinaia: la portinaia aveva dei parenti in campagna e ci ripagava in castagne, mele e patate.

Mio fratello studiava medicina e ci volevano sempre dei soldi, ora per il microscopio, ora per i libri e le tasse. Mio padre credeva che sarebbe diventato un grand'uomo: non c'era forse una ragione per crederlo ma lo credeva: aveva cominciato a pensare così fin da quando Valentino era piccolo e adesso forse gli riusciva difficile smettere. Mio padre stava tutto il giorno in cucina e farneticava da solo: s'immaginava quando Valentino sarebbe stato un medico famoso e sarebbe andato ai congressi nelle grandi capitali d'Europa e avrebbe scoperto nuove medicine e malattie. Valentino invece non pareva che avesse voglia di diventare un grand'uomo: in casa, di solito si divertiva con un gattino; e faceva

369

dei giocattoli per i bambini della portinaia, con un po' di segatura e qualche vecchio scampolo di stoffa: faceva dei cani e dei gatti e anche dei diavoli con delle grosse teste e dei lunghi corpi a bitorzoli. Oppure si vestiva tutto da sciatore e si guardava nello specchio: a sciare non andava un gran che, perché era pigro e soffriva il freddo: ma si era fatto fare da mia madre un completo da sciatore tutto nero con un gran passamontagna di lana bianca: si trovava molto bello cosí vestito e passeggiava davanti allo specchio prima con una sciarpa buttata intorno al collo e poi senza; e s'affacciava al balcone per farsi vedere dai bambini della portinaia.

Molte volte si era fidanzato e poi sfidanzato e mia madre s'era data da fare a pulire la saletta da pranzo e a vestirsi per bene. Era successo già molte volte e cosí quando ci disse che si sposava entro il mese non credemmo e mia madre si mise stancamente a pulire la saletta da pranzo e indossò il suo vestito di seta grigia che era quello per gli esami al Conservatorio delle sue allieve e per le fidanzate.

Cosí aspettavamo una delle solite ragazzine che lui giurava di sposare e piantava dopo quindici giorni e ormai ci pareva d'aver capito il tipo di ragazze che gli piaceva: ragazzine con dei berrettini che andavano ancora al liceo. Di solito eran molto intimidite e non ci facevano spavento un po' perché sapevamo che le piantava e un po' perché somigliavano tanto alle allieve di piano di mia madre.

Allora quando lui arrivò con la nuova fidanzata eravamo cosí sbalorditi che nessuno aveva fiato di parlare. Perché questa nuova fidanzata era qualcosa che non avevamo potuto immaginare. Portava una lunga pelliccia di martora e delle scarpe piatte con la suola di gomma ed era piccola e grassa. Aveva degli occhiali cerchiati di tartaruga e dietro gli occhiali ci fissava con degli occhi severi e rotondi. Aveva un naso un po' sudato e dei baffi. In testa aveva un cappello nero tutto schiacciato da una parte: dove non c'era il cappello si vedevano dei capelli neri striati di grigio, ondulati al ferro e spettinati. Doveva avere almeno dieci anni piú di Valentino. Valentino parlava e parlava perché noi stavamo zitti.

Valentino diceva cento cose insieme, sul gatto e sui bambini della portinaia e sul microscopio. Voleva subito condurre la fidanzata nella sua stanza a vedere il microscopio ma mia madre si oppose perché la stanza era ancora in disordine. E la fidanzata disse che del resto lei ne aveva visti tanti di microscopi. Allora Valentino andò a cercare il gatto e glielo portò. Gli aveva messo un nastro al collo e un sonaglio perché facesse una buona impressione. Ma il gatto era molto spaventato per via del sonaglio e s'arrampicò sulla tenda e di là ci guardava e soffiava col pelo tutto irto e gli occhi feroci e mia madre si mise a gemere per la paura che le sciupasse la tenda.

La fidanzata accese una sigaretta e cominciò a parlare. Parlava con la voce di chi è abituato a dare dei comandi e ogni cosa che ci diceva pareva che ci desse un comando. Disse che voleva bene a Valentino e aveva fiducia in lui; aveva fiducia che la smettesse di giocare col gatto e fare giocattoli. E disse che lei aveva moltissimi soldi e cosí potevano sposarsi senza aspettare che Valentino guadagnasse. Era sola e libera perché i suoi genitori erano morti e non aveva bisogno di render conto a nessuno di quel che faceva.

D'improvviso mia madre si mise a piangere. Fu un momento un po' penoso e non si sapeva bene cosa fare. Perché non c'era nessuna specie di commozione in quel pianto di mia madre, ma solo dispiacere e spavento: io lo sentivo e mi pareva che anche gli altri dovessero sentirlo. Mio padre le batteva dei colpettini sulle ginocchia e faceva dei piccoli schiocchi con la lingua, come si fa per consolare un bambino. La fidanzata si fece a un tratto molto rossa in viso e s'accostò a mia madre: i suoi occhi splendevano inquieti e imperiosi e capii che avrebbe sposato Valentino a ogni costo. « Ecco la mamma che piange — disse Valentino — la mamma ha sempre le lagrime in tasca ». « Sí — disse mia madre, e s'asciugò le lagrime e si lisciò i capelli e si raddrizzò. — Sono un po' debole in questo periodo e mi viene da piangere sovente. La notizia m'ha colto un po' di sorpresa: ma Valentino ha sempre fatto quello che ha voluto ». Mia madre era

stata educata in un collegio signorile; era molto beneducata
e aveva un grande controllo di sé.

Allora la fidanzata spiegò che quel giorno lei e Valen-
tino sarebbero andati a comprare i mobili per il salotto. Al-
tro non dovevano comprare perché c'era già tutto il neces-
sario in casa sua. E Valentino disegnò a mia madre la pianta
della casa, dove già abitava dall'infanzia la fidanzata e dove
avrebbero abitato insieme: una villa a tre piani, col giardino,
in un quartiere tutto di giardini e villette.

Quando se ne furono andati, per un po' restammo zitti
a guardarci; poi mia madre mi disse d'andare a chiamare mia
sorella e io andai.

Mia sorella abitava all'ultimo piano d'una casa in peri-
feria. Tutto il giorno batteva a macchina degl'indirizzi per
una ditta che le dava un tanto ogni busta. Aveva sempre male
ai denti e stava con una sciarpa intorno alla bocca. Le dissi
che la mamma voleva parlarle; chiese cos'era, ma non glielo
dissi. Era tutta incuriosita e si prese in collo il suo bambino
piú piccolo e venne con me.

Mia sorella non aveva mai creduto che Valentino sarebbe
diventato un grand'uomo. Non lo poteva soffrire e faceva una
faccia cattiva ogni volta che ne parlava, e subito le venivano
in mente tutti i soldi che mio padre spendeva per farlo stu-
diare, mentre lei doveva battere indirizzi. Cosí mia madre le
aveva tenuto nascosto il completo da sciatore e quando mia
sorella veniva da noi bisognava correre nella stanza di Va-
lentino e guardare che non ci fosse in giro quel vestito o le
altre cose nuove che s'era fatto.

Adesso era difficile raccontare a mia sorella Clara cos'era
successo. Che c'era una donna con tanti soldi e coi baffi che
voleva pagarsi il lusso di sposare Valentino e che lui ci stava.
Che si era lasciato indietro tutte le ragazzine coi berrettini
e girava per la città con una signora dalla pelliccia di mar-
tora a cercare dei mobili per il salotto. Aveva ancora pieni
i cassetti di fotografie di ragazzine e di loro lettere. E nella
nuova vita, con quella donna con gli occhiali di tartaruga
e coi baffi, avrebbe armeggiato in modo da svignarsela di

quando in quando per incontrarsi con le ragazzine dai berrettini; e avrebbe speso un poco di denaro per farle divertire: un poco di denaro: non molto, perché era fondamentalmente avaro nello spendere per gli altri il denaro che pensava gli appartenesse. Clara restò ad ascoltare mio padre e mia madre e alzò le spalle. Aveva molto male ai denti e doveva battere indirizzi; e poi doveva fare il bucato e aggiustare le calze dei bambini. Perché l'avevamo scomodata a farla venire fin da noi, cosí che aveva perso il pomeriggio? Non voleva sapere niente di Valentino, cosa faceva e con chi si sposava: quella lí era certo una pazza, perché nessuna donna con la testa a posto poteva pensare sul serio a sposarsi con Valentino; oppure era una puttana che aveva trovato il suo merlo e probabilmente la pelliccia era finta: papà e mamma di pellicce non ci capivano niente. Ma mia madre disse che la pelliccia era proprio vera; e quella era una signora perbene e aveva un fare proprio da signora perbene e non era pazza. Soltanto era brutta da fare spavento: e mia madre si coprí la faccia con le mani e di nuovo si mise a piangere nel ripensare com'era brutta. Ma mio padre disse che non era lí la questione; e voleva dire dov'era la questione e stava cominciando tutto un discorso ma mia madre non lo lasciò finire: perché mia madre non gli lasciava mai finire i discorsi a mio padre e lui restava con le parole strozzate in gola e s'agitava e soffiava.

Si sentí un gran chiasso nel corridoio ed era Valentino che rientrava. Aveva trovato il bambino di Clara e gli faceva festa. Lo alzava su alto al soffitto e poi lo rimetteva a terra: e di nuovo lo faceva volare su alto e il bambino rideva forte. E per un momento Clara sembrò contenta di quelle risate del suo bambino: ma subito la sua faccia divenne amara e cattiva come sempre quando si trovava Valentino davanti.

Valentino si mise a raccontare che avevano scelto i mobili per il salotto. Erano mobili impero. Diceva quanto costavano, diceva delle cifre che ci sembravano enormi: si fregava forte le mani e gettava quelle cifre con gioia nella nostra piccola stanza. Tirò fuori una sigaretta e l'accese: aveva un accendisigari d'oro. Gliel'aveva regalato Maddalena, la sua fidanzata. Non s'era accorto che noi eravamo muti e a disagio. Mia madre evitava di guardarlo. Mia sorella aveva preso in collo il bambino e gl'infilava i guanti. Da quando aveva visto l'accendisigari, s'era messa a sorridere a bocca stretta: si coprí quel sorriso con la sciarpa, e andò via col suo bambino in collo. « Che maiale », disse dentro la sciarpa, sulla soglia. Aveva detto quella parola pianissimo, ma Valentino sentí. Voleva rincorrere Clara giú per le scale e sapere perché aveva detto maiale, e mia madre lo trattenne a stento. « Perché maiale? — chiese Valentino a mia madre. — Perché m'ha detto maiale quella vigliacca? Perché mi sposo, mi dice maiale? Ma cosa crede quella brutta vigliacca? »

Mia madre si lisciava le pieghe del vestito e sospirava e taceva; e mio padre si riempiva la pipa con le dita che tremavano forte. Poi sfregò un fiammifero contro la suola della scarpa per accender la pipa, ma allora Valentino s'accostò con l'accendisigari. Mio padre guardò un momento la mano di Valentino con l'accendisigari acceso: e a un tratto respinse da sé quella mano, scagliò via la pipa e lasciò la stanza. Poi di nuovo riapparve sulla porta, e annaspava e soffiava come se stesse per cominciare un discorso: ma invece se ne andò senza dir nulla, sbattendo forte la porta.

Valentino era rimasto senza fiato. « Ma perché? — chiese a mia madre. — Ma perché s'è arrabbiato? Che cos'hanno? cos'ho fatto io? »

« È una donna brutta da fare spavento — disse piano mia madre. — È proprio un orrore, Valentino. E siccome dice che è tanto ricca, la gente penserà che lo fai per i soldi. Lo pensiamo anche noi, Valentino. Perché non possiamo mica credere che ti sei innamorato, te che correvi sempre dietro alle ragazze carine, e una non ti pareva mai carina abbastanza. E queste cose in casa nostra non son mai successe: mai nessuno di noi ha fatto una cosa soltanto per i denari ».

Valentino allora disse che non avevamo capito niente.

La sua fidanzata non era brutta: almeno lui non la trovava brutta e in fin dei conti non doveva piacere solo a lui? Aveva begli occhi neri e un portamento distinto: e poi era molto intelligente, molto intelligente, con una grande cultura. Era stufo di tutte quelle ragazzine che non sapevano parlare di niente, e invece con Maddalena lui parlava di libri e d'un mucchio di cose. Non si sposava per i soldi: non era un maiale. Tutt'a un tratto si offese e andò a chiudersi nella sua stanza.

Nei giorni che seguirono, fece ancora l'offeso e l'uomo che sta per fare un matrimonio contrastato dalla famiglia. Era serio, dignitoso, un po' pallido, e non ci parlava. Non ci mostrava i regali della sua fidanzata, ma ogni giorno ne aveva uno nuovo: al polso aveva un orologio d'oro a cronometro con un bracciale di pelle bianca; e aveva un portafogli di coccodrillo e ogni giorno una cravatta nuova.

Mio padre disse che sarebbe andato a parlare con la fidanzata di Valentino. Mia madre invece non voleva che andasse: un po' perché mio padre era malato di cuore e non doveva emozionarsi; e un po' perché lei non aveva nessuna fiducia nelle cose che poteva dire. Mio padre non diceva mai niente di sensato: forse il fondo del suo pensiero era sensato ma non arrivava mai a dire il fondo del suo pensiero: si perdeva in tante parole inutili e digressioni e ricordi d'infanzia e cincischiava e annaspava. Cosí in casa non gli riusciva mai di concludere un discorso perché non avevamo pazienza: e lui rimpiangeva sempre il tempo che ancora faceva scuola, perché là poteva parlare quanto voleva e non c'era nessuno che lo mortificasse.

Mio padre era sempre stato molto timido con Valentino: mai aveva osato rimproverarlo neppure quando era stato bocciato agli esami: e mai aveva smesso di credere che sarebbe diventato un grand'uomo. Adesso invece pareva che avesse smesso di crederlo: aveva un'aria infelice e pareva diventato vecchio tutt'a un tratto. Non voleva piú stare da solo in cucina: diceva che si sentiva impazzire in quella cucina senz'aria e si metteva seduto in un caffè sotto casa a bere il chinotto; oppure si spingeva fino al fiume e guardava pescare e ritornava a casa soffiando e farneticando fra sé.

Cosí mia madre, perché avesse pace, acconsentí che andasse dalla fidanzata di Valentino. Mio padre si vestí dei suoi vestiti migliori e mise anche il suo cappello migliore e dei guanti: e io e mia madre restammo affacciate al balcone a guardarlo mentre s'allontanava. E mentre lo seguivamo con gli occhi, ci prese un po' di speranza che le cose potessero ancora aggiustarsi nel migliore dei modi: non sapevamo come, e non sapevamo neppur bene che cosa sperare di preciso, e non riuscivamo a immaginare che cosa potesse dire mio padre; ma fu per noi un pomeriggio sereno, come da un pezzo non ce n'erano stati. Mio padre rientrò tardi, e pareva molto stanco: volle mettersi subito a letto, e mia madre l'aiutò a spogliarsi e intanto lo interrogava: ma questa volta invece lui pareva che non avesse voglia di parlare. Quando fu a letto, con gli occhi chiusi, con un viso grigio come la cenere, disse: «È una brava donna. Ho pietà di lei». E dopo un poco disse: « Ho visto la villa. Una gran bella villa, di gran lusso. Noialtri di un lusso cosí non ne abbiamo mai sentito nemmeno l'odore da lontano». Rimase per un momento in silenzio, e poi disse: « Io tanto creperò fra poco».

Alla fine del mese ci fu il matrimonio: e mio padre scrisse a un suo fratello per chiedergli un prestito, perché tutti dovevamo esser vestiti con decenza e non far sfigurare Valentino. Mia madre si fece fare un cappello, dopo tanti anni: un cappello alto e complicato, con un nodo di nastro e una veletta. E tirò fuori la sua vecchia volpe con un occhio di meno: se puntava la coda contro il muso non si vedeva che mancava l'occhio: mia madre aveva già speso tanto nel cappello, che non voleva piú sborsare neanche una lira per quel matrimonio. Io ebbi un abito nuovo, di lanetta celeste, con delle guarnizioni di velluto: al collo avevo anch'io una piccola volpe, piccolissima, me l'aveva regalata la zia Giuseppina quando avevo compiuto nove anni. La spesa piú grossa fu l'abito per Valentino: un abito di panno blu marin,

con una sottilissima riga bianca. Erano andati a sceglierlo
lui e la mamma, e lui allora aveva smesso di fare l'offeso
ed era felice e diceva che l'aveva sognato tutta la sua vita,
un abito blu marin con una sottilissima riga bianca.

Clara disse che lei al matrimonio non ci veniva, perché
non voleva immischiarsi nelle porcherie di Valentino e non
voleva spendere dei soldi: e Valentino mi disse di farle sa-
pere che stesse pure a casa ed era contento di non vedere
il suo brutto muso la mattina che si sposava. E Clara disse
che il muso l'aveva forse ancora peggio la sposa di lei: l'ave-
va vista solo in fotografia ma bastava. E invece poi comparve
anche Clara quel mattino in chiesa, col marito e la bambina
piú grande: e s'erano dati da fare anche loro a vestirsi per
bene e mia sorella s'era fatta arricciare i capelli.

Per tutto il tempo della chiesa mia madre mi tenne stret-
ta la mano e stringeva sempre piú forte: e nel momento che
loro s'infilavano gli anelli chinò il viso e mi disse che le
faceva troppo male guardare. La sposa era vestita di nero
con la solita pelliccia lunga e la nostra portinaia che aveva
voluto venire rimase delusa perché si aspettava i fiori d'aran-
cio e il velo: e ci disse poi che non era stato tanto un bel
matrimonio come aveva sperato dato che in giro correva la
voce che Valentino si sposava con una molto ricca. Oltre
alla portinaia e alla giornalaia dell'angolo non c'era nessuno
che conoscevamo noi: e la chiesa era piena dei conoscenti
di Maddalena, signore ben vestite con pellicce e gioielli.

Poi andammo nella villa e fu servito un rinfresco. Ades-
so che non c'era piú la portinaia e la giornalaia ci sentivamo
proprio sperduti, mia madre e mio padre e io e Clara e il
marito di Clara. Ce ne stavamo accosto alla parete e Valen-
tino venne un attimo a dirci che non stessimo tutti insieme a
fare tribú: ma noi continuammo a stare insieme. Le stanze
terrene della villa e il giardino eran piene di quella gente
che c'era in chiesa: e fra quella gente Valentino si muoveva
tranquillo e loro gli parlavano e rispondeva: era molto fe-
lice col suo vestito blu marin dalla riga bianca sottile sottile
e prendeva le signore a braccetto e le accompagnava al

buffet. La villa era proprio molto di lusso, come aveva detto mio padre: e pareva un sogno che ora Valentino abitasse lí.

Poi gl'invitati se ne andarono via e Valentino e sua moglie salirono in automobile: andavano in riviera per tre mesi in viaggio di nozze. Noi ritornammo a casa. La bambina di Clara era molto eccitata per le cose che aveva mangiato al *buffet* e per tutto quello che aveva visto: saltava e non faceva che parlare e raccontava che aveva girato per il giardino e si era spaventata di un cane e poi era stata anche in cucina dove c'era una gran cuoca tutta vestita di celeste che macinava il caffè. Ma appena a casa noi cominciammo a pensare a quel debito che avevamo fatto col fratello di mio padre; eravamo stanchi e di cattivo umore e mia madre andò nella stanza di Valentino e si mise a sedere sul letto disfatto e pianse un poco. Ma poi prese a riordinare ogni cosa e mise in naftalina il materasso e coprí i mobili con le fodere e chiuse le imposte.

Pareva che non ci fosse piú niente da fare senza Valentino, senza piú niente da spazzolare e stirare e smacchiare con la benzina. Parlavamo poco di lui; io mi preparavo agli esami e mia madre andava spesso da Clara che aveva un bambino ammalato. E mio padre andava in giro per la città perché non gli piaceva piú star da solo in cucina: andava a trovare certi suoi vecchi colleghi e cercava di fare con loro quei suoi lunghi discorsi ma poi finiva col dire che tanto lui sarebbe morto fra poco e non gli dispiaceva di morire perché la vita non gli aveva dato un gran che. Qualche volta saliva su da noi la portinaia per portare un po' di frutta, in cambio delle ripetizioni che avevo dato ai suoi figli: e sempre chiedeva di Valentino e diceva com'eravamo stati fortunati che Valentino si fosse sposato con una tanto ricca: cosí lei gli avrebbe messo su uno studio quando fosse stato dottore e noi potevamo dormire tranquilli che Valentino era a posto. E se lei non era bella meglio ancora, cosí almeno si poteva esser certi che non gli avrebbe messo le corna.

Passò l'estate e Valentino ci scrisse che ancora non ritornava; facevano i bagni e andavano in barca a vela e contavano di andare anche nelle Dolomiti. Era una bella vacanza e volevano godersela a lungo perché in città poi ci sarebbe stato da lavorare sul serio. Lui aveva gli esami da preparare e sua moglie si occupava sempre d'un mucchio di cose: doveva amministrare le sue terre e poi anche beneficenza e roba cosí.

Era già settembre inoltrato quando ce lo vedemmo arrivare a casa un mattino. Eravamo felici di vederlo: eravamo cosí felici che quasi ci pareva che non fosse piú niente importante la moglie che aveva preso. Era di nuovo seduto in cucina, con la sua testa riccia e i denti bianchi e la profonda fossetta nel mento e le grosse mani. Carezzava il gatto e diceva che voleva portarselo con sé: c'erano dei topi nella cantina della villa e cosí avrebbe imparato a mangiare i topi che adesso invece aveva paura. Rimase un pezzo con noi e volle mangiare un po' di salsa di pomodoro sul pane, perché la cuoca loro non faceva la salsa cosí buona come noi a casa. Si portò via il gatto in un cestino ma lo riportò dopo qualche giorno: l'avevano messo in cantina che mangiasse i topi ma aveva cosí paura di quei grossi topi che piangeva tutta la notte e la cuoca non poteva dormire.

Fu un inverno duro per noi: il bambino di Clara stava sempre male, pareva che avesse qualcosa di brutto nei bronchi e il medico aveva ordinato un vitto sostanzioso e abbondante. E poi avevamo sempre la preoccupazione di quel debito col fratello di mio padre, che cercavamo di pagare un poco alla volta. Cosí anche se non avevamo piú spese per Valentino facevamo fatica lo stesso ad arrivare alla fine del mese. Valentino non ne sapeva niente delle nostre preoccupazioni; lo vedevamo di rado, perché doveva prepararsi agli esami; comparivano a volte lui e la moglie, mia madre li riceveva in salotto, si lisciava le pieghe del vestito e c'erano lunghi silenzi: mia madre stava seduta in poltrona, diritta, col suo bel viso bianco e delicato fra le ciocche dei capelli bianchi, lisci e fini come la seta: e c'erano lunghi silenzi, interrotti ogni tanto dalla voce gentile e spenta di mia madre. Al mattino andavo a comprare a un mercato lontano, per vedere di risparmiare un po' sulla spesa. Quella passeggiata che facevo al mattino mi piaceva molto, soprattutto all'andata quando avevo la sporta vuota: camminavo nell'aria fredda e libera e mi dimenticavo per un poco le preoccupazioni che c'erano in casa: e invece mi chiedevo tutte le cose che si chiedono di solito le ragazze, se mi sarei sposata e quando e con chi. Non sapevo proprio con chi mi potevo sposare perché in casa non venivano mai giovanotti: ancora quando c'era Valentino ne capitava ogni tanto qualcuno ma adesso piú niente. E mio padre e mia madre pareva che non pensassero mai che io mi potevo sposare: parlavano di me come se avessi dovuto restare sempre con loro e parlavano di quando avrei vinto il concorso di maestra e avrei portato un po' di soldi a casa. Certe volte mi stupivo dei miei genitori, che non si chiedessero mai se mi sarebbe piaciuto sposarmi, o anche soltanto avere un vestito nuovo e uscire qualche domenica con delle ragazze. Mi stupivo, ma non provavo nessuna specie di rancore: a quell'epoca io non avevo dei sentimenti molto dolorosi e profondi: e mi sentivo piena di fiducia che presto o tardi le cose si mettessero meglio per me.

Un giorno mentre ritornavo dal mercato con la sporta, vidi la moglie di Valentino: era in automobile e guidava lei: fermò e mi disse di salire che m'avrebbe accompagnato a casa. Mi disse che lei ogni mattina s'alzava alle sette, faceva una doccia fredda e andava a vedere le sue terre a diciotto chilometri dalla città: e Valentino intanto rimaneva a letto e mi chiese se era sempre stato tanto pigro. Io le dissi del bambino di Clara che era sempre malato e lei allora si fece molto scura in viso e disse che non ne sapeva niente: Valentino gliene aveva appena accennato come a una cosa di poca importanza e mia madre non gliene aveva parlato. « Mi trattate proprio come un'estranea: tua madre non mi può vedere e me ne sono accorta fin dalla prima volta che son venuta. Non vi passa nemmeno per la testa che potrei aiutarvi quando siete nei guai. E pensare che viene da me della gente sconosciuta a chiedermi aiuto e io mi muovo sempre ».

Era molto arrabbiata e non sapevo che dirle: eravamo arrivate sotto casa mia e timidamente la invitai a salire ma disse che non le piaceva venire a trovarci perché lo sapeva benissimo che mia madre ce l'aveva con lei.

Ma quel giorno stesso andò da Clara e si trascinò dietro Valentino che non andava a casa di Clara da un pezzo, da quando lei gli aveva detto maiale. Maddalena per prima cosa spalancò le finestre, perché trovava che c'era molto cattivo odore. E disse che era una cosa vergognosa come Valentino se ne infischiava dei suoi: e lei che non aveva nessuno si scaldava per gente sconosciuta e faceva chilometri. Mandò Valentino a chiamare il suo medico di fiducia: e il medico disse che il bambino era meglio portarlo in clinica e lei disse che avrebbe pagato le spese. Clara era tutta spaventata e stordita mentre preparava la valigia con le cose del bambino: e Maddalena intanto la sgridava e la maltrattava e mia sorella si confondeva ancora di più.

Ma quando il bambino fu entrato in clinica sentimmo un grande sollievo. Clara si chiedeva cosa poteva fare per sdebitarsi. Si consigliò con mia madre e comprarono una grande scatola di cioccolatini, e Clara andò a portarla a Maddalena: ma allora Maddalena le disse che era una vera cretina a spender soldi in cioccolatini con tutte le preoccupazioni che aveva, e cos'erano queste scemenze di sdebitarsi. Disse che tutti noialtri avevamo delle idee storte in fatto di denaro: mio padre e mia madre che non sapevano come tirare avanti e mi mandavano a un mercato lontano per risparmiare qualche lira e sarebbe stato tanto semplice che si fossero rivolti a lei per aiuto: e Valentino che se ne infischiava e si comprava una quantità di vestiti nuovi e poi si guardava nello specchio e faceva lo scimmiotto. E disse che d'ora innanzi ci avrebbe fatto avere del denaro ogni mese e poi della verdura tutti i giorni perché io non dovessi più andare a quel mercato lontano, lei di verdura ne aveva sempre tanta dalle sue terre e le marciva in cucina. E Clara venne da noi a pregare che accettassimo quel denaro: perché avevamo sempre fatto tanti sacrifici per Valentino ed era giusto che adesso sua moglie ci aiutasse un poco. Cosí ogni mese veniva l'amministratore di Maddalena col denaro dentro una busta: e ogni due o tre giorni trovavamo in portineria una cesta di verdura e io non dovevo piú andare al mercato e potevo dormire di piú.

Alla fine dell'inverno, mio padre morí. Io e mia madre eravamo andate a trovare il bambino di Clara alla clinica. Cosí era solo mio padre quando morí. Tornammo a casa e lo trovammo già morto: s'era messo sul letto e aveva sciolto certe sue compresse in una tazza di latte, perché forse si sentiva male: ma poi non aveva bevuto. Nel cassetto del comodino trovammo una lettera per Valentino, che doveva aver scritto qualche giorno prima: una lunga lettera, dove si scusava d'aver sempre sperato che Valentino diventasse un grand'uomo; invece non c'era nessun bisogno che diventasse un grand'uomo, e bastava che diventasse un uomo, né grande né piccolo: perché adesso era soltanto un bambino. Vennero Valentino e Maddalena e Valentino pianse; e Maddalena per la prima volta fu molto buona con mia madre, delicata e gentile; telefonò all'amministratore che s'occupasse dei funerali, e restò con mia madre tutta la notte e anche il giorno dopo. Quando se ne fu andata, feci osservare a mia madre com'era stata gentile; ma mia madre disse che anche quando era gentile non la poteva sopportare e si sentiva una stretta al cuore ogni volta che la vedeva accanto a Valentino: e disse che era sicura che mio padre era morto per quello, per il dispiacere che Valentino si fosse sposato soltanto per i denari.

Nell'estate Maddalena ebbe un figlio: e credevo che mia madre si sarebbe commossa e intenerita e che si sarebbe affezionata al bambino: e mi pareva che il bambino avesse una piccola fossetta nel mento e che rassomigliasse a Valentino. Ma mia madre diceva che non c'era nemmeno l'ombra d'una fossetta: era molto triste e abbattuta mia madre; pensava sempre a mio padre e si faceva rimorso d'essere stata poco affettuosa con lui; non aveva mai pazienza di lasciargli finire un discorso e lo zittiva e lo mortificava. Invece adesso capiva che mio padre era stata la meglio cosa che aveva avuto nella sua vita: non poteva lamentarsi di Clara e di me, ma pure non le facevamo tutta la compagnia che avremmo dovuto; e Valentino si era presa quella moglie soltanto per i denari. A poco a poco smise di dar lezioni di pianoforte, perché aveva l'artrite e le dolevano molto le mani; e del resto quella busta che ci portava ogni mese l'amministratore bastava per noi due. L'amministratore lo ricevevo io nella saletta da pranzo, e mia madre si chiudeva in cucina e non voleva che le parlassi di quella busta: ma pure era di quello che mangiavamo ogni giorno.

Maddalena venne a dirmi se volevo passare l'agosto al mare con loro: sarei stata molto contenta di andare ma non volevo lasciar sola mia madre, e cosí rifiutai. Maddalena mi disse ch'ero una scema e non sapevo staccarmi da casa: e cosí era escluso che trovassi marito e mi mettessi pure il cuore in pace. Le dissi che non me ne importava di trovare marito: ma non era vero e fu un agosto lungo e malinconico; e io accompagnavo mia madre la sera a prendere il fresco nei viali e sul fiume con la sua lunga mano sformata dall'artrite al mio braccio e avevo una voglia tremenda di camminare in fretta e da sola e di poter parlare con qualcuno che non fosse mia madre. Poi cominciò a non alzarsi piú dal letto perché anche la schiena le doleva e si lamentava continuamente. Pregavo Clara di venire spesso ma aveva un gran daffare a battere indirizzi per quella sua ditta. Aveva mandato i bambini in campagna, anche quello ch'era stato malato e adesso era guarito bene; tutta la settimana batteva indirizzi come una furia, e la domenica andava dai suoi bambini. Cosí ero sola in casa quando morí mia madre, la domenica di ferragosto: tutta la notte si era lamentata di quel male alle ossa, e smaniava e voleva da bere e s'irritava perché non ero svelta a portarle l'acqua e a levarle i cuscini: al mattino andai a chiamare il medico e mi disse che non c'era speranza. Mandai un telegramma a Valentino e anche a Clara in campagna: ma quando loro arrivarono la mamma era morta.

Io le avevo voluto molto bene. Adesso avrei dato tutto per fare di nuovo quelle passeggiate serali che m'annoiavano, con la mano lunga e storta di mia madre appoggiata al mio braccio. E mi facevo rimorso di non essere stata abbastanza affettuosa con lei. Certe volte stavo affacciata sul cortile a mangiar le ciliege e non mi voltavo quando lei mi chiamava: lasciavo che mi chiamasse per un pezzo e restavo appoggiata alla ringhiera e non mi voltavo. Adesso m'era venuto in odio quel cortile, quel balcone e le nostre quattro stanze vuote: eppure non volevo niente: non volevo andar via.

Ma venne Maddalena e mi disse d'andare a stare da loro. Era molto gentile con me, cosí com'era stata con mia madre quando era morto mio padre: era molto gentile e carezzevole e non comandava. Disse ch'ero libera di fare come volevo ma non aveva senso che stessi in quella casa da sola: c'erano tante stanze nella sua casa dove avrei potuto studiare tranquilla e quando fossi stata malinconica loro m'avrebbero tenuto compagnia.

Cosí lasciai quella casa dov'ero cresciuta e che sapevo a memoria, tanto che mi sembrava impossibile di poter vivere in un'altra casa. Mentre riordinavo le stanze prima d'andar via, trovai dentro un baule le lettere e le fotografie di quelle ragazzine coi berrettini che si fidanzavano con Valentino una volta: e io e Clara passammo un pomeriggio a leggere quelle lettere e a ridere e alla fine le bruciammo tutte sul gas. Il gatto lo lasciai alla portinaia: e quando tornai a vederlo dopo qualche mese aveva imparato a mangiare i topi ed era diventato un grosso gatto robusto e indifferente e non aveva piú niente da fare col nostro gattino sparuto e feroce che s'arrampicava sulle tende quando si spaventava.

Nella villa di Maddalena avevo una stanza con un grande tappeto azzurro. Mi piaceva molto quel tappeto e ogni mattina quando mi svegliavo mi rallegravo a vederlo. Ci posavo sopra i piedi nudi ed era caldo e soffice. Mi sarebbe piaciuto stare un po' a letto al mattino ma ricordavo che Maddalena non aveva stima della gente che s'alzava tardi, e difatti sentivo la sua scampanellata violenta e la sua voce imperiosa che dava gli ordini per la giornata. Poi usciva fuori con la sua pelliccia lunga e il cappello schiacciato da una parte: strillava ancora un po' con la cuoca e la balia e saliva in automobile sbatacchiando forte lo sportello. Andavo a prendere il bambino e lo tenevo un po' in collo. M'ero affezionata a quel bambino, e speravo che s'affezionasse a me. Valentino scendeva a far colazione, insonnolito, con la barba lunga: gli chiedevo se avrebbe dato gli esami ma girava il discorso. Poi veniva l'amministratore, il Bugliari, quello che ci portava sempre le buste quando stavo nel nostro alloggio col papà e la mamma: e veniva un cugino di Maddalena che chiamavano Kit. Valentino si metteva a giocare a carte con loro: ma quando si sentiva il rumore dell'automobile nel giardino, nascondevano in fretta le carte perché Maddalena non voleva che Valentino perdesse il tempo a giocare. Maddalena arrivava, spettinata e stanca, e con la voce rauca perché aveva gridato coi contadini; e si metteva a litigare con l'amministratore e tiravano fuori certi registri e discutevano un pezzo lí sopra. Io mi stupivo che non chiedesse neppure del bambino e non andasse a vederlo: pareva che non gliene importasse molto del bambino: quando la balia glielo portava lo prendeva un attimo in collo, e per un attimo il suo viso diventava giovane, mite e materno; ma subito annusava il bambino alla nuca e diceva che non aveva un buon odore pulito e lo ridava alla balia perché lo lavasse.

Kit aveva quarant'anni. Era lungo e magro, un po' calvo, con pochi capelli umidi e lunghi sulla nuca che parevano i capelli d'un bambino appena nato. Non aveva nessuna professione precisa: possedeva delle terre vicino a quelle di Maddalena ma non aveva mai voglia d'andarle a vedere;

pregava Maddalena di darci un'occhiata e lei si lamentava sempre che con tutto il da fare che aveva le toccava anche vedere le terre di Kit. Kit passava le giornate da noi: giocava col bambino e chiacchierava con la balia e faceva qualche partita a carte con Valentino e stava buttato nel fondo d'una poltrona a fumare. Poi, verso sera, lui e Valentino andavano a sedersi in un caffè del centro e guardavano passare le donne eleganti.

Ero molto preoccupata per Valentino perché mi pareva che non studiasse mai. Si metteva nella sua stanza col microscopio e coi libri e con un teschio, ma non riusciva a stare un momento al tavolo e suonava che gli portassero uno zabaione e poi accendeva una candela dentro il teschio e faceva tutto buio nella stanza e chiamava la cameriera per spaventarla. Da quando s'era sposato aveva dato due esami e gli erano andati bene: di solito gli esami gli andavano bene perché aveva la parola facile e riusciva a far credere di sapere anche quello che non sapeva. Ma gli restavano ancora molti esami prima della laurea e certi suoi amici che avevano cominciato con lui erano già laureati da un pezzo. Girava sempre il discorso quando gli parlavo dei suoi esami e non sapevo come fare. Maddalena quando ritornava a casa gli chiedeva: « Hai studiato? » e lui diceva di sí e lei gli credeva: o forse aveva trafficato e litigato tutto il giorno per i suoi affari e non aveva piú voglia di litigare ancora a casa sua. Si metteva sdraiata sul divano e Valentino si sedeva sul tappeto vicino a lei. Allora io la vedevo diventare vile di fronte a Valentino. Prendeva la sua testa fra le mani e l'accarezzava, e il suo viso diventava luminoso, materno e mite. « Valentino ha studiato? » chiedeva anche a Kit. « Ha studiato », rispondeva Kit. E lei chiudeva gli occhi e stava quieta e passava e ripassava le dita sulla fronte di Valentino.

Maddalena ebbe un altro figlio e ce ne andammo al mare per l'estate. Faceva i figli senza nessuna fatica, e per tutto il tempo della gravidanza continuava a andare e venire per le sue terre. Poi, quando li aveva fatti, mandava a cercare una balia che li allattasse e non se ne interessava piú. Le bastava sapere che c'erano. E anche con Valentino era la stessa cosa: le bastava sapere che c'era ma passava le giornate lontano da lui: le bastava ritrovarselo a casa la sera quando ritornava, e accarezzargli un momento i capelli e star distesa con la sua testa nel grembo. Mi ricordavo quello che lui aveva detto a mia madre, che con Maddalena poteva parlare di qualunque cosa, di libri e di tutto: ma io non m'accorgevo che parlassero mai. Intanto c'era sempre Kit; e Kit era sempre lui a parlare, certe storie noiose e senza fine della sua serva che era mezza cieca e scema, e dei mali che lui si sentiva e del suo medico. E quando Kit non c'era, Maddalena gli faceva telefonare che venisse subito.

Dunque andammo al mare, e con noi vennero Kit e il Bugliari, la cameriera e la balia. Stavamo in albergo, un albergo molto elegante; e io mi vergognavo dei miei pochi vestiti, ma non volevo chiedere dei soldi a Maddalena e lei pareva che non ci pensasse a offrirmene: del resto anche lei non era niente elegante, sempre con lo stesso prendisole a palle bianche e blu; e diceva che non voleva spendere per i vestiti perché Valentino spendeva già tanto per farsene lui. Valentino sí era elegante, con i calzoni di tela, con canottiere e maglioni che si cambiava continuamente; era Kit che lo consigliava per i vestiti, anche se lui aveva sempre gli stessi calzoni un po' consumati perché diceva che era troppo brutto e non gli dava piacere vestirsi. Valentino se ne andava via in barca a vela con Kit, e Maddalena e io e il Bugliari stavamo ad aspettarli sulla spiaggia; e Maddalena diceva ch'era già stufa di quella vita perché non era capace di stare al sole senza niente da fare. Valentino e Kit andavano anche a ballare la sera: e Maddalena gli diceva di portare anche me a ballare ma Valentino diceva che a ballare ci si va senza sorelle.

Tornammo in città e io presi il diploma di maestra: ottenni una supplenza in una scuola e ogni mattina Maddalena m'accompagnava alla scuola in automobile prima di partire per le sue terre. Le dissi che ora avrei potuto star da sola e pensare a me stessa: ma si offese e mi disse che non vedeva cos'avrei fatto da sola, quando c'era la sua casa cosí grande e sempre con tanta roba da mangiare: non vedeva perché avrei dovuto affittarmi una stanzetta e cuocermi la minestrina su un fornellino. Non vedeva perché. E i bambini mi s'erano affezionati e potevo un po' sorvegliarli quando non c'era lei: e potevo sorvegliare anche Valentino, che studiasse.

Allora presi coraggio e le dissi che ero preoccupata per Valentino: mi pareva che studiasse sempre meno e adesso Kit gli aveva detto d'imparare a cavalcare e ogni mattina andavano al maneggio. Valentino s'era fatto fare un costume da cavalleriźzo, con gli stivaloni e la giacchetta stretta e il frustino: e a casa si guardava nello specchio e agitava il frustino e salutava con il berretto. Allora Maddalena chiamò Kit e gli fece una sfuriata: e gli disse che se lui era un ozioso e un fallito, Valentino non doveva diventare un fallito e lo lasciasse tranquillo. Kit restò ad ascoltare con gli occhi socchiusi, spalancando la bocca e carezzandosi le mascelle: e Valentino intanto gridava che cavalcare gli faceva bene, e stava molto meglio di salute da quando cavalcava. Maddalena allora corse a prendere il costume da cavallerizzo, gli stivali e il berretto e il frustino, fece un pacco e disse che andava a buttarlo nel fiume: e uscí fuori con quel gran pacco sotto il braccio: era di nuovo incinta e la pancia le sporgeva fuori della pelliccia e correva un po' zoppicando per il peso della pancia e del pacco. Valentino uscí dietro a lei: e restammo soli io e Kit. «Ha ragione», disse Kit, e diede un sospiro profondo; si grattava quei pochi capelli e faceva una faccia cosí buffa che mi venne da ridere. «Maddalena ha ragione, — disse ancora, — io non sono che un ozioso e un fallito. Ha ragione. Per un tipo come me non c'è nessuna speranza. Ma non c'è nessuna speranza nemmeno per Valentino: è come me: è un tipo come me. Anzi è

peggio, perché non gliene importa niente di niente: e a me
invece me ne importa un po' delle cose: poco, ma un po' sí».
« E pensare che mio padre credeva che Valentino diven-
tasse un grand'uomo », dissi, e lui disse: « Ah, davvero? »
e ruppe a un tratto in una gran risata, con tutta la bocca
aperta: si cullava nella poltrona e stringeva le mani tra le
ginocchia e rideva. Ebbi una sensazione spiacevole e lasciai
la stanza: e quando ritornai se n'era andato. Valentino e
Maddalena non rientrarono per mangiare, e venne buio e
non si vedevano ancora; ero già coricata da un po' quando
li sentii nelle scale, e ridevano e sussurravano e capii che
avevano fatto la pace. L'indomani Valentino andò al ma-
neggio col suo costume da cavallerizzo: Maddalena non l'ave-
va buttato nel fiume: soltanto la giacchetta s'era un po' sgual-
cita e si dovette stirarla. Kit non si fece vedere per qualche
giorno, ma poi ricomparve: aveva le tasche piene di calzini
da rammendare e li diede alla cameriera, perché a casa sua
nessuno gli rammendava i calzini, stava solo con quella vec-
chia serva mezza cieca che non rammendava.

Nacque il terzo figlio di Maddalena: era di nuovo un
maschio, e lei diceva ch'era contenta d'avere soltanto dei
maschi, perché se nasceva una bambina avrebbe avuto trop-
pa paura che da grande le assomigliasse, e avesse il suo viso:
e il suo viso le pareva tanto brutto che non si sentiva d'au-
gurarlo a nessuna donna. Lei adesso era contenta lo stesso
anche col suo brutto viso, perché aveva i bambini e Valenti-
no: ma da ragazza aveva pianto molto e non si dava pace, e
temeva di non sposarsi mai; temeva d'invecchiare sola in
quella grande villa, coi tappeti e coi quadri. Adesso forse
faceva tanti bambini per dimenticarsi di quella paura che
aveva avuto, e perché fossero piene le stanze di giocattoli e
di pannolini e di voci: ma i bambini una volta che li aveva
fatti non se ne occupava un gran che.
Andarono a fare un viaggio Valentino e Kit. Valentino
aveva dato un altro esame, gli era andato bene e diceva

d'aver bisogno d'un po' di riposo. Andarono a Parigi e a Londra, perché Valentino non aveva mai visto niente: e Kit diceva ch'era vergogna non conoscere le grandi città. Diceva che Valentino aveva un fondo molto provinciale: e bisognava sprovincializzarlo e portarlo in giro nei dancing e nelle grandi gallerie di quadri. Io tutte le mattine facevo scuola e il pomeriggio stavo nel giardino a giocare con i bambini: e cercavo di fabbricare giocattoli con la stoffa e la segatura, come faceva un tempo Valentino per i figli della portinaia. Quando Maddalena non c'era, la balia e la· cameriera e la cuoca venivano a sedersi in giardino con me: mi dicevano che non si sentivano niente in soggezione con me, mi volevano molto bene e si toglievano le scarpe e le posavano sull'erba lí accanto; e si facevano dei cappelli di carta e leggevano i giornali di Maddalena e fumavano le sue sigarette. Trovavano che io facevo una vita troppo solitaria e in disparte e che Maddalena avrebbe dovuto portarmi un po' a divertire: ma lei aveva sempre la testa soltanto alle sue terre. E dicevano che cosí era difficile che io trovassi marito: in casa non ci veniva quasi mai nessuno, salvo il Bugliari e Kit: il Bugliari era troppo vecchio, e cosí decisero che dovevo sposare Kit: era molto buono ma cosí scombinato, non andava mai a dormire la notte e passeggiava per la città fino a tardi: e forse gli ci voleva proprio una donna che pensasse a rammendargli i calzini e si prendesse cura di lui. Ma avevano una gran paura di Maddalena e appena sentivano il rumore dell'automobile si rimettevano svelte le scarpe e scappavano in cucina.

Andavo qualche volta da Clara, ma mi accoglieva male e diceva che ormai a me non me ne importava piú niente di lei e dei suoi bambini: e volevo bene soltanto ai figli di Valentino. Ormai s'era scordata di quando Maddalena s'era data da fare per il suo bambino ch'era ammalato e l'aveva fatto entrare alla clinica pagando le spese: ce l'aveva con Maddalena e diceva che Valentino s'era rovinato del tutto con quel matrimonio: adesso si trovava ogni giorno la minestra servita e potevamo dare un caro addio alla speranza che prendesse la laurea. Adesso si sarebbe mangiato tutti i soldi della moglie a poco a poco. Mentre mi parlava continuava a battere indirizzi: a forza di battere indirizzi le eran venuti dei calli alle dita, e poi aveva sempre un dolore alle spalle, e la notte dormiva poco per il mal di denti. Avrebbe dovuto fare una cura molto costosa e non le bastavano i soldi. Le proposi di chiedere un prestito a Maddalena ma si offese e disse che lei non voleva soldi da quel tipo di gente. Cosí presi a portarle il mio stipendio ogni mese: tanto io avevo da mangiare e da dormire e non mi occorreva nulla: e speravo che fosse piú serena e andasse dal dentista e s'affaticasse un po' meno a battere indirizzi. Ma invece batteva indirizzi lo stesso e dal dentista non ci andava: diceva che aveva dovuto fare il cappotto alla bambina e comprare le scarpe al marito e che io non avevo un'idea delle sue condizioni e se un giorno mi fossi sposata avrei visto che gioia. Perché era sicura che se io mi sposavo andavo a cascare con uno senza niente come era successo a lei e ormai nella nostra famiglia c'era già stato Valentino che aveva fatto un matrimonio coi soldi, e un'altra volta non potevamo aspettarcela una fortuna cosí. E del resto pareva una fortuna ma era una disgrazia, perché a Valentino i soldi gli servivano soltanto a fare l'ozioso e a mangiarseli tutti a poco a poco.

Valentino e Kit ritornarono e partimmo tutti per il mare: ma Valentino era molto di malumore e lui e Maddalena litigavano di continuo. Valentino se ne andava via solo in automobile al mattino presto e non diceva dove andava: e Kit stava sdraiato sotto l'ombrellone con noi ed era molto triste. A mezzo agosto Valentino disse che ne aveva abbastanza del mare e voleva andare nelle Dolomiti: cosí partimmo tutti per le Dolomiti, ma là pioveva e al bambino piú piccolo venne la febbre. Maddalena disse allora che era colpa di Valentino se il bambino s'era ammalato, perché aveva voluto partire cosí di furia dal mare dove stavamo bene, e l'albergo dov'eravamo adesso era scomodo e c'entrava aria

391

da tutte le parti. Ma Valentino disse che lui avrebbe anche potuto venirsene via da solo: non ci aveva chiesto di venirgli tutti dietro ma noi gli stavamo sempre alle costole e lui era stufo di bambini, di balie e di tutto il nostro corteo. Kit andò di notte con la macchina a cercare un medico: e quando il bambino si fu rimesso tornammo tutti in città. Tutt'a un tratto i rapporti fra Maddalena e Valentino parevano peggiorati e non c'era piú pace quand'erano insieme. Maddalena era molto nervosa e appena s'alzava al mattino cominciava a gridare con la cameriera e la cuoca. Era molto nervosa anche con me e s'irritava ogni volta che le parlavo. E li sentivo litigare forte lei e Valentino fino a notte tardi: e lei gli diceva che era un ozioso e un fallito proprio come Kit. Ma almeno Kit era buono e invece Valentino non era buono, era un egoista e pensava soltanto a sé: e buttava via i denari per i vestiti e per altre cose che lei non sapeva. E Valentino allora gridava ch'era lei che l'aveva rovinato: e gli pareva d'impazzire al mattino quando sentiva la sua voce e aveva orrore di sedersi a tavola con lei davanti. Qualche volta poi facevano la pace, lui le chiedeva perdono e piangeva e anche lei chiedeva perdono: e per un poco stavano tranquilli come una volta, lui seduto sul tappeto e lei sul divano a carezzargli i capelli: e chiamavano Kit e lo ascoltavano raccontare tutte le notizie della città. Ma duravano poco quei momenti e si facevano sempre piú rari: e c'erano lunghe giornate di visi scuri e silenzio e poi scoppi di voce a notte alta.

La cameriera si licenziò per una scena che le aveva fatto Maddalena; e Maddalena mi chiese d'andare a cercare una cameriera in un paese di campagna vicino alle sue terre, dove le avevan dato degl'indirizzi. M'avrebbe accompagnato Kit con la macchina. E partimmo un mattino io e Kit. La macchina correva nella campagna e non parlavamo: guardavo di tanto in tanto quel buffo profilo di Kit, con il piccolo basco sulla testa calva e il naso un po' a fischietto; alle mani aveva i guanti di Valentino. « Sono i guanti di Valentino? »

gli dissi, per rompere il silenzio: e staccò un momento le mani dal volante e se le guardò. « Sí, sono i guanti di Valentino. Non voleva prestarmeli: è geloso delle cose sue ». Posai la fronte al vetro a guardare la campagna: e provai un senso di sollievo e di pace al pensiero di quella giornata che m'aspettava, libera, lontano da quella casa dove si litigava sempre: e pensai che dovevo andarmene da quella casa: non ci stavo piú bene, ci stavo troppo a disagio: m'era venuto in odio perfino il tappeto azzurro che c'era nella mia stanza e che prima mi piaceva tanto. Dissi: « Che bella mattina ». E Kit allora disse: « Sí, e troveremo una bella cameriera e faremo colazione in un'osteria che so io, dove hanno del vino buono. Sarà una vacanza, una piccola vacanza d'una giornata: per te dev'essere pesante la vita, con quei due che non vanno d'accordo e non trovano pace ». « Sí, — dissi — certe volte non se ne può piú. Vorrei andarmene via ». « Dove via? » disse. « Oh non so, in qualche posto ». « Si potrebbe andare via insieme, io e te, — disse, — cercarci un piccolo posto tranquillo, e lasciare che se la sbrighino da soli quei due. Anch'io ne ho abbastanza di loro. Al mattino tante volte mi alzo e dico: non andrò da loro; ma poi càpito sempre lí. Ormai è un'abitudine: sono abituato a mangiare da Maddalena da tanti anni: e sto al caldo e m'aggiustano i calzini. Casa mia è una vera topaia; c'è una stufa a carbone che non tira e finirà che morirò asfissiato: e c'è la serva che mi chiacchiera sempre. Dovrei far fare l'impianto del termosifone: Maddalena qualche volta viene da me e mi dice tutte le cose che dovrei fare. Io le dico che non ho i denari: ma lei mi dice che me li trova i denari, basterebbe far fruttare quelle mie terre: vendere qui, comperare là, lei sa tutto come bisognerebbe fare. Ma io non ho voglia di decidere niente di nuovo. Maddalena poi dice che dovrei prendere moglie: ma questo credo proprio che non lo farò mai. Non ci credo nel matrimonio. Quando Maddalena e Valentino m'hanno detto che si sposavano, sono stato una giornata intera a cercare di dissuaderli. E allora a Valentino glie l'ho detto in faccia che non avevo stima di lui. E vedi, se m'avessero dato retta. Vedi adesso in che imbroglio si trovano: sempre a litigare, sempre a farsi amara la vita».

«Non hai stima di Valentino?» dissi.

«No. Perché tu forse hai stima di lui?»

«Io gli voglio bene, perché è mio fratello», dissi.

«Voler bene è un altro discorso. Può essere che anch'io gli voglia molto bene». Si grattò la testa di sotto al basco. «Ma non ho stima di lui. Non ho stima neppure di me: e lui è come me: un tipo proprio come me. Un tipo che non farà mai niente di bello. La sola differenza tra me e lui è questa: che a lui non gliene importa niente di niente: né cose, né persone, né niente. Lui venera soltanto il suo corpo: il suo sacro corpo, che bisogna nutrire bene ogni giorno e vestire bene e badare che non manchi niente. E a me invece me ne importa un poco delle cose e delle persone; ma non ho nessuno che gliene importi di me. Valentino è felice, perché l'amore per se stessi non delude mai; e io sono un disgraziato, e non ho un cane che gliene freghi niente di me».

Eravamo arrivati al paese che ci aveva detto Maddalena e lui fermò la macchina: «Ora andiamo a cercare questa cameriera», disse.

Chiedemmo indicazioni nel paese e ci mostrarono una casa lontana, su alto sulla costa della collina, dove forse c'era una ragazza disposta a venire in città. Salimmo su per un viottolo tra le vigne e Kit era senza fiato e si faceva vento col basco. «Anche cercargli la cameriera dobbiamo, — diceva, — è un po' troppo. Che tipi che sono. Io le scarpe me le pulisco da me».

La ragazza era andata a lavorare nei campi e si dovette aspettarla. Ci sedemmo in una piccola cucina buia e la madre della ragazza ci offerse del vino e delle piccole pere grinzose. Kit parlava svelto in dialetto con la donna e lodava il vino e le faceva infinite domande minuziose sul lavoro dei campi; e io bevevo il vino in silenzio e a poco a poco mi si confondevano i pensieri: era un vino molto forte e ad un tratto mi sentii felice in quella cucina, con i liberi prati dietro ai vetri e il sapore del vino, e Kit con quelle gambe lunghe e col basco e col suo naso a fischietto: pensavo: « Ma com'è simpatico questo Kit! »

Poi uscimmo fuori al sole e ci sedemmo su una panca di pietra davanti alla casa. Mangiavamo le pere e godevamo il sole e Kit mi disse: « Come stiamo bene ». Prese un attimo la mia mano e mi levò il guanto e la guardò: « Hai le dita come Valentino » disse. D'un tratto buttò via la mia mano. « Sul serio tuo padre credeva che Valentino diventasse un grand'uomo? » « Sí, — dissi, — lo credeva. Abbiamo fatto molti sacrifici perché potesse studiare; avevamo la vita dura e non sapevamo mai come arrivare alla fine del mese. Ma a Valentino non gli è mancato mai niente; e mio padre diceva che poi saremmo stati ricompensati, il giorno che Valentino sarebbe diventato un medico famoso, di quelli che fanno delle grandi scoperte ».

« Ah sí », disse. Per un momento sembrò che lo pigliasse quel suo riso convulso, com'era successo quella volta in salotto quando avevamo parlato della stessa cosa. Si dondolò sulla panca con le mani strette fra le ginocchia; ma subito guardò la mia faccia e si rifece serio.

« Sai, — disse, — i padri hanno sempre delle strane idee. Il mio credeva che sarei diventato ufficiale d'aviazione. Ufficiale d'aviazione, io che non posso andare neppure in ottovolante perché mi vengono le vertigini a guardare giú ».

Arrivò la ragazza; aveva i capelli rossi e due grosse gambe con le calze nere arrotolate sotto i polpacci: Kit cominciò a farle una serie interminabile di domande minuziose e meticolose in dialetto: e pareva competentissimo su tutto quello che deve saper fare una cameriera. La ragazza era disposta a venire a servizio; avrebbe preparato le cose sue e fra due o tre giorni sarebbe partita.

Scendemmo al paese a pranzare e passeggiammo a lungo fra le case e nei campi. Kit non aveva nessuna voglia di ritornare. Spalancava ogni porta che vedeva e curiosava nei cortili: e una volta venne fuori una vecchia tutta infuriata e scappammo via e la vecchia ci tirò dietro una scarpa. Camminammo a lungo nella campagna: Kit aveva ancora le tasche piene di quelle piccole pere e me ne dava ogni tanto. « Vedi come stiamo bene lontano da quei due, — ripeteva, — vedi come siamo contenti. Ce ne dobbiamo andare via insieme, in un posto tranquillo ». Era buio quando risalimmo in automobile. « Vuoi sposarmi? » disse ad un tratto. Teneva le due mani sul volante e non faceva partire la macchina: e faceva una faccia cosí buffa, spaventata e severa, col basco tutto storto sulla fronte e le sopracciglia aggrottate: « Vuoi sposarmi? » ripeté con rabbia: e io risi e dissi di sí. Allora accese il motore e partimmo.

« Non sono innamorata » dissi.

« Lo so; e neppur io sono innamorato. E io nel matrimonio non ci credo. Ma chi sa? Potrebbe anche andarci bene, a noialtri due; sei una ragazza cosí tranquilla, cosí dolce, mi pare che staremmo cosí tranquilli. Non faremmo delle cose strane, non faremmo dei grandi viaggi: soltanto andremmo ogni tanto a vedere un paese come quello di oggi, a spalancare delle porte e a curiosare nei cortili ».

« Ti ricordi la vecchia che ci ha tirato la scarpa? » dissi.

« Ah sí, — disse, — com'era infuriata! »

« Credo che dovrò pensarci ancora un poco » dissi.

« Pensare a che cosa? »

« Se sposarci o no ».

« Ah sí, — disse, — pensiamoci bene. Ma sai, non è la prima volta che io l'ho pensato: ti guardavo, e dicevo: "Che cara ragazza". Io sono una brava persona: ho dei gravi difetti, sono pigro, lascio sempre le cose come sono: in casa mia le stufe non tirano, e le lascio stare. Ma nell'insieme sono una brava persona. Se ci sposiamo, farò aggiustare le stufe: e poi mi occuperò delle mie terre. Maddalena sarà molto contenta ».

Davanti a casa, aperse lo sportello e mi salutò. « Non salgo, — disse, — metto la macchina in garage e vado a dormire. Sono stanco ». Si tolse i guanti e mi disse: « Restituiscili a Valentino ».

Trovai Valentino in salotto. Maddalena era già andata a

dormire. Valentino stava leggendo *I misteri della giungla nera*. « La cameriera l'avete trovata?, — mi chiese, — dov'è Kit? » « È andato a dormire: ti restituisce i guanti, — dissi, e glieli buttai. — Ma non sei un po' troppo vecchio per leggere *I misteri della giungla nera?* »

« Non parlarmi con questo tono da maestra di scuola » rispose.

« Sono una maestra di scuola » gli dissi.

« Lo so; ma non parlarmi con questo tono ».

M'avevano lasciato la cena su un tavolino lí in salotto e sedetti a mangiare: Valentino leggeva sempre. Dopo mangiato, andai a mettermi accanto a lui sul divano. Gli posai la mano sui capelli. Brontolò sottovoce e s'acciglió, senza staccare gli occhi dalla pagina. « Valentino, — disse, — forse sposerò Kit ».

Lasciò cadere il libro: mi guardò. « Sul serio? » disse. « Sul serio, Valentino » gli dissi. Fece allora un sorriso tutto storto, un sorriso come vergognoso; e si scostò da me.

« Non lo dici sul serio? »

« Ma sí ».

Restammo un poco in silenzio. Faceva sempre quel sorriso storto: non potevo guardarlo, perché non mi piaceva quel sorriso: era un sorriso che non capivo, un sorriso dove c'era della vergogna: non capivo quella vergogna: non capivo che cosa sentisse.

« Io non sono tanto giovane, Valentino, — cominciai a dire. — Ho quasi ventisei anni. E non sono tanto una bella ragazza e sono povera: e mi piacerebbe sposarmi, non vorrei diventare vecchia da sola. Kit è una brava persona: io non sono innamorata ma se ragiono trovo che è una brava persona, un uomo semplice e sincero e buono. Cosí se mi vuole sposare io sono contenta: perché mi piacerebbe avere dei figli, e una casa per me ».

« Ah sí, — disse, — capisco. Allora vedi un po' tu. Io non sono bravo a dare consigli. Ma pensateci ancora ».

S'era alzato in piedi, si stirava le braccia e sbadigliava. « È sporco, — disse, — non si lava bene ».

« Ma questo è un difetto piccolo » dissi.

« Ti dirò, non si lava proprio niente. Non è un difetto piccolo. A me non piace la gente che non si lava. Buonanotte » disse, e mi fece una piccola carezza. Era molto raro avere delle carezze da Valentino, e gli fui grata. « Buonanotte, caro Valentino », gli dissi.

Pensai tutta la notte se dovevo sposare Kit. Ero molto agitata e non riuscivo a dormire. Pensavo a tutta quella giornata che avevamo passato insieme, ricordavo ogni cosa: il vino, le piccole pere, la ragazza coi capelli rossi, i cortili e i campi. Era stata una giornata cosí felice: m'accorgevo ora come avevo avuto poche giornate felici nella mia vita: poche giornate libere, solo per me.

L'indomani mattina, Maddalena venne a sedersi sul mio letto. « Ho sentito che ti sposi con Kit, — disse. — Può darsi che non sia un'idea tanto cattiva, dopo tutto. Avrei preferito che ti trovassi un uomo piú a posto: Kit è uno scombinato e un ozioso, glielo dico sempre; e poi non ha molta salute. Ma può darsi che a te riesca di tirarlo fuori da quella vita storta che fa. Non è detto che non ti riesca. Certo, devi essere molto ferma con lui: la sua casa è una vera cantina: bisogna far fare l'impianto per il riscaldamento e dare il bianco alle stanze. E lui deve andare ogni giorno a vedere le sue terre, cosí come faccio io: sono buone terre, e frutterebbero se lui ci stesse un po' dietro: devi darti da fare anche tu. Mi dirai che anch'io dovrei essere piú ferma con Valentino: mi ci provo sempre a stargli dietro che studi, ma finiamo col litigare terribilmente e va male. Va proprio male e certe volte penso che dovremmo dividerci; ma abbiamo i bambini e non ho coraggio di farlo. Ma adesso lasciamo stare queste cose tristi: ti sei fidanzata, e bisogna essere allegri. Kit lo conosco da quando era piccolo, siamo cresciuti insieme come fratelli: è molto buono di cuore, e gli voglio molto bene e spero che sia felice ».

Il mio fidanzamento con Kit durò venti giorni. Per questi venti giorni girammo con Maddalena a vedere dei mobili:

ma Kit non si decideva mai a comprare niente. Non furono
giorni molto felici: ripensavo sempre a quel giorno ch'era-
vamo andati a cercare la cameriera, io e Kit, e aspettavo che
tornasse per noi la felicità di quel giorno; ma non tornò mai
quella felicità. Si girava per i negozi degli antiquari, veniva
sempre anche Maddalena e Kit e Maddalena litigavano per-
ché lui non si decideva a comprare niente: e Maddalena di-
ceva che cosí ci si lasciava scappare delle buone occasioni.
La ragazza coi capelli rossi era arrivata, era vestita col grem-
biule nero e la cuffietta di pizzo e mi riusciva difficile rico-
noscere la contadina infangata di quel giorno: ma ogni vol-
ta che vedevo quei suoi capelli rossi, ricordavo le piccole pere
e il vino e la cucina buia e la panca di pietra davanti alla
casa e la distesa dei campi: e mi chiedevo se anche Kit si
ricordava. Mi pareva che avremmo dovuto stare un po' soli
insieme qualche volta, io e Kit: ma lui pareva che non lo
desiderasse: e pregava sempre Maddalena di venire con noi
quando andavamo a vedere dei mobili, e quando eravamo in
casa giuocava a carte con Valentino come avevano sempre
fatto.

In casa tutti mi facevano festa: e la cuoca e la balia si
rallegravano e ricordavano che me l'avevano detto sempre,
che io e Kit ci dovevamo sposare. Io avevo chiesto un'aspet-
tativa di tre mesi alla scuola, per motivi di salute; e mi ri-
posavo e mi divertivo coi bambini in giardino, quando non
bisognava andare a cercare dei mobili con Maddalena e con
Kit. Maddalena m'aveva detto che avrebbe pensato lei al mio
corredo: e da Clara volle andare lei a dirle che m'ero fidan-
zata. Clara aveva visto Kit due o tre volte e non lo poteva
soffrire: ma era sempre molto intimidita davanti a Madda-
lena e non osò dir niente; e poi forse le faceva impressione
che mi sposassi con uno che aveva delle terre, e non con uno
senza niente come aveva sempre creduto.

Un pomeriggio mentr'ero in giardino e dipanavo la la-
na, m'avvisarono che c'era Kit in salotto e cercava di me.
Andai con la lana e pensavo di chiedergli che mi reggesse

la matassa. Maddalena era fuori e Valentino dormiva: pensavo che avevamo qualche ora per stare un po' soli.

Lo trovai seduto nel salotto. Non si era tolto il soprabito e sgualciva il basco fra le mani. Era molto pallido e abbattuto e stava buttato nel fondo della poltrona con le sue lunghe gambe distese.

« Stai male? » dissi.

« Sí: non sto bene. Ho dei brividi. Forse mi verrà l'influenza. Non ti reggerò la matassa, — disse guardando la lana che avevo sul braccio, e agitava il lungo dito indice a dire di no. — Scusa. Sono venuto a dirti che non ci possiamo sposare ».

S'era alzato e passeggiava su e giú per la stanza. Sgualciva il basco e d'un tratto lo scagliò via. Si mise davanti a me e restammo in piedi uno davanti all'altro, e mi posò le mani sulle spalle. La sua faccia era quella d'un neonato vecchissimo, con i pochi capelli ravviati e umidi sulla lunga testa.

« Mi dispiace tanto d'averti detto che t'avrei sposato. Invece non mi posso sposare. Sei una cara ragazza, cosí quieta, cosí dolce, e io mi ero inventato tutta una storia di noi due insieme. Era una bella storia ma tutta inventata, niente vera. Ti prego di perdonarmi. Non mi posso sposare. Ho spavento ».

« Va bene, — dissi, — non importa, Kit. — Avevo molta voglia di piangere. — Non sono innamorata, te l'ho detto. Se mi fossi innamorata di te, sarebbe stato difficile; ma cosí non è tanto difficile. Si volta la testa dall'altra parte, e non ci si pensa piú ».

Voltai la testa verso la parete. Avevo gli occhi pieni di lagrime.

« Io non posso proprio, Caterina — disse. — Non devi piangere per me, Caterina: non ne vale la pena. Io sono uno straccio. Ho pensato tutta la notte, come dovevo dirtelo; e tutti questi giorni non ho avuto pace. Mi dispiace tanto d'averti dato dolore: una cara ragazza come sei. Ti saresti pentita a morte dopo poco tempo: perché avresti capito che sono uno straccio, proprio di quelli che ci si pulisce per terra ».

Tacevo e giocherellavo con la lana: « Ora posso reggere la matassa, — disse lui, — ora ti ho parlato, e sono tranquillo. Mi sentivo tutto sossopra, mentre venivo qui. E stanotte non ho dormito un momento ».

« No; non ho voglia della lana ora, — dissi, — grazie ». « Perdonami, — disse. — Non so come farmi perdonare da te. Dimmi cosa posso fare perché tu mi perdoni ».

« Ma niente, — dissi, — proprio niente, Kit. Non è successo niente: non avevamo ancora comperato i mobili, era tutto così in aria. Era una cosa detta così, mezzo per scherzo ».

« Sí sí, mezzo per scherzo, — disse. — In fondo, nessuno ci credeva. Ma potremmo fare ancora qualche gita insieme, che quel giorno è stato così bello: ti ricordi la vecchia con la scarpa? »

« Sí ».

« Nessuno ci proibisce di fare qualche gita insieme. Non c'è bisogno d'essere sposati per questo. Andremo ancora, no? » « Sí. Andremo ancora ».

Salii a piccoli passi nella mia stanza. Avevo quella lana da dipanare, e a un tratto mi pareva così faticoso dipanare la lana, e anche tirar su i piedi nel salire le scale, e dovermi spogliare, e piegare i vestiti sulla sedia e mettermi a letto. Volevo chiamare la cameriera e dirle che avevo mal di testa e non sarei scesa a cena: ma non volevo vedere la cameriera, non volevo vedere i suoi capelli rossi e ricordare quel giorno. Pensavo che dovevo andarmene da quella casa subito, il giorno dopo: non vedere piú Kit. E pensavo come non c'era niente di bello nella mia sofferenza, perché io non amavo Kit: sentivo solo vergogna: vergogna che m'avesse detto che ci saremmo sposati e poi che non si poteva fare. E mi pareva che in tutti quei giorni avessi speso tanti sforzi inutili, per cancellare tutte le cose che non mi piacevano di Kit, per accendere quelle che mi piacevano, per imparare a vivere col suo viso di neonato vecchio: quanti sforzi inutili,

inutili! quanti sforzi inutili e umilianti! E com'era buffo Kit, cosí tutto spaventato di dovermi sposare davvero!

Quando Maddalena venne da me, le dissi che Kit e io d'accordo avevamo deciso di non sposarci e che volevo andarmene via di casa per un po' di tempo. Parlavo a voce bassa, e tenevo la faccia voltata verso la parete: avevo pensato a lungo quelle parole dentro di me, e ora le recitavo piano piano, fiaccamente e come una cosa successa già da tanto tempo; avevo pensato di dire cosí perché Maddalena non se la prendesse con Kit, ma anche era per non avere tanta vergogna; ma invece Maddalena non credette che d'accordo avessimo deciso di no.

« Tutt'e due vi siete pentiti? No, solo lui » disse, e non pareva stupita.

« Tutt'e due, — ripetei fiaccamente. — Tutt'e due ».

« Solo lui, — disse. — Lo conosco bene. Tu sei di quelli che non cambiano idea. Be', non è poi una gran disgrazia; ne troverai un altro molto meglio di Kit. È cosí scombinato, questo Kit. Domani verrà a dirti che ti vuole di nuovo. Lo conosco. Ma tu lascialo perdere: vedi com'è scombinato, com'è indeciso: vedi che anche per i mobili non si decideva mai ».

« Voglio andare un po' via » dissi.

« Dove, via? »

« Non so. Un po' da sola, un po' da qualche parte ».

« Come ti pare », disse, e mi lasciò.

Partii l'indomani mattina, prima ancora che Valentino s'alzasse: Maddalena m'aiutò a fare le valige, volle darmi del denaro e venne alla stazione con me. « Ciao » disse, e mi baciò. « Non litigare troppo con Valentino », le dissi. « No, — disse, — cercherò di non litigare: e tu non piangere e non farti amara la vita. Non ne vale la pena, per quello scemo di Kit ».

Andai dalla zia Giuseppina. La zia Giuseppina era la sorella di mia madre; stava in campagna, nel paese dove aveva fatto scuola tutta la vita: adesso non faceva piú scuola e passava le giornate a lavorare a maglia: le pagavano un po'

quei lavori e viveva della pensione e di quello. Non la vedevo
da tanti anni, e mi colpí la sua rassomiglianza con mia ma-
dre: e quando guardavo il suo piccolo *chignon* bianco e il
suo profilo delicato, mi sembrava proprio di essere con mia
madre. Le avevo detto che ero stata malata e che avevo bi-
sogno di riposo; ed era piena di premure per me, badava
che non mi mancasse niente, mi preparava le pietanze che
mi piacevano; passeggiavo con lei prima di cena, piano pia-
no, con la sua mano magra posata sul mio braccio, e mi pa-
reva di passeggiare con mia madre.

Ogni tanto arrivavano le lettere di Maddalena, brevi, del-
le brevi notizie: le cose con Valentino andavano cosí cosí,
i bambini stavano bene, mi ricordavano e aspettavano il mio
ritorno. Raccontavo alla zia Giuseppina dei bambini di Va-
lentino e dei bambini di Clara, si ripetevano sempre le stesse
parole, la zia Giuseppina rifaceva sempre le stesse domande:
soprattutto la incuriosiva quella moglie di Valentino tanto
ricca, quella sua villa con tanti servitori e tappeti: e si stu-
piva un po' che avessi lasciato quella bella villa per venire
da lei, nel suo povero paese fangoso e cosí fuori mano.

Ero già da due mesi dalla zia Giuseppina, e s'avvicina-
va il tempo che dovevo ritornare a far scuola: e scrissi alla
nostra portinaia d'una volta perché m'indicasse una stanza,
perché non volevo piú abitare da Maddalena. E cosí mi pre-
paravo a ripartire: e con la zia Giuseppina facevo il giro
delle sue conoscenze, per dire addio e promettere cartoline.

Un mattino ricevetti una lettera da Valentino. Era tutta
sgorbiata e sconnessa. Diceva: « Con Maddalena non ci pos-
siamo piú stare insieme. Sono molto addolorato. Cerca di
venire presto qui ». E al fondo della pagina c'era scritto:
« Avrai saputo della morte di Kit ».

Io non sapevo niente. Era morto, Kit? E mi sembrò di
vederlo, morto, disteso, con le sue lunghe gambe diventate
rigide. Avevo cercato di non pensare a lui per tutto quel
tempo, perché non l'amavo ma pure era duro che non mi
avesse voluto: e intanto lui era morto, Kit!

Piansi. Ricordavo la morte di mio padre, poi la morte

di mia madre; quei visi che a poco a poco perdevano ogni traccia nella memoria, e inutilmente ci si sforzava di ricordare tutte le cose che dicevano sempre; e cosa diceva lui, Kit? « Ti ricordi la vecchia con la scarpa? » diceva. « Chi ci proibisce di fare qualche gita insieme? Io sono uno straccio, — diceva, — proprio di quelli che ci si pulisce per terra ». Dissi addio alla zia Giuseppina. In treno rilessi ancora la lettera di Valentino, quegli sgorbi sconnessi. Aveva litigato ancora con Maddalena: ormai c'ero abituata a vederli litigare, e chi sa, forse li avrei ritrovati già di nuovo in pace. Ma quella frase mi faceva impressione: « sono addolorato ». Quella frase mi suonava strano: perché non era una frase da Valentino. E anche era strano che m'avesse scritto, lui che aveva orrore di prendere in mano la penna.

Dalla zia non leggevo giornali, perché lei non ne comperava e del resto in quel piccolo paese arrivavano sempre in ritardo di qualche giorno. Cosí non avevo saputo della morte di Kit. Ma perché Maddalena non m'aveva scritto? Avevo il cuore stretto d'angoscia e tremavo, mi pareva di avere la febbre: il treno correva forte nella campagna e rivedevo i luoghi che avevo visto quel giorno in automobile, quel giorno che ero stata con Kit a cercare la cameriera ed eravamo stati cosí felici: e ricordavo il vino e le piccole pere, e la vecchia che ci aveva tirato la scarpa.

Arrivai alla villa ch'erano le quattro del pomeriggio. I bambini mi vennero incontro in giardino e mi fecero festa. La balia lavava sotto l'androne, il giardiniere innaffiava le aiuole; dunque tutto pareva come il solito. Salii nel salotto.

Maddalena era seduta in poltrona, con gli occhiali bassi sul naso e con un gran mucchio di calze da rammendare. Di solito non era a casa a quell'ora, e in ogni modo non rammendava le calze. « Ciao », disse, guardandomi di sopra agli occhiali: e mi parve a un tratto che fosse diventata molto vecchia: una vecchia signora.

Chiesi: « Dov'è Valentino? »

« Non piú qui. Non vive piú qui. Ci siamo separati. Siediti ».

Sedetti. « Non ti stupire se rammendo le calze, — mi disse, — calma i nervi. E poi non voglio piú vivere come prima: voglio rammendare le calze e occuparmi della casa e dei bambini e stare molto seduta. Sono stufa di andare in giro per le mie terre e urlare e trafficare. Di soldi ne abbiamo: e adesso non c'è piú Valentino a buttarli via per i suoi vestiti e le altre cose. Valentino, gli ho detto che gli manderò un tanto al mese: una busta ».

« Valentino verrà ad abitare con me — dissi. — Prenderemo due stanze. Fino a quando non vi sarete riconciliati ».

Non rispose. Rammendava molto accuratamente, stringendo forte le labbra e aggrottando la fronte.

« Ma forse presto farete la pace, — dissi. — Avete litigato altre volte, e poi avete rifatto pace. Lui m'ha scritto che è molto addolorato ».

« Ah, t'ha scritto? — disse. — Che cosa t'ha scritto? »

« M'ha scritto che è molto addolorato, e nient'altro, — dissi. — E allora sono venuta subito qui. E m'ha scritto che è morto Kit ».

« Ah, te l'ha scritto — disse. — Sí, Kit s'è ammazzato ». Parlava con voce fredda, lontana. D'un tratto posò la calza che rammendava, con l'ago infilato. Si strappò via gli occhiali e mi sgranò in faccia degli occhi cattivi.

« È successo cosí, — disse, — s'è ammazzato. Ha mandato via di casa la serva con una scusa, ha acceso nella stanza da letto quella sua stufa a carbone, l'ha scoperchiata e ha chiuso il tiraggio. Ha lasciato una lettera per Valentino. Io l'ho letta ».

Respirò forte e si passò il fazzoletto sul viso, sulle mani e sul collo.

« Io l'ho letta. E poi allora ho frugato in tutti i cassetti. C'erano fotografie di Valentino, e lettere. Non lo voglio vedere mai piú, Valentino ». D'un tratto si mise a singhiozzare convulsamente. « Non lo voglio vedere mai piú — diceva — non me lo fate vedere mai piú. È una cosa che non posso sopportare. Avrei sopportato qualunque cosa, qualunque storia con una donna. Ma non questa cosa qui. — Tirò su la faccia e mi fissò di nuovo con gli occhi cattivi. — Anche te, non ti voglio piú vedere. Vai via».

« Dov'è Valentino? » dissi.

« Non lo so. Il Bugliari lo sa. Stiamo facendo le pratiche per la separazione. Digli che stia tranquillo: ogni mese il Bugliari verrà con la busta».

« Ciao, Maddalena » dissi.

« Ciao, Caterina, — disse. — Non venire piú. Preferisco non vedere nessuno della vostra famiglia. Preferisco stare tranquilla. — S'era messa di nuovo a rammendare. — Vedrò di farti incontrare sovente i bambini — disse — ma non qui. Combineremo con l'avvocato. E ogni mese manderò la busta».

« Non importa la busta » dissi.

« Importa — disse — importa».

Già scendevo le scale quando mi richiamò. Ritornai. E allora m'abbracciò di nuovo e pianse, ma questa volta piangeva senza rabbia, quietamente e pietosamente. « Non è vero che non voglio piú vederti — disse — torna ancora da me, Caterina, mia carissima Caterina». E piansi anch'io e restammo a lungo abbracciate. E poi uscii nel pomeriggio soleggiato e calmo, e andai a telefonare al Bugliari per sapere dov'era Valentino.

Adesso io e Valentino viviamo insieme. Abbiamo due piccole stanze con la cucina e un ballatoio davanti. Il ballatoio guarda su un cortile che somiglia molto al cortile della casa dove stavamo col papà e la mamma. Certe mattine, Valentino si sveglia con idee di commercio: e si viene a sedere sul mio letto e fantastica a lungo con cifre, damigiane d'olio e navi; e allora se la piglia col papà e la mamma che l'hanno fatto studiare, mentre lui sarebbe stato cosí bravo a occuparsi d'affari. Lo lascio dire.

Io faccio scuola al mattino e nel pomeriggio ho delle lezioni private: e allora dico a Valentino di non farsi vedere in cucina, perché in casa sta sempre con una vecchia vesta-

glia che ormai è diventata come un cencio. Valentino è abba-
stanza ubbidiente e docile con me: ed è anche abbastanza
affettuoso e quando torno da scuola infreddolita e stanca mi
prepara la borsa dell'acqua calda. È ingrassato, perché non
fa piú nessuno sport; e si vede qualche ciocca grigia nei
suoi ricci neri.

Al mattino, di solito non esce: ciondola per casa nella
sua vestaglia lacera, legge dei giornaletti e fa le parole cro-
ciate. Nel pomeriggio si fa la barba, si veste e va fuori: lo
seguo con gli occhi finché svolta l'angolo: e poi, dove vada,
non so.

Una volta la settimana, il giovedí, i bambini vengono
da noi. Li accompagna la *nurse*: ora hanno una *nurse*, e la
balia è andata via. E Valentino fabbrica di nuovo per i suoi
bambini quei giocattoli con la stoffa e la segatura, che fa-
ceva una volta per i figli della portinaia: gatti e cani e dia-
voli tutti bitorzoluti.

Non parliamo mai di Maddalena, Valentino e io. Non
parliamo neppure di Kit. Tratteniamo le nostre parole ben
ferme su piccole cose, su quello che mangiamo o sulla gente
che abita di fronte. Vedo Maddalena qualche volta. È diven-
tata molto grossa, tutta grigia, e fa proprio la vecchia signo-
ra. Si occupa dei suoi bambini, li porta a pattinare e orga-
nizza per loro delle feste in giardino. Ora va di rado nelle
sue terre: è stanca, e dice che di soldi ne ha fin troppi. Sta
in casa degl'interi pomeriggi, e il Bugliari le tiene compa-
gnia. È contenta di vedermi, ma non devo parlarle molto di
Valentino: e con lei come con Valentino, sto attenta a trat-
tenere le parole sulle cose che non fanno male: i bambini,
il Bugliari, la *nurse*. Cosí non ho nessuno con cui dire le
vere parole: le vere parole, di tutta la nostra storia cosí co-
m'è stata: e me le tengo dentro, e certe volte mi pare che mi
strozzino il fiato.

Certe volte mi viene una gran rabbia contro Valentino.
Me lo vedo lí, a ciondolare per casa nella sua vestaglia lace-
ra, a fumare e a fare le parole crociate, lui che mio padre
credeva che diventasse un grand'uomo. Lui che si è preso

sempre tutto quello che la gente gli ha dato, senza sognarsi di dare mai niente, senza trascurare un sol giorno di carezzarsi i ricci davanti allo specchio e di farsi un sorriso. Lui che certo non ha mancato di farsi quel suo sorriso allo specchio, neppure il giorno della morte di Kit.

Ma non dura a lungo la mia rabbia contro di lui. Perché lui è la sola cosa che rimanga nella mia vita; e io sono la sola cosa che rimanga nella sua. Cosí, sento che da quella rabbia io mi devo difendere; devo restar fedele a Valentino, e restare ferma al suo fianco, che mi trovi se si volta dalla mia parte. Lo seguo con gli occhi quando esce per strada, lo accompagno con gli occhi fino all'angolo: e mi rallegro che sia sempre cosí bello, con la piccola testa ricciuta sulle spalle forti. Mi rallegro del suo passo ancora cosí felice, trionfante e libero: mi rallegro del suo passo, dovunque lui vada.

MARIO SOLDATI

TRE COMPONIMENTI IN VERSI

FILASTROCCA
DELLE CINQUE VOCALI

per J.

Con le altre donne — della mia vita
ho chiuso bene o male la partita:
ultimo errore — di gioventù
resti soltanto tu.

Da dodici anni — l'errore dura,
e del volersi bene la tortura:
so ch'è la via — della virtù;
ma a volte non so più.

Quand'ero paggio — la via maestra
al centro non cercai, sinistra o destra:
boccia la boccia — secca colpì:
io ero tutto lì.

Alta la ferrea — boccia levavo
o carezzevole al suol rotolavo:
carezze e baci — se vuol così
alla vecchia Fanny.

Ma poi cercavo — baci e carezze
e da vere Fanny svenevolezze:

rosse di fuoco — ocra, lillà,
ed anche un po' più in là.

Era ogni volta — fuoco di paglia,
velo di neve al sole che lo squaglia,
gioco, ricerca — se va la va,
indove non si sa.

E di che cosa — ricerca o gioco
se la felicità mi parve poco?
quando l'argentea — pioggia cadé,
andarsene, perché?

Alte campane — l'argentea aria
frangevano a Zurigo solitaria:
basta la Svizzera — così com'è,
e scordarmi di te!

Eppure addio — Svizzera, laghi:
ora memoria e crudeltà mi paghi.
Cupa dolcezza — ripeterò:
la mia vita passò.

Tra bimbi e moglie — dolcezza ed ire,
come tanti mariti anch'io morire;
e se misuro — i contro i pro,
sto bene come sto.

NOTA. — *Ferrea boccia, Fanny.* Nella Francia meridionale le bocce
sono chiodate. E in ogni campo è appesa al muro l'oleografia di una don-
nina seminuda, che, tirandosi su con due dita la sottoveste nera o rosa,
volta al pubblico il sedere e un viso dall'espressione *canaille*: la Fanny.
Quando uno dei due avversari, o dei due gruppi di avversari (coppie, tri-
plette, quadrette), perde a zero o, come si dice da noi, prende cappotto,
è obbligato a baciare il sedere della Fanny; che è insieme un'umiliazione
e una consolazione. I perdenti eseguono la cerimonia togliendosi il ber-
retto e marciando con buffonesca solennità e compunzione fino all'oleo-
grafia, tra le risa le grida gli evviva degli avversari e di tutti gli astanti.
Nella Repubblica delle Bocce, che un amico genovese vagheggiò in altri
tempi, tale costume dovrebbe diventar legge.

TRENO
ritornando in seno alla famiglia

Orti prati alberi
fiori primavera
gettarmi giù mordere
terra fresca nera.

Verso il cielo volgermi,
velo unito bianco,
di rimorsi d'opere
di volontà stanco.

Nella terra morbida
affondare meglio
d'ogni notte, rapido
e senza risveglio.

Eppure, se ridere
vedo i volti amati
ringrazierò libero
che mi sono nati:

dolore dolcissimo
straziata gioia
essi mi continuano,
e la morte muoia.

A GIACOMO NOVENTA
perché non abbandoni l'Italia ma soltanto la cosa pubblica
e torni finalmente agli ozi poetici, ai veri amici

Troppo tempo ormai muta la musa,
Giacomo, tua, l'esilio additi

411

dove cercarti, e sprezzi gl'inviti
degli amici che l'età non usa.

Dunque la stagione sempre chiusa
nel modesto inferno dei politici
non ti fu già esilio? né i riti
d'una scienza servilmente astrusa?

Lascia la plebe abbietta od atroce,
e trascura l'effimera scoria
dal tuo fuoco sparsa: riberremo

vecchio Barbaresco; riudremo,
corona a te d'amici e di gloria,
il violoncello della tua voce!

CARLOS FUENTES

NUEVA TENOCHTITLAN *

Esta sangre me punza como filo de maguey, corre por ella la parálisis desenfrenada que todas las auroras debe teñir de coágulos sin más consideración que su calidez de salto mortal hacia mañana; juego, acción fe, día a día -no sólo el día del premio o del castigo: veo mis poros oscuros y sé que me está vedado. El duende de Anáhuac no machaca uvas — corazones; no bebe néctares — su vino, gelatina de osamentas; no persigue la piel alegre, se caza a sí mismo en una catársis negra de piedra torturada y ojos de jade opaco. Hincado, coronado de nopales, flagelado por su propia mano. Bailando, colgado de un asta de plumas, o de la defensa de un camión; muerto en una guerra florida, en la riña de cantina, a la hora de la verdad, a la única hora puntual. Poeta de la insinceridad, artista del tormento, lépero cortés, ladino ingenuo, mi plegaria desarticulada se pierde en el albur y en el relajo. Dañarme, a mí siempre más que a los otros. Guerrero en el vacío, visto la coraza de la bravuconada; pero mis sienes sollozan, y no cejan en la búsqueda de lo suave: la patria, el clítoris, el azúcar del esqueleto, el cántico quejumbroso y aterciopelado que rasgan los aullidos miméticos de bestia enjualada. Vida de espaldas, por miedo a « darlas », cuerpo

---

* Fragmento de la novela, en preparación, « La región más transparente del aire ».

413

fracturado, de trozos centrífugos, gimientes de enajenación, ciego a las invasiones. Vocación por la libertad. Libertad que se escapa en la red de encrucijadas de la opción. Y con sus restos mojamos los pinceles, y nos sentamos a la vera del camino para jugar con los colores... Al nacer, muerto, quemaste tus naves para que otros fabricaran la epopeya con tu carroña; al morir, vivo, desterraste una palabra: «hermano». Te detuviste en el último sol; después, la victoria azorada inundó de materia, de títulos, — de ornamentos, tu cuerpo hueco, inmóvil. Escucha... los atabales aun dictan sus ecos, sobre el ruido de motores y sinfonolas, entre el sedimento del valle, cerca de la prisión de basalto. En tus urnas dormitan las serpientes, animales con historia. En tus ojos, brilla la jauría de soles. En tu cuerpo, un cerco de púas. ¡No te rajes, mano! Saca tus pencas, afila tus cuchillos, niégate, niégate, no hables, no compadezcas, no mires. Deja que tu nostalgia emigre, todos tus cabos sueltos; comienza, todos los días, en el parto. Y recobra la llama en el momento, imperceptible, del organillo callejero, del rasgueo contenido, cuando parecería que todas tus memorias se hicieran más claras, se ciñeran. Recóbrala, solo: tus héroes no regresarán. Has venido a dar, conmigo, sin saberlo, a esta meseta de joyas fúnebres. Aquí vivimos, en las calles se cruzan nuestros olores de sudor y pátchuli, de ladrillo nuevo y gas subterráneo, nuestras carnes ociosas y tensas, jamás nuestras miradas. Jamás nos hemos hincado juntos, tú y yo, a recibir la misma hostia; desgarrados juntos, creados juntos, sólo morimos para nosotros, aislados. Aquí caímos. Qué le vamos a hacer. Aguantarnos, manito. A ver si algún día mis dedos tocan los tuyos. Ven, déjate caer en la cicatriz lunar de nuestra ciudad, ciudad omisión de sangre, ciudad puñado de alcantarillas, ciudad cristal de vahos y escarcha mineral, ciudad presencia de todos nuestros olvidos, ciudad inclusión de indiferencias, ciudad de acantilados carnívoros, ciudad dolor inmóvil, ciudad de la brevedad inmensa, ciudad a fuego lento, ciudad con el agua al cuello, ciudad del letargo pícaro, ciudad de los nervios negros, ciudad de los tres ombligos, ciudad de la risa gualda, ciudad del hedor torcido, ciudad

414

rígida entre el aire y los gusanos, ciudad vieja en las luces,
vieja ciudad en su cuna de aves agoreras, ciudad nueva junto
al polvo esculpido, ciudad a la vera del cielo gigante, ciudad
de barnices oscuros y pedrería, ciudad bajo el lodo esplenden-
te, ciudad de víscera y cuerdas, ciudad de retazos rojos, humi-
llación ostentada, ciudad de nichos y estofados, ciudad de la
derrota violada, ciudad del tianguis sumiso, carne de tinaja,
ciudad de las calzadas rotas, ciudad del asiento, ciudad del
lago de caracoles, ciudad bocina del mudo, ciudad reflexión
de la furia, ciudad del fracaso ansiado, ciudad en tempestad
de cúpulas, ciudad abrevadero de las fauces rígidas del her-
mano empapado de sed y costras, ciudad tejida en la amnesia,
resurrección de infancias, encarnación de pluma, pirámide de
huesos, ciudad perra, ciudad famélica, suntuosa villa, ciudad
lepra y cólera hundida ciudad. Tuna incandescente. Aguila
sin alas. Serpiente de estrellas. Aquí nos tocó. Qué le vamos
a hacer. En la región más transparente del aire.

— ¡Boinas!

El barrendero le dió un empujón en las nalgas, y Gladys respiró la mañana helada. Echó el último vistazo al espejo gris, a los vasos ahogados de colillas del cabaret. Chupamirto bostezaba sobre el bongó. Las luces limón se apagaron, devolviendo su opacidad descascarada a las pilastras de palmera. Algún gato corría entre los charcos de la calle. Gladys se quito los zapatos, descansó, encendió el último (boquita trompuda, dientes cincelados de oro), el cigarrillo que le tocaba cada quince minutos. En Guerrero ya no había inundación y pudo calzarse. Empezaban a correr las bicicletas por Bucareli; algunos tranvías, ya. La avenida parecía una cornucopia de basura: rollos de diario derelicto, los desperdicios de los cafés de chinos, los perros muertos, la anciana clavada, hurgando en un bote, los niños dormidos, removiéndose en la nidada de periódicos y carteles. La luz del más tenue de los cirios fúnebres. Del Caballito a los Doctores, arrancaba un ataúd de asfalto, anárquico — triste como la mano tendida — y habría que pensar en un supremo esfuerzo, casi en una resurrección, para dar sangre y pálpitos a este collar de erisipela. Pero ya en el sol, ¿vivía? Desde la ¡ erspectiva de Carlos IV y su corte de neones enanos, Gladys no podía hablar, de las fritangas y los gorros de papel de los voceadores y sus soldaderas panzonas, porque desconocía lo diurno, del aire viejo, empolvado, que va masticando los contornos de las ruinas modernas de la aldea enorme. Iba caminando sola, su cuerpecillo de tamal envuelto en raso violeta brillante, ensartado en dos palillos calados sobre plataformas: bostezaba para rascarse los dientes de oro: la mirada, bovina, sus ojitos de capulín. ¡Qué aburrido caminar sola por Bucareli a las seis y cuarto! Tarareaba la letanía que noche tras noche le había enseñado el pianista gordo del « Bali-Hai », *mujer, mujer divina*

esa me la cantaba Beto; ése sí que me trajo al trote, con eso de ser ruletero y sacarme a pasear en el coche; ¡qué machote, y qué vacilador! Vieja que se sube al coche, vieja que me bombeo, decía;

— *¿Estás sola, chata?*

— *Estoy contigo, ¿me siento?*

ya Chupamirto lo conocía, y le dedicaba sus mambos por el micrófono, *yo soy, el ruletero, que sí, que no, el ruletero.*

— *Estás muy buena chata ...aaaajayyyyy... por abajo anda el jarabe.*

— *No te calientes, granizo...*

— *¡Pa' su!.......*

— *Ay, qué siento, qué siento...*

que sí, que no, el ruletero y chanceador como él solo, como me gusta,

— *¿A tí no te agarró alguien de puerquito en la escuela chata?*

— *¿En la escuela? Estás chanceando.*

— *Conmigo se metía un tipo así de grandote, le decían el Mayeya y me traía malhoreado. Yo todo tilique en aquella época, y él grandote, torciéndome las orejas. Hasta que maté a un cuate y me mandaron dos años a la peni; ya estaría... ¡Lo vieras ahora! Me lo encuentro y no es sonrisota de cua-*

tacho la que me hace. Pero yo tampoco me meto con nadie. Ya ves los líos que tiene uno ruleteando: que se bajan, que te la mientan. Pues que me la mienten. ¿Qué es peor? ¿Morirte en la cama? ¿o que un cristiano venga y te mande al otro barrio? Para qué hacerle un favor a nadie.

Pero ya se lo había dicho; no le había tomado el pelo: — Tendría harta lana si no fuera por las viejas y el bailecito. Todos los días tengo que meterme a bailar. Suave, chánchararachanchanchacha, chánchara... Qué quieres. Así me hicieron.

Así me hicieron. No había vuelto a sentir lo que con él. Pero los prietos prefieren a las güeras, y ésta se lo llevó. Beto. Y ahora, el viejecillo flaco y con halitosis que la buscaba todos los viernes en la noche presumiendo de alto funcionario de alguna Secretaría. El único que le dejaba lana. Se las ponía de nevero, le apretaba la cintura y gritaba: — ¡Raza de bronce, cabrona raza de bronce! y luego le contaba el gran chiste de cómo venía los viernes porque ese día le daba a su mujer la excusa del balance de fin de semana. Pero no era lo mismo que con Beto,

— ¿Le gusta el chou del Bali-Hai?

— Me encanta, jajay, me encantas tú...

— Venga más seguido, pues. Mire cómo será que nomás los viernes. Si no es obligación.

— Ya te he dicho que los viernes hago pato a la vieja; mira, ese día nos pasan...

Aquí había nacido Gladys, entre los palacios de tierra de la meseta, en la gran ciudad chata y asfixiada. En la ciudad, extendiéndose cada vez más como una tiña irrespetuosa. Un día quisieron llevarla a Cuernavaca unos abarroteros con automóvil, y el coche se descompuso en Tlalpam. No sabía de montañas o de mar; la brizna del jaramago, el encuentro de arena y sol, la dureza del níspero, la hermosura primaria... qué rete chula ha de ser la mar... Amarrada al cemento, a la acumulación de brillantes despeperdicios, a la casa del avaro loco que va almacenando polvo y mierda y olvido tras de los postigos cerrados. Llegó al fin a los Doctores, rendida. Encendió la veladora Vos sois rica y nosotros pobres; Vos todo lo tenéis y nosotros no tenemos nada ¿por ventura no sois la madre de misericordia? la jicotera no tiene cintura y se acostó. ¿Borregos? Fichas, fichas cayendo sin eco sobre una mesa, hasta llegar a diez pesos. Ya no hacía tanta lana. Se le apretaban los clientes. *¿Vieja? Treinta años. ¿Jodida? Que lo diga Beto.* Por primera vez, se le ocurrió pensar qué iba a ser de ella cuando ya no pudiera ganarse la vida en el « Bali-Hai ». ¿Cómo se gana la vida? *Voy a ir mañana a un comercio, a ver cuánto pagan de vendedora.* Tenía que impresionar. Liliana le prestaría el zorro, o si no el conejo propio. *¿Dónde está ese perfume que me regalaron a la entrada de un cine?* Rimmel a chorros; no hay nada peor que una carota de gringa desabrida... Fichas, fichas, acurrucada contra el muro frío, iluminada por la veladora, sentir que se perdían las piernas y el vientre se le hacia grande, grande la cucaracha no pué caminá que vuestro virginal manto cubra siempre a vuestros hijos, guardadlos, son vuestros para siempre, son vuestros para siempre, ¡oh celeste tesorera del Corazón de Jesús! a vuestros hijos.

Salió de la tienda de modas a la avenida. La lluvia se soltó, confundida con los edificios grises. Es lluvia de ciudad. Contagiada de olores. Mancha las paredes. No se mete a la tierra. Espuma de hierro, el desconcierto de las cabezas bajas, sumisas al lívido cimbal del cielo, cabezas gachas, mojadas de lluvia y vaselina. Surtidores del cielo mexicano: esperando en silencio desesperado, esperando junto a los muros, los cuerpos enjutos y grasientos, junto a la lluvia. Bajo la lluvia, disueltos en en vaho de gasolina y asfalto, momias de un minuto, junto a la lluvia. Los letreros despintados, el bostezo de las piedras, la ciudad como una nube tullida, olores viejos de piel y vello, de garnacha y toldos verdes, murmullo chirriante de las ruedas, chisguetes de canción: el cielo se abría sin otorgar, el cemento y los mexicanos no pedían: que luchen lluvia y polvo, que se muerdan viento y rostros, que se espere pegado a las paredes, ensopado, los bigotes lacios, los ojos vidriosos, los pies húmedos, comprimido en su carne espesa, maloliente e insano, plagado de cataratas y furúnculos, dormido en los nichos como ídolo eterno, de cuclillas junto a los muros acribillados de soledad, escarbando en la basura algo que roer, murciélagos pegados a la pared. Que se espere. Que se espere allí, más cerca del origen oscuro, más cerca de los rincones: lluvia en los rincones, voces pequeñas, ¡ay, que se abrazaran, solos, juntos bajo la lluvia! Un abrazo de todos, cuando el perfil del firmamento negro dice: tú aquí, ellos allá. Gladys sorbía las gotas en su nariz. El rimmel le escurría como llanto de noche. El conejo apestaba. Se paró y sacó la mano.

(— Muy guaje, ¿no? Miren: mucho'ojo. Eso se saca uno por meterse con apretados. ¡A la chingada! ¿Hora? Seis. Abren a las nueve. Y está lloviendo a trancazos).

¡Ora si t'enjuagates, chilindrina! pasó una bicicleta frenando. Se abría la noche, su noche, la noche que le reservan los ángeles y el vacío. La ciudad olía a gas mientras Gladys ambulaba por la Avenida Juárez. ¿Dónde estaban, los demás, su pueblo, las gentes a quienes querer? ¿No había, por ahí, una casa caliente donde meterse, un lugar donde caber con los otros? Sus gentes...

el viejo era pajarero; salía muy de mañana a agarrarlos, mientras la madre le hacía el café con piquete y nosotros arreglábamos las jaulas. Me pusieron Gaudencia... quién me manda nacer el veintidós de enero. Junto al puente de Nonoalco. Las láminas ardían en verano, y a todos se les calentaba la sangre. En un catre, los viejos y el escuincle. En el otro, yo con mis hermanos. Ni me di cuenta, ni supe cuál de ellos me hizo la desgraciadura. Pero las láminas ardían, todos estábamos muy calientes, muy chamacos. Tenía trece años. Así comienza uno. Y luego ya no los vuelve a ver.

Frente al Hotel del Prado, se topó con una comitiva de hombres altos y mujeres rubias, alhajadas, que fumaban en boquillas. Ni siquiera eran gringos, hablaban español...

— Rápido, Pichi, vamos a tomar un libre...

— Voy, chéri. Déjame arreglarme el velo.

— Nos vemos en casa de Bobó, Norma. No llegues tarde:
para las orgías, puntualidad británica...

— Y ademá, el canalla de Bobó cambia sin avisar de la
Viuda a Ron en cuanto se levantan los coros de las bacantes.

— ¡Chao, viejita!

— Too-toot.....

y parecían dioses que se levantaban como estatuas, aquí
mismo, en la acera, sobre las orugas prietas de los demás,
¡qué de los demás!, sobre ella que estaba fundida, inconscien-
te, con los vendedores, con los mendigos y los ruleteros, con
el arroyo de camisetas manchadas de aceite, rebozos, panta-
lones de pana, cacles rotos, que venía hollando la avenida.
Pero en el siguiente puesto, entre uno de bolsas de cocodrilo
y otro de cacahuate garrapiñado, gastó dos pesos en una bo-
quilla de aluminio.

JORGE GUILLÉN

PENTECOSTÉS

Un viento de tormenta,
Tormenta sin nublado
De atmósfera,
Encendido fragor irresistible,
Sonó.
Y todos los discípulos,
Férvida compañía,
Alzaron las miradas
Hacia un tumulto de relampagueos.
El trance:
Algo que nos ocurre y no se entiende.
Un soplo superior al hombre asiste
— Con una violencia sin sentido
Que deslumbra y no alumbra —
Al hombre.

Miraban, esperaban
Los preparados a lo portentoso.
Y el tumulto de luz fulgió con luces.
Innumerables luces como lenguas
En vibración de fuego
Buscaban, descendían
Arrebatadamente.

Muy próximos
A las cabezas de los elegidos,
Aquellos muchos haces fogueantes
Eran cielo exaltado,
Un maná torrencial,
A golpes
Radiosos invasor,
Gloria que regalara
Secretos,
Penumbras de los rayos más remotos,
Revelación tal vez
De las últimas claves:
Inspiración, inspiración sagrada.

Y todos los creyentes
Llegaron a la cumbre de sus voces:
Lengua desconocida
Por los así parlantes
Con un vigor que exige
Su forma, su vocablo,
Caliente aún y más allá del fuego,
Sin gesticulaciones
— A través de las nubes peligrosas —
Don de la gran palabra,
Una alegría sin embriaguez,
Don de Espíritu Santo,
Aquella inspiración
Ascendía a verdades
Rectoras,
Superaba al vidente siempre humilde.

OCTAVIO PAZ

EL RÍO

La ciudad desvelada circula por mi sangre como una abeja.
Y el avión que traza un gemido en forma de S larga, los
    tranvías que se derrumban en esquinas remotas,
ese árbol cargado de injurias que alguien sacude a media
    noche en la plaza,
los ruidos que ascienden y estallan y los que se deslizan
    y cuchichean en la oreja un secreto que repta,
abren lo oscuro, precipicios de aes y oes, túneles de vocales
    taciturnas,
galerías que recorro con los ojos vendados, el alfabeto som-
    noliento cae en el hoyo como un río de tinta,
y la ciudad va y viene y su cuerpo de piedra se hace añicos
    al llegar a mi sien,
toda la noche, uno a uno, estatua a estatua, fuente a fuente,
    piedra a piedra, toda la noche
sus pedazos se buscan en mi frente, toda la noche la ciudad
    habla dormida por mi boca
y es un discurso incomprensible y jadeante, un tartamudeo de
    aguas y piedra batallando, su historia.

Detenerse un instante, detener a mi sangre que va y viene,
    va y viene y no dice nada,
sentado sobre mí mismo como el yoguín a la sombra de la
    higuera, como Buda a la orilla del río, detener el instante,

un solo instante, sentado a la orilla del tiempo, borrar mi
imagen del río que habla dormido y no dice nada y me
lleva consigo,
sentado a la orilla detener el río, abrir el instante,
penetrar por sus salas atónitas hasta su centro de agua,
beber en la fuente inagotable, ser la cascada de sílabas
azules que cae de los labios de piedra,
sentado a la orilla de la noche como Buda a la orilla de sí
mismo ser el parpadeo del instante,
el incendio y la destrucción y el nacimiento del instante y
la respiración de la noche fluyendo enorme a la orilla
del tiempo,
decir lo que dice el río, larga palabra semejante a labios,
larga palabra que no acaba nunca,
decir lo que dice el tiempo en duras frases de piedra, en
vastos ademanes de mar cubriendo mundos.
A mitad del poema me sobrecoge siempre un gran desamparo,
todo me abandona,
no hay nadie a mi lado, ni siquiera esos ojos que desde atrás
contemplan lo que escribo,
no hay atrás ni adelante, la pluma se rebela, no hay comienzo
ni fin, tampoco hay muro que saltar,
es una explanada desierta el poema, lo dicho no está dicho,
lo no dicho es indecible,
torres, terrazas devastadas, babilonias, un mar de sal negra,
un reino ciego,
No,
detenerme, callar, cerrar los ojos hasta que brote de mis
párpados una espiga, un surtidor de soles,
y el alfabeto ondule largamente bajo el viento del sueño y
la marea crezca en una ola y la ola rompa el dique,
esperar hasta que el papel se cubra de astros y sea el poema
un bosque de palabras enlazadas,
No,
no tengo nada que decir, nadie tiene nada que decir, nada ni
nadie excepto la sangre,

nada sino este ir y venir de la sangre, este escribir sobre lo
    escrito y repetir la misma palabra en mitad del poema,
    sílabas de tiempo, letras rotas, gotas de tinta, sangre que
    va y viene y no dice nada y me lleva consigo.

Y digo mi rostro inclinado sobre el papel y alguien a mi
    lado escribe mientras la sangre va y viene,
y la ciudad va y viene por su sangre, quiere decir algo, el
    tiempo quiere decir algo, la noche quiere decir,
toda la noche el hombre quiere decir una sola palabra, decir
    al fin su discurso hecho de piedras desmoronadas,
y aguzo el oído, quiero oír lo que dice el hombre, repetir
    lo que dice la ciudad a la deriva,
toda la noche las piedras rotas se buscan a tientas en mi
    frente, toda la noche pelea el agua contra la piedra,
las palabras contra la noche, la noche contra la noche, nada
    ilumina el opaco combate,
el choque de las armas no arranca un relámpago a la piedra,
    una chispa a la noche, nadie da tregua,
es un combate a muerte entre inmortales, ay, dar marcha atrás,
    parar el río de sangre, el río de tinta,
parar el río de las palabras, remontar la corriente y que la
    noche vuelta sobre sí misma muestre sus entrañas de oro
    ardiendo,
que el agua muestre su corazón que es un racimo de espejos
    ahogados, un árbol de cristal que el viento desarraiga
(y cada hoja del árbol vuela y centellea y se pierde en una luz
    cruel como se pierden las palabras en la imagen del poeta),
que el tiempo se cierre y sea su herida una cicatriz invisible,
    apenas una delgada línea sobre la piel del mundo,
que las palabras depongan armas y se cierren y sea el poe-
    ma un resplandor implacable que avanza,
el llano después del incendio, el pecho lunar de un mar
    petrificado que no refleja nada
sino la extensión extendida, el espacio acostado sobre sí mismo,
    las alas inmensas desplegadas,

y sea todo como la llama que se esculpe y se hiela en la roca
de entrañas transparentes,
piedra de sol contra la noche de piedra, piedra contra el
silencio y la palabra, piedra contra el jadeo.

Y el río remonta su curso, repliega sus velas, recoge sus imá-
genes y se interna en sí mismo.

CARLOS BARRAL

CIUDAD MENTAL

Aspira lo profundo
a envés de su materia sepultada
Peldaños de repente,
el vértigo y los límites porfían.
El corazón intenta.
Sube la tierra desolada. Sigue,
sucumbe el aire demasiado grave.

Umbral no más lejano
que el pie remoto.
                    ¿Dónde?
¿Qué silenciosa curva te interroga?
Atreve.
        Todo en vilo,
pendiente.
           Cruza a ciegas
la linde del consuelo.

Clara avenida, dulce
ciudad del hombre.
Porque piensas la línea más externa,
¡oh! sita en el comienzo

¡oh! sita en el comienzo
de estar en tí,
                qué mundo ya seguro.
El orden de los ojos adelanta
hacia tu multitud.
Como una aurora insomne
pasa la paz descalza por la acera.

Ventanas, cielo casi
recíproco¿ Quién sabe
qué espesura de búsqueda se asoma?
¿Qué precursor, qué tiempo
apenas antes ya culmina,
como un bloque difícil en lo alto
que estaba?
             Que ahora sin estrépito,
irreparable entorno de negación,
existe.
        Equidistante,
                cierta,
como cristal,
         la plaza.

Expresa un nombre extraño.
Aquí, desde este centro sin rumores
las sílabas se imparten. Indecibles
objetos, voces nunca aplicadas.

Detrás de las almenas,
más allá de los pórticos habría
si un instante durase...
« Este fué el edificio de la Opera.
Un frontón de cartílago y de lágrimas
en lugar de estos hierros,
bajo el gran lomo verde
coronado de musgos y reptiles ».

Detrás la piedra ardiente.
De atmósfera labrada,
cautelosa de encuentros proseguía
la ciudad a deshora.

Vegetal de dormidos sin cesar
se iban siglos inmóviles.

Era el hotel, la casa
experta en vez de rápido desnudo,
distribución de soledad, presencia
optativa del cuerpo.
Verás las indudables
huellas,
           Quizás la voz futura
oigas de otra hacinada muchedumbre
parietal. Como si abrieran
miríadas de poros y exultase
aquel gas elocuente,
húmedo de burbujas murmuradas.
¡Qué dimensión de nadie!

Impactos sobre el muro
a parcelas de trágico.

¿Altera el mundo una pared?

La tierra se coagula
al pie de la lentísima substancia.

La tierra grumo a grumo, inhabitable,
amargamente impuesta en el vacío.
Terminada la tierra.

429

Como un viento,
a ráfagas, la tierra que se ignora.

Horribles aberturas, lienzos turbios,
agujas rotas, bloques corrompidos
clamaban por su nombre ante tus ojos.
Mira a través de la pared.
¿Qué ramas
valederas explican los desagües?
Vientre abajo es la especie,
un líquido a intervalos
que destilan los órdenes de muertos.
Porque el espacio celular no cesa
de golpe. Todavía
no ha sido la cuadrícula invalida
y el ondulado rastro de los peines
y los adverbios de temor y el humo
flotan en las estancias acabadas.

En vano escrutas la intemperie. Solo.
Sólo el muro sumerje
sus vísceras tenaces en lo obscuro.
Se inserta en lo ocurrido, reconoce,
palpa las mutaciones del vacío.
El muro vence en soledad.
El muro porque quema
más que el incendio,
el muro de dos caras necesarias.
Alterno, cristalino en el salto
mortal
   a les techumbres
      fugitivas.

Sin párpados ¿qué esperas,
de las ondas nocturnas, qué intersticio
supones que de pronto se ilumine?

Son ya las gradas de estupor.
                              ¿No sientes
tirar de ti despacio
disolverte la sombra tan delgada?
Te buscan las raíces,
los móviles internos
que se detienen sin saber.
                              Oculto
alud.
     En adelante,
qué rápidos los cambios.

Regresa la materia
cismática.
          Del ojo se desprende
y expira en lo profundo.

TRADUZIONE DELL'ODE
SOPRA UN'URNA GRECA DI KEATS

DI

AUGUSTO FRASSINETI

Tu della quiete ancora inviolata sposa,
alunna del silenzio e del tempo tardivo,
narratrice silvestre, che un racconto
fiorito puoi cosí piú che la nostra
rima dolcemente dire,
quale leggenda adorna d'aeree fronde si posa
intorno alla tua forma?
Di deità, di mortali o pur d'entrambi,
in Tempe, o nelle valli
d'Arcadia? Quali uomini
son questi o quali dèi,
quali ritrose vergini,
qual folle inseguimento, qual paura,
quali zampogne e timpani,
quale selvaggia estasi?

Dolci le udite melodie: piú dolci
se non udite. Dunque voi seguite,
tenere cornamuse, il vostro canto,
non al facile senso, ma, piú care,
silenziosi concenti date all'intimo cuore.
Giovine bello, alla fresca ombra mai
può il tuo canto languire, né a quei rami
venir meno la fronda.

432

Audace amante e vittorioso, mai
mai tu potrai baciare,
pur prossimo alla meta, e tuttavia
non darti affanno: ella non può sfiorire
e, pur mai pago, quella
per sempre tu amerai, bella per sempre.

O fortunate piante cui non tocca
perder le belle foglie,
né, meste, dire addio alla primavera.
Te felice, cantore non mai stanco
di sempre ritrovare
canti per sempre nuovi.
Ma piú felice Amore, piú felice,
felice Amore,
fervido e sempre da godere e giovane
ed anelante sempre,
tu, che di tanto eccedi ogni vivente
passione umana,
che in cuore un solitario
dolore lascia e sdegno: amara febbre.

Chi son questi venienti al sacrificio?
E, misterioso sacerdote, a quale
verde altare conduci
questa, che mugghia ai cieli,
mite giovenca di ghirlande adorna
i bei fianchi di seta?
Qual piccola città, presso del fiume
o in riva al mare costruita, o sopra
il monte, fra le sue placide mura,
si è vuotata di questa
folla festante, in questo pio mattino?
Tu, piccola città, quelle tue strade
sempre saranno silenziose e mai

non un'anima tornerà, che dica
perché sei desolata.

O pura attica forma! Leggiadro atteggiamento,
cui d'uomini e fanciulle
e rami ed erbe calpestate intorno
fregio di marmo chiude,
invano invano il pensier nostro ardendo
fino a te si consuma,
pari all'eternità, fredda, silente,
imperturbata effige.
Quando, dal tempo devastata e vinta,
questa or viva progenie anche cadrà,
fra diverso dolore, amica all'uomo,
rimarrai tu sola,
"Bellezza è verità" dicendo ancora:
"Verità è bellezza. Questo a voi
sopra la terra di sapere è dato:
questo, non altro, a voi, sopra la terra,
è bastante sapere".

Algeria, Campo 127,
Ottobre 1943

RENÉ CHAR

POEMS

TRANSLATED BY DENIS DEVLIN AND JACKSON MATHEWS

WIND AWAY

Camped on the hillsides near the village are fields of mimosa. During the gathering season, it may happen that, some distance away, you meet an extremely sweet smelling girl whose arms have been busy during the day among the fragile branches. Like a lamp with a bright nimbus of perfume, she goes her way, her back to the setting sun.

To speak to her would be sacrilege.

The grass crushed beneath her slippers. Give her right of way. You may be lucky enough to make out on her lips the chimaera of the damp of Night.

THE BASKET-WEAVER'S LOVE

I loved you. I loved your face, like a well-spring ravined by storms, and the secret of your domain enclosing my caress. Some rely on a round imagination, like the earth. For me going is enough. I brought back from despair a basket so small, my love, it could be woven of willow.

YOUTH

Far from the ambush of roofs and the alms of country shrines you take your birth, hostages of the birds, O fountains. Man's decline in the nausea of his ashes, man's struggle with his vindictive providence, not even these can disillusion you.

Praise, praise, we have come to terms with ourselves.

« If I had been mute as the trusty stone step beneath the sun heedless of its wound sewn with ivy », she said, « if I had been childlike as the white tree receiving the fright of bees, if the hills had lived on into summer, if the lightning had opened its gates to me, if your night had forgiven me... »

Eyes, the orchard of stars, the gorse, the solitude are not part of you. A song finishes exile. The lamb-wind brings back new life.

LIVING

Pass.
The sidereal spade, in other times,
Plunged and was swallowed up here.
To-night a whole village of birds
Passes over, exulting.

Hear, in the stony head
Of presences gone,
The word that will make your sleep
Warm like a September tree.

See, they tremble, the intertwining
Certitudes that have come

436

Among us to their quintessence,
O my Crossroads, my anxious Thirst!

The bitterness of living prowls
Ceaselessly lusting after exile.
Under a thin almond rain,
Gentle and in liberty,
Alchemy your nurse was born,
O my Love!

POSTSCRIPT

Stand you away from me who wait nor speak;
I was born at your feet but you have lost me;
Too well my flames have marked their kingdom out;
My treasure sank that struck your chopping-block.

The desert where the one firebrand took refuge
Has never called me out, nor given me up.

Stand you away from me who wait nor speak:
The clover of passion is iron in my hand.

In the dazed air through which I go my ways,
Time will clean up my face, little by little,
Like a horse aimless at his bitter ploughing.

HYMN IN A LOW VOICE

Hellas! broad shore of a sea of genius from which the
breath of knowledge and the magnetism of intelligence arose
at dawn, swelling with equal fertility forces that seemed
endless, you are, further back, an atlas of strange mountains:
a volcano chain that smiles at the magic of heroes, at the

437

serpentine loves of goddesses, and guides the nuptial flight of man, free at last to know himself a bird and die a bird; you are the answer to everything, even to the usury of birth, even to the ways of the labyrinth. But you, mass of earth made of the diamond of light and snow, earth incorruptible beneath the feet of a people victorious over death but mortal as proof of purity, there is a foreign belief that would chastise your perfection, thinking to stifle the murmur of your wheat.

O Greece! mirror and body three times martyred, to imagine is to restore you. Your healers are in your people and your health is in your right. Your blood incalculable, I call upon it, the only living thing for which liberty has ceased to be sickly; it breaks open my mouth, the blood with silence, I with a shout.

LILY OF THE VALLEY

I stood guard over their fate, that couple. I stood by them in their dark fidelity. The aged mountain stream had read me its page of thanksgiving. A new storm was coming. The light of the earth brushed against me. And while on the window-pane the childhood of the justicer was being written (clemency being dead), my patience exhausted, I broke down in sobs.

MARTHA

Martha whom these old walls cannot take over, fountain reflecting my lonely monarchy, how could I forget you since I do not have to remember you: you are the present, accumulating. We shall come together without having to approach or prepare for each other, as two poppies in love make a giant anemone.

I will not enter your heart to shorten its memory. I will not engage your mouth so that it cannot open to the blue air and thirst for departure. I want to be freedom for you, and the wind of life crossing the threshold of always before night becomes undiscoverable.

TO THE HEALTH OF THE SERPENT

I

I sing the heat that is like a new-born babe, desperate heat.

II

It is bread's turn to break man, to be the beauty of daybreak.

III

He who believes in the sunflower will not meditate in the house. All thoughts of love will become his thoughts.

IV

Within the swallow's loop, a storm searches, a garden grows.

V

There will always be a drop of water to outlast the sun, without shaking the sun's ascendancy.

VI

Bring forth that which knowledge would keep secret, knowledge with its hundred corridors.

VII

That which comes into the world to cause no trouble deserves neither respect nor patience.

VIII

How long will man's failure last, this dying at the centre of creation because creation has dismissed him.

IX

Each house was a season. The town in this way repeated itself. Together the inhabitants knew only winter, in spite of their heated bodies, in spite of the day that would not go.

X

You are in essence always a poet, always at the height of your love, always hungry for truth and justice. It is doubtless a necessary evil that you cannot be so, assiduously, in your conscience.

XI

You shall make of the non-existant soul a man better than her.

XII

Look how your country glows in the light of daring; this pleasure for a long time has not been yours.

XIII

Many there are who wait till the reefs lift them over and the goal passes them by, to clarify themselves.

XIV

Be thankful to him who cares nothing for your remorse. You are his equal.

XV

Tears despise their sympathiser.

XVI

The depth remains measurable where the sands subdue destiny.

XVII

My love, it matters little that I was born; you come into sight where I disappear.

XVIII

Would I could walk, without deceiving the bird, from the heart of the tree to the ecstasy of the fruit.

XIX

That which calls to you through pleasure is nothing but the mercenary gratitude of memory. The presence you have chosen bids no farewells.

XX

Stoop only to love. If you die, you still love.

XXI

The glooms in which you steep yourself are still subject to your lusty, solar sovereignty.

XXII

Have nothing to do with those in whose eyes man is only a passing shade of the colour lying on earth's tormented back. Let them reel off their long protestation. The red of the poker and the glow of the cloud are one.

XXIII

It is unworthy of the poet to puzzle the lamb, to invest himself with its fleece.

XXIV

If we live in a lightning flash, it is the heart of eternity.

XXV

Eyes that thought to create the day, but woke the wind, what can I do for you, I am oblivion.

XXVI

Poetry is of all clear streams the one that lingers least about her reflected bridges.
Poetry, life's future held in man requalified.

XXVII

A rose that it may rain. At the end of innumerable years, that is your wish.

THE METEOR OF THE 13th OF AUGUST

Black will be that night when, in the absence of truth, man will suppress the superstition of truth.

The three phases of the meteor correspond to the three fates or, if you prefer, to the three *crossed* ways along which our life springs forward, pauses, and burns out, life almost completely deprived of free will. These describe three sovereign states, but it is impossible to say which has especial precedence, as each gives the illusion of being the most deeply, the most desperately and the most joyously felt, in equal measure and *almost* at once. In the following brief paragraphs, we have attempted a domification which, unfortunately, can only be approximate.

[THE METEOR OF THE 13th OF AUGUST]

The very moment you appeared to me, my heart had the whole sky to light its way. It was mid-day in my poem. I knew anguish was asleep...

[NOVAE]

The first ray, trembling between a curse under torture and magnificent love.

The optimism of philosophy is no longer adequate.

The light on the rock shelters a major tree. We are advancing to where it is visible.

Ever wider the marriage of eyes. The tragedy that is unfolding will rejoice even at our limits.

Danger wiped out our melancholy. We spoke without looking at each other. Time held us together. Death avoided us.

Larks of the night, stars, circling about the springs of surrender, be progress to these sleeping heads.

I jumped out of my bed bordered with hawthorn. Barefooted, I talk to the children.

[THE MOON CHANGES GARDENS]

Where am I to rid me of this legacy of excrement that escorts me like a lamp?

Tentative hymns! hymns denied!

Woman, mad and to the night obedient — star.

Stormy liberty in the swaddling-clothes of thunder, over the supremacy of the void, in the small hands of man.

Don't daze yourself with tomorrows. What you are looking at is winter striding over wounds, gnawing at the windows; and on the porch of death, the inscrutable torture.

Those that sleep in wool, those that run in the cold, those that offer mediation, those that are not ravishers for want of something to do, are in accord with the meteor, the cock's enemy.

I have the illusion of being at the same time in my soul and outside it, far beyond the window pane and yet against it, a burst saxifrage. My desire is infinite. Nothing obsesses me but life.

Nomad spark dying in its conflagration.

Give yourself to love, O dweller by the riverside. Spend your truth. The grass that hides the gold of your love will never know the frost.

On this earth with its dangers, I marvel at the idolatry of life.

May my presence, that stirs in you a secret malaise, an unremitting hatred, be a meteor in your soul.

A birdsong surprises the branches of morning.

TO AN IMAGE OF WARRIOR ARDOUR

Our-Lady-of-Lights alone on your rock, at odds with your church, friendly to her rebels, we owe you nothing but a little charity.

I have sometimes destested you. You were never naked. Your mouth was unclean. But I know now that I was wrong, for those that kissed you had fouled their table.

Transients that we are, we have never insisted on sleep until we were tired out. Protectress of endeavour, you bear no mark, save that of those who showed you little love.

You are the moment of a revealed lie, the bludgeon befouled, the guilty torch. I have the strength of heart, fool that you are, to strike you or take your hand... It is for you to defend yourself.

Too many clever fools are watching you, waiting for you to take fright. You have no choice but complicity. The awful disgust, having to obey their orders, and in return serve as their ally.

I have broken silence because they have all gone and left you nothing but your clump of pines. Ah! run down to the road, make friends for yourself, be woman, but yielding woman...

The world has been through so much since your coming that it is nothing but a pot of bones, a will to cruelty. O faded Lady, bold, shameless country girl, the lights are cold where men are born.

(From *FUREUR ET MYSTÈRE*, Gallimard, Paris 1948).

FLUSHED WITH JOY, THOSE THAT RISE IN THE MORNING...

Evidence and its near-hits are collective. Truth is personal.

Take care: all men are not trustworthy.

A welcome for him who comes to me in labour and sweat, saying: « I have come to deceive you ».

O, great black helm, on your way to death, why should it always be your task to point out the lightning?

I

The state of mind of the rising sun is gladness in spite of the cruel day and the memory of night. The hue of dried blood becomes the redness of dawn.

II

Those whose mission is to arouse, begin by taking a morning wash in the river. The first enchantment and the first shock are for one's self.

III

Force your luck, clasp your happiness, and go to meet your risk. Seeing you, they will get used to your doing so.

IV

At the height of the storm, there is always a bird to comfort us. The unknown bird. It sings, and flies away.

V

The wise thing is not to collect in the mass but, in common nature and creation to seek out your number, your reci-

procity, your differences, your passage, your truth, and the small bit of despair that is its goad and moving fog.

VI

Go straight to the essential: don't you need young trees to rebuild your forest?

VII

Intensity is silent. Its image is not. (I like the man who dazzles me and then accentuates my inner darkness).

VIII

How this world suffers in becoming the world of man, shaped between the four walls of a book! That it should then be given over to speculators and fools who urge it on faster than it can go, — how are we not to see in this more than bad luck? To fight at all cost against that inevitable end with the help of our own magic, to make endless forays along the route, or what we use for the route, that is the task of the Morning people. Death is but a sleep complete and pure, with the plus sign for pilot to help it cleave the wave of becoming. Why take fright at your alluvial condition? Quit taking the branch for the trunk and the root for the void. That is at least a beginning.

IX

You must breathe on sparks to make a good light. Beautiful burnt-out eyes will complete the offering.

X

Woman, fear-inspiring, with madness in her bite and a mortal cold in her body: that knowledge which, born of a noble ambition, in the end finds its measure in our tears and *our subjugation. Make no mistake, O best of men whose strong arm she covets and whose weakness she lies in wait for.*

XI

When we feel the pressure to break with our luck and our courage, and to accept the various simplifications, something that owes nothing to man, but wishes us well, exhorts us: « Rebels, rebels, rebels... »

XII

The personal adventure, the abundant adventure: community of our mornings.

XIII

Conquest and the unlimited preservation of the conquest that lies ahead of us murmuring of our shipwreck, deflecting our disillusion.

XIV

We have the peculiarity sometimes of swaying when we walk. Time is light, the ground agreeable, our foot turns where it knows.

XV

When we say: the heart (and say it regretfully), what we mean is the smouldering heart, clothed in our common, miraculous flesh, which can at any moment stop beating and giving.

XVI

Between your greatest good and their least bad, poetry flares.

XVII

The swarm, the lightning, and anathema: three slopes of the same mountain.

XVIII

To stand firmly on the ground and give your arm to a love unacceptable to those who sustain you, to build what you think is your house without that first stone, which will always inconceivably be missing, that is the curse.

XIX

Do not complain because you live nearer death than mortals do.

XX

We seem to be born always half-way between the beginning and the end of the world. We grow up in open rebellion, almost as furiously against what draws us on, as against what holds us back.

XXI

Imitate men as little as possible in their enigmatic passion for tying knots.

XXII

Death is not detestable except in the way it attacks each of our five senses one by one, then all of them together. If need be, hearing could ignore her.

XXIII

We can build multiformly only on error. This is what allows us to think, at each renewal, that we are happy.

XXIV

When the ship sinks, her sails find harbor inside us. Her masts rise out of our blood. Her fresh impatience gathers strength for further obstinate voyages. Is it not so, you, who are blind upon the sea? Staggering through all that blue, O sadness rising on the farthest waves?

XXV

We are passers-by schooled *to pass by, and therefore to sow disturbance, to impose our heat, to speak our exuberance. That is why we interrupt! That is why we are untimely and unusual! The plume we flaunt means nothing. Our usefulness is directed against the employer.*

XXVI

I can despair of myself and keep my hope in You. I have fallen from my brightness, and you do not notice death, in plain view, bracken in the wall, woman walking by my side.

XXVII

Finally if you will destroy, let it be with nuptial implements.

DIVERGENCE

The horse with the narrow head
Has beaten down his enemy,
The poet with the lazy heels
Knows winds more masterful
Than those that breathe in his voice.
The devastated earth recovers
Though wounded by an endless sword.

Go back in patience to your farms;
Over the almond-trees in Spring
Youth and age pour in streams.
Death smiles at the edge of Time
Giving it some nobility.

It is upon the heights of summer
That the poet's revolt begins,
And it is from the harvest's fire
He draws his madness and his torch.

THE ADVICE OF THE LOOK-OUT

Fruit springing beneath the knife
Beauty whose echo is a taste,
Dawn with your pincer jaws,
Lovers the world would pull apart,
Woman in your apron,
Nail scratching on the wall,
Desert! Desert!

PYRENEES

Mountains of the great and wronged,
On your feverish tower-tops
The last light fades.

Naught but the void, the avalanche,
Grief and regret!

Those troubadours, crossed in love,
Watched their kingdom bitter-sweet
Turn white in one summer.

Ah! inexorable the snow
Would have them at its feet in pain,

Would have them die in ice
Who have lived among the sands.

ON LEAVE

The ogre that is everywhere:
On her face you're waiting for
And in your longing for that face,
In the migration of the birds,
Beneath their feigned tranquillity:
The ogre that serves us all
And is never thanked,
In the house you built yourself
Despite the migraine of the wind;
The ogre, hooded a chimaera;
Ah! if he were free to tell us
That he is the serving man of Death,
Our anguish would become resigned
But what a desert were the mind.

NIGHTS OF FULFILLMENT

With a stronger wind,
A lamp less dim,
We should reach the wayside halt
At which night will say « Pass on »;
And we shall know it's true
When the glass goes black.

O earth all tenderness!
O branch my joy grows on!
The maw of heaven is white.
What's shimmering there is you,
My fall, my love, my prey.

452

FULLY

When our bones had touched land,
And through our faces crumbling come,
My love, nothing ended there.
Love came freshly in a cry
Reviving and restoring us.
Though our heat was silenced,
Something there kept on
(Different from dying life)
Unfolding to infinity.
That which we had seen afloat
Edge to edge with grief
Was there, as in a nest,
Its two eyes bringing us
Together in new-born consent.
Despite the wool of swaddling-clothes
Death had not grown up,
And happiness not yet begun
Was listening for us;
The grass was bare and trampled on.

WHEREFORE YIELD?

Oh! Woman discovered, our wings go side by side
And high heaven is their faithful air.
But what is that still shining above us?

It is the dying reflection of our daring.
When we have made our way through it,
We shall distress the earth no more:
We shall see each other.

(From *LES MATINAUX*, Gallimard, Paris 1950).

POÈMES

CONGÉ AU VENT

A flancs de coteau du village bivouaquent des champs fournis de mimosas. A l'époque de la cueillette, il arrive que, loin de leur endroit, on fasse la rencontre extrêmement odorante d'une fille dont les bras se sont occupés durant la journée aux fragiles branches. Pareille à une lampe dont l'auréole de clarté serait de parfum, elle s'en va, le dos tourné au soleil couchant.

Il serait sacrilège de lui adresser la parole.

L'espadrille foulant l'herbe, cédez-lui le pas du chemin. Peut-être aurez-vous la chance de distinguer sur ses lèvres la chimère de l'humidité de la Nuit?

LA COMPAGNE DU VANNIER

Je t'aimais. J'aimais ton visage de source raviné par l'orage et le chiffre de ton domaine enserrant mon baiser. Certains se confient à une imagination toute ronde. Aller me suffit. J'ai rapporté du désespoir un panier si petit, mon amour, qu'on a pu le tresser en osier.

JEUNESSE

Loin de l'embuscade des tuiles et de l'aumône des calvaires, vous vous donnez naissance, otages des oiseaux, fontaines. La pente de l'homme faite de la nausée de ses cendres, de l'homme en lutte avec sa providence vindicative, ne suffit pas à vous désenchanter.

Éloge, nous nous sommes acceptés.

« Si j'avais été muette comme la marche de pierre fidèle au soleil et qui ignore sa blessure cousue de lierre, si j'avais été enfant comme l'arbre blanc qui accueille les frayeurs des abeilles, si les collines avaient vécu jusqu'à l'été, si l'éclair m'avait ouvert sa grille, si tes nuits m'avaient pardonnée... ».

Regard, verger d'étoiles, les genêts, la solitude sont distincts de vous! Le chant finit l'exil. La brise des agneaux ramène la vie neuve.

POÈMES

CONDUITE

Passe.
La bêche sidérale
autrefois là s'est engouffrée.
Ce soir un village d'oiseaux
très haut exulte et passe.

Écoute aux tempes rocheuses
des présences dispersées
le mot qui fera ton sommeil
chaud comme un arbre de septembre.

Vois bouger l'entrelacement
des certitudes arrivées
près de nous à leur quintessence,
ô ma Fourche, ma Soif anxieuse!

La rigueur de vivre se rode
sans cesse à convoiter l'exil.
Par une fine pluie d'amande,
mêlée de liberté docile,
ta gardienne alchimie s'est produite,
ô Bien-aimée!

POST-SCRIPTUM

Écartez-vous de moi qui patiente sans bouche;
A vos pieds je suis né, mais vous m'avez perdu;
Mes feux ont trop précisé leur royaume;
Mon trésor a coulé contre votre billot.

Le désert comme asile au seul tison suave
Jamais ne m'a nommé, jamais ne m'a rendu.

455

Écartez-vous de moi qui patiente sans bouche:
Le trèfle de la passion est de fer dans ma main.

Dans la stupeur de l'air où s'ouvrent mes allées,
Le temps émondera peu à peu mon visage,
Comme un cheval sans fin dans un labour aigri.

HYMNE A VOIX BASSE

L'Hellade, c'est le rivage déployé d'une mer géniale d'où s'élancèrent à l'aurore le souffle de la connaissance et le magnétisme de l'intelligence, gonflant d'égale fertilité des pouvoirs qui semblèrent perpétuels; c'est plus loin, une mappemonde d'étranges montagnes: une chaîne de volcans sourit à la magie des héros, à la tendresse serpentine des déesses, guide le vol nuptial de l'homme, libre enfin de se savoir et de périr oiseau; c'est la réponse à tout, même à l'usure de la naissance, même aux détours du labyrinthe. Mais ce sol massif fait du diamant de la lumière et de la neige, cette terre imputrescible sous les pieds de son peuple victorieux de la mort mais mortel par évidence de pureté, une raison étrangère tente de châtier sa perfection, croit couvrir le balbutiement de ses épis.

O Grèce, miroir et corps trois fois martyrs, t'imaginer c'est te rétablir. Tes guérisseurs sont dans ton peuple et ta santé est dans ton droit. Ton sang incalculable, je l'appelle, le seul vivant pour qui la liberté a cessé d'être maladive, qui me brise la bouche, lui du silence et moi du cri.

LE MUGUET

J'ai sauvegardé la fortune du couple. Je l'ai suivi dans son obscure loyauté. La vieillesse du torrent m'avait lu sa page de gratitude. Un jeune orage s'annonçait. La lumière de la terre me frôlait. Et pendant que se retraçait sur la vitre l'enfance du justicier (la clémence était morte), à bout de patience je sanglotais.

MARTHE

Marthe que ces vieux murs ne peuvent pas s'approprier, fontaine où se mire ma monarchie solitaire, comment pourrais-je jamais vous oublier puisque je n'ai pas à me souvenir de vous: vous êtes le présent qui s'accumule. Nous nous unirons sans avoir à nous aborder, à nous prévoir comme deux pavots font en amour une anémone géante.

Je n'entrerai pas dans votre cœur pour limiter sa mémoire. Je ne retiendrai pas votre bouche pour l'empêcher de s'entr'ouvrir sur le bleu de l'air et la soif de partir. Je veux être pour vous la liberté et le vent de la vie qui passe le seuil de toujours avant que la nuit ne devienne introuvable.

A LA SANTÉ DU SERPENT

I

Je chante la chaleur à visage de nouveau-né, la chaleur désespérée.

II

Au tour du pain de rompre l'homme, d'être la beauté du point-du-jour.

III

Celui qui se fie au tournesol ne méditera pas dans la maison. Toutes les pensées de l'amour deviendront ses pensées.

IV

Dans la boucle de l'hirondelle un orage s'informe, un jardin se construit.

V

Il y aura toujours une goutte d'eau pour durer plus que le soleil sans que l'ascendant du soleil soit ébranlé.

VI

Produis ce que la connaissance veut garder secret, la connaissance aux cent passages.

VII

Ce qui vient au monde pour ne rien troubler ne mérite ni égards ni patience.

VIII

Combien durera ce manque de l'homme mourant au centre de la création parce que la création l'a congédié?

IX

Chaque maison était une saison. La ville ainsi se répétait. Tous les habitants ensemble ne connaissaient que l'hiver, malgré leur chair réchauffée, malgré le jour qui ne s'en allait pas.

X

Tu es dans ton essence constamment poète, constamment au zénith de ton amour, constamment avide de vérité et de justice. C'est sans doute un mal nécessaire que tu ne puisses l'être assidûment dans ta conscience.

XI

Tu feras de l'âme qui n'existe pas un homme meilleur qu'elle.

XII

Regarde l'image téméraire où se baigne ton pays, ce plaisir qui t'a longtemps fui.

XIII

Nombreux sont ceux qui attendent que l'écueil les soulève, que le but les franchisse, pour se définir.

XIV

Remercie celui qui ne prend pas souci de ton remords. Tu es son égal.

XV

Les larmes méprisent leur confident.

XVI

Il reste une profondeur mesurable là où le sable subjugue la destinée.

XVII

Mon amour, peu importe que je sois né: tu deviens visible à la place où je disparais.

POÈMES

XVIII

Pouvoir marcher, sans tromper l'oiseau, du coeur de l'arbre à l'extase du fruit.

XIX

Ce qui t'accueille à travers le plaisir n'est que la gratitude mercenaire du souvenir. La présence que tu as choisie ne délivre pas d'adieu.

XX

Ne te courbe que pour aimer. Si tu meurs, tu aimes encore.

XXI

Les ténèbres que tu t'infuses sont régies par la luxure de ton ascendant solaire.

XXII

Néglige ceux aux yeux de qui l'homme passe pour n'être qu'une étape de la couleur sur le dos tourmenté de la terre. Qu'ils dévident leur longue remontrance. L'encre du tisonnier et la rougeur du nuage ne font qu'un.

XXIII

Il n'est pas digne du poète de mystifier l'agneau, d'investir sa laine.

XXIV

Si nous habitons un éclair, il est le coeur de l'éternel.

XXV

Yeux qui, croyant inventer le jour, avez éveillé le vent, que puis-je pour vous, je suis l'oubli.

XXVI

La poésie est de toutes les eaux claires celle qui s'attarde le moins aux reflets de ses ponts.
Poésie, la vie future à l'intérieur de l'homme requalifié.

XXVII

Une rose pour qu'il pleuve. Au terme d'innombrables années, c'est ton souhait.

RENÉ CHAR

LE MÉTÉORE DU 13 AOUT

> Mauvaise sera la nuit où, à défaut de
> la vérité même, l'homme supprimera la
> superstition de la vérité.

Les trois phases du météore correspondent aux trois fatalités ou
si l'on préfère aux trois directions *contrariées*, en vertu desquelles s'élan-
ce, s'ajourne et brûle notre vie, à peu près complètement dépourvue de
libre arbitre. Elles traduisent trois états souverains, mais il est impos-
sible d'écrire lequel a plus particulièrement barre sur l'autre, chacun
offrant l'illusion d'être le plus profondément, le plus désespérément, le
plus allègrement ressenti par nous à l'instar de ses pareils et *presque*
à la fois. Dans cette succession de brefs paragraphes nous avons tenté
une domification qui ne peut être, hélas, qu'approximative.

[LE MÉTÉORE DU 13 AOUT]

*A la seconde où tu m'apparus, mon coeur eut tout le ciel pour
l'éclairer. Il fut midi à mon poème. Je sus que l'angoisse dormait.*

[NOVAE]

*Premier rayon qui hésite entre l'imprécation du supplice et le ma-
gnifique amour.*

L'optimisme des philosophies ne nous est plus suffisant.

*La lumière du rocher abrite un arbre majeur. Nous nous avançons
vers sa visibilité.*

*Toujours plus larges fiançailles des regards. La tragédie qui s'éla-
bore jouira même de nos limites.*

*Le danger nous ôtait toute mélancolie. Nous parlions sans nous re-
garder. Le temps nous tenait unis. La mort nous évitait.*

Alouettes de la nuit, étoiles, qui tournoyez aux sources de l'abandon, soyez progrès aux fronts qui dorment.

J'ai sauté de mon lit bordé d'aubépines. Pieds nus, je parle aux enfants.

[LA LUNE CHANGE DE JARDIN]

Où vais-je égarer cette fortune d'excréments qui m'escorte comme une lampe?

Hymnes provisoires! hymnes contredits!

Folles, et, à la nuit, lumières obéissantes.

Orageuse liberté dans les langes de la foudre, sur la souveraineté du vide, aux petites mains de l'homme.

Ne t'étourdis pas de lendemains. Tu regardes l'hiver qui enjambe les plaies et ronge les fenêtres, et, sur le porche de la mort, l'inscrutable torture.

Ceux qui dorment dans la laine, ceux qui courent dans le froid, ceux qui offrent leur médiation, ceux qui ne sont pas ravisseurs faute de mieux, s'accordent avec le météore, ennemi du coq.

Illusoirement, je suis à la fois dans mon âme et hors d'elle, loin devant la vitre et contre la vitre, saxifrage éclaté. Ma convoitise est infinie. Rien ne m'obsède que la vie.

Étincelle nomade qui meurt dans son incendie.

Aime riveraine. Dépense ta vérité. L'herbe qui cache l'or de ton amour ne connaîtra jamais le gel.

Sur cette terre des périls, je m'émerveille de l'idolâtrie de la vie.

Que ma présence qui vous cause énigmatique malaise, haine sans rémission, soit météore dans votre âme.

Un chant d'oiseau surprend la branche du matin.

A UNE FERVEUR BELLIQUEUSE

Notre-Dame-des-Lumières qui restez seule sur votre rocher, brouillée avec votre église, favorable à ses insurgés, nous ne vous devons rien qu'un peu de charité.

Je vous ai quelquefois détestée. Vous n'étiez jamais nue. Votre bouche était sale. Mais je sais aujourd'hui que j'ai exagéré car ceux qui vous baisaient avaient souillé leur table.

Les passants que nous sommes n'ont jamais exigé que le repos leur vînt avant d'être épuisés. Gardienne des efforts, vous n'êtes pas marquée, sinon du peu d'amour qui vous fut témoigné.

Vous êtes le moment d'un mensonge éclairé, le gourdin encrassé, la lampe punissable. J'ai le coeur assez fort, folle, pour vous gifler ou vous prendre la main. A vous de vous défendre.

Trop de coquins vous guettent et guettent votre effroi. Vous n'avez d'autre choix que la complicité. Le sévère dégoût qu'obéir à leur voix, de devoir en retour leur servir d'affidée!

J'ai rompu le silence puisque tous sont partis et que vous n'avez rien qu'un bois de pins pour vous. Ah! courez à la route, faites-vous des amis et femme devenez, mais femme qui se plie...

Le monde a tant marché depuis votre venue qu'il n'est plus qu'un pot d'os, qu'un voeu de cruauté. O Dame évanouie, campagnarde effrontée, les lumières sont froides où les hommes sont nés!

(*FUREUR ET MYSTÈRE*, Gallimard, Paris 1948).

POÈMES

ROUGEUR DES MATINAUX

(ENCLAVE DÉLÉBILE)

L'évidence et ses à-peu-près sont collectifs. La
vérité est personnelle.

Prenez garde: tous ne sont pas dignes de la
confidence.

Accolade à celui qui, émergeant de sa fatigue
et de sa sueur, s'avancera et me dira: « Je suis
venu pour te tromper ».

O grande barre noire, en route vers ta mort,
pourquoi serait-ce toujours à toi de montrer
l'éclair?

I

*L'état d'esprit du soleil levant est allégresse malgré le jour cruel
et le souvenir de la nuit. La teinte du caillot devient la rougeur de
l'aurore.*

II

*Quand on a mission d'éveiller, on commence par faire sa toilette
dans la rivière. Le premier enchantement comme le premier saisisse-
ment sont pour soi.*

III

*Impose ta chance, serre ton bonheur et va vers ton risque. A te
regarder, ils s'habitueront.*

IV

*Au plus fort de l'orage, il y a toujours un oiseau pour nous rassurer.
C'est l'oiseau inconnu. Il chante avant de s'envoler.*

V

*La sagesse est de ne pas s'agglomérer, mais dans la création et
dans la nature communes, de trouver notre nombre, notre réciprocité,
nos différences, notre passage, notre vérité et ce peu de désespoir qui
en est l'aiguillon et le mouvant brouillard.*

463

VI

Allez à l'essentiel: n'avez-vous pas besoin de jeunes arbres pour reboiser votre forêt?

VII

L'intensité est silencieuse. Son image ne l'est pas. (J'aime qui m'éblouit puis accentue l'obscur à l'intérieur de moi).

VIII

Combien souffre ce monde, pour devenir celui de l'homme, d'être façonné entre les quatre murs d'un livre! Qu'il soit ensuite remis aux mains de spéculateurs et d'extravagants qui le pressent d'avancer plus vite que son propre mouvement, comment ne pas voir là plus que de la malchance? Combattre vaille que vaille cette fatalité à l'aide de sa magie, ouvrir dans l'aile de la route, de ce qui en tient lieu, d'insatiables randonnées, c'est la tâche des Matinaux. La mort n'est qu'un sommeil entier et pur avec le signe plus qui le pilote et l'aide à fendre le flot du devenir. Qu'as-tu à t'alarmer de ton état alluvial? Cesse de prendre la branche pour le tronc et la racine pour le vide. C'est un petit commencement.

IX

Il faut souffler sur quelques lueurs pour faire de la bonne lumière. Beaux yeux brûlés parachèvent le don.

X

Femelle redoutable, elle porte la rage dans sa morsure et un froid mortel dans ses flancs, cette connaissance qui, partie d'une noble ambition, finit par trouver sa mesure dans nos larmes et dans notre jugulation. Ne vous méprenez pas, ô vous entre les meilleurs dont elle convoite le bras et guette la défaillance.

XI

A toute pression de rompre avec nos chances, notre morale, et de nous soumettre à tel modèle simplificateur, ce qui ne doit rien à l'homme, mais nous veut du bien, nous exhorte: « Insurgé, insurgé, insurgé... ».

XII

L'aventure personnelle, l'aventure prodiguée, communauté de nos aurores.

XIII

Conquête et conservation indéfinie de cette conquête en avant de nous qui murmure notre naufrage, déroute notre déception.

XIV

Nous avons cette particularité parfois de nous balancer en marchant. Le temps nous est léger, le sol nous est facile, notre pied ne tourne qu'à bon escient.

XV

Quand nous disons: le coeur (et le disons à regret), il s'agit du coeur attisant que recouvre la chair miraculeuse et commune, et qui peut à chaque instant cesser de battre et d'accorder.

XVI

Entre ton plus grand bien et leur moindre mal rougeoie la poésie.

XVII

L'essaim, l'éclair et l'anathème, trois obliques d'un même sommet.

XVIII

Se tenir fermement sur terre, et, avec amour, donner le bras à un fruit non accepté de ceux qui vous appuient, édifier ce qu'on croit sa maison, sans le concours de la première pierre qui toujours inconcevablement fera faute, c'est la malédiction.

XIX

Ne te plains pas de vivre plus près de la mort que les mortels.

XX

Il semble que l'on naît toujours à mi-chemin du commencement et de la fin du monde. Nous grandissons en révolte ouverte presque aussi furieusement contre ce qui nous entraîne que contre ce qui nous retient.

XXI

Imite le moins possible les hommes dans leur énigmatique maladie de faire des noeuds.

XXII

La mort n'est haïssable que parce qu'elle affecte séparément chacun de nos cinq sens, puis tous à la fois. A la rigueur, l'ouïe la négligerait.

XXIII

On ne bâtit multiformément que sur l'erreur. C'est ce qui nous permet de nous supposer, à chaque renouveau, heureux.

XXIV

Quand le navire s'engloutit, sa voilure se sauve à l'intérieur de nous. Elle mâte sur notre sang. Sa neuve impatience se concentre pour d'autres obstinés voyages. N'est-ce pas, vous, qui êtes aveugle sur la mer? Vous qui vacillez dans tout ce bleu, ô tristesse dressée aux vagues les plus loin?

XXV

Nous sommes des passants appliqués à passer, donc à jeter le trouble, à infliger notre chaleur, à dire notre exubérance. Voilà pourquoi nous intervenons! Voilà pourquoi nous sommes intempestifs et insolites! Notre aigrette n'y est rien. Notre utilité est tournée contre l'employeur.

XXVI

Je puis désespérer de moi et garder mon espoir en Vous. Je suis tombé de mon éclat et la mort vue de tous, vous ne la marquez pas, fougère dans le mur, promeneuse à mon bras.

XXVII

Enfin si tu détruis, que ce soit avec des outils nuptiaux.

DIVERGENCE

Le cheval à la tête étroite
A condamné son ennemi,
Le poète aux talons oisifs,
A de plus sévères zéphyrs
Que ceux qui courent dans sa voix.
La terre ruinée se reprend
Bien qu'un fer continu la blesse.

Rentrez aux fermes, gens patients;
Sur les amandiers au printemps
Ruissellent vieillesse et jeunesse.
La mort sourit au bord du temps
Qui lui donne quelque noblesse.

C'est sur les hauteurs de l'été
Que le poète se révolte,
Et du brasier de la récolte
Tire sa torche et sa folie.

CONSEIL DE LA SENTINELLE

Fruit qui jaillissez du couteau,
Beauté dont saveur est l'écho,
Aurore à gueule de tenailles,
Amants qu'on veut désassembler,
Femme qui portez tablier,
Ongle qui grattez la muraille,
Désertez! désertez!

PYRÉNÉES

Montagne des grands abusés,
Au sommet de vos tours fiévreuses
Faiblit la dernière clarté.

Rien que le vide et l'avalanche,
La détresse et le regret!

Tous ces troubadours mal-aimés
Ont vu blanchir dans un été
Leur doux royaume pessimiste.

Ah! la neige est inexorable
Qui aime qu'on souffre à ses pieds,
Qui veut que l'on meure glacé
Quand on a vécu dans les sables.

LE PERMISSIONNAIRE

L'ogre qui est partout:
Sur le visage qu'on attend
Et dans le languir qu'on en a,
Dans la migration des oiseaux,
Sous leur feinte tranquillité;
L'ogre qui sert chacun de nous
Et n'est jamais remercié,
Dans la maison qu'on s'est construite
Malgré la migraine du vent;
L'ogre couvert et chimérique;
Ah! s'il pouvait nous confier
Qu'il est le valet de la Mort,
L'angoisse se résignerait.
Mais le désert s'établirait.

LES NUITS JUSTES

Avec un vent plus fort,
Une lampe moins obscure,
Nous devons trouver la halte
Où la nuit dira « Passez »;
Et nous saurons que c'est vrai
Quand le verre s'éteindra.

O terre devenue tendre!
O branche où mûrit ma joie!
La gueule du ciel est blanche.
Ce qui miroite, là, c'est toi,
Ma chute, mon amour, mon saccage.

PLEINEMENT

Quand nos os eurent touché terre,
Croulant à travers nos visages,
Mon amour, rien ne fut fini.
Un amour frais vint dans un cri
Nous ranimer et nous reprendre.
Et si la chaleur s'était tue,

La chose qui continuait,
Opposée à la vie mourante,
A l'infini s'élaborait.
Ce que nous avions vu flotter
Bord à bord avec la douleur
Etait là comme dans un nid,
Et ses deux yeux nous unissaient
Dans un naissant consentement.
La mort n'avait pas grandi
Malgré des laines ruisselantes,
Et le bonheur pas commencé
A l'écoute de nos présences;
L'herbe était nue et piétinée.

POURQUOI SE RENDRE?

Oh! Rencontrée, nos ailes vont côte à côte
Et l'azur leur est fidèle.
Mais qu'est-ce qui brille encore au-dessus de nous?

Le reflet mourant de notre audace.
Lorsque nous l'aurons parcouru,
Nous n'affligerons plus la terre:
Nous nous regarderons.

(*LES MATINAUX*, Gallimard, Paris 1948).

469

ROBERT LOWELL

IL CIMITERO DEI QUACCHERI A NANTUCKET
(PER WARREN WINSLOW, PERITO IN MARE)

L'uomo abbia il dominio sui pesci del mare
e gli uccelli dell'aria e le bestie e su tutta
quanta la terra, e su ogni creatura che si
muove strisciando sulla terra.

1

Un'amara lingua di basso fondale al largo di Madacket —
il mare si rompeva ancora violento e la notte
era entrata rapida nella nostra flotta del Nord Atlantico,
quando il marinaio annegato afferrò la rete. La luce
balenò dal suo capo scarruffato e dai piedi di marmo;
egli si aggrappò alla rete
con i muscoli delle coscie rigidi e attorti:
il cadavere era esangue, a chiazze rosse e bianche,
gli occhi aperti e fissi
erano opache luci morte,
oblò di una stiva incagliata
grave di sabbia. Noi solleviamo il corpo, gli chiudiamo
gli occhi e lo rendiamo al mare donde venne,
là dove lo squalo dal muso di tacco si spella il naso
nel vuoto di Ahab e nella fronte; e il nome
è scritto in maiuscoletto col gesso giallo.
Marinai che alzate questo portento al mare,

dove le corazzate testimonieranno
la sua divinità infernale,
quando nulla potete
a rinsaldare questo baluardo dell'Atlantico, davanti a cui
    si erge
lo scuotitor della terra, verde, instancabile, casto
nelle sue scaglie d'acciaio: non chiedete liuto d'Orfeo
per riafferrare col suono la vita. I cannoni della flotta
    d'acciaio
balzano indietro e poi ripetono
il rauco saluto.

II

Allorché i venti si muovono e il loro soffio
preme sui baluardi stretti a questo molo,
le rondini del mare e i gabbiani tremano alla tua morte
in queste acque casalinghe. Marinaio, le senti
le ali del marino Pequod *che battono verso terra, che ricadono*
a capofitto e si infrangono sulla nostra muraglia atlantica
al largo di 'Sconset, dove i cutter inclinati
con gli spinnaker rigonfi, copron di spruzzi la boa,
mentre la corda aggrovigliata, stridendo, libera
le carrucole: al largo di Madacket, dove i marinai d'acqua
    dolce
sferzano la densa risacca e gettano le lunghe esche di piombo
per i pesci azzurri. Gabbiani socchiudono le loro gravi pal-
    pebre
verso il mare. Le ali dei venti percuotono le pietre,
cugino, o gridano per te e gli artigli si avventano
alla gola del mare e la torcono nella fanghiglia
di questo antico cimitero quacchero dove le ossa
si lamentano nella lunga notte per la bestia ferita
che riaffiora presso le baleniere di Ahab ad oriente.

III

Quanto recuperasti da Posidone perì
con te, cugino, e l'acqua solcata
è sterile sulla azzurra barba del dio,
distesa di qui verso i castelli di Spagna,
porto di Nantucket volto ad occidente. Verso Cape Cod
i cannoni, adagiati sulla marea,
squarciano i sargassi in un orologio ad acqua
di fondaccio e risucchio, intorbidano sale e sabbia
sferzando il palco della terra, cullano
le nostre navi da guerra nella mano
del grande Dio, dove la contrizione del tempo inazzurra
quanto quei marinai quaccheri persero
nella furiosa lotta per la vita. Morirono
quando l'età era ad occhi spalancati,
rozza e bambina; solo ossa dimorano
là, nel nulla ignoto, dove le loro navi furono scagliate
alte verso il cielo, là dove i marinai avevano favoleggiato
di Colui che è, il mostro bianco. Ciò che ad essi costò
è il loro segreto. Nella scia del capodoglio
vedo i quaccheri annegare e odo il loro grido:
« Se Dio stesso non fosse stato con noi,
se Dio stesso non fosse stato con noi,
quando l'Atlantico si levò contro di noi, ecco,
allora ci avrebbe ingoiato subito vivi ».

IV

È finita la rotta delle balene, e la balena
che vomitava le ossa di Nantucket sull'onda trebbiata
e muoveva in vortici le acque inquiete
per mandare il Pequod spedito all'inferno:
è finita per loro, pazzi per tre quarti,
aggrappati a fili di paglia per far vela
sempre più verso l'alto dietro alla virante balena,
che sputa sangue e acqua mentre si rotola,

fradicia come un cane, a queste atlantiche secche:
Clamavimus, o abissi. Gemano per l'acqua i gabbiani,

per il profondo dove l'alta marea
mormora ferita a se stessa, mormora e rifluisce.
Le onde si voltolano nel loro risucchio, vanno sempre più
    al largo,
lasciano solo il funebre crepitìo dei granchi,
mentre il lido cresce, e il suo enorme grugno
succhia il fianco dell'oceano.
S'è finito di correre sulle onde;
siamo riversati come acqua. Chi farà balzare
il signore dei Leviatani legato all'albero
da questo campo di quaccheri nelle loro tombe senza pietra?

V

Quando le viscere della balena si infrangono e l'onda
della sua corruzione invade questo mondo
al di là di Nantucket spoglia di alberi, e di Wood's Hole
e di Martha's Vineyard, o marinaio, sibilerà la tua spada
e piomberà e affonderà nel grasso?
A Giosafat nella gran fossa di ceneri
le ossa invocano piangendo il sangue della balena bianca,
le grasse pinne s'inarcano e la percuotono intorno agli
    orecchi,
la lancia di morte zàngola nel santuario, strappa
il cuore brunito in brandelli che si sollevano a flagello,
e sminuzza fuori la vita attorcigliata: scava e tende
e squarcia il diaframma della balena,
pezzi di grasso volano al vento, o marinaio,
e gabbiani girano intorno alle assi sfondate
dove le stelle del mattino cantano insieme
e il tuono squassa la bianca schiuma e straccia
la rossa bandiera inchiodata alla testa dell'albero. Nascondi
il nostro acciaio, Giona Messia, nel tuo fianco.